ELEMENTS
OF
ECONOMICS

PHILIP LEE

ELEMENTS OF ECONOMICS

David W. Rasmussen

Charles T. Haworth

The Florida State University

SCIENCE RESEARCH ASSOCIATES, INC.
Chicago, Henley-on-Thames, Sydney, Toronto
A Subsidiary of IBM

Acquisition Editor	*Michael Zamczyk*
Project Editor	*Gretchen Hargis*
Compositor	*Graphic Typesetting Service*
Illustrator	*Pat Rogondino*
Cover and Text Designer	*Carol Harris*
Cover Photo	*Tom Tracy*
Part Opener Photos	*Terry Zabala*

Library of Congress Cataloging in Publication Data

Rasmussen, David W.
  Elements of economics.

  Includes index.
  1. Economics. I. Haworth, Charles T. II. Title.
HB171.5.R24 1984   330   83-20390
ISBN 0-574-19450-9

10 9 8 7 6 5 4 3 2

Contents

Preface

Economic theory, we believe, is a body of thought with clear applications, a tool that can be used to explain and predict economic phenomena. Governments use these explanations and predictions to try to control economic conditions (such as unemployment, inflation, and pollution) and to improve the standard of living. Throughout this book, we emphasize the practical applications of economic theory, while at the same time indicating the complexity of economic problems.

This text surveys the economic issues that confront all societies—how to achieve affluence, economic stability, and an acceptable distribution of income. Economics provides (1) concepts that help us understand how economies work, (2) a perspective on the roles played by the public and private sectors, and (3) insights for solving economic problems. It is an exciting field. We are dealing with some of today's most pressing problems: unemployment, inflation, pollution, economic growth, poverty, inequality, discrimination, and the efficiency of the private sector relative to the public sector.

The field of economics does not, however, offer definitive solutions to these problems. Economics is a social science; its principles are axioms about the behavioral tendencies of individuals and groups. It is not a science of great precision; unlike the law of gravity, its "laws" cannot be readily verified. An economy is so complex, so intertwined with the economies of other nations, so affected by the factors that shape people's economic behavior that precise predictions about economic phenomena are usually impossible. It is clear to economists—and it soon becomes clear to students of economics—that in this profession there are no sages, no one who has all the answers. Students will soon realize that economics must operate in the context of a political decision-making process. Solutions to existing problems may be different from those thought appropriate a decade ago. Economic theory is a dynamic body of thought that enables us to conceptualize broad issues and problems—a body of thought that is pushed continually to new frontiers as we endeavor to learn more about economic relationships in society.

Our experience as teachers of economics tells us that many students of introductory economics simply memorize facts, neglecting the processes necessary to an understanding of the material. After an examination, for example, some students—particularly those who only memorize facts—find themselves with test scores lower than they expected. In this regard students will find it helpful to use the Study Guide designed to accompany this text. The Study Guide includes projects and problems as well as sample true/false and multiple-choice questions with detailed answers.

Many economists have contributed directly and indirectly to the writing of this book. We appreciate the cordial and productive working environment provided by our colleagues at The Florida State University. We are also grateful to the following reviewers for their insightful comments and suggestions: David Abel (Mankato State University), Richard C. Cahaan (Ohio State University), Daniel Gropper (Florida State University), Randolph Martin (University of South Carolina), Robert Michaels (California State University), G. R. Miller (Morehead State University), Sidney Wilson (Rockland Community College), and H. Zabinsky (Loyola University).

Part 1

INTRODUCTION

Chapter 1

What Is Economics?

"Why should I study economics?"

This is usually one of the first questions raised by a beginning student in an introductory course in economics. It is a simple question that has several answers.

One major reason to study economics is to become a better-informed citizen. A knowledge of economics helps you understand economic questions facing the society and to evaluate the statements of political leaders on economic matters.

The study of economics also helps you to understand other societies besides the United States because economics deals with universal problems. Every society must decide what to produce, how to produce it, and who will receive the benefits. Many principles are the same, whether in the United States or elsewhere.

Perhaps the least helpful definition of economics is the tongue-in-cheek observation, "Economics is what economists do." Fortunately the activity of economists can be summarized in a more helpful way. Economics is the study of (1) the way societies choose to allocate scarce resources among alternative uses, (2) the way they distribute the fruits of production among various individuals and groups, and (3) the sources of economic growth and the causes of fluctuations in economic activity. Rather than continue to define economics in general terms, let us show the relevance of economics by discussing some of the issues covered in this book.

THE RELEVANCE OF ECONOMICS

How Do Markets Work?

The economy of the United States uses what is called the market system to allocate its production of goods and services. There is no central council or board of planners to decide who manufactures what, or how much of it, or who buys it at what price. Yet many economic wants are satisfied. People in Chicago go to the supermarket confident that they can buy oranges grown 1000 miles away. Florida growers cultivate their trees hoping that people they have never seen will buy the fruit and that the growers will make a profit. Decentralized decision making is characteristic of the market mechanism.

Individual workers in a market economy seek to perform those tasks which yield them the highest reward. Business firms produce goods or services that will maximize their profits. In their search for "best advantage," individual business firms within the market system produce commodities that people are willing and able to purchase, and in the process they organize production. Growing oranges requires many different people and products before the fruit can be bought by the consumer. Florida growers must buy fertilizers and sprays from chemical manufacturers hundreds of miles from the groves. Ladders may be "imported" from Tennessee, crates and boxes from Washington or Georgia, and sprayer equipment from California. Those who pick the crops may come from as far away as Maine. Trucks deliver the oranges to wholesalers who in turn sell them to super-

At the supermarket, shoppers make choices that help determine how profitable the production of various foods is. *(Photo by Richard Kalvar, Magnum Photos, Inc.)*

markets. In the stores, local workers unpack and price the fruit before the final consumers purchase it. Self-interest directs the behavior of each person in this chain, yet their conduct benefits the consumers as well. As Adam Smith, who first elaborated the workings of the market mechanism, noted, "It is not from the benevolence of the butcher, the brewer, or the baker, that we expect our dinner, but from their regard to their own interest. We address ourselves, not to their humanity but to their self-love, and never talk to them of our own necessities but of their advantage." The study of how markets work belongs to the branch of economics called *microeconomics.*

The fact that individual self-interest can produce a social good is a paradox of this form of organization. Yet, while unplanned markets work reliably in bringing oranges from the groves of Florida, Texas, and California to households all over the nation, in other circumstances they do not work at all. For instance, they do not work in national defense. Most Americans are willing to pay for a commodity called national defense in order to guard against a possible attack by a foreign power. Yet no private business firm offers to "sell" this protection. Providing national security and growing oranges both require productive resources, yet the government supplies national security while the private market mechanism organizes the production of fruit. Economics analyzes the circumstances under which private markets work well and those under which governmental organization seems superior. Such questions are basic to economics, a discipline not without controversy.

Can We Avoid Unemployment and Inflation?

A modern economy such as ours is subject to periodic fluctuations, in which the production of goods and services declines. In human terms,

the most painful consequence is that some people wishing to work cannot find jobs. The most dramatic decline in economic activity was the Great Depression of the 1930s. In 1929 President Hoover took office with a pledge to eliminate poverty in the United States only to find himself, three years later, presiding over a crippled economy. Man-hours of work in manufacturing fell 45 percent between 1929 and 1932. National income declined from $87 billion to $39 billion. At the depth of the depression, one of every four workers was out of a job.

How could the Great Depression happen? The factors that account for production—land (which includes all natural resources), labor, and capital—were intact. Capital—the machines and buildings that raise the productivity of workers—was idle while people sought work, yet somehow the two could not be combined into a productive process. People wanted to work, employers preferred to have factories in operation so they could make a profit, raw materials were available; yet the economic system floundered as abysmally as its most severe critics had ever predicted.

What does a decline in economic activity really mean? The effects are far more dramatic than economic data suggest, for cold statistics cannot reflect the resulting human suffering. In his oral history of the Great Depression, Studs Terkel reports a psychiatrist's impressions of miners during the 1930s:

I did a little field work among the unemployed miners in Pennsylvania. Just observing. What the lack of a job two, three, four, five years did to their families and to them. They hung around street corners and in groups. They gave each other solace. They were loath to go home because they were indicted, as if it were their fault for being unemployed. A jobless man was a lazy good-for-nothing. The women punished the men for not bringing home the bacon by withholding themselves sex-

For many people, the lack of jobs during the Great Depression led to not only hunger but also psychological depression. *(Photo by Dorothea Lange, Magnum Photos, Inc.)*

ually. By belittling and emasculating the men, undermining their paternal authority, turning to the eldest son. Making the eldest son the man of the family. These men suffered from the depression. They felt despised, they were ashamed of themselves. They cringed, they comforted one another. They avoided home.*

---

* Studs Terkel, *Hard Times: An Oral History of the Great Depression* (New York: Pantheon, 1970), p. 196.

In the late 1970s and early 1980s, inflation—the rising prices of goods and services—joined unemployment as a substantial and persistent economic problem. When the general price level rises, the purchasing power of the dollar falls. Each dollar we hold will buy fewer goods and services. In 1979 the price level rose by 13.3 percent, and the following year it rose another 12.4 percent. Over the span of two years prices rose 25.7 percent. By the end of 1980, a dollar bought only three-quarters of the amount it could buy at the beginning of 1979.

A major portion of the economics discipline, called *macroeconomics* because it is concerned with the entire economy, is directed to the study of economic growth and instability. Macroeconomics has a public-policy orientation that focuses on three distinct but related goals: sustaining a desired rate of economic growth, maintaining stable prices to avoid inflation, and keeping unemployment as low as possible. Achieving these goals would greatly increase our national economic well-being.

How Is the Distribution of Income Determined?

One of the issues facing the United States is the unevenness with which the national income is distributed. The U.S. Census Bureau's official definition of poverty is based on a food budget designed for "temporary or emergency use when funds are low." Such a budget by definition does not meet the basic needs of a family over an extended period; yet it represents a level of existence that many families and individuals do not attain. In 1980 25.3 million persons were living in poverty in the United States—11.2 percent of the population! The outstanding feature of the poverty profile is that many poor people are not able to improve their economic status. Over 8.4 million persons under the age of 15 lived in poor families in 1980; almost 3.6 million people

Finding the Facts

Many times people engage in discussions and debates which are needlessly prolonged because the participants lack the necessary facts. Statistics on social questions are readily available and should be sought out to shed light on problems of interest.

The best way to track down quantitative aspects of many other economic and social questions is to begin with *The Statistical Abstract of the United States.* When this volume does not present the exact data sought, it usually offers references which guide you to an appropriate source. Of special interest to students of economics are sections on geography and environment, labor force, employment and earnings, social insurance and welfare services, income, expenditures and wealth, prices, government finances and employment, banking, finance and insurance, business enterprise, manufacturers, distribution and services, comparative international statistics, and metropolitan area statistics. A detailed index is included.

A valuable source for information regarding current economic conditions is the annual *Economic Report of the President.* This document is based on materials supplied by the President's Council of Economic Advisors and is a source of both data and analysis. The monthly *Federal Reserve Bulletin* is another good source for current information on the economy. It is the primary source for information on banking, money, and credit conditions.

The U.S. Bureau of the Census publishes the *Census of the Population* every 10 years. Its many volumes provide detailed and cross-tabulated data for social and economic characteristics of the population. Of particular interest to economics students are data on employment, income, occupation, race, mobility, and place of residence. The Census Bureau's *Census of Manufactures* appears every five years. This is the basic source for data on the nation's manufacturing industries: their shipments, employment, payrolls, inventories, and capital expenditures. Data on farms, crops, and livestock are published every five years in the *Census of Agriculture.* The *Census of Business* presents data on the size and type of business, sales and payroll for retail, wholesale, and the service trades. Census Bureau publications usually present data for the entire United States, as well as regional units, states, and major metropolitan areas. The *Census of Government* every five years presents data on public finance and employment at state and local levels.

over age 65 were officially classed as living in poverty. Thus, of the 25.3 million "poor," 12.0 million or 47 percent had virtually no control over their economic situation.

Some public policies, such as civil rights legislation, have been based on the notion that many able-bodied workers cannot rise out of poverty because of discrimination in the labor market. Three out of 10 blacks—a minority group thought to suffer heavily from inequitable employment opportunities—lived in poverty in 1980. Women, although not a minority, are perhaps most in need of better job opportunities. In 1978, about 30 percent of female heads of household lived in poverty. Many such women cannot work full time because day-care facilities for their children are inadequate; when they do work full time, they often are paid wages far below those required to support their families.

In the past two decades, economists have studied poverty and the economics of discrimination in considerable depth. The most effective way to provide an adequate living for those who cannot support themselves has also been the subject of much research and considerable debate. Many questions arise from the distribution of income and wealth. For example, what determines the portion of national income each individual will receive? Does a prizefighter really "earn" $10 million by fighting another person on a rope-enclosed platform for an hour? If we desire to change the distribution system to assist those who live in poverty, can we do it in a way that does not stifle the incentive to work? Is there justification for taxing the earnings of one person in order to give the money to another person? Basic issues of property rights and the distribution of income and wealth are an important and controversial part of economic analysis. Questions of income distribution are included in microeconomics.

ECONOMIC GROWTH

Throughout human history, the problem of producing material goods has been of foremost importance. Poorly endowed for survival in the natural state, humanity has had to use reason to create a more hospitable environment. The purpose of production is to ensure human survival. We must produce clothing and shelter to insulate ourselves from the elements, and we must find sustenance in agriculture. Survival instinct leads to production of life's necessities. (Humanity's desire for material comforts is not satiated when survival is assured, for the quality of life is associated with the level of physical well-being. Technical improvements that accompany economic development greatly enhance the human situation: personal comfort is advanced, longevity is increased, and perhaps most important, less work time is required to guarantee the necessities of life. The latter benefit of economic growth is the source of culture and civilization, which improve the human experience. The drive to produce greater material output is an integral part of Western culture and is based on the desire to improve the human condition.)

The world has by no means experienced uniform success in the acquisition of wealth. Indeed,

poverty and a scarcity of material goods typify the human condition. Considerably less than 25 percent of the world's population can be said to approach anything near what we might call affluence. And there is no obvious pattern of success. National income per capita is shown for several countries in Exhibit 1-1. Here we see that the United States, a large country, has a high standard of living, as does a very small nation, Sweden. India, with 586 million people, is a very poor country, yet its neighbor Afghanistan with only 19 million people is even poorer. The amount of natural resources does not appear to be the crucial determinant of a society's affluence. Brazil with a per capita income of $2067 is very rich in natural resources, whereas Japan, a relatively wealthy country, has very few natural resources. Nor does ideology appear to be an important influence. Socialist countries are both rich and poor, and capitalist countries similarly differ. Differences in national income among countries stem from many things, but

Exhibit 1-1 National income per capita for selected countries, 1980

Country	Per Capita Income
United States	$11,231
Sweden	11,028
Canada	9,875
Denmark	9,826
France	9,420
Belgium	8,571
Japan	8,163
Finland	6,864
United Kingdom	5,323
Italy	5.308
Venezuela	3,396
Brazil	2,067
Mexico	2,044
Afghanistan	207
India	202
Ethiopia	129

SOURCE: Herbert Block, *The Planetary Product in 1980: A Creative Pause?*, Bureau of Public Affairs, U.S. Department of State.

Exhibit 1-2 Annual production possibilities for a hypothetical society

Mix of Civilian and War Production	Units of Civilian Products	Units of War Materials
a	25	0
b	24	5
c	20	13
d	14	20
e	8	24
f	0	26

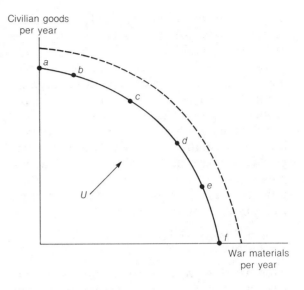

Exhibit 1-3 Production-possibilities frontier

The production-possibilities frontier shows the maximum amount a society can produce during a given period of time. If society is operating inside the curve, at say u, some resources are unemployed. When the curve shifts from a-f to the dotted production-possibilities frontier, we say economic growth has occurred.

the most important are the nation's resources and the way in which effort is mobilized and allocated. Methods of mobilizing and allocating effort are studied when economists analyze the quest for material well-being.

What Is Economic Growth?

Economic growth is best described using a production-possibilities frontier. The production possibilities for a hypothetical society are shown in Exhibit 1-2 and illustrated graphically in Exhibit 1-3. This society could produce 25 units of civilian output if it were to allocate all its resources toward the production of civilian products. This possibility is shown in commodity mix *a*. On the other hand, 26 units of war materials and no civilian products could be produced if society allocated all its resources toward the production of war materials. The intervening points show the various combinations the society could produce between all-out civilian production and total war production, given the level of resources and the state of technology.

The production-possibilities frontier shown in Exhibit 1-3, points *a* through *f*, shows the maximum amount society can produce by fully utilizing its available resources during a given period of time. Since a society can produce more in a year than in a month, the production-pos-

sibilities frontier must be placed within a particular time reference if it is to identify correctly the quantity of output a society is capable of producing.

When an economy is operating on its production-possibilities frontier, it is fully utilizing all its resources of land, labor, and capital. Any point beyond this frontier, of course, is unattainable, because either the resources or the technology is unavailable to produce more. When an economy is operating *inside* its production-possibilities frontier—say, at point *u* in Exhibit 1-3—resources are less than fully utilized. Some factors of production—land, capital, or labor—are unemployed because society could produce more of both goods and services by moving to the production-possibilities frontier. In our example, society could get more of both civilian goods and war materials, as shown by the arrow from point *u*. When *economic growth* occurs, the production-possibilities frontier shifts outward. Thus, when a society moves from production-possibilities frontier *a–f* to the dotted possibilities frontier in Exhibit 1-3, economic growth has occurred. Society can now produce more civilian goods, as well as more war materials during a given period of time.

Economic Growth in the United States

This nation's production-possibilities frontier has shifted outward over the past century. The dollar value of output produced in a year, when adjusted for inflation, is called real Gross National Product (GNP), and provides a measure of the change in productive capacity over time. The increase in real GNP in the United States for the past century—1874 to 1980—is shown in Exhibit 1-4. The value of output produced in 1980 was 42 times that produced in 1874, an impressive growth record. It is important to add one qualification, however. Although overall output increased 42 times over the 1874–1980 period, the economic well-being of individuals increased at a much slower rate because the nation's population was increasing as well. Output *per person* rose only 8.2 times over the period shown in Exhibit 1-4.

THE ECONOMIC PROBLEM: CHOOSING AMONG ALTERNATIVES

Definitions of economics usually focus on the subject matter of the discipline. The description of economics at the beginning of this chap-

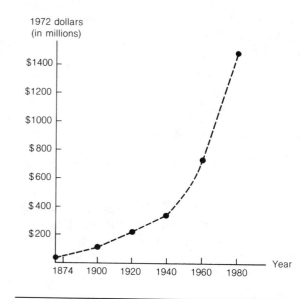

Exhibit 1-4   Growth of output in the United States, 1874-1980

ter told you that our subject deals with the production, distribution, and consumption of goods and services. In a more fundamental sense, economics deals with the basic problem of choosing among alternative courses of action relating to how resources are to be allocated. This problem affects everyone. The manufacturer of automobiles must decide which of many alternative inputs to use in the production process. As individuals we must choose among goods and services competing for the limited number of dollars we have to spend. When we have only $10 to spend on an evening's entertainment, the options of attending a movie, eating out, bowling, or going to a night spot must be weighed against one another if we are to get the most for our $10. Or another choice may be to study at the library and save the $10 for another time. Similarly, we must choose among alternative allocations of our most precious resource—time.

The economic way of thinking is fundamentally designed to help individuals make decisions among alternative courses of action. The production-possibilities frontier shown in Exhibit 1-3 illustrates the necessity of making these choices. Along the frontier, we must give up civilian goods if we are to produce more war materials. On the solid frontier *a* through *f*, increasing the production of war material from 13 to 20 (point *c* to point *d*) requires that civilian production be reduced from 20 to 14. We cannot escape this sacrifice. Growth allows us to consume more of both goods, yet along any higher production-possibilities frontier we must still sacrifice one good when we desire more of the other. Increasing wealth does not alleviate the problem of choice that is central to the study of economics.

The production-possibilities frontier illustrates a general proposition in economics: we must always give up one thing to obtain something else. In popular terms, this basic rule of economics is expressed: For society there is no such thing as a free lunch. Even if you receive a "free" lunch from a friend, society has used resources that cannot be used to produce something else. *Opportunity cost* is defined to be the highest valued alternative that must be given up when a choice is made. This necessity of choosing among alternatives and the idea that every alternative has an opportunity cost is at the core of the economic way of thinking.

ECONOMICS AS A SOCIAL SCIENCE

Economists, like all other social scientists, use a tool called *theory* to help unravel complex problems. Using theory we look at a problem in an abstract way in order to discover significant cause-and-effect relationships. In many ways, theoretical reasoning is more efficient than common sense. Common sense, for example, deals with particular events, while theory deals with generalities. Common sense is oriented toward tangible problems, while theory is concerned primarily with the ideas and concepts behind a problem.

Theory is sometimes ridiculed as impractical, abstract, and out of touch with reality, whereas common sense is viewed as practical and helpful to the solution of problems. Common sense, however, is not always the reliable guide to knowledge that many sidewalk philosophers would have us believe. An apparently reasonable proposition, based on experience, is that the earth is flat. Empirical evidence verifies common sense, for last year we drove an automobile across the United States and stayed

---

One-Armed Economists

A U.S. senator got tired of hearing expert witnesses say, "On one hand . . . but then on the other hand . . ." The senator expressed an interest in one-armed economists. Economists agree on many issues, and on these well-understood matters the senator would not get many "two-handed answers." However, many economic problems are very complex, and answers cannot be definitive. An economist who offers definitive, one-armed answers to these problems is simply misleading people. Policymakers should expect two things from economists who provide advice on complex issues. First, economists should make clear how effectively they believe they can answer the questions being asked. Second, whenever possible they should identify what is required to get better answers. Important economic issues require that we ask very difficult questions, but no one is well-served by inaccurate simplistic answers.

upright in the seat the entire time. Today we find this kind of reasoning laughable, yet for centuries common sense led people to believe it. In many cases, theory is more likely than common sense to yield an accurate description of reality.

Economic science, called *positive economics,* is dedicated to finding out how the economy works and to discovering key economic relationships. Positive economics is a description, or an analysis, of what *is* rather than what *should be* and therefore attempts to be value-free and ethically neutral. Economists engaged in positive or scientific analysis can describe the implications of different policy options that reflect different social values. For example, economists have often described how the minimum wage law can make it more difficult for teenagers to find employment. This is an implication of an economic policy that economists can point out without taking a stand as to the overall desirability of the law. The scientific observation tells policy makers that they had better consider this fact when assessing the overall desirability of the minimum wage law.

But economists do not remain exclusively in the scientific arena, where they must suppress personal opinion and bias. *Normative economics* is the branch of the discipline that addresses what ought to be. Ethical judgments and individual values are often at the core of debates about what constitutes a better world. It is in the arena of normative economics that economists advocate particular public policies. Normative statements, because they are inevitably rooted in one's conception of how the world ought to be, cannot be empirically tested or confirmed with scientific analysis. Only positive statements describing the world as it is can be verified through the scientific process that is at the core of economics.

Common Errors in Positive Economics

Depicting the world in its precise form can be a difficult task. The economy is complicated and the effects of many events and policies intermingle to produce a particular outcome. As a result, careful analysis is required if we are to understand the implications of various policy alternatives and the consequences of economic events. For instance, it is important to understand three common errors in positive economics—violation of the ceteris paribus condition, the fallacy of composition, and the causation problem.

Violation of Ceteris Paribus Assumption When attempting to identify a particular economic relationship, economists frequently use the ceteris paribus assumption. *Ceteris paribus,* a Latin phrase, means "all other things held equal." An economist might say, "Other things constant, an increase in the number of people who want to buy personal computers will cause the price of computers to rise." If you try to verify this statement, you might find that more people are indeed buying computers, but that the price of computers is falling. In this case we observe that all other things are *not* equal, because rapid technological advance in the personal computer industry has allowed a rapid decline in the cost of production. Hence it is possible to observe both the rise in the demand for computers and the falling price. When verifying a positive economic statement it is necessary to identify the circumstances—the ceteris paribus conditions—under which the statement applies. Given the complex and rapidly changing world in which we live, few statements are true without careful specification of the ceteris paribus conditions.

In spite of the rising demand for personal computers, their price is declining—because of technological advances that make producing them cost less and less. *(Photo by Ellis Herwig, Stock, Boston)*

The Fallacy of Composition   One of the most frequent mistakes in economics is to assume that what is true for individuals is also true for society as a whole. This is the *fallacy of composition*, of which there are many examples. One person might attend school to get a good job as an electrical engineer. But if everyone were trained as an electrical engineer, the profession would hold no promise. The fallacy of composition also applies in reverse: what makes sense for society does not necessarily make sense for an individual.

The Problem of Determining Causation   It is sometimes difficult to identify the specific cause of a given effect. Late in the nineteenth century an English economist named W. Stanley Jevons studied the problem of fluctuations in economic activity. He observed that from 1721 to 1878 business cycles seemed to correspond to the frequency of sunspots. This led him to hypothesize that sunspots caused fluctuations in economic activity. The theory is not as ridiculous as it may at first appear. Jevons thought that sunspots caused weather cycles, which in turn affected crops. The resulting fluctuations in agricultural output were transmitted to industrial production and employment. Therefore, Jevons concluded that business cycles were related uniquely to sunspots.

Jevons' theory could obviously be tested. If the hypothesis were true, observing the frequency of sunspots would enable one to predict business cycles. Unfortunately for Jevons, the theory did not hold true. In fact, even his initial observations that sunspots and business cycles were closely related broke down when further evidence was collected on sunspots. Nevertheless, it is interesting to consider whether Jevons' theory could have predicted business cycles. If so, would we conclude that business cycles were caused by the weather cycles related to sunspots? In short, how are we to assess the theory? To what degree do we equate successful predictions with causation? By what criteria do we judge our theory good or bad?

One of the most famous contemporary economists, Nobel Prize winner Milton Friedman of the University of Chicago, argues that successful prediction should be the only judge of theory. Had Jevons been right, Professor Friedman would presumably have advised the federal government to combat business cycles as if they were caused by sunspots. However, if we use predictability as our only criterion for success, we are obviously not interested in determining causation.

An alternative criterion, seeking to determine causation among social phenomena, is fraught with difficulty. Eighteenth-century philosopher David Hume once observed that you can never prove causality with empirical evidence. Because two things happen together does not necessarily mean that one caused the other. And if A and B are related in a systematic way, does A cause B, or does B cause A? Although the social scientist's search for an understanding of the social system is difficult, theories are best judged by how well they help us discover causation. Thus, while we may judge a theory useful because its predictions contribute to successful public policies, ultimately we hope to understand how the social system works.

SUMMARY

1. Economics is the study of (1) the way societies choose to allocate scarce resources among alternative uses, (2) the way they distribute the fruits of production among individuals and groups, and (3) the sources of economic growth and the causes of fluctuations in economic activity.

2. The market system solves economic problems through a decentralized decision-making process based on self-interest. In some circumstances the government must intervene if society is to achieve the best allocation and distribution of resources.

3. Microeconomics analyzes the way societies allocate scarce resources, combine factors in the production process, and divide the fruits of production. Macroeconomics is the study of the total economy, its growth and stability.

4. There are three factors of production: land, labor, and capital. Land includes all natural resources, labor all human inputs, and capital all man-made items used in the production process.

5. The production-possibilities curve shows the maximum amount a society can produce when it fully utilizes its available resources during a given period of time. Economic growth occurs when the production-possibilities curve shifts outward.

6. Opportunity cost reflects the necessity of choosing among alternatives because it measures the highest valued option given up when a choice is made.

7. Positive economics describes how the economy works and attempts to be value-free and ethically neutral. Normative economics includes discussions about how the economic world ought to be.

KEY CONCEPTS

market system	opportunity cost
microeconomics	positive economics
factors of production	normative economics
macroeconomics	*ceteris paribus*
production-possibilities curve	fallacy of composition

QUESTIONS FOR DISCUSSION

1. Describe a world in which economic problems do not exist. Feel free to make any assumptions about the society you wish—even the notion of food falling like manna from heaven. Can you eliminate economic problems?
2. Economics is sometimes defined as the study of how to allocate scarce resources in the face of unlimited human wants. Do you think human wants are insatiable? How do you think people's wants change as they achieve higher levels of well-being?
3. Some people argue that the interdependence of modern economic life suggests a need for more planning and less decentralized decision making in markets. Do you agree? How do you justify your position?
4. Capital is defined as something man-made and used in the productive process. Typical examples are machines, tools, and buildings. Can you think of reasons why people may be called human capital?
5. When is the government justified in taxing the earnings of one person in order to give the money to another?

Appendix: USING GRAPHS IN ECONOMICS

Economists frequently use graphs to illustrate theories and to clarify analysis of economic problems. You have already seen an example in the production-possibilities frontier graph used to illustrate economic growth. Basic economic concepts (such as supply and demand) and economic data (such as unemployment or production statistics) are often presented in graph form. It is therefore necessary to understand what information a graph conveys and to be able to translate economic ideas into graphs. This appendix provides a brief review of graphs for those who are not comfortable working with them.

From Tables to Graphs

A graph can be a "picture" of a table of numbers. Our first task is to understand how pairs of numbers can be represented on a graph. Exhibit 1A-1 contains a table with six pairs of numbers. One column is labeled *x* and the other *y*. In row *A*, 0 is the *x* value and 1 the *y* value. Similarly, in row *C* the *x* value is 4 and the *y* value is 3.

An accompanying graph presents all data contained in the table. The graph has two axes, one for the *x* column and one for the *y* column. By convention, the *x* column is always placed on the horizontal line and the *y* column on the vertical line. Each line is marked off to indicate the number of units, with the corner (called the origin) representing 0 units of both *x* and *y*. We can now plot each pair of points in the table on this graph. Row A has an *x* value of 0 and a *y* value of 1; starting from the origin, *x* is at 0 and we move up the *y*-axis to the first mark. This is point *A* on the graph. For point *B*, the pair of

Exhibit 1A-1   Six pairs of numbers

	x	*y*
A	0	1
B	2	2
C	4	3
D	6	4
E	8	5
F	10	6

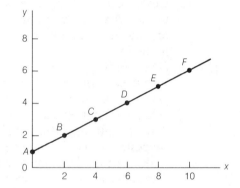

numbers shown in row B, we move out two units on the *x*-axis and two up the *y*-axis. Points *C* through *F* are found the same way. The points are joined with a line to show that there is a specific relationship between *x* and *y*—*y* increases as the *x* value becomes larger.

Examples of Graphs in Economics

Economists use graphs to analyze concepts and information about the well-being of people. We are not therefore interested in abstract *x*'s and

Exhibit 1A-2   Data for two variables

	Number of Cars Parked/Day	Price of Parking/Day
A	100	$10
B	200	8
C	300	6
D	400	4
E	500	2

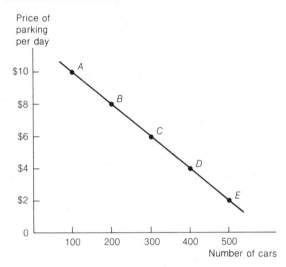

emerges from this table is that as the price of parking falls, more people are willing to pay to park their cars.*

Graphs are also very useful to illustrate trends in economic data. Exhibit 1A-3 shows the percentages of black women and of white women in the labor force from 1955 to 1980. The data are also shown in graph form. The horizontal axis denotes the year; the vertical axis the percentage of women 20 years or older in the labor force. From both the table and the graph we see that black women are more likely to be in the labor force than white women. However, the disparity between them is becoming smaller: in 1955 the percentage of black women in the labor force was 13.5 percentage points higher than that of white women, while in 1980 the difference was only 5.3 percentage points.

This data provides an opportunity to indicate how graphs can be used to misrepresent data. The diagram in Exhibit 1A-3 appears to show that black women were about three times more likely than white women to be members of the labor force in 1955. But this is an illusion created by a break in the graph; that is, we do not show the percentages from 0 through 35. Trends can be made to look very different by changing the scale on either or both axes. For example, the data for white women from Exhibit 1A-3 is reproduced in Exhibit 1A-4 for the years 1970–80. The trend in this second graph looks much steeper because the years have been moved closer together on the horizontal axis and the percentages further apart on the vertical axis.

Graphs can be helpful because they give a more vivid picture of data than a table. However, when preparing a graph or reading one prepared by

y's but in specific economic relationships. A common economic relationship is shown in Exhibit 1A-2. The table in this illustration shows a series of five points; the first column shows the number of cars parked each day while the second column shows the price of parking a car for a day. Once again we must translate the table into a graph. Point A, the number of cars parked per day, is 1 (that is, 100 since we are measuring in units of 100); this is represented by 1 unit on the horizontal axis and 10 units on the vertical axis, for the price of $10. The other points are plotted in the same way. The "picture" that

---

*When showing a relationship between price and quantity, it is customary to put the price on the y-axis and the quantity on the x-axis.

Exhibit 1A-3   Percentage of women (20 years or older) in the labor force, 1955–80

Year	White	Black
1955	34.0%	47.5%
1960	36.2	49.9
1965	38.0	51.1
1970	42.2	51.8
1975	45.3	51.4
1980	50.6	55.9

SOURCE: *Economic Report of the President*, 1982.

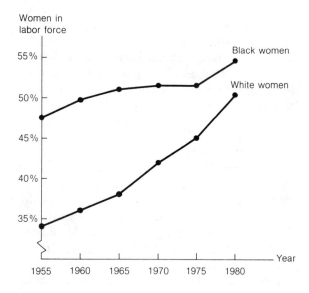

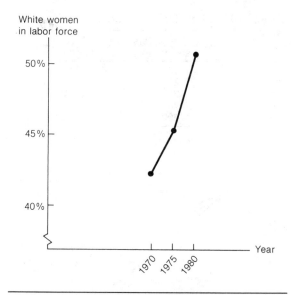

Exhibit 1A-4   Percentage of white women (20 years or older) in the labor force, 1970-80

someone else, it is important to be sure that the picture is an accurate portrayal of the data.

Slope

The slope of a straight line is defined as the change in the y value divided by the change in the x value. Put another way, it is the vertical change divided by the horizontal change. In Exhibit 1A-5 the line at the left has a slope of 3

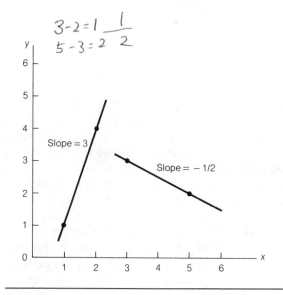

Exhibit 1A-5   Two lines with varying slopes

because y changes from 1 to 4 when x changes from 1 to 2. The change in y is 4 minus 1, or 3, when the change in x is 1 (2 minus 1). The slope is 3/1. In the case of the line at right, when x increases from 3 to 5, we see that y falls from 3 to 2. The change in y is -1 when the change in x is 2. The slope is therefore $-1/2$. The slope of a straight line is the same at any point along the line.

The slope of a curved line varies from point to point. The slope of a curved line is defined to be the slope of a straight line drawn tangent to the curve. A tangent line is one that just touches the curved line but does not cross it. Exhibit 1A-6 shows the production-possibilities frontier that was used in Exhibit 1-2. At point D a line has been drawn tangent to the curve. The line has a slope of -1 because a 1-unit increase in x is associated with a 1-unit decrease

in y. Recall that we used the production-possibilities curve to show that there was no free lunch; to get more war material, we have to sacrifice civilian goods when we are on the production-possibilities frontier. The slope of the curve tells us exactly how much we must give up at any point. If we are at point D, the slope of the curve tells us that we must give up 1 unit of civilian goods for every additional unit of war materials.

Graphs Without Numbers

In order to illustrate an economic principle, an instructor will often draw graphs without a table of numbers. For example, Exhibit 1A-2 shows that more people want to park their cars when the price of parking falls; the relationship also can be shown in an abstract way. All that is needed is a negatively sloping line on a graph in which the price of parking is shown on the vertical axis and the numbers of cars per day on the horizontal axis. We may not know the exact relationship (i.e., we don't know the slope), but we do know the direction of the relationship. These abstract graphs play a major role in the learning of economic principles.

A word of caution is in order. Students often try to cram for an economics examination by memorizing graphs. A memorized graph turns out to be nothing but a jumble of lines under the pressure of the examination when the professor does not ask a question in the precise way the graph has been memorized. The purpose of graphs is to clarify economic principles—the graphs themselves have no other importance. Rather than memorizing graphs, the student who does well in economics will be able to explain the graphs in English and be able to express in graphical form ideas and principles stated in English.

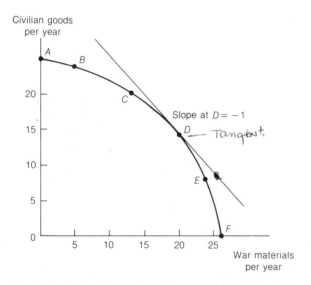

Exhibit 1A-6   Production-possibilities frontier

Chapter 2

Overview of the Market Mechanism

In economics we are concerned with allocating resources. Microeconomics focuses on how individual decisions affect these allocations. It seeks to explain how individual choices help to determine the price and quantity of goods supplied and purchased, and thus cause resources to be channeled into those products with the greatest demand.

Economists often talk about the laws of supply and demand, and cite them to explain many oddities of economic life. For example, "Why is air free but fur coats expensive even though we need air to survive and fur coats are not essential to our existence?" The answer is supply and demand: the supply of air is greater than we demand, whereas fur coats are scarce relative to their demand. We might also ask, "Why did the price of steak rise faster than the prices of other commodities?" The answer again is found in the concepts of supply and demand.

What do we mean then by supply and demand? This chapter will define and describe these two terms. We will also explore how interaction between supply and demand establishes a market price and determines the actual quantity bought and sold. This chapter will present a brief overview of how a market works.

DEMAND

The Definition of Demand

If coffee costs 50¢ a cup, how many cups would you want this morning? And if we lower the price to 15¢, or 10¢, or 5¢, how many cups of coffee would you buy at each price? These are typical questions that economists ask in studying demand. In economics, demand has a special meaning. It defines the relationship between the amount of a good that buyers are willing and able to purchase during a given period of time at various prices. We are not interested in how much people would *like* to purchase but in what they *will* actually purchase when their tastes, preferences, income, and the environment remain the same.

Obviously, demand assumes both that the consumer wants to buy a good *and* is able to buy the good. Neither characteristic is relevant without the other. For example, if you want to buy a Jaguar XKE but cannot afford it, you cannot influence the market for Jaguars. Alternatively, you may have the money but not be interested in buying a luxury car (maybe you don't drive); again, you will not influence the market for Jaguars. Only if you have both the desire and the ability to pay for a good will you have an influence in the marketplace.

Demand Schedule

Economists find it useful to compile a table or schedule showing prices and quantities of a good demanded at each price. Exhibit 2-1 shows such a *demand schedule* for semiprecious stones for two persons. The quantity that each consumer would purchase at each price is indicated. For example, at $1.50 per stone, Stuart would purchase six stones. At the same price, Ann would purchase only three stones. The total amount demanded (for both Stuart and Ann) at $1.50 would be nine stones. We can calculate the total quantity demanded for semiprecious stones at a given price for any group by merely adding up the separate demand schedules of the individuals.

We have been reading the schedule as if the quantity demanded were a function of price. That is, price causes consumers to increase or decrease the quantity they demand. The schedule shows that at higher prices each person demands fewer stones. Such a relationship is consistent with

Exhibit 2-1 Monthly purchase of semiprecious stones

Price	Number of Stones Purchased by Stuart	Number of Stones Purchased by Ann	Total Quantity Demanded, Stuart and Ann
$2.00	4	2	= 6
1.50	6	3	= 9
1.00	8	4	= 12
.50	10	5	= 15

Silver items are typically high-priced "luxury" goods, and so the quantity demanded is relatively low. *(Photo by Patricia Hollander Gross, Stock, Boston)*

our own experience; we tend to buy more when the price of an item is lowered. In fact, this is the purpose of specials or sales—merchants want to sell a greater quantity than they could expect to sell at the higher, presale price.

Law of Demand

While the specific price-quantity relationship shown in Exhibit 2-1 may be interesting to a semiprecious-stone producer, the general trend illustrated by the demand schedule is important to an economist. We note, for example, that as the price of semiprecious stones increases

the quantity demanded decreases. This decline reflects a normal consumer reaction to increasing prices, a relationship between price and quantity that occurs consistently. The relationship has been given a name, *the law of demand*, which is stated as follows: The quantity demanded of a good increases as the price decreases assuming always that all other things which might affect demand—such as income, tastes, preferences, period of time, and the prices of other goods—remain the same.

The law of demand can be stated in another way. We could say that the *quantity* demanded of a particular good *decreases* as the price

Exhibit 2-2 Hypothetical demand curve for
semiprecious stones

Price	Quantity Demanded
$2.00	6,000
1.50	9,000
1.00	12,000
.50	15,000

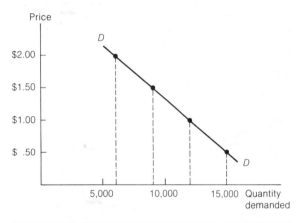

*A hypothetical demand schedule for semiprecious
stones is given in the upper half of the exhibit.
Another way of indicating the same information is to
plot the points from the demand schedule on a graph
of price and quantity. These points are plotted in the
lower half of the exhibit. When the points are
connected, a demand curve is created. (Remember,
the demand curve can be a straight line.) The demand
curve is identified by the letter D on both ends of the
line segment and is referred to as demand curve DD.
This demand curve is consistent with the law of
demand, which states the consumers will purchase
more of a good as the price declines.*

increases. In either case, we are expressing an
inverse relationship between the price of a good
and the quantity demanded. This inverse relationship is the law of demand.

Rather than present demand as a table of

numbers, it is often useful to represent the relationship between price and quantity on a graph.
Exhibit 2-2 shows a demand schedule for semiprecious stones for 2000 people like Stuart and
Ann and the graph representing the schedule.
These 2000 people are the only people in the
economy willing and able to purchase semiprecious stones at any price. Hence, they compose
the individual units on the demand side of the
market. In these graphs, by convention, we place
the price per unit on the vertical axis of the
graph and the quantity demanded per unit of
time on the horizontal axis. It is then possible
to show the demand schedule by a line which
starts higher at the leftmost points on the graph
and slopes downward. In our demand schedule
the line is straight with a slope down to the
right. The relationship between price and quantity demanded is not necessarily represented by
a straight line, however. It might be bumpy or
curved although it will always slope downward
for normal products. Whether it is straight or
curved, it is termed a *demand curve.*

The downward-sloping demand curve exists
because people are willing to pay a relatively
high price for a small amount of a particular
commodity. However, as they obtain more and
more of the commodity their willingness to pay
high prices decreases. For example, if you have
drunk three cups of coffee in an hour a fourth
cup is likely to give you less satisfaction than
the first. Each additional cup will decline in value
to you; the price you are willing to pay will
decrease as well.

Changes in Demand Schedules

Now that you are familiar with the basic law
of demand and how it is reflected in the demand
curve and demand schedule, it is possible to
investigate more interesting questions. Two

types of changes in a demand schedule should be distinguished.

Change in Quantity Demanded What happens when the price of a particular commodity changes? Our demand schedule or demand curve gives us the answer: in Exhibit 2-2, if the price of a semiprecious stone doubles from 50¢ to $1 we can see, from either the demand schedule or the demand curve, that the quantity will drop from 15,000 stones per month to 12,000.

In general the law of demand tells us that as the price increases the quantity demanded decreases. This response is reflected in the shape of the curve: it slopes downward from left to right. In the specific case, the demand for stones decreased when the price increased from 50¢ to $1. Changes in price result in *changes in the quantity demanded* and this is reflected in the demand curve or the demand schedule. That is, we are simply moving along the demand curve, or up or down the demand schedule, in order to learn the impact of a change in price on the quantity demanded.

Change in Demand If you were hired as an economist for the SPS Production Corporation you might want to learn what would happen if a person's income or preference for semiprecious stones changed. The demand curve can help. You will recall that a demand curve or schedule is based on the assumption that all variables, like taste, preference, and disposable income, remain constant except the quantity demanded for a particular good and its price. But suppose one of the other variables changes. Suppose, for example, that Ann receives a $1000 increase in income. How will this affect her demand for semiprecious stones at any given price? If these stones are a desirable good, she will purchase a larger quantity than she previously had bought

Exhibit 2-3 Shifts and movements in demand

P	Q Demanded before Income Increase	Q Demanded after Income Increase
$2.00	6,000	11,000
1.50	9,000	14,000
1.00	12,000	16,000
.50	15,000	19,000

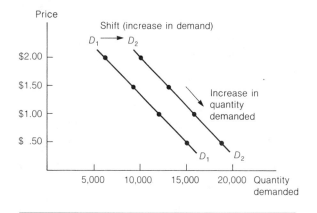

This figure illustrates the difference between a movement along a demand curve and a shift in a demand curve. Curve D_1D_1 shows the relationship between price and quantity for a group of individuals. This group receives an increase in income and as a result demands more semiprecious stones (at the same price) than they did before. The new demand curve is shown as D_2D_2.

Shift – income change.

at the same price. If we graph this new demand and relationship, we find that the new demand curve lies to the right of the original demand curve. Such a shift is illustrated in Exhibit 2-3. It does not necessarily shift to the right by the same amount at every price, but it certainly shifts outward from its original position based on the old income level.

Other changeable factors besides income can influence demand. Take sales of antifreeze in a mild climate. When the weather forecasters predict the first "hard freeze" of winter, the original demand curve for antifreeze shifts to the right as car owners feel an urgent need to protect their cars. Or consider the recent demand curve for tennis equipment. More tennis gear has been demanded at every price because our *preference* for tennis increased. In these cases we are not moving along a demand curve but rather shifting the whole curve to the right. (Of course, a demand curve may shift to the left if a smaller quantity is demanded at each price. Can you think of an example?)

Shifts in the demand curve result from a change in forces outside the specific market for the commodity in question. A demand curve does not shift as a result of changes in price. Shifts are the result of changes in such variables as income, tastes, and preferences, or perhaps the price of other related commodities. You will recall that the demand schedule and the demand curve were constructed on the assumption that certain conditions would not change. We assumed that a person's income, tastes, preferences, and the prices paid for other goods stayed the same. But when one of these factors does change, it may shift the demand curve either left or right depending upon how the change affects our demand for a particular commodity.

Prices of **Complements** and **Substitutes**

Coffee - cig.
Beer - peanuts.

Changes in prices of related goods can shift a demand curve. Suppose you regard coffee as an incomplete product unless accompanied by a doughnut. That is, coffee is only mildly interesting to you unless you can obtain a doughnut at the same time. In this case we regard doughnuts and cups of coffee as *complementary goods.* Consequently, how many cups of coffee you buy depends not only on the price of coffee but also on whether you can obtain doughnuts at some

acceptable price. Suppose the price of a doughnut declines from 35¢ to 25¢. Although the price decrease may not have an obvious impact on the coffee market, it may make additional cups of coffee more desirable, since you can now obtain more doughnuts at a lower price. You may demand more coffee to go with those cheaper doughnuts. In this case, the price of another commodity has influenced the demand schedule for cups of coffee. The demand curve shifts; you have probably already realized that the shift will be to the right. The new demand schedule will reflect more quantity demanded at any given price than the old schedule because the price of a complementary good went down. Undoubtedly, you can think of other complementary goods such as cars and gasoline, homes and electricity, cameras and film, and others.

Suppose, on the other hand, you drink both coffee and tea and regard tea as an adequate substitute for coffee. When these two beverages have the same price, you may prefer coffee to tea. However, if the price of tea drops to 10¢ per cup when the price of coffee remains at 25¢, your demand schedule for coffee may change considerably. Nothing has happened to the price of coffee; hence, you are not moving *along* your demand schedule. But an event outside the coffee market has left you unwilling to demand the same number of cups of coffee. Hence, your demand curve for coffee shifts left—as the result of a decrease in the price of tea. Goods such as coffee and tea which a consumer is willing to substitute one for another are called *substitute goods.* When the price of a substitute good decreases, the demand curve for the original good shifts to the left. When the price of a complementary good decreases, demand for the original good increases and the curve shifts to the right.

Obviously, we are also assuming that your tastes and preferences have not changed. But

When a substitute good becomes much cheaper, demand for the original good is likely to decline. *(Photo by Steve Potter)*

they do change. Activities which were highly desirable when we were 12 years of age may seem ridiculous at age 19. The lifestyle of a young married couple with children is often very different from that enjoyed by singles. Experience, age, and changing situations cause most people to have very different tastes and preferences at various points in their lives. When something happens to change your tastes and preferences, there is a corresponding shift in your demand schedules or demand curves.

A person's expectation regarding future income and prices also affects his or her current demand for a good. If we expect car prices to be higher in the future we are likely to buy more cars now regardless of price, than if we expect car prices to decline in succeeding years. Hence, our demand curve for cars will shift right when we expect future prices to rise and shift left if we expect future prices to go down.

To review, demand curves shift when something occurs external to the market for the goods. Changes in forces external to the market, such as income, tastes, and preferences, or prices of substitute or complementary goods, shift the demand schedule for any given commodity. When nothing external occurs and only the price of a given commodity changes, our demand schedule or curve reflects what will happen to the quantity demanded. This we call a *movement* along a demand curve.

SUPPLY

We have discussed demand as if goods are always available for purchase. In fact, the supply of goods is also related to price. Whether or not we decide to market semiprecious stones depends on whether the cost of the mine, the equipment, and the labor is low enough to provide an adequate return on our time and money when we sell the stones.

One way to assess whether we obtain a good return is to compare it to alternative uses of our time and money. This alternative return is called our *opportunity cost* as defined in Chapter 1. Opportunity cost is the amount we lose when we decide to produce semiprecious stones instead of some other commodity. Consequently the good we finally produce should use our resources better than any other alternatives.

Supply Schedule

Exhibit 2-4 is a hypothetical supply schedule for semiprecious stones. It indicates that at a

Exhibit 2-4 Hypothetical supply schedule for
semiprecious stones

Price	Quantity (per month)
$2.00	20,000
1.50	16,000
1.00	12,000
.50	8,000

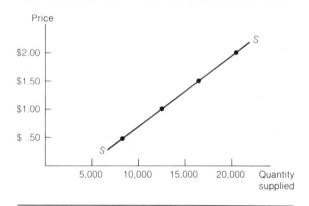

*This hypothetical supply schedule shows the response
of producers to higher prices. At low prices the
producers are willing to supply small quantities. At
higher prices they are willing to supply more. When
the schedule is plotted, curve SS illustrates the law of
supply.*

price of 50¢ per stone, 8000 stones per month
would be supplied, whereas at $1.00, 12,000
stones per month would be forthcoming. When
prices rise even higher, additional amounts
would be supplied. Why is the supply schedule
shaped this way? Let us remember that while
price is an obstacle for consumers to overcome
in order to purchase a good, it also serves as an
incentive for those producing the good. The
higher the price the greater the incentive to produce the good.

Supplying additional goods, however, is usually accompanied by higher costs of production.
Imagine that you dig semiprecious stones in a
mine that you own. At 50¢ you are willing to
dig and sell the easily reached stones, but if you
wish to produce at a higher rate of output you
will need additional equipment and labor
because you must dig deeper to find more stones.
These additional inputs yield more stones, but
costs per stone also rise.

Of course, the supply schedule can be graphed
in the same way as the demand schedule. The

Court Recognizes Opportunity Cost

The Maryland Court of Appeals has recognized
the role of opportunity cost by admitting the value
of a wife's housework. The ruling occurred in a
1978 case in which the 10 children of a murdered
Prince George's County woman asked the State
Criminal Injuries Compensation Board to compensate them for the loss of their mother's
domestic services. The board ruled that the loss
of her services did not constitute financial hardship since the household duties were assumed
by the two eldest daughters.

On appeal, the board's decision was over-
ruled by the Maryland Court of Appeals, which
noted, "Clearly, Mrs. Holmes might have increased
her earnings by purchasing care for her children,
thereby emancipating herself for additional paid
work. Although she chose to perform the paren-
tal services herself, we nevertheless believe that
the economic position of the Holmes family was
enhanced by the value of those services." (A
labor economist calculated her household chores
to be worth $634 a month at 1978 prices.) This
decision was an explicit recognition of the monetary value of a factor—its opportunity cost—
even when the factor was not paid.

supply curve of Exhibit 2-4 is lower at the left side of the curve than at the right side. It indicates that as the price of a good rises, the quantity supplied increases—just as the supply schedule showed.

The *law of supply* states that *the quantity of a good supplied usually varies directly with the price of the good, assuming all other factors related to supply do not change.* "Directly" means that as the price of a good increases, the quantity supplied also increases (the upward-sloping supply curve). Supply schedules are related to costs.

Change in Supply

As in the demand curve, two cases of change in the supply curve should be discussed.

Change in Quantity Supplied A movement along a supply schedule is a change in the quantity supplied. As shown in Exhibit 2-5, an increase in price from $1 to $3 increases the amount supplied from 10,000 to 20,000 units. This movement along the supply curve S_1S_1 is illustrated by the movement from point *a* to point *b*.

Change in Supply When factors external to the market do not remain constant, a shift in the supply curve may result. Such a change is also illustrated in Exhibit 2-5. The change in supply shown means that at *the same price* the producers are willing to provide less than they previously would. The change from point *b* to point *c* illustrates such a decrease in supply: that is, a shift to the left S_2S_2. What would cause such a shift? Two explanations are most common: (1) a change in production technology and (2) a change in the cost of the factors used in the production process. For example, the introduc-

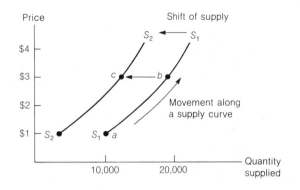

Exhibit 2-5 Shifts in supply

This figure illustrates the difference between a movement along a supply curve and a shift in a supply curve. Curve S_1S_1 shows the relationship between price and quantity for a group of producers. Points a and b on the supply curve S_1S_1 reflect a movement along a supply curve. Curve S_2S_2 shows a shift in supply which causes a smaller quantity to be supplied at the same price (for example, point b to point c).

tion of the mechanical cotton-picker had a significant impact on the production of cotton, shifting the supply curve to the right. A factor price change occurred in the electric utility industry during the 1974–75 period. When fuel oil costs rose, large utilities' supply curves for electricity shifted left by a large amount.

MARKETS: WHERE DEMAND AND SUPPLY INTERACT

A supply schedule does *not* tell us what price will be charged for a cup of coffee nor how many cups will be sold or produced. Nor does the demand schedule yield that information. These questions can be answered only by considering supply and demand simultaneously and, even then, only when all characteristics of the supply/demand interaction are known. When the process of interaction takes place economists call it a *market*. The price established by the interaction of supply and demand is called the *market price*.

A large number of prices exist at which producers will supply *some* quantity of output. There are also a large number of prices at which buyers will purchase *some* goods. But there is only one *equilibrium price*, or stable price, at which the quantity supplied and the quantity demanded are equal. At equilibrium, there are no forces working in the market to change the price until there is a shift in the demand or supply schedule.

The role of market forces in establishing an equilibrium price is illustrated in Exhibit 2-6, which combines the demand and supply schedules for semiprecious stones seen earlier (in Exhibits 2-2 and 2-4). It shows the equilibrium price at which the quantity supplied and the quantity demanded are equal, and there are neither shortages nor surpluses. At the $1 price there is no pressure to change either quantities supplied or quantities demanded.

But note what happens when the price is not at its equilibrium level. For example, at a price of $2, producers supply 20,000 semiprecious stones but consumers demand only 6000. Thus, there is a surplus of 14,000 stones per month at a price of $2. Sellers may temporarily hold the price at $2, but if they do, inventories of unsold stones will build up. Eventually competitive forces among the sellers will force them to lower the market price in order to reduce their large inventories. (Who wants to pay increased storage costs for unsold stones?) Lowering prices will increase their sales.

If the market price is below equilibrium, say

Exhibit 2-6   Combining hypothetical supply and demand schedules for semiprecious stones

P	Q_D	Q_S	Pressure on Prices
$2.00	6,000	20,000	↓
1.50	9,000	16,000	↓
1.00	12,000	12,000	Neutral
.50	15,000	8,000	↑

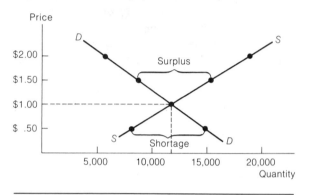

The intersection of supply (SS) and demand (DD) curves indicates an equilibrium price. At prices above the equilibrium, there is a surplus. At prices below equilibrium, there is a shortage. Only at the equilibrium price does the quantity of goods that producers are willing to supply equal the quantity of goods that consumers desire.

50¢, similar pressures exist. More semiprecious stones will be demanded than will be supplied; 15,000 demanded minus 8000 supplied equals 7000 shortage at 50¢. Competition among consumers for the limited number of stones will bid the market price up. This upward pressure on price will continue until it reaches the equilibrium price ($1) where quantity supplied equals quantity demanded. Exhibit 2-6 shows the surplus and shortage associated, respectively, with the nonequilibrium prices $1.50 and 50¢.

Shifts in Supply and Demand

An equilibrium price can be changed by a shift in either supply or demand. Exhibit 2-7a illus-

FREEZE

Shortage   ORANGE JUICE.

Apple Juice, water

Tynenol capsults.

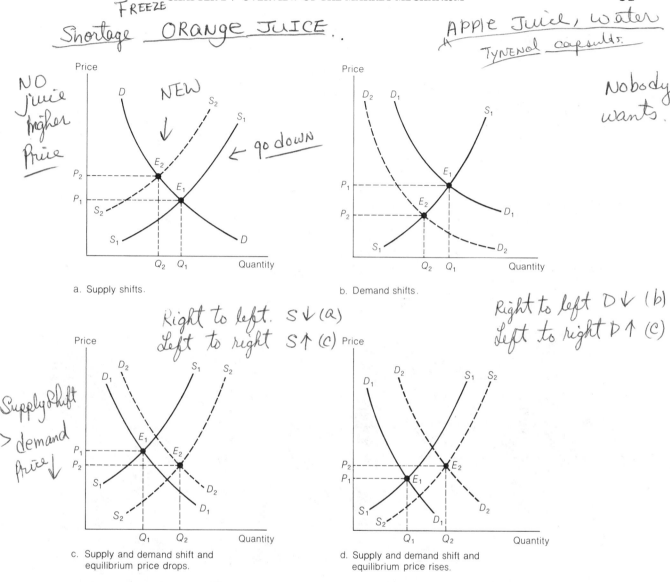

NO
juice
higher
price

NEW
↓

← go down

Nobody
wants.

a. Supply shifts.

b. Demand shifts.

Right to left. S↓ (a)
Left to right S↑ (C)

Right to left D↓ (b)
Left to right D↑ (C)

Supply shift
> demand
price ↓

c. Supply and demand shift and
   equilibrium price drops.

d. Supply and demand shift and
   equilibrium price rises.

Exhibit 2-7 Shifts in supply and demand

*This figure illustrates the impact upon the
equilibrium price and quantity when shifts occur in
either supply or demand. D_1D_1 and S_1S_1 form the
initial price (P_1) and quantity (Q_1). After a shift has
occurred, the new equilibrium conditions are shown
by P_2 and Q_2.*

trates the effect of a shift in the supply schedule. Suppose that supply and demand for oranges
are in equilibrium as shown by the solid curves
S_1S_1 and *DD*. Imagine that a deep freeze hits
the orange groves in Florida, reducing the quantity of oranges available at each price level and

causing a shift in the supply function to the dotted line S_2S_2. After the shift of the supply curve, sufficient oranges are no longer available at the old equilibrium price. There is an orange shortage. Consumers start bidding for the limited supply, and the market price begins to rise along the demand curve from P_1, the original equilibrium price, to P_2. At the higher price, more oranges are supplied and fewer are demanded. The adjustment to a shift in the orange supply occurs through the interaction of supply and demand. At the higher price, more expensive recovery methods, such as handpicking, are used to supply a larger quantity. At the same time a higher price keeps some consumers out of the market. Equilibrium is achieved at a higher price as indicated by point E_2.

A parallel situation occurs in Exhibit 2-7b, with a demand shift. Suppose that some bad news is released about a product (for example, reports of its radiation level being unsafe) which shifts the demand curve to the left (to D_2D_2). As a result P_1 is no longer an equilibrium price. Now suppliers are unable to sell all the goods that they produce. Inventories build up, and the seller competition drives the price down along the supply curve to the new equilibrium P_2. At this lower price consumers are willing to purchase

Because of rising oil costs, people have looked to alternate sources of energy, thus affecting demand for oil. *(Photo by Dean Abramson, Stock, Boston)*

more, and producers supply less. The result is that at E_2 a new equilibrium is reached.

When only one side of a market shifts, we can predict the direction of the price and quantity change. For example, when supply shifted left, the new equilibrium was at a higher price and a lower quantity than the original equilibrium. If supply had increased at every price, indicating a shift to the right, then the new equilibrium price would be lower and more would be sold than previously. (Can you make similar statements about demand shifts, left or right?) However, when both sides of the market shift at the same time it is not so easy to generalize about the resulting equilibrium. Two possibilities are shown in Exhibit 2-7c-d. Both show a shift in demand and supply and an increase in the equilibrium quantity. However, Exhibit 2-7c shows a decrease in the price, since supply shifted more than demand, and Exhibit 2-7d shows an increase in the equilibrium price. A simple shift on one side of the market is easy to analyze, but the interaction of shifts in both sides of the market is not.

Prices as an Allocation System

The changes in the equilibrium price brought about by shifts in the supply and demand curves can be viewed as a system of signals to both producers and consumers. When the quantity demanded exceeds the quantity supplied at a given price, the actions of individuals bidding for the limited supply of the good force the price up. The higher price is a signal to consumers to use less of the good because it is in short supply. At the same time, the higher price serves as a signal to producers that more of the good is desired and that more resources should be allocated to producing it.

Similarly, falling prices usually indicate a market surplus and signal producers to allocate

---

Scalping

The impact of shifts in demand can be seen clearly by the case of "scalping" tickets (charging more for a ticket than the official price) which occurs at some athletic contests. At the beginning of a season the number of tickets available for each home game is fixed by the number of seats available (ignoring standing room). The demand for each event is based on people's expectations as to the importance and value of that event. As the season progresses, a team may fare better or worse than expected. A game that wasn't supposed to mean much can suddenly take on added importance at the end of the season—e.g., Texas and Oklahoma end up playing for the national championship or Stanford and Southern California play to determine the Rose Bowl representative. The demand curve for tickets shifts right, but the supply is limited by the number of seats. People who want to see the game and do not have a ticket must bid the tickets away from those who have them. The original supplier (the athletic ticket office) cannot add to supply. Tickets that originally sold for $20 a pair may be valued at $30 and higher. In this case price serves as a device to allocate tickets based upon intensity of desire to see the game. The change in preferences for the tickets has caused a shift to the right in the demand curve and, since supply is constant, has caused the ticket price to increase.

---

less resources to the production of the good. In Part III we will discuss this method of resource allocation in greater detail, but for now we will present a brief outline of the process. Although there are delays and imperfections in such a system, a market-oriented economy uses the information provided by the market to allocate scarce resources.

It is important to remember that some allocation procedure is necessary in any society as long as shortages exist. The primary allocation device in the United States today is market price, but other devices also exist. Illustrations are not hard to find. For example, parking space near most universities is a scarce resource. Many students and staff must park their cars on the streets. Demand for parking close to campus far exceeds the supply of parking places because the price is zero. To alleviate this problem, the desirable parking places, if privately owned, could be allocated in any one of several ways. Parking slots could be auctioned to the highest bidder. Or a lottery could be held, with all students and/or staff having an equal chance. (However, if the winners "scalped" their winning location we would be back to a price system.) Desirable parking could be assigned in alphabetical order, or to the strongest (determined by who lasted longest in a brawl), or to the most beautiful, or to the most overweight, or by giving the most desirable places to seniors, second most desirable to juniors, and so forth. A common solution is to reserve the closest parking lots for members of the administration, faculty, and staff.

The alternatives usually adopted, however, are other rules just like the pricing scheme. The "fairness" of an allocation method is a normative question—a matter of values or personal choice. However, it should be clear that *some* allocation method or rule is necessary as long as there is a scarcity of the things people want.

SUMMARY

1. A demand schedule or demand curve reflects a set of prices for a good and the quantity of that good which an individual or group of individuals would purchase at the given price. The law of demand states that there is an inverse relation between price and quantity demanded.

2. A demand curve can *shift* with a change in the price of other goods, consumers' income, tastes, preferences, expectation of future prices and incomes, or some other factors external to the market.

3. A supply schedule or supply curve shows the amount of goods that will be provided at a given price. These goods are produced when their opportunity cost is higher than for producing any other goods. Opportunity cost is determined by comparing one use of resources with the best possible alternatives. The law of supply indicates a direct relationship between quantity supplied and price.

4. A market is the interaction of supply and demand. There is usually only one price, the equilibrium price, at which the quantity demanded is equal to the amount that suppliers are willing to supply. At any other price, there are pressures which tend to drive the market price toward equilibrium.

5. A market mechanism is just one method of allocating resources. However, as long as there is unfulfilled demand for goods some allocation device is necessary.

KEY CONCEPTS

demand schedule	supply schedule
law of demand	supply curve
demand curve	law of supply
change in the quantity demanded	change in quantity supplied
change in demand	market
complementary goods	market price
substitute goods	equilibrium price
opportunity cost	allocation of resources

QUESTIONS FOR DISCUSSION

1. Suppose you were estimating the demand curve for automobiles in 1990. What are some of the factors you would need to consider in developing the demand curve?
2. Would reducing the price of autos shift the demand curve? Would it affect the quantity demanded? What is the difference between these two questions?
3. Americans are buying more fish per capita now than 20 years ago even though the price of fish has increased over that period. Does this disprove the law of demand?
4. During the 1950s the U.S. government stockpiled large quantities of copper and other strategic metals. If a decision had been made to use these stockpiles to keep the price of copper from rising above a certain price, how could this have been accomplished? What would the copper supply curve look like?
5. You are told that the equilibrium price of gidgets has dropped from $10 to $8 but no other information is given you. Can you say the price change is due to a shift in demand, supply, or both?
6. Providing manpower for the military has been a controversial subject for many years. It is essentially an allocation question. In the United States, three methods have been used over the last 20 years: the volunteer or high-wage system, the draft with a lottery to determine priority, and the previous draft which granted widespread exemptions. Is one of these systems "fairer" than the others? What do you mean by fair? Do you think a volunteer system would work during a war? Why?

Chapter 3

An Overview of the U.S. Economy

The economy of the United States is an extremely complex mechanism composed of a large number of components working together in a myriad of processes. For convenience the components and processes are usually grouped together in aggregates. Newspaper headlines herald reductions in interest rates or increases in unemployment. However, these aggregates are composed of widely varying components that hide the variances. A national unemployment rate of 9 percent may disguise such extremes as 16 percent joblessness in Detroit but only 4 percent in Houston.

Similarly we speak of a piece of legislation as being "pro-business." But does "business" in this case refer to General Motors with 750,000 employees or a mom-and-pop grocery store with two employees? Is it likely that these two dissimilar business entities would have similar views on most legislation?

In the first part of this chapter we discuss the major players on the economic stage: consumers, business, government, and foreign factors affecting the U.S. economy. In the second portion we address current economic trends and problems.

PLAYERS ON THE ECONOMIC STAGE

Consumers

The key to the success of any business is being able to sell its products or services. No product or service is developed unless a business thinks consumers will buy it. Businesses that were once large and prosperous, such as the A&P grocery store chain, International Harvester, and Braniff Airlines, have been hurt badly or failed because they were unwilling or unable to adjust to changes in the marketplace. Yet small firms can grow and prosper when they accurately predict a trend; Apple Computer, Coppertone, and Kindercare are recent examples.

The demographic composition of the population is constantly changing, and these changes set the stage for major consumption decisions. Businesses need to recognize these changes if they are to anticipate shifts in tastes and needs among different groups. For example, the average age of the population and the ratio of males to females may affect the relative demand for certain broad categories of goods: large houses versus apartments, baby goods versus stereo equipment, tennis rackets versus soccer shoes. Although averages sometimes conceal wide shifts

in population composition, a brief discussion of certain averages will show how our economy is shifting.

In 1979 the median age of the U.S. population reached 30 years, meaning that half the population was older than 30. This was the second time in U.S. history that this figure was reached. In 1950 the median age of the population hit 30.2 years. Back in 1890 the median was only 20.9. Thereafter the median age started to rise. After passing the age-30 threshold in 1950, the median age fell during the "baby boom" years of the 1950s, when American couples were having a record number of babies. The median age reached a modern low of 27.9 years in 1970 and has been creeping upward since then. By the year 2000 the median age is expected to be 35.

Such changes in population age levels may forecast a greater need for facilities for the aged than now exist. Simultaneously the changes may present opportunities for new products and innovations supporting different life styles.

The sexual composition of the population has been changing, too. The 1950 census counted 99 men for every 100 women. The male/female ratio has since dropped to 95 men per 100 women and is expected to decrease even further.

Households are smaller, too. In 1930, the average household numbered 4.1 persons. By 1974 the average had dropped to 3.0 and continues to fall, having reached 2.8 in 1982. Census Bureau projections forecast that an average household will consist of 2.3 persons in 1995.

Geographically the center of U.S. population—the point on the map at which exactly half the population lives to the west and half to the east—has been moving westward throughout the 200 years of U.S. history. In the 1790 census, the nation's population center was near Baltimore; by 1880, it had moved west to the Cincinnati area. It was even farther west, in Illinois, between 1950 and 1980. In 1980 a milestone of sorts was reached when the center of

Retirees are becoming a bigger and bigger segment of the U.S. population. *(Photo by Terry Zabala)*

population moved across the Mississippi River into Missouri. The center is expected to remain in Missouri for the next 50 years.

As Exhibit 3-1 shows, population growth has varied widely among the states during recent years. The Sun Belt of the Southeast and South-

Exhibit 3-1   The ten fastest and ten slowest growing states, 1970–80

Fastest Growing States	Percent Increase in Population	Slowest Growing States	Percent Change in Population
1. Nevada	63.5%	1. New York	−3.8%
2. Arizona	53.1	2. Rhode Island	−0.3
3. Florida	43.4	3. Pennsylvania	0.6
4. Wyoming	41.6	4. Massachusetts	0.8
5. Utah	37.9	5. Ohio	1.3
6. Alaska	32.4	6. Connecticut	2.5
7. Idaho	32.4	7. New Jersey	2.7
8. Colorado	30.7	8. Illinois	2.8
9. New Mexico	27.8	9. Iowa	3.1
10. Texas	27.1	10. South Dakota	3.6

SOURCE: *Demography*, March 1982.

west has gained population relative to the northeastern and north central states.

The two-earner family has also become more common. Between 1968 and 1978, the number of families in which two persons were earning income grew by 4.5 million. This dramatic shift has had a powerful effect upon family activities. The demographic characteristics of two-earner families are different from those of one-earner families. The two-earner families have fewer children, higher income, and a greater amount of education. They spend more on conveniences and services such as food preparation, laundry, child care, transportation, and vacations.

Consumers have also responded to changes in the relative prices of goods. As houses became relatively more expensive, more people began to buy smaller houses. The size of the average single-family house in the United States fell from 2200 square feet in 1970 to 1700 square feet in 1980. Experts estimate that houses will shrink even further, to 1200 square feet, by 1990. Thus a major industry, housing, has been strongly affected by both changing demographic factors and relative prices. Builders who anticipated these trends have survived; others have faltered.

The importance of the consumer in the economy cannot be overemphasized. Firms that do not satisfy consumer wishes will not prosper.

Businesses

Businesses produce the goods and services that provide for the material wants of society. They employ the labor, use the capital, and rent the land. Businesses come in many sizes and forms. Like the consumer, they play a major role in the economic process.

The U.S. business structure is continually changing. Looking at the major trends over time, one can see how some sections of the economy have grown while others have declined. Before

and after the Civil War, agriculture was the dominant economic activity in the United States, with three of every five workers engaged directly in farming. Countless other workers were indirectly associated with agriculture, through the production of farm equipment, transportation of agricultural goods, and retail sales to farmers.

In the following three decades other sectors of the economy grew rapidly. Railroads, in particular, took large amounts of capital and labor; the growth of the Western railroads and the resulting ease of transportation changed the character of other sectors. Large factories supplying goods to the whole country replaced small shops providing manufactured goods for local or regional markets. As cities grew, the tasks of providing electricity, water, and transportation became more important. Rapid growth in utilities and manufacturing dominated the economic scene at the turn of the century. By the end of World War I, the United States had changed from an agricultural nation to an industrial nation. Exhibit 3-2 illustrates the shift from agricultural to non-agricultural employment.

While these broad changes were occurring, other changes went on within individual sectors. Even though manufacturing continued to grow after World War I, all forms of manufac-

Exhibit 3-2 Percentage of workforce engaged in agriculture

Year	Percentage
1800	74.6%
1840	68.6
1860	59.8
1900	39.4
1920	21.0
1940	16.8
1960	7.2
1970	4.0
1982 (estimated)	2.7

turing did not share in this growth. For example, the manufacture and sale of ice for home iceboxes was once a significant activity in every city and town, but the development of the electric refrigerator soon reduced commercial ice-making to a minor activity. In the energy sector, fuel oil and natural gas superseded coal for home heating, causing a decline in coal-mining employment. In the post–World War II era, passenger transportation by railroad was almost eliminated as airplanes, automobiles, and buses became more popular.

Exhibit 3-3 shows some of the changes that occurred in nonagricultural employment between 1940 and 1982. As shown in this exhibit, industries have taken different paths since 1940. For example, mining employs the same number of people now as it did more than 40 years ago, but the number of government employees has more than tripled. Such changes within individual industries are continuing even today.

In addition, the composition of an industry changes. Some firms grow and prosper, while others disappear. Among auto producers, such one-time giants as Duesenberg, Stutz, Locomobile, Chandler, Nash, Studebaker, and Packard have stopped producing autos, but General Motors, Ford, and Chrysler continue to operate.

Among railroads, the once profitable and fashionable New York Central and Pennsylvania railroads declined and suffered a series of annual losses until absorbed into the government-backed Conrail System. Meanwhile, the well-run Southern and Western railroads prosper.

The United States is a very large market. Serving this market, however, does not necessarily require large firms. One interesting aspect of U.S. businesses is the lack of giant corporations in many sectors. Manufacturing remains the largest sector and has numerous large firms.

An indication of conditions in manufacturing is the size of the firms that make up that sector. The 50 largest manufacturing firms account for more than 25 percent of production, and their share continues to grow.

Multinational firms have grown rapidly, although firms operating in more than one country are not new. Royal Dutch Shell (Shell Oil in the United States) has produced, transported, and sold petroleum products all over the world since the beginning of the twentieth century. Similarly, Nestle's, a Swiss firm, has manufactured and sold food products, and the British-based Lever Brothers has sold soaps worldwide. However, the post–World War II era has seen an acceleration in the number and size

Exhibit 3-3 Shifts in nonagricultural employment, 1940 and 1982

Industry	1940		1982	
	Number of Employees (in millions)	Percentage	Number of Employees (in millions)	Percentage
Manufacturing	11.0	34%	20.9	24%
Trade	6.8	21	20.1	22
Service	3.7	11	17.0	19
Government	4.2	13	15.6	17
Transportation and utilities	3.0	9	5.1	6
Finance, insurance, real estate	1.5	5	4.9	5
Contract construction	1.3	4	4.2	5
Mining	.9	3	.9	1
Total employment	32.4	100	88.7	100

of companies that view the world as their market. These firms are able to move assets, funds, and production technologies from one country to another. Some observers contend that no country can exercise effective control over a multinational firm. Other observers disagree. Although no definitive statement can be made about their behavior, undoubtedly multinational firms are growing in importance.

The Labor Force

The U.S. labor force of 114 million persons is the most important element in the economy. These workers both produce the goods and use their wages to purchase goods. The wages received by the workforce make up about two-thirds of all personal income.

The following trends dominated the labor force during the 1970s and have continued through the early 1980s:

1. Manufacturing is declining in importance.
2. Labor unions are declining in both relative and absolute size.
3. Women are playing a more important role in the labor force.
4. The workforce is growing older and the 60-plus age group is increasing.
5. The job market is changing.

Let us discuss each of these trends.

Although manufacturing has always been the largest sector of the economy, it is becoming less important. The high technology and service sectors are growing rapidly and are providing the growth opportunities. Exhibit 3-4 shows this shift in the type of employment between 1950 and 1980.

Labor unions grew relative to the labor force from 1930 to 1970 but have since declined in

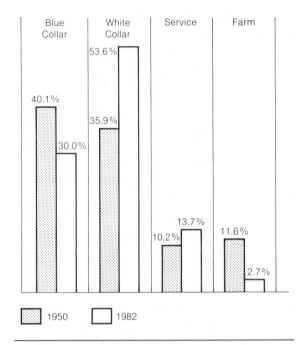

Exhibit 3-4   Where the workers are—by share of total employment, 1950–82

both relative and absolute size. Part of this decline reflects the shift in demand from manufactured goods to service goods. The huge industrial unions, largely representing the workers in the manufacturing industries, have not been able to recruit as successfully in the service sector. Unions now represent less than 21 percent of the entire labor force, the smallest share since World War II.

The increased representation of women in the labor force can be seen in the following data:

Year	Adult Women in the Labor Force
1950	33.9%
1960	37.7
1970	43.3
1980	52.1

Behind the Aggregates

One of the problems of aggregate numbers, like a 9 percent unemployment rate, is that they hide wide variations within the components. In the midst of the 1979–80 recession, with unemployment at 9 percent, some companies were desperately short of technicians. One company even went to a bounty system, paying a $1000 bonus to any employee who helped recruit a microwave and stress analysis technician. While 18 percent of U.S. steelworkers were laid off, nurses were in such demand that some hospitals could not operate all their wards.

Recessions do not affect all sectors, regions, and demographic groups equally. Unemployment rates provide the best example. In January 1982, when overall joblessness rose only 0.1 percentage point to 7.0 percent of the labor force, the unemployment rate for blacks rose 0.5 percent to 15.2 percent. Worse still, the rate for teenage blacks soared nearly four full points, to 40.3 percent. Bleak as that picture was, blacks in other areas showed considerable progress. For example, in banking the number of bank officers who were black rose from 7.2 percent to 8 percent during 1981. Similarly, women in many of the traditional heavy industries were suffering from layoffs, yet women were moving into professional and managerial positions at a rapid rate.

These differences by demographic groups to a large extent reflect different employment patterns by industry. During the 1982 recession the troubled steel and auto industries were operating at only 60 percent of capacity. Blacks made up close to 18 percent of workers in these hard-hit industries. The recession's effect on the steel and auto industries also caused hardships in the upper Midwest, with Detroit and Cleveland especially hard hit. At the same time, the growing demand for both home and business computers put Silicon Valley in California and the Boston-area electronic firms in a hiring mode.

Although unemployment rates and inflation rates are good indicators of general conditions, they hide wide differences of the impact by industry, region, age, education, and skill. These differences are very important in terms of policy and well-being of the nation.

It appears that this trend will continue and that eventually women without small children will participate in the labor force in the same proportion as men.

Since 1970, as noted above, the median age of the population in the United States has increased from 28 to 30. The increase reflects the declining birth rate of the late 1950s and 1960s that decreased the number of young workers. In addition, the 60-plus age group is increasing, due to a decline in mortality rates. The maturing of the labor force will be associated with increased productivity as the proportion of experienced workers increases; it will also mean more competition for career advancement as experienced workers vie for promotion. There will be fewer workers for the prime-age workers to supervise. This maturing will also drain Social Security funds. Currently there are six persons of working age for each person over 65. By the year 2000 the ratio could be as low as 4 to 1.

The job market of the future will be different than at present. The number of traditional production-line, blue-collar jobs will either remain stagnant or decline as production jobs are automated. Certain white-collar jobs may increase, but not all can be expected to do so. It is estimated that fewer opportunities will exist for farm workers, teachers, and unskilled laborers.

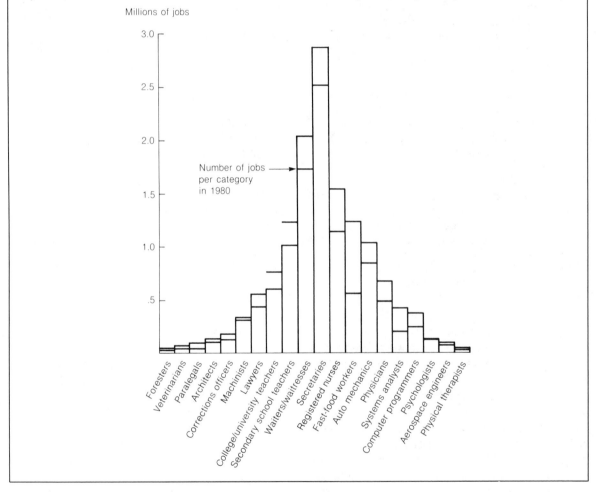

Jobs in 1990

According to the U.S. Bureau of Labor Statistics, the number of jobs in the United States will increase by 1990, but in an uneven manner. Fast-food chains, for example, will add nearly 800,000 jobs, but the number of teachers (at both the secondary school and college/university levels) will continue to drop.

By contrast, computer programmers, technicians, scientists, and administrators will be in increased demand. Rapid technological change will make the acquiring and updating of skills a necessity.

Government

In the Market   The role of the government in economic matters has been the subject of much recent inquiry. This interest has been associated with the growth in importance of government of all levels in the economy. In 1929, the government share of Gross National Product was less than 11 percent. In 1983 government receipts amounted to more than one-third of GNP, and government spending totaled more than $1100 billion.

Some of the activities by which the government receives and spends money do not differ markedly from those of private business organizations. For example, the Tennessee Valley Authority (TVA) and the Bonneville Power Administration (BPA) generate and sell hydroelectric power. TVA and BPA hire labor and buy equipment at market-determined prices and sell their power at prices similar to those of private organizations.

On the other hand, some government activities have no relationship to market activity. The majority of federal government activities fall into this category. Transfer payments—payments for which no services are performed, such as unemployment compensation and Social Security—are an example. The budget of the U.S. Department of Health and Human Services, which dispenses many transfer payments, is the largest of any government agency, having surpassed that of the U.S. Department of Defense in 1970. The Department of Defense also, of course, allocates resources outside the market. In sum, federal nonmarket activity is large and growing.

As shown in Exhibit 3-5, civilian federal employment in 1980 exceeded 2.8 million, not including another 2 million in the armed forces. State government employed 3.7 million; local government employed more than federal and state government combined—a total of 9.4 million in 1980. Thus total government employment, including military personnel, amounted to approximately 18 million, a significant part of a total labor force of 110.2 million.

Exhibit 3-5   Federal, state, and local government expenditures and employment

Government Level	Expenditures (billions)
Federal	$527
State	173
Local	259
Total	959

Government Level	Employment (millions)
Federal civilian	2.865
State	3.726
Local	9.377
Total civilian	15.968*
Federal military	2.062
Total civilian and military	18.030

*14.5 percent of 1980 total labor force (110.2 million)

Patterns of Federal Receipts and Expenditures   The federal government's largest source of income is the individual income tax (45 percent), followed by Social Security contributions (31 percent) and corporate income tax (14 percent). Such items as customs duties and tariffs, gift taxes, and excise taxes amount to only 10 percent of government receipts.

Expenditures, however, are more varied. As shown in Exhibit 3-6, Social Security payments are the largest category of expenditure, amounting to approximately 34 percent of the budget. National defense, with 23 percent, is the second largest. Interest at 11.2 percent, health at 10 percent, education (including training, employment, and social services) at 5.4 percent, and a miscellaneous set of other activities make up the remainder.

Shifts in Federal Government Spending   The federal budget serves not only as an accounting procedure but also as an index of national policy and trends. Exhibit 3-6 shows the percentage of federal expenditures going to various purposes in 1960, 1970, and 1980. Trends become clearer

Exhibit 3-6   Federal government expenditures, 1960–80

Area	Percent Distribution of Total Expenditures		
	1960	1970	1980
Social Security	19.8%	21.9%	33.9%
National defense	49.0	40.0	23.1
Interest	9.0	9.3	11.2
Health (primarily Medicare)	0.9	6.7	10.0
Education*	1.1	4.4	5.4
Veterans benefits	5.9	4.4	3.7
Transportation	4.4	3.6	3.5
Community and regional development	0.2	1.2	1.5
Revenue sharing	0.2	0.3	1.5
Commerce and housing	1.7	1.1	1.0
Miscellaneous†	7.8	7.1	5.2

*Includes training, employment, and social services.
†E.g., energy development, agriculture support, science, and technology.
SOURCE: *Statistical Abstract of the United States*, 1980, page 261.

when comparisons are made between 1960 and 1980, two years when there was no extensive military involvement by the United States that might otherwise distort the trends.

The dominant trend has been the declining share of federal expenditures going to national defense between 1960 and 1980. This decline from 49 to 23 percent has almost been matched by the increase in Social Security payments from 20 to 34 percent and in Medicare expenditures, from 0.1 to 10 percent. The other categories have remained rather stable.

Government As a Regulator   Government strongly affects the economy through the employment of millions of individuals and by purchasing billions of dollars worth of goods and services. However, government also plays an important role in the economy indirectly. Government influences virtually every economic decision made by business managers and their employees, by investors, by farmers, and by consumers.

As a starting point government provides the framework for the functioning of the economy.

It provides the police protection and the judicial system that safeguards property and enforces contracts. It provides a monetary system that lubricates the wheels of commerce.

Who Reads Their Mail?

In 1981 Congress required banks of the Federal Reserve System to explain to customers the intricacies and protection built into the method of paying of bills by means of electronic transfers. Like other financial institutions, the Northwestern National Bank was directed to draw up and mail a pamphlet about the new rules to each of its 120,000 customers. The bank felt that the $69,000 mailing cost was not justified, since its customers had shown no interest in the process. But the federal regulators insisted on the mailing, so to prove its point the bank devised a readership test: 100 of the 120,000 pamphlets were printed with the sentence, "Any customer who receives a disclosure that includes this paragraph can get $10 simply by writing 'Regulation' and [the customer's] name and address and mailing it to the bank." Not a single person redeemed the $10.

Regulatory Success

One of the successes of government regulation has been in the banking sector. The Federal Deposit Insurance Corporation (FDIC) was founded during the depression to insure depositors' accounts against bank failure. During the 1920s some 600 banks failed every year, unable to repay their customers' money in full. In the early 1930s that figure rose to 2000 per year. Since the founding of the FDIC in 1933, however, failures have averaged about 12 a year.

The agency is financed by an annual levy on member banks. Most of this money goes into a trust fund. When a bank fails, the FDIC uses the trust fund to pay off depositors, then assumes the bank's assets and sells them to replenish the trust fund. In 50 years, not a single depositor has lost a penny of his FDIC insured deposit, and the trust fund has grown to $12.3 billion.

In addition, government serves as a regulator of the private sector. Government intervention in the economy has been expanding since the founding of the United States, and by the late 1970s had become so pervasive that it had become a major political issue. The election of President Reagan in 1980 signaled a lull in the growth of regulation. Whether or not the Reagan victory indicates a reversal of the long-term trend will be determined by the election results during the 1980s. Regardless, the important point is that the cost of regulation is very large. The Center for the Study of American Business of Washington University estimates that in 1981 the annual price tag for government regulation was $130 billion. Most of that expense is picked up by consumers. In many programs the costs are clearly justified, in others the value received per dollar of cost seems small. Clearly each program of government regulation should be reviewed to see whether the benefits justify the costs, but this consideration has not always entered into the thinking of Congress when legislating new regulations.

Foreign Trade

Foreign trade is an important part of the U.S. economy and one that is growing rapidly. The evidence can be seen in the cars we drive, the television sets we watch, the oil that heats our homes, even the knives and forks on our tables.

Foreign economic conditions and the price of foreign currencies affect all Americans, from the farmers in Kansas whose wheat is sold in Europe, to the Datsun dealer in South Carolina whose car prices are determined by the exchange rate for yen. When the English pound increases in value relative to the dollar, U.S. consumers will see the price of English woollens rise. At the same time a drop in the exchange rate of the Canadian dollar will make a vacation in Quebec more attractive than it was before the drop.

Production of goods has become much more international than ever before. A television set may contain a picture tube from Japan and circuits from Singapore, be assembled in Mexico, and sold in the United States. In short, foreign commerce has an effect upon almost everyone's pocketbook.

Immediately after World War II the United States was relatively self-sufficient. It had productive capacity undamaged by the war, technological leadership in many fields, and stable economic and political institutions that attracted capital. This era has passed. What is known as the law of comparative advantage has reasserted itself. This economic principle says that some countries can provide certain products more efficiently than others because of better or differential access to raw materials, access to inexpensive labor, access to technological

Exhibit 3-7 Largest U.S. imports and exports, 1981

Largest U.S. Imports	Dollar Value (billions)
1. Petroleum	$78.5
2. Motor vehicles, parts	27.4
3. Iron, steel	12.1
4. Electrical machinery, parts	9.4
5. TV sets, radios, phonographs	9.2
6. Clothing	8.0
7. Nonferrous metals	7.1
8. Natural gas	5.8
9. Chemicals	5.6
10. Special-purpose machinery	5.3

Largest U.S. Exports	Dollar Value (billions)
1. Motor vehicles, parts	$16.1
2. Aircraft, parts	14.7
3. Industrial machinery	11.5
4. Office machinery, computers	9.8
5. Power-generating machinery	9.5
6. Chemicals	9.2
7. Corn	8.0
8. Wheat	7.8
9. Soybeans	6.2

advances, or other material endowments (e.g., fertile lands).

Exhibit 3-7 illustrates this phenomenon for the United States. The largest exports (in terms of dollar value) reflect U.S. technology in electronics, aircraft, and computers. The corn, wheat, and soybean exports reflect the efficiency of U.S. agriculture and plentiful farmland. The largest import, petroleum, is a result of the material endowment of the Middle East. On the other hand, imports of autos and iron and steel show the effect of high U.S. labor costs and aging production facilities.

Consumer purchases of foreign goods that reflect the benefits of other nations' comparative advantage have stimulated U.S. international trade to expand at a faster rate than the economy. U.S. exports grew from 2 percent of U.S. output in 1960 to 8 percent in 1981. There were 4.8 million workers in jobs in the United

States associated with the export of manufactured products. In addition, the export of agricultural products plays an important role in the income of farmers.

Exports and Imports Exhibit 3-8 shows the size and scope of trade activity. Purchases of foreign production—imports—accounted for $264.1 billion in 1981. Canada and Japan remain the largest suppliers of imports in the United States. Canadian sales to the United States reflect the complex and extensive interaction of the two neighboring countries. Imports from Canada cover a wide range of products, from raw materials (such as petroleum and natural gas) and agricultural products to extensive consumer products produced and sold along the long open border. Imports from Japan, by contrast, tend to be concentrated in the auto (Datsun, Toyota) and electronics (Sony, Panasonic) industries.

To pay for these imports, a country needs to sell to the consumer in other nations. In 1981 the United States exported $236.3 billion worth of products. The difference between U.S. exports and imports reached a near-record negative $27.8 billion. However, a merchandise trade deficit is not the whole story. U.S. firms also receive payments from foreign firms for sales of services (banking services, insurance services, data processing services, and communication services). In addition, the profits of U.S. multinational corporations that are returned to the United States help reduce the trade deficit on goods. When these transactions are combined, the United States in 1981 had a small surplus of $4.5 billion on total foreign transactions. Although the net figures on foreign trade appear small, the two components have been growing rapidly. This growth is shown in Exhibit 3-9, where we see that imports have now become almost 9 percent of GNP. Foreign trade is one of the most dynamic components of the U.S.

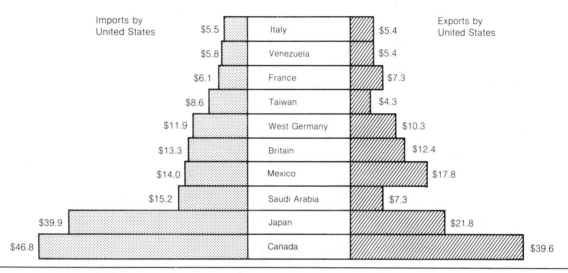

Imports by United States | Exports by United States

	Imports		Exports	
Italy	$5.5		$5.4	
Venezuela	$5.8		$5.4	
France	$6.1		$7.3	
Taiwan	$8.6		$4.3	
West Germany	$11.9		$10.3	
Britain	$13.3		$12.4	
Mexico	$14.0		$17.8	
Saudi Arabia	$15.2		$7.3	
Japan	$39.9		$21.8	
Canada	$46.8		$39.6	

Exhibit 3-8   The largest trading partners (in billions) of the United States, 1981

economy. This is an area where the comparative advantage of different nations can help to improve the living standards of both trade partners.

CURRENT ECONOMIC PROBLEMS

Economies are never without problems; only the degree and emphasis change. By 1980 a series of years of double-digit inflation had left a con-

Exhibit 3-9   Exports and imports of merchandise, 1960–79

Year	Total Merchandise Exports (billions)	Total Merchandise Imports (billions)
1960	$ 20.6	$ 14.7
1965	27.5	21.3
1970	43.2	39.8
1975	107.6	96.5
1979	181.8	205.9*

*8.7 percent of 1979 GNP ($2368 billion)

siderable number of people wondering whether the United States could ever solve its problem of inflation. There was a general consensus that inflation was the nation's major economic problem. Three years later, with inflation at least temporarily diminished, public attention turned to high interest rates and/or unemployment as the economy's burning questions. Commentators who previously were sure that inflation could never be reduced were now saying that interest rates would never come down.

This change in public perception of "the economic problem" is primarily a change in emphasis. There remains a continuing desire for stability and growth in the economy.

THE GOALS OF MACROECONOMIC POLICY

Macroeconomics is the study of the overall economy and is primarily concerned with stabilizing economic activity. Three goals guide the

---

European Unemployment

After years of relatively low unemployment, 1982 brought painfully high levels of joblessness to Europe. Part of this unemployment was the result of a demographic double whammy. Europe's postwar baby boom came later than that in the United States, and the resulting flood of school leavers coincided with an ebb in the number of people leaving the workforce through retirement. Europeans reaching age 65 represent the very lean birthrate years of World War I, 1914–18. This age cohort, already small, then lost additional numbers as casualties in World War II. Hence, there were few retirees but many new jobseekers.

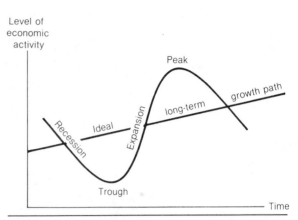

Exhibit 3-10　The business cycle and the desired stable, long-term growth path

Business cycles are typical in a free-enterprise economy. The goal of macroeconomic policy is to achieve steady growth so we avoid unnecessary unemployment and excess inflation.

formulation of macroeconomic policy. First, the government wishes to maintain full employment, which means that any person seeking a job can find one within a reasonable length of time. Second, it is desired that the price level not rise too rapidly; that is, we seek to avoid inflation. Finally, in order to maintain and increase the level of material comfort, it is desirable to keep the economy growing at an optimum rate. *The purpose of macroeconomic policy is to maintain a steady rate of economic growth with relatively stable prices and minimum unemployment.*

The Business Cycle

In a perfect world, the economy's path over time would be a smooth upward sloping line reflecting a constant rate of growth, as shown in Exhibit 3-10 (the *ideal long-term growth path*). History has not been so kind, and economic reality is instead depicted in Exhibit 3-10 as a series of business cycles around the long-term growth path. Periods of declining economic activity are called *recessions*. At its lowest level, the business cycle is said to be in its trough; the subsequent recovery is called the *expansion* which eventually hits a peak, after which the process starts again. The goal of macroeconomic policy is to "flatten" the business cycle around the ideal long-term growth path. This means that we strive to make recessions as brief as possible, with the trough as close to the long-term trend as possible. Similarly, because expansions above the long-term growth potential are destined to turn into recession, we wish to minimize the chance of such a decline by keeping growth under control so it may be sustained in the long run.

The goals of full employment, economic growth, and price stability must be achieved within the framework of the world economy. These goals can only be achieved in the United States if the economy is in a sort of "balance" with that of the rest of the world. Economists therefore add a fourth goal of macroeconomic policy, one of "external balance," so it is pos-

In Part II we will analyze how national income is determined in a modern economy and the economic policies that can affect income determination. Macroeconomic policy is complicated by the fact that its goals are sometimes mutually exclusive. Lowering the rate of unemployment may lead to a higher price level. Maintaining external balance may result in a lower rate of economic growth. These tradeoffs between policy goals produce many political debates. Conflicting interests are clear. People on fixed incomes, such as the retired, suffer a decline in purchasing power when prices rise. But they don't suffer from an increased rate of unemployment, a major concern of people who want to be employed. The balancing of these sometimes conflicting goals is an important part of successful macroeconomic policy.

THE IMPORTANCE OF STABILITY

Economic stabilization is an important aspect of government policy. While the contribution of economic stability to the welfare of society is not clear, the menace of instability is substantial. It is very easy to discuss macroeconomic conditions in rather clinical fashion: "The unemployment rate increased 2 percentage points, while the price level remained constant." Two percent is a small number but it has a large impact on individual welfare. In 1983 a two percentage point increase in unemployment meant that an additional 2 million people were looking for jobs! There is evidence such an increase in unemployment will not be shared equally by the entire population. The overall unemployment rate in 1983 was 10.1 percent. This varies among subgroups of the population. About 7.0 percent of the males who headed families were out of work, while 23.2 percent of

U.S. policy on Japanese imports such as cameras is one factor affecting "external balance," the fourth goal of macroeconomic policy. *(Photo by Richard Kalvar, Magnum)*

sible to maintain economic stability and growth. Interest in external balance with the rest of the world stems, of course, from our desire for domestic stability. Our interest in the international goal is indirect. As individuals we don't care about external balance in the same way we care about economic growth and keeping our jobs. We are concerned about external balance only because it may affect our ability to achieve other goals—economic growth, full employment, and price stability.

teenagers seeking work were unemployed. In general, the unemployment rate for blacks was roughly twice that of their white counterparts.

The Cost of Unemployment

Many of the unemployed suffer deeply from their plight. They don't blame the system for denying them employment, but blame themselves. Studs Terkel in his *Hard Times: An Oral History of the Great Depression* found this feeling common in the 1930s: "The suddenly-idle hands blamed themselves, rather than society. True, there were hunger marches and protestations to City Hall and Washington, but the millions experienced a private kind of shame when the pink slip came. No matter that others suffered the same fate, the inner voice whispered, 'I'm a failure.' "* When unemployment exceeded 10 percent in 1982, it was clear Americans had not escaped this mentality. Inability to provide for their families caused some people to feel a diminished sense of self-worth.

Recent studies suggest that physical and mental health are related to unemployment. Unemployment brings increased rates of suicide, alcohol abuse, automobile accidents, and homicide. Stress brought about by unemployment may lead to high blood pressure, which then increases the risk of heart attacks. One researcher predicted that the recession of 1974–76 would eventually cause a 15 to 25 percent increase in heart attack deaths!

Violation of the law seems to rise with unemployment. Criminologists and police officials say that the level of crime varies with economic depression or prosperity. Crimes against property, such as shoplifting and robbery, increase as unemployed workers can no longer support themselves or their families. In times of rapid inflation, those on fixed incomes experience a similar inability to support themselves. Crimes against persons, like assault and murder, also increase. One sociologist argues that personal arguments leading to such incidents are associated with alcohol and guns—and claims that both drinking and gun possession increase with unemployment.

If recession develops into deep depression, the same frustration may lead to attacks on fundamental social institutions. Most members of society demand a job so that they may live as they have become accustomed. If society is unable to provide for these needs, the body politic may demand (or be receptive to) a change. During the Great Depression of the 1930s, a great many American intellectuals were attracted to socialism and communism, believing that capitalism had ceased to function properly. While Americans were not prone to full-scale social revolution, the fear was occasionally voiced. The dean of the Harvard Law School admitted, "Capitalism is on trial and on the issue of this trial may depend the whole future of Western civilization."*

The most prominent of those who have argued that economic instability can cause social revolution is Karl Marx. Indeed, Marx based his theory of the collapse of capitalism on ever-worsening business cycles. He argued that instability, coupled with the workers' realization that they are victimized by the owners of capital, would doom capitalism. The 1930s provided uncomfortable verification of the great instability of modern market economies. And the demand for government to undertake efforts to stabilize economic activity was partly a demand to eliminate a greater danger of increased social unrest.

*Studs Terkel, *Hard Times: An Oral History of the Great Depression* (New York: Pantheon Books, 1970), p. 5.

*David A. Shannon, *The Great Depression* (Englewood Cliffs, N.J.: Prentice-Hall, 1960), p. 115.

Social revolution was feared by some as a possible result of the Great Depression. *(Photo courtesy of Terry Zabala)*

HOW EFFECTIVE IS MACROECONOMIC POLICY?

A review of the efforts at stabilization in the past 40 years helps to keep perspective on the present. Economists since the late eighteenth century believed that full employment was the natural equilibrium state of the economy. Any deviations would surely be modest and self-correcting. This view and the reasoning behind it is discussed in Chapter 6. When the Great Depression struck in 1929, the prevailing advice to President Hoover was to sit tight, balance the federal budget, and wait for recovery.

His opponent in the 1932 election, Franklin D. Roosevelt, won not because he advocated policies that were different from Hoover's, but because he was not Hoover. Presidents normally are not reelected during hard economic times. Roosevelt eventually responded to the public's cry for action, although economic theory did not provide much guidance. In 1936 John Maynard Keynes offered a theoretical basis for government policies to control business cycles. Keynes showed that there was no built-in tendency for capitalism to operate at full employment. If a government wanted to achieve full employment, it must adopt *policies* to make it happen. Although some economists anticipated Keynes, his treatise, *The General Theory of Employment, Interest, and Money*, was not accepted as economic doctrine for many years.

The Keynesian theory was widely accepted by the mid-1950s. However, it still was not translated into public-policy action. President Dwight D. Eisenhower, like most Republicans of the period, considered an increased government role in stabilization an unwarranted intrusion into the workings of the market. And the recession of 1957–58 was largely ignored by the federal government. Not until after the election of John F. Kennedy were Keynesian economics and government stabilization activities welcome in the White House. Richard Nixon pronounced some years later, "We are all Keynesians now," indicating bipartisan support for the new orthodoxy.

After a successful swing through the 1960s with uninterrupted economic growth, economists became increasingly comfortable with their new approach to stabilizing the economy. In a requiem for the business cycle, Nobel Prize winner Paul A. Samuelson, while adding a cautionary note that inflation might remain a problem, wrote, "We must redefine the cycle so that stagnant growth below the trend-potential of growth is to be called a recession, even though

absolute growth has not vanished."* Such confidence seemed misplaced only one year later, as economic activity *declined* two straight quarters in 1974.

The period 1976–80 saw some of the worst peacetime inflation and unemployment combinations in the history of the United States. The election of President Reagan in 1980 brought new economic policies to Washington including an income tax cut to increase aggregate demand.

Belief that we could now control the economy to prevent major downturns was obviously in error. Both economists and the public at large had apparently forgotten the inexact nature of social science. Macroeconomic policy is crude and, perhaps more important, it is very new. Efforts to control the economy date back only to the early 1960s and hardly provide a backlog of experience to inspire confidence. Since social science experiments cannot be repeated, the value of our brief experience as a guide for future policy seems modest.

In Part II we will discuss the basic ideas of modern macroeconomic theory and its application to public policy. The relative stability of the post–World War II era suggests that we have learned a great deal about controlling the business cycle. But social organisms are complicated and it is difficult to identify lines of causation. This difficulty is responsible for a major debate over macroeconomic policy among economists.

Economists need not apologize that the key to economic stability has not been uncovered. It is unrealistic to expect precision from a the-

---

*Paul A. Samuelson, *Economics*, ninth ed. (New York: McGraw-Hill, 1973), pp. 266–67. Normally we say a recession has occurred when the level of gross national product corrected for price changes falls two successive quarters.

ory which was revolutionary only 45 years ago. However, the search for better policy tools in a constantly changing world makes macroeconomics a particularly interesting aspect of economics.

Can Normal Policy Deal with Super Cycles?

A Russian economist, Nikolai Kondratyev, discovered in the 1920s what appeared to be long waves in the level of economic activity in capitalist countries. These "super cycles" seem to exist for diverse measures of economic activity in both Western Europe and the United States. The cycles seem to last about 50 years each. Peaks in economic activity occurred about 1812–19, 1865–74, and 1920–29. Although Kondratyev did not offer a theoretical basis for these cycles, he did not believe that they were random events. One possible explanation is that declining portions of the long wave represent consolidation of gains from previous growth, a self-cleansing mechanism that provides the basis for another period of sustained expansion.

Unfortunately for Kondratyev, the idea that long-term decline could set the stage for renewed growth in capitalist countries upset Josef Stalin. It is reported that Kondratyev died in Siberian exile. His research had drastic implications for him personally. And if he was correct, it may have important implications for the United States as well. The last Kondratyev peak was 1920–29, which means another 50-year cycle would have peaked between 1970 and 1979. Perhaps we are on the down side of a long wave. But unlike any previous long cycle, we now use macroeconomic policies in an attempt to stabilize the economy. It will be interesting to see if the statistically based Kondratyev long cycle can withstand the onslaught of public policy.

SUMMARY

1. The U.S. economy is an extremely complex mechanism composed of a large number of components, working together in a myriad of processes. For convenience, the components and processes are usually grouped together in aggregates—e.g., unemployment and Gross National Product (GNP).

2. Consumers are a key element in the economy. Businesses that fail to fulfill consumers' desires will not prosper and survive. Consumers' tastes are affected by the age and sex composition of the population. Two-earner families have different consumption patterns than single-earner families.

3. Businesses produce the goods and services that provide for the material wants of society. They employ the labor, use the capital, and rent the land. They come in many sizes and forms. Among the major trends has been the shift from agriculture to manufacturing. Among the largest sectors in the U.S. economy are services, government, and trades.

4. The labor force of 114 million individuals (in 1982) plays a very important role in the U.S. economy. The share of women in the labor force has been growing steadily. The workforce is also aging. At the same time the proportion of the workforce with union membership has been declining.

5. The role of government in the U.S. economy has grown. Government spending accounts for one-third of GNP. Federal expenditures and receipts serve as an index of national policy and trends. Government regulation influences business decision makers.

6. Foreign trade is an important and growing part of the U.S. economy. Exports reflect the

resource endowment and technology of the United States.

7. Economies are never without problems—just the severity and emphasis change. Macro-economic policy attempts to reduce the severity of the business cycle.

KEY CONCEPTS

multinational firms

labor force

transfer payments

government regulation

exports and imports

business cycles

stabilization function of government

QUESTIONS FOR DISCUSSION

1. In the U.S. economy, what businesses have had the greatest success lately? What characteristics have these businesses had? What about business failures?

    health spa
    video store
    Disney

2. Do you think the recent reduction in the share of the labor force in labor unions is a temporary or permanent feature of the U.S. economy?

3. Is the growth of government regulation a permanent feature of the U.S. economy?

4. Which economic problem would be less painful to you: 10 percent inflation with 6 percent unemployment or 4 percent inflation with 8 percent unemployment? Why?

5. Why can an aggregate figure such as 10 percent unemployment cover a lot of potential problems? What type of problems?

Part II
MACROECONOMICS

Chapter 4

Measuring Economic Activity

People usually view national economic conditions from the vantage point of their personal situation. This characteristic led to one observer's facetious definition of macroeconomic developments: "A recession is when my neighbor has been laid off; a depression is when I get laid off." But this definition is clearly not appropriate for economic analysis. To analyze and control economic fluctuations, we need measures of aggregate economic activity. The most frequently used and most important aggregate economic indicator is Gross National Product (GNP).

This measure and related measures from the national income accounts are used to describe the level and growth of economic activity. Inflation and unemployment are also important indicators of economic performance. In this chapter we describe the way we measure economic growth, inflation, and unemployment.

PATTERNS OF GNP
IN THE UNITED STATES

In Chapter 1, Exhibit 1-4 showed GNP in the United States from 1874 to 1980. Economic activity in this century has had two important characteristics:

1. There has been a strong upward trend in Gross National Product over the last 100 years. Even if we allow for the effect of inflation, the GNP figures in Exhibit 1-4 show a rapid increase during this century. This average annual increase of 3.5 percent illustrates the economic growth that has been the dominant feature of the U.S. economy during the twentieth century.

2. Economic growth has not been steady. We previously described the Great Depression of 1930–39 as a period of high unemployment—one of four workers was out of work

in 1933. From 1930 to 1933, national output declined by over 30 percent. Exhibit 4-1 shows fluctuations in GNP since the Great Depression. We see that the highest peak (i.e., the most rapid economic growth) occurred during World War II (1940–44). The Korean War (1950–51) was another time of particularly rapid growth. In general terms the 1950s were a decade of some fluctuation, the 1960s were characterized by reasonably steady growth with no years of negative growth, and the 1970s were typified by a return of economic instability. From 1970 through 1980, annual GNP actually declined four times—in 1970, 1974, 1975, and 1980.

Comparative Economic Statistics for 1980

In 1980, most developed nations suffered lower growth, higher inflation, and more unemployment than they had in the past. As shown in the table, only one country, Great Britain, grew more slowly than the United States in 1980; Italy and Japan were the fastest growing nations. The United States had somewhat higher unemployment than most nations, although the inflation rate of 9 percent compares favorably with the inflation rates of all but two countries.

Nation	Growth of GNP	Unemploy-ment Rate	Inflation Rate
Italy	4.0	3.9%	20.4%
Great Britain	− 1.8	7.5	18.8
Sweden	1.4	2.0	11.6
France	1.3	6.6	11.5
Australia	2.1	6.1	11.1
Canada	0.1	7.5	10.5
United States	− 0.2	7.1	9.0
Federal Republic of Germany	1.8	3.3	5.1
Japan	4.2	2.0	3.2

SOURCE: *Statistical Abstract of the United States*, 1981.

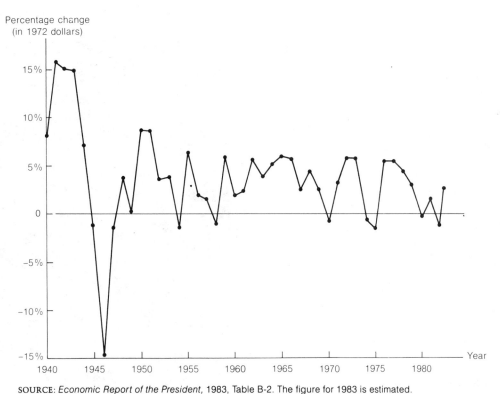

Percentage change
(in 1972 dollars)

SOURCE: *Economic Report of the President*, 1983, Table B-2. The figure for 1983 is estimated.

Exhibit 4-1 Annual growth of GNP, 1940–83

It is important to remember that the ups and downs shown in Exhibit 4-1 can be translated into significant disturbances in the economic well-being of many people. Unemployment and all the costs associated with being out of work, bankruptcy of firms, and unused equipment are among the casualties of downturns in economic activity.

WHAT IS GNP?

During the past 25 years GNP has become a household word, but though widely used it is often misunderstood. Politicians compare U.S. GNP with that of other countries either to alarm or comfort their audiences. Stock market analysts relate individual stock projections to GNP forecasts. Businesses adjust expansion plans in accordance with changes in GNP. State and federal authorities take budget actions guided by the latest GNP figures. In these and countless other activities we use GNP data in the decision-making process. For our current purpose the actual GNP numbers are less important than the concept of GNP. National accounting concepts, of which GNP is the most important, are central to much of macroeconomics. We will elaborate on their meaning and use in this section.

A simple way to think of GNP is to imagine a small island with a single product. A count of the units produced could serve as the Gross National Product. For instance, if coconuts were the island's only crop, a count of the number harvested each year would constitute the entire GNP figure for the economy. Economic growth might be stated as 712 coconuts in 1984 and 730 coconuts in 1985. The annual coconut count would reflect both economic growth and the level and fluctuations in economic activity.

Modern economies, of course, have more than one product, raising problems of measurement. Take the example of a country, Paradise, that produces only two products—coconuts and apples. The national accounts might read:

1985 harvest

number of coconuts	=	6000
number of apples	=	4000

Unfortunately, this measure of economic activity cannot be compared with either the Gross National Product of other countries or activity from different time periods in Paradise. Suppose that the 1984 GNP figures for Paradise had been:

1984 harvest

number of coconuts	=	5000
number of apples	=	5000

Since we cannot add apples and coconuts, we do not know whether the residents of the country are better off in 1985 than in 1984. They have increased coconut production but cut back on apples. If the people of Paradise enjoy coconuts more than apples, they are better off. On the other hand if apples are more desirable than coconuts, then they are worse off. And if coconuts and apples are identical in value, economic welfare in 1984 and 1985 would be equal.

In order to make a valid comparison, it is necessary to attach weights to the different goods.

The total GNP for a given year is the monetary value of all the final goods and services produced by that economy during the year. *(Photo by Peter Vandermark, Stock, Boston)*

Using the market prices of apples and coconuts to measure society's relative evaluation of them is one means of establishing these weights. Suppose coconuts and apples have been 10¢ and 5¢ respectively in both years under consideration. We can then use the 5¢ and 10¢ prices as our weights and calculate the value of total production (GNP) in Paradise.

GNP 1984

5000 coconuts @ 10¢ = $500
5000 apples @ 5¢ = $250
GNP = $750

GNP 1985

6000 coconuts @ 10¢ = $600
4000 apples @ 5¢ = $200
GNP = $800

Using prices allows us to measure and compare the economic output for the two years. We see that GNP in Paradise increased by $50 or 6.7 percent between 1984 and 1985.

A real economy with many sectors and numerous final products is treated analogously. That is, the total GNP for a given year is the monetary value of all the final goods and services produced by that economy during the year. In an economy such as that of the United States, millions of products and services are included.

PROBLEMS IN MEASURING GNP

Problem of Changing Prices

One of the major uses of GNP calculations is to make period-to-period comparisons within a country. In Exhibit 4-1 the level of GNP was used to identify periods of recession and expansion. However, calculating the monetary equivalents of total output creates a problem when prices change over time.

To compare Paradise's GNP in 1984 and 1985 we assumed that the prices of coconuts and apples did not change. In the example, this meant that GNP grew from $750 to $800, indicating that residents of Paradise valued its goods and services more in 1985 than in 1984. Suppose, however, that a rapid inflation occurred in 1986, resulting in a doubling of the prices of coconuts

and apples. Suppose also that output fell to a level of 5000 apples and 2500 coconuts. GNP in 1986 is

5000 apples @ 10¢ + 2500 coconuts @ 20¢ = $1000

Output measured by GNP rose from $750 in 1984 to $1000 in 1986 even though apple production was unchanged and coconut output fell to one-half its 1984 level. Since output is unambiguously lower, the inflation of 1986 shows clearly that changing prices are a serious problem for measuring output with GNP.

To solve this problem we compare the physical output in the two years by using the same prices—for example, we could estimate the value of output in both years by using 1984 prices. Alternatively, we could use 1986 prices to evaluate the output in both 1984 and 1986.

For example, if GNP for 1984 and 1986 is to be calculated in 1984 prices, we do the following:

$$\text{GNP}_{1984} = (\text{quantity of apples}_{1984}$$
$$\times \text{ the price of apples}_{1984})$$
$$+ (\text{quantity of coconuts}_{1984}$$
$$\times \text{ the price of coconuts}_{1984})$$

Using symbols or abbreviations, we can write the same statement as:

$$\text{GNP}_{84} = (Qa_{84} \times Pa_{84}) + (Qc_{84} \times Pc_{84})$$

Putting in the appropriate prices and quantities, we can calculate GNP for 1984 as follows:

$$\text{GNP} = (5000 \times 5¢) + (5000 \times 10¢)$$
$$= \$250 + \$500 = \$750$$

Thus, GNP for 1984 is $750 using 1984 quantities and 1984 prices. Since prices have gone up in 1986, to compare the two time periods requires an adjustment for the price increase. By using the 1984 prices with the 1986 levels of production, we can adjust for the effect of inflation. Using 1984 prices to adjust for inflation in 1986 is referred to as "deflating" to 1984

Exhibit 4-2   Measuring GNP when prices change over time

	Output in Physical Units		
Harvested In	Coconuts	Apples	
1984	5000	5000	
1985	4000	6000	
1986	2500	5000	

	Calculating GNP				
	Coconuts		Apples		Total
	Prices	Value	Prices	Value	GNP Value
1984 GNP (1984 prices)	10¢	$500	5¢	$250	$ 750
1985 GNP (1984 prices)	10¢	$600	5¢	$200	$ 800
1986 GNP (1986 prices)	20¢	$500	10¢	$500	$1000
1986 GNP (1984 prices)	10¢	$250	5¢	$250	$ 500

price levels. This makes the 1984 and 1986 GNP figures comparable. The calculation is given below:

$$GNP_{1986} \text{ (deflated to 1984 prices)}$$
$$= (Qa_{86} \times Pa_{84}) + (Qc_{86} \times Pc_{84})$$

$$GNP_{86} = (5000 \times 5¢) + (2500 \times 10¢)$$
$$= \$250 + \$250 = \$500$$

These calculations are summarized in Exhibit 4-2.

When 1986 GNP is deflated to 1984 prices, the results show what is obvious from the production data: output fell from 1984 to 1986. When we measure national output in terms of the prices prevailing in the same year (that is, using 1986 prices to value 1986 output), the result is what we call *money GNP*. When we adjust the calculation by using some base year price level to control the effect of changing prices, the result is called *real GNP*. Real GNP is a measure of output that is valued by using the prices prevailing in an arbitrarily chosen base year. In Exhibit 4-2 we measured real GNP in terms of 1984 prices. This was an arbitrary choice. Prices in any year can serve as the base

year to transform money GNP into real GNP. When we express the price level in one year in terms of some base year, we are using a *price index*.

Price Indexes

In the United States we use the GNP *price deflator* to deflate money GNP into real GNP. This deflator is the ratio of money GNP in a year to the real GNP in that year multiplied by 100. The formula is:

$$GNP \text{ deflator} = \frac{\begin{array}{c}\text{Current year output} \\ \text{valued at} \\ \text{current year prices}\end{array}}{\begin{array}{c}\text{Current year output} \\ \text{valued at} \\ \text{base year prices}\end{array}} \times 100$$

Exhibit 4-3 shows the GNP deflator for Paradise; the doubling of the price level reported in 1986 shows up as a GNP price deflator of 200. Exhibit 4-4 shows money and real GNP for the United States from 1930 to 1982. The base year for the deflator is 1972; in this year the value

Exhibit 4-3 GNP deflator in Paradise (base year = 1984)

Year	Current Year Output Valued at Current Year Prices (1)	Base Year Prices (2)	GNP Deflator ((col. 1 ÷ col. 2) × 100)
1984	$ 750	$750	100
1985	800	800	100
1986	1000	500	200

Exhibit 4-4 Money and real GNP (in billions) in the United States, 1930–82
(GNP deflator base year = 1972)

Year	Money GNP (Y)	GNP Deflator (P)	Real GNP	Year	Money GNP (Y)	GNP Deflator (P)	Real GNP
1930	$ 90.7	31.8	$ 285.2	1960	$ 506.5	68.7	$ 737.3
31	76.1	28.9	263.3	61	524.6	69.3	757.0
32	58.3	25.7	226.8	62	565.0	70.6	800.3
33	55.8	25.1	222.3	63	596.7	71.7	832.2
34	65.3	27.3	239.2	64	637.7	72.8	876.0
1935	72.5	27.8	260.8	1965	691.1	74.4	928.8
36	82.7	30.0	275.7	66	756.0	76.8	984.4
37	90.9	29.3	310.2	67	799.6	79.1	1010.9
38	85.0	28.7	296.2	68	873.4	82.5	1058.7
39	90.9	28.4	320.0	69	944.0	86.8	1087.6
1940	100.0	29.1	343.6	1970	992.7	91.4	1086.1
41	125.0	31.2	400.6	71	1077.7	96.0	1122.6
42	158.5	34.4	461.8	72	1185.9	100.0	1185.9
43	192.1	36.1	532.1	73	1326.4	105.7	1254.9
44	210.6	37.0	569.2	74	1434.2	114.9	1248.2
1945	212.6	37.9	560.9	1975	1549.2	125.5	1244.4
46	209.8	44.0	476.8	76	1718.0	132.1	1300.5
47	233.1	49.5	470.7	77	1918.0	139.8	1371.9
48	259.5	53.0	489.6	78	2156.1	150.0	1437.4
49	258.3	52.5	492.0	79	2413.9	162.8	1482.7
1950	286.5	53.6	534.5	1980	2626.1	177.4	1480.6
51	330.8	57.1	579.2	81	2922.2	193.6	1509.4
52	348.0	57.9	601.0	82	3073.0	206.9	1485.4
53	366.8	58.8	623.8				
54	366.8	59.6	615.4				
1955	400.0	60.9	657.0				
56	421.7	62.8	671.5				
57	444.0	65.0	683.1				
58	449.7	66.0	681.2				
59	487.9	67.6	721.7				

$$\frac{206.9}{100} = 2 \qquad \frac{3073}{2} = 1536.5$$

SOURCE: *Economic Report of the President*, 1982.

of the deflator is 100. Note that the GNP deflator is less than 100 for the years before 1972. This shows prices were on average lower in these years than they were in 1972.*

The GNP deflator has a built-in shortcoming: it is not possible to correct adequately for changes in product quality. For some commodities, such as food, quality differences over time are slight; other products, however, may change substantially. Comparing a 1950 car to a 1982 model illustrates this point, since the later model is more comfortable, gets better gas mileage, and offers greater safety. Television sets and calculators are examples of products whose performance greatly improved while prices were falling. Although the GNP deflator can capture the falling prices of these items, the improved picture on color TV sets and the greatly increased capacity of calculators are not included in the price index. The Bureau of Labor Statistics (BLS) recognizes the problem, but so far has been unable to eliminate the bias from the GNP price deflator.

Value Added: A Concept That Prevents Double Counting

Throughout our discussion we have described a simple economy in which only final products are purchased by consumers from producers. Suppose, however, that gadgets produced by Firm X are used by Firm Y in the production of supergadgets. Now gadgets would be considered an "intermediate good." Continuing the Paradise example, suppose that a change in the tastes of the population makes applesauce highly popular. Apples are no longer desired for themselves, but become intermediate products in the pro-

---

*To determine real GNP from money GNP it is important to remember that the price ratio is multiplied by 100. Real GNP is therefore (money GNP divided by the deflator) × 100.

duction of applesauce. The production stages can be specified as:

Stage I:	Value of apples sold by orchards to cannery	$250
Stage II:	Value of applesauce sold by cannery to stores	$350
Stage III:	Value of applesauce sold by stores to consumer	$400

A possibility of double counting in the GNP calculations now arises. The $400 final sales to consumers includes the value of apples at the earlier stages of production. If we were to add $250 + $350 + $400 to arrive at a $1000 total, we would be incorrectly including the intermediate processing, already counted at the earlier stage.

Double counting can be avoided in two ways. The first and easiest is to ensure that only the final product is included in the GNP calculation. The GNP contribution for apples would be encompassed in the $400 final figure from Stage III, omitting Stages I and II transactions.

Another method of avoiding double counting is to include only the amount of *value added* at each stage in the production process, by subtracting the value of products purchased from other firms from the final sales of the producing firm. If we assume that apple growers need no inputs from other firms, we can make the following value-added calculations.

Stage	Value of sales	Purchases from other firms	Value added
I	$250	0	$250
II	$350	$250	$100
III	$400	$350	$ 50
		Total value added:	$400

The $400 total value added is equal to the total **final** product of $400 since the definition of GNP does not include any double counting.

In actual practice the U.S. Department of Commerce uses both the value-added and the final-products calculations in determining GNP.

Depreciation

Why do we speak of *Gross* National Product? The term *Gross* indicates that the total output as measured includes no consideration of wear and tear on machinery caused by the production process. For example, suppose that in order to produce this year's output of $100,000, we must wear out machinery that cost $15,000. This wearing-out process is referred to as *depreciation* or the *capital consumption allowance*. When depreciation is not considered, the amount produced is the Gross National Product. When the value of output is reduced by the value of equipment worn out during the year, the figure represents the *Net National Product* (NNP). That is, GNP minus depreciation equals NNP. A useful rule of thumb for the United States is that

depreciation is approximately 10 percent of GNP, or put another way, NNP is roughly 90 percent of GNP.

OTHER MEASURES OF ECONOMIC ACTIVITY

GNP and NNP perform well as indices of national output and will be used extensively in the following chapters. However, mention should be made of three other measures of economic activity reported by the U.S. Department of Commerce. These are national income, personal income, and disposable personal income. The definitions of each and their relationship to one another are summarized in Exhibit 4-5.

National Income

National income represents NNP minus indirect business taxes, which include excise taxes,

Exhibit 4-5 Relation of GNP, national income, and personal income (in billions), 1970 and 1980

	Item	1970	1980
	Gross National Product	$992.7	$2626.1
less:	Capital consumption allowances	88.1	287.3
equals:	Net national product	904.7	2339.3
plus:	Subsidies *less* current surplus of government enterprises	2.9	4.6
less:	Indirect business tax and nontax liability	94.3	212.2
equals:	National Income	810.7	2119.5
less:	Corporate profits	71.4	180.7
	Net interest	41.4	179.9
	Contributions for social insurance	58.6	203.7
plus:	Government transfer payments to persons	76.1	283.8
	Personal interest income	69.4	256.2
	Dividends	22.2	54.4
	Business transfers	4.1	10.5
equals:	Personal Income	811.1	2160.2
less:	Personal tax and nontax payments	115.8	338.5
equals:	Disposable personal income	695.3	1821.7
less:	Personal outlays	639.5	1720.4
equals:	Personal Saving	55.8	101.3

SOURCE: *Statistical Abstract of the United States,* 1981, Table 707.

gasoline taxes, sales taxes, and cigarette stamps. These are subtracted because they do not represent income to the firm; the firm merely collects them for the government. Subsidies to business firms are added to national income while surpluses or profits of government enterprises are subtracted to obtain the final national income figure. Exhibit 4-5 shows that these adjustments are modest compared to the size of indirect business taxes.

Personal Income

Personal income measures the amount of income received by households. To calculate that figure, we must first subtract certain items included in national income but not actually received by individuals. These include payments into the Social Security fund, corporate profits, and net interest. Government transfer payments to persons (such as welfare and Social Security checks), personal interest income, dividends, and business transfers are counted as personal income, however. Exhibit 4-5 shows that personal income was $2.1 trillion in 1980, making up about 82 percent of GNP.

Disposable Personal Income

Disposable personal income is the amount individuals actually have to spend. It represents the remainder after all tax payments and other payments to the government have been subtracted from personal income. Disposable personal income constituted 69 percent of GNP in 1980. Exhibit 4-5 shows that $1.7 trillion, or 94 percent of personal income, was consumed while the remainder was saved.

GNP AS A MEASURE OF WELL-BEING

It is often implicitly or explicitly assumed that human welfare is directly related to Gross

---

Work That Doesn't Count

One of the largest categories of goods and services not counted in the Gross National Product is in the household sector.

The housework performed by an average American housewife was worth $4705 in 1972, according to a study published by the Social Security Administration. That figure rose with inflation and was estimated at $10,200 in 1981. For housewives in their late twenties or early thirties with young children, the 1981 figure was estimated at $12,700.

These estimates were derived from a study in which a representative sample of housewives was surveyed to determine how many hours they spent at various household activities—child care, cleaning, cooking, dishwashing, washing clothes, and so on. Their reported time was multiplied by the prevailing hourly wage for each activity, including those of dishwashers, cooks, cleaning women, appliance repairmen, clothing maintenance specialists, handymen, accountants, and chauffeurs, to determine the equivalent amount the housewife's tasks would cost in the marketplace.

However, even though the value of the goods and services provided by housewives can be estimated, this value does not enter in the calculation of GNP because they are not market transactions.

National Product. Examples can be found in international comparisons of GNP per capita. The reasoning is that since Country *A* has twice the GNP per capita of Country *B*, residents of Country *A* are twice as well off. Similarly, comparisons are sometimes made for time periods within the same country. If GNP has risen, the well-being of the residents is presumed to have increased too.

There are three problems in equating GNP per capita with the well-being of the residents of a country: (1) the problem of measuring GNP, (2) the offsetting nature of certain economic activity, and (3) the materialistic orientation of the accounting process.

Measurement Problems

A major deficiency in GNP accounting is that some valuable activities do not enter the GNP calculations. One example is housework. If a person is hired to do housework for $5000 per year, GNP calculations include the $5000. But if the same work is performed by a household member, no wage is paid and there is no addition to GNP. The inconsistency can be illustrated by the frequently used example of the bachelor who marries his housekeeper. The marriage reduces GNP by $5000 even though the same economic activities are accomplished.

Another measurement problem arises because certain economic transactions are not officially observed and therefore are not counted in the national accounting framework. Sometimes this happens because the transactions are illegal—drug traffic, gambling, and prostitution are examples. Other activity is legal and valuable but may not be fully reported through official channels. Persons who receive tips may not report all this income to the Internal Revenue Service, nor may casual workers or babysitters who are paid in cash. In still other cases, legal activity may be conducted in a way to evade income taxes, such as "skimming" profits from a small business or doing work "off the books."

Although it is inevitably difficult to measure economic activity that is intentionally conducted to go unobserved, the so-called underground economy is large and growing. According to Edgar Fiege of the University of Wisconsin, unobserved economic transactions in 1979 amounted to more than $600 billion, about 27

The Underground Economy

Uncounted economic activity—the so-called underground economy—distorts economic statistics in that the economy actually may appear to be in worse shape than it is. An example will clarify this. An unemployed carpenter decided to build his parents a house and hired four other carpenters who were out of work and receiving unemployment compensation to help him. The carpenters received half of their wage from unemployment compensation and half from the couple building the house. Although they worked full time, the five were counted as unemployed and their income was not reported. Economic growth was underestimated and unemployment exaggerated as a result. In many industrialized countries, such data problems appear to be substantial. In France the underground economy is estimated to be 25 percent of measured economic activity; in Italy about 35 percent; and in the United Kingdom 15 percent.

---

percent of GNP.* Economists disagree about the accuracy of Fiege's estimate, but they do agree that the problems of measuring GNP became more serious during the 1970s.

Offsetting Activities

Some economic activities generate not only desirable products but also undesirable side effects. In such instances, additional economic activity may be required to correct the undesirable results of the first activity. However, since both the cost of the original activity and the cost of the corrective action enter into the cal-

---

*Edgar L. Fiege, "A New Perspective on Macroeconomic Phenomena—The Theory and Measurement of the Unobserved Sector of the United States Economy—Causes, Consequences, and Implications," mimeo, August 1980.

culation of GNP, the addition to national well-being is overstated. For example, suppose that a stand of virgin timber in a remote area is cut down and sold for $10 million. As one result, rain run-off creates flood problems for cities downstream, which must then spend $15 million on flood control construction. According to national income accounting, the economy has grown by $25 million. However, in another sense society has suffered a net loss of $5 million.

With increased public concern over air, water, and noise pollution, the amount of offsetting activity has increased in the last few years. Some of the U.S. GNP growth has not been a true increase in well-being, but merely additional costs of removing pollution.

Materialistic Orientation

Another important problem is a conceptual one—the difference between value and price. Simon Kuznets, America's second Nobel Prize winner in economics, noted as early as 1946 that one major omission of national income accounting is that it excludes the human cost of turning out the product, calculating only the salary received by the worker. He cited the shorter workweek as a source of increased well-being not included in the calculation of GNP. Similarly, a pleasant walk in the woods does not enter into the accounts, but the airplane overhead whose noise lessens the enjoyment of the walker does count as an increment in national output.

After noting these problems, you might wonder why national accounts are used at all. It is important to remember that national accounts are not designed to measure human welfare. Instead, their purpose is to provide systematic indices of economic activity that can be used for policy guidance. Used for macroeconomic measurement, GNP performs well. Used as an index for well-being, it has serious weaknesses.

The GNP calculation do not take into account the value of activities that do not already have a price attached. *(Photo by Marshall Berman)*

UNEMPLOYMENT

Unemployment is the second measure used to assess the health of an economy. Exhibit 4-6 shows the annual rate of unemployment from 1948 to 1983 in the United States. It demonstrates that the unemployment rate has fluctuated from a low of 2.9 percent in 1953 to a high of 9.7 percent in 1982. These statistics often conceal the importance of what appears to be a "modest" increase in the unemployment rate from, say, 5 to 6 percent. In 1983 the labor force was about 100 million people. Thus, an increase of one percentage point in the unemployment

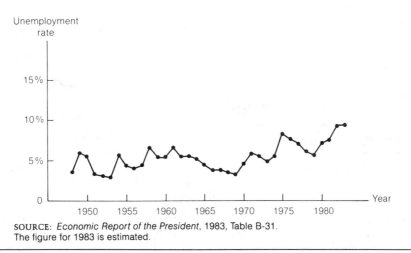

SOURCE: *Economic Report of the President*, 1983, Table B-31.
The figure for 1983 is estimated.

Exhibit 4-6 Annual rate of unemployment in the United States, 1948–83

rate means that one million more people are not working but looking for a job.

Each month interviewers hired by the U.S. Department of Labor visit 60,000 representative American households to determine the employment status of family members. The interviewers ask which family members worked at a job the previous week. Those who worked are questioned further about where they worked and for how many hours. Those who did not work are asked about their job-seeking activity. Did they apply for a job? Were they actively looking for work? If not, were they in school, on vacation, ill, retired, keeping house?

Based on these interviews, all persons over 16 years of age are classified as (1) employed, (2) not employed but looked for work within the preceding four weeks, or (3) not employed and not seeking employment. Those who fit in the first two categories make up the labor force. The unemployed are those members of the labor force who are not employed but are seeking work. Also counted among the unemployed are people

who are not looking for work because they are on layoff or who are waiting to start a new job within 30 days.

On the basis of the sample, the Bureau of Labor Statistics projects employment totals for the nation. The sample is much larger than those of public opinion polls because of the statistical requirement that specific demographic subgroups, like blue-collar workers aged 35–55, be adequately represented. Of course, the validity of the projections still depends upon the accuracy of the responses, but outside studies and corroborating data support the validity of the published statistics.

In a market economy people leave jobs for many reasons. At any moment some persons are moving from one job to another or entering the labor force. Others quit to find better employment, because they are angry at the boss, because they want to travel, or for a myriad of other personal reasons. Still others are laid off. In 1982, when unemployment was 9.7 percent of the labor force, these were the causes of unemployment:

Lost last job	5.6%
Left last job	0.8
Reentered labor force	2.2
Never worked before	1.1
Total	9.7

Unemployment is not evenly spread throughout the economy. Some demographic groups have higher unemployment rates than others. Teenagers, for example, had an unemployment rate of 20 percent in 1981. At the same time married men living with their wives had an unemployment rate of only 4 percent. Blacks are twice as likely to be unemployed as whites. Unemployment rates vary among cities as well as across population groups. Exhibit 4-7 shows the unemployment rate for selected metropolitan areas in 1981. Unemployed workers accounted for 7.4 percent of the labor force in the nation as a whole, but only 4.1 percent of Houston's labor force was out of work. In sharp contrast

was Detroit, with 14.4 percent of its labor force looking for work. Altoona and Fresno also had unemployment rates far higher than the national average.

An often overlooked category of persons not working might be called the *discouraged workers*. Some people are not seeking employment because they don't believe they can find a job. The presence of discouraged workers raises the amount of wasted human resources in an economy. But the number of discouraged workers is difficult to define, since we do not know whether or not their employment expectations are reasonable. Almost anyone would work if wages were high enough and working conditions pleasant enough. But it is not clear whether the discouraged workers should lower their expectations or government policies should encourage them to continue to search for acceptable work.

Exhibit 4-7 Unemployment in selected U.S. metropolitan areas, January 1981*

Area	Unemployment Rate
Altoona, Penn.	15.3%
Detroit, Mich.	14.4
Charleston, W.V.	12.4
Fresno, Calif.	12.1
Buffalo, N.Y.	10.7
Akron, Ohio	10.3
Spokane, Wash.	9.5
Birmingham, Ala.	9.4
Chicago, Ill.	9.2
Newark, N.J.	7.5
Omaha, Neb.	6.6
Boston, Mass.	6.4
Greenville-Spartanburg, S.C.	6.3
Los Angeles-Long Beach, Calif.	6.3
Macon, Ga.	6.3
Denver, Colo.	5.8
Tucson, Ariz.	5.4
Washington, D.C.	4.6
Houston, Texas	4.1

*U.S. average unemployment was 7.4 percent at this time.

INFLATION

We have already discussed the GNP deflator as a measure of changing prices in the economy. Inflation (the rising of the price level) and deflation (the falling of the price level) can also be measured by the Consumer Price Index (CPI). The CPI is designed to measure changes in the price of a representative "market basket" of goods and services purchased by typical households in urban areas of the country. The formula for the index is:

final Exam

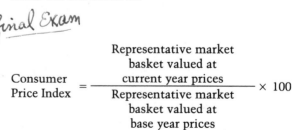

$$\text{Consumer Price Index} = \frac{\text{Representative market basket valued at current year prices}}{\text{Representative market basket valued at base year prices}} \times 100$$

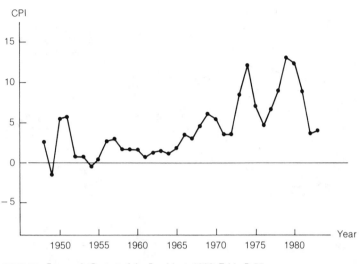

SOURCE: *Economic Report of the President*, 1983, Table B-55.
The figure for 1983 is estimated.

Exhibit 4-8   Annual changes in the Consumer Price Index, 1948–83

Since the CPI includes only items that are purchased by a typical family and the GNP deflator includes price changes for all output, the CPI is a more commonly used measure of the impact of price changes on consumers. Exhibit 4-8 shows annual changes in the CPI from 1948 to 1983.

Mechanics of the CPI

Suppose a person wanted to develop an index of the costs of homemade lunches. If he or she kept track from month to month of the total cost of buying a loaf of bread, a pound of peanut butter, and a pint of jelly, these numbers would provide the basis for constructing an index of food prices, much like the CPI. All that would be left to do would be to divide the total cost of homemade lunches in each month by the cost in the first month. This would yield a measure of the relative change in costs of homemade

lunches (for example, peanut butter-and-jelly sandwiches). As in the CPI, the quantities of the goods are held constant over time—a pound of peanut butter and a pint of jelly—so that the index measures the changes in the prices of the components.

The major problem in constructing a price index is to determine which items and what quantity to include. For the person who eats only peanut butter-and-jelly sandwiches, the task is easy. But constructing an index appropriate to the spending patterns of over 200 million people is much more difficult. Consumers purchase a wide variety of goods and services, which vary in quantity, durability, and type. Some items, like artichokes, are consumed by only a few people and are not durable. Other items, like housing, are consumed by most people for use over a long time. Each item used in the CPI must be weighted according to its importance

The CPI attempts to reflect the spending patterns of all Americans. *(Photo by Mike Mazzaschi, Stock, Boston)*

in the consumption pattern of people. These weights, for the CPI, are based on a periodic survey of actual consumer spending patterns. Exhibit 4-9 shows the major categories of expenditures for a typical urban wage earner and the weights that the various categories carry in

Exhibit 4-9   Relative importance of various categories in the Consumer Price Index

Category	Percentage
Shelter	31.9%
Transportation	19.3
Food and beverages	17.6
Other housing	14.1
Medical care	4.9
Apparel and upkeep	4.6
Other goods and services	4.0
Entertainment	3.6

SOURCE: U.S. Department of Labor, Bureau of Labor Statistics, *CPI Detailed Report*, April 1982.

the current CPI. (Do they reflect your spending patterns?)

Prices of more than 400 separate items are used to construct the CPI. Trained representatives from the Bureau of Labor Statistics periodically go around the United States and price the various items in the index, from pens to used cars to basketballs. Prices used in the index are those actually paid at the stores and include excise and sales taxes.

Shortcomings of the CPI

The CPI attempts to measure the cost of consumer goods to the "average" urban wage earner. But admittedly the CPI is only an approximation of any particular family's costs. For example, food constitutes 18 percent of the CPI. When food prices rise the CPI understates the effect on low-income groups, who devote 30 percent of their spending to food. At the same time it overstates the effect on higher-income groups, whose food bills account for only 10 percent of their total spending.

A second problem with the CPI is that its market basket is assumed to be unchanged even when prices are changing. If the price of coffee suddenly rises rapidly, many people may choose to drink tea instead of coffee. The typical market basket assumes that people continue to consume the same amount of coffee as before, despite the price change. Whenever the price of one item rises rapidly and there are available substitutes (such as chicken for beef), the CPI will tend to overestimate the actual effect of the price change on households. Of course, if the change in relative prices is permanent, the bias will be removed when the market basket is revised.

SUMMARY

1. Gross National Product measures the dollar value of goods and services produced in a nation over a period of time. As such, it is a key measure of economic activity and is used in major public policy questions.

2. In order to adjust for changes in prices over time, it is necessary to convert *money* GNP into *real* GNP by use of a price index. This index, called the GNP deflator, is based on current year output valued at current prices divided by current year output valued at base year prices. Base year prices are expressed as 100 on this index.

3. Some production is used as an input into other products. In order to avoid counting the same product several times the value-added calculation is used. Value added is determined by subtracting the purchase of input(s) from other firms from the final sales of the producing firms. *value-added*

4. Net National Product is Gross National Product less depreciation.

5. GNP is an indicator of the level of production of goods and services, not a measure of human welfare.

6. The unemployment rate, another measure used to reflect the state of the economy, is the proportion of the labor force that is not employed but seeking work.

7. Inflation, the rising of the price level, has an impact on households that is measured by the Consumer Price Index. It is designed to measure changes in the price of a representative market basket of goods and services.

KEY CONCEPTS

Gross National Product	depreciation
money GNP	Net National Product
real GNP	Consumer Price Index
price index	national income
GNP deflator	personal income
value added	disposable personal income
unemployment rate	

QUESTIONS FOR DISCUSSION

1. Convert money GNP in the following years to real GNP (in billions):

Year	Money GNP (in billions)	GNP Deflator (base = 1972)
1930	$ 90.7	31.8
1933	55.8	25.1
1939	90.9	28.4
1959	487.9	67.6
1969	944.0	86.8
1981	2922.2	193.6

    How much did the economy grow between 1930 and 1933? Between 1969 and 1981? Calculate your answer in terms of both money and real GNP. Could you use this data to calculate real GNP in 1969 in terms of 1981 prices?

2. When an executive marries her butler what is the effect upon GNP? Why?

3. In 1933 gross investment in the economy was $1.4 billion. Depreciation in that year was $6.9 billion. What do we mean by depreciation? How could net investment be negative?

4. Using the data in Exhibit 4-8, estimate how much a salary had to rise between 1979 and 1981 to keep the same "real income." *20% Raise*

5. What is the purpose of national income accounting?

6. Have you contributed to the size of the underground economy? What forces might have caused this unobserved sector to become much larger in recent years?

7. If the typical workweek were to suddenly shift from 40 hours per week to 30 hours per week what would probably happen to real GNP? Would this mean that the country was "worse off"? What do you mean by worse off?

8. "Under no circumstances should we consider discouraged workers when we are assessing the employment of the labor force." Defend a positive or negative reaction to this statement.

PHILIP
LEE

• PHILIP H
  LEE

Chapter 5

Interdependence in a Modern Economy

The previous chapter on GNP prepared us to discuss the fundamental principle of modern macroeconomics: *the output of a society is equal to the income of that society.* This simple identity of output and income underlies most macroeconomic theory and policy. Our example of the island of Paradise shows its simplest form. When Paradise's total production is 5000 coconuts, it is clear that 5000 coconuts is equal to the income available to the people residing on the island. When fewer coconuts are harvested, the residents' income is reduced. A similar relationship exists for even the most developed societies, but the complexity of a modern economy makes this interrelationship difficult to see.

THE CIRCULAR FLOW OF INCOME

One method of clarifying the interrelationship of production and income is the diagram of the *circular flow of income* shown in Exhibit 5-1. Here we see a simplified economy with no saving or investment, no government expenditures, and no foreign trade. We also temporarily assume away the questions of capital consumption, retained corporate earnings, and transfer payments.

The result is an economy made up of two components—households (including the entire population) and business firms. The diagram shows an inner loop reflecting the movement of goods and services and factors of production. The outer loop is the money used to purchase the goods and services, as well as the money used to pay the factors of production.

Inner Loop: Physical Flows

In our diagram the business firms own no property or plants. They merely bring together factors of production such as land, labor, and capital to produce goods. The households provide

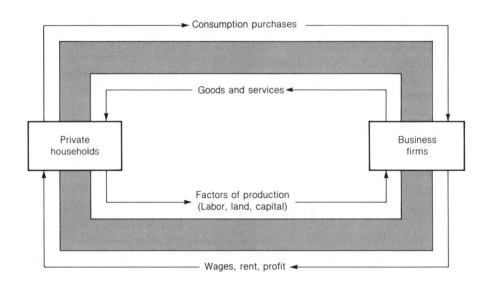

Exhibit 5-1   Circular flow of income

The diagram illustrates the circular flow between households and business firms. The upper half of the diagram reflects the movement of goods and services from the business sector to households. The lower half reflects the movement of the factors of production from the households that own them to the business sector. The inner loop represents the
movement of real physical units (dozens of coconuts, hours of labor, acres of land). The outer loop reflects monetary payments for the real physical units. For example, the lower half of the outer loop includes the wages paid to households for providing labor to the business firm, and the lower inner loop includes the actual hours of labor provided to business firms.

the factors and at the same time they consume the goods produced. These transactions in real physical units are shown in the inner loop.

Outer Loop: Monetary Flows

The factors of production will be supplied by the household only if they receive compensation. Similarly, a firm requires payments for the goods it sells. The payments, in money form, are shown by the outer loop. The bottom half of the loop shows payments from the firm to the factors of production (*factor payments*). By custom these payments require special terminology: *rent* is a payment to the owner of real property in return for its use, *wages* are a payment to labor, *interest* is the payment to capital, and *profit* is the payment to the *entrepreneur(s)*. The top half of the loop is the payment by the public to businesses for the goods and services received. Since we have assumed there are no retained profits, the flows represented by the two loops are equal.

We can illustrate the circular flow with a simple economy that consists of only one industry—a farm. The annual economic statement of this economy is shown in Exhibit 5-2. The top half of the economic statement reflects the use of real things—worker-years of labor, acres of land, and pounds of corn. This is shown schematically as the inner loop in Exhibit 5-3.

As discussed in the previous chapter, a simple economy carrying out transactions by barter would require no money. The farm could pay the factors of production, such as the five workers, in pounds of corn, according to each worker's contribution to the final product. Such an arrangement is conceptually feasible for a farm whose products can be used directly and are easily transported. However, barter would not be feasible at a steel plant or auto factory where workers would have to be paid in tons of steel or parts of a car. Thus, in order to avoid barter, the farm sells corn to the public and receives 50¢ per pound, or a total of $24,000. The farm in turn pays its factors of production $24,000. These transactions make up the outer, or money, loop. Note that payments to factors equal payments received, since the farm retained no profit. Also note that the GNP of the economy (consisting of one farm) could be measured either by the final sale of products ($24,000) or by total payments to factors ($24,000).

Exhibit 5-2   Annual economic statement of a hypothetical farm

	Factors and Goods	
	Factors supplied to farm	Product produced on farm
Physical Flows (inner loop)	5 worker-years (labor) 1000 acres (land) 5 tractors (capital)	48,000 pounds corn

	Money Payments	
	Firm's payments to factors	Payment to firm for product
Monetary Flows (outer loop)	$10,000 ($2,000 per worker) $12,000 ($12 per acre) $2,000 ($400 per year per tractor)	$24,000 (50¢ per pound)

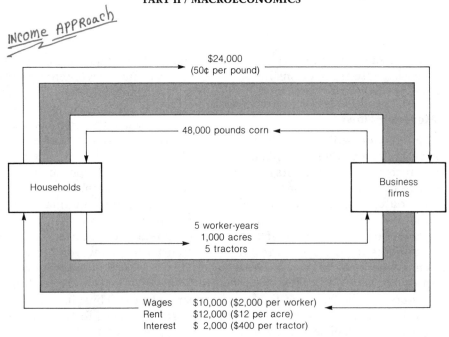

INCome APPRoach

$24,000
(50¢ per pound)

48,000 pounds corn

Households

Business firms

5 worker-years
1,000 acres
5 tractors

Wages $10,000 ($2,000 per worker)
Rent $12,000 ($12 per acre)
Interest $ 2,000 ($400 per tractor)

Exhibit 5-3   Circular flow of a simple hypothetical economy

This exhibit illustrates the circular flow of economic goods between households and firms in a simple economy consisting of only one industry—a farm. The inner loop shows the 48,000 pounds of corn produced by the farm, which goes to households for consumption, and the 5 worker-years, 1000 acres, and 5 tractors required to produce the corn. The upper half of the outer loop reflects the purchase of corn by households for $24,000. The lower half of the outer loop shows payment by the farm to the households, which have provided the labor, land, and capital necessary to produce the corn. Since the farm retains no profit, the payments to the factors equal the payment received for the product.

A MORE COMPLEX CIRCULAR FLOW

The economy has several important sectors that are not included in the circular flow of income shown in Exhibits 5-1 and 5-3. In addition to households and business firms we must include the financial sector (banks, savings and loan associations, and other financial institutions), the government sector (including federal, state, and local levels), and the foreign sector (including all nations that buy our products or sell their output to us). To show the circular flow of income when all these sectors are included, we show only monetary flows without reference to the corresponding physical flows contained in the previous exhibits.

Exhibit 5-4 shows an overview of an economy and the interdependence of these key sectors. One way to measure the GNP of the economy shown in this exhibit is to measure the expenditures for final products. This is shown in the upper loop. The diagram shows four basic types of expenditures received by business firms. Three of these are expenditures by households for consumption of goods and services, purchases of capital goods (investment), and purchases by government. Items imported from

Payments to the factor Production.

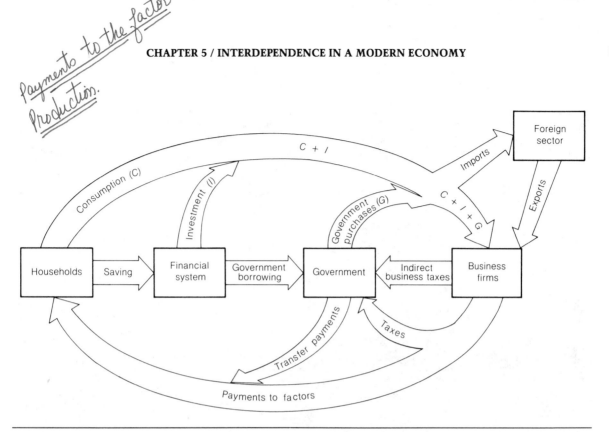

Exhibit 5-4   Circular flow of expenditures

This circular flow diagram shows GNP from both the income and expenditure viewpoints. The upper portion shows consumption expenditures coming from households, investment expenditures from the financial system, and government expenditures. To obtain total spending, net exports must be added to consumption, investment, and government expenditures. Net exports are shown as import expenditures flowing away from business firms and

export sales causing funds to flow to the firms. The lower portion shows business firms producing national income and paying indirect business taxes to the government. Capital consumption allowances (depreciation) are not shown. Taxes and government borrowing provide to the government the funds for transfer payments and government purchases. Saving provides the financial system resources for investment expenditures.

foreign countries involve a flow of expenditures out of the country and therefore lower the stream of expenditures to business firms. Thus the import arrow in Exhibit 5-4 points away from the flow of expenditures going to business firms. However, exports (items bought by citizens of other countries) represent flows to business firms. Measuring total expenditures requires that we add consumption, investment, government purchases, and exports minus imports. Exports minus imports is called *net exports*.

In Exhibit 5-3 we showed that GNP could also be measured by counting the payments to factors of production. This is called the *income approach* to GNP. The lower half of Exhibit 5-4 shows that business firms make payments to factors of production—wages to labor, rents to the owners of real property, interest for the use of capital, and profit to successful entrepreneurs. Without government or a financial system, all of these payments are received by households. Taxes, like death, are generally

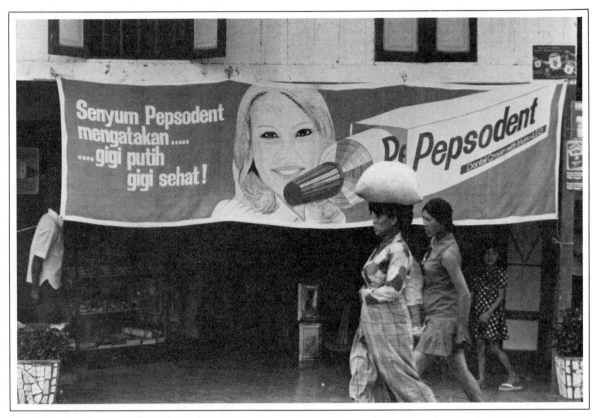

Goods that have been produced in the United States but are sold in other countries return money to the United States. *(Photo by George Bellerose, Stock, Boston)*

considered one of the inevitable facts of life. Thus some of these payments are siphoned off from households via taxes. These are returned to the income stream in one of two ways. The first is for the government to buy goods and services (such as airplanes and tanks for national defense, or a county health service on a local level). In this case the circular flow of income is completed but bypasses the households. The second way for government to return tax payments to the income stream is to give the money to households via programs such as Social Security or welfare expenditures. These are called *transfer payments.*

We also know that people do not spend all their income on goods and services. Lack of spending would break the circular flow of income if the money were put in a mattress or buried in the backyard. Instead income saved is generally placed in one of a variety of financial institutions that loan the money to individuals or business firms wanting to buy capital goods.

The purchase of capital goods (machines, buildings, and inventories) is called *investment*. Investment must offset saving to keep the circular flow of income in balance.

TWO VIEWS OF GNP

The circular flow of income makes clear that there are two ways of looking at GNP. Specifically:

$$\left.\begin{array}{c}\text{Total flow of}\\\text{expenditures for}\\\text{final output}\end{array}\right\} = \text{GNP} = \left\{\begin{array}{c}\text{Total flow of}\\\text{income from}\\\text{final output}\end{array}\right.$$

The *expenditures approach* is the upper half of the circular flow of Exhibit 5-1; the *income approach* is the lower half. Exhibit 5-5 shows the components of the expenditure and income flows.

A few additional comments about the identity of income and production may clarify other points that sometimes confuse students. When goods are produced, claims upon them are produced at the same time. Farm workers who add value by doing their jobs earn wages that enable them to buy products. Similarly, investors who loan money to a firm receive interest payments as their share of final output. Generally, all recipients of these kinds of payments have agreed in advance to the terms of payment; workers are to receive $6 per hour, for instance, regardless of the profitability of the firm. The entrepreneur who brought together the factors of production agrees to pay these *contractual claims*, which include wages, rent, interest, and some taxes. For his efforts the entrepreneur has a *residual claim* on the revenue remaining after the contractual claims have been paid. If the revenue generated by the firm's operations is greater than the contractual claims, the entrepreneur makes a profit; if the contractual claims exceed revenue, the entrepreneur suffers a loss.

Quite often several of these functions are performed by one person. An individual might own a business (loan capital to himself or herself), work in the business (labor), and serve as an entrepreneur. In such a case, the "profits" of firms include factor payments as well as the profit which we have called a residual claim.

Exhibit 5-5   Two views of GNP

Expenditure Viewpoint		Income Viewpoint
Flow of product		*Flow of income*
Household sector (personal consumption expenditures) +		Wages Rent
Government sector (government purchases of goods and services) +	= GNP =	Interest Profit Proprietors' income +
Business sector (gross private domestic investment) +		Nonincome expenses Indirect business taxes Depreciation of capital
Foreign sector (net exports of goods and services)		

GNP from the Expenditure Viewpoint

Expenditures are grouped into the four types shown in Exhibit 5-5. The sum of these expenditures comprises GNP, as shown in Exhibit 5-6. Here we give a more detailed description of these categories.

Personal Consumption Expenditures (C) Expenditures made by households fall into this category. They include spending on durable consumer goods (e.g., automobiles, desks, refrigerators, television sets), nondurable consumer goods (e.g., food, beer, razor blades, gasoline), and consumer services (e.g., medical care, barbers, garbage collection, bowling).

Gross Private Domestic Investment (I) There are three components of this seemingly complicated term: (1) new construction, (2) producers' durables, and (3) changes in business inventories. However, we should differentiate between the everyday meaning of the word "investment" and the definition used by economists. In everyday language, an individual who pur-

chases stocks or bonds is making an investment. Economists, however, use the term "investment" to mean an addition to the stock of real productive capital. The purchase of stocks or bonds from others is merely a transfer of existing assets, not an investment in the economists' sense. However, purchase of a new piece of machinery is considered an investment by economists. Here are the components of investment as defined by economists:

1. *New construction.* Building new factories or stores clearly creates new productive capacity. However, residential construction is also included as investment, because apartments and houses are long-lived assets that create flows of services over time, such as the provision of housing services for which rent is paid. A property owned by an investor provides rental income over a long time. Rather than make an artificial distinction between investor-owned homes and occupant-owned homes, all construction is included in the investment category.

Exhibit 5-6   Gross National Product (in billions), 1981

Expenditure Viewpoint			Income Viewpoint		
Personal consumption expenditures		$1858.1	Wages		$1771.7
Nondurable will NOT LAST — Food	711.7		Interest		215.0
Durable will LAST — CAR.	269.4		Rent		33.6
Services	877.0		Profit		189.0
Gross private domestic investment		450.6	Proprietors' income		134.4
Nonresidential	338.9		Nonincome expenses		572.7
Residential	94.6		Depreciation	321.5	
Changes in business inventories	17.1		Indirect business taxes	251.2	
Government spending		589.7	Miscellaneous		5.8
Federal	228.6				
State and local	361.1				
Net exports		23.8			
Exports	366.7				
Imports	342.9				
Gross National Product		2922.2			2922.2

SOURCE: *Economic Report of the President*, 1982.

An increase in inventories constitutes an increase in investment. *(Photo by Terry Zabala)*

2. *Producer durables.* The purchase of machinery and tools used in the production process is a straightforward case of investment.

3. *Changes in inventory.* Inventories are a form of investment for a business, since the presence of goods in warehouses and storerooms allows firms to meet consumer demands. A store without adequate inventories will lose sales; a manufacturer without inventories will not be able to meet orders promptly from stores. If the amount of goods in inventory did not change from year to year, GNP would not be affected. However, when inventories are reduced, GNP must be reduced accordingly, since goods produced in a previous time period have been sold. Similarly, an increase in inventories constitutes an increase in investment that represents goods produced during the year.

The term "gross" is an important modifier in "gross private domestic investment." It signifies that we are including all investment goods produced during the year—including those used to replace machinery, equipment, and buildings that have worn out. Occasionally we measure only *net* private domestic investment, which is the gross investment less an allowance for the capital stock used up during the year.

In a growing economy additions to capital stock are usually greater than the amount of capital stock that wears out. Net investment is then positive. When there is little need or incentive to replace depreciated capital, such as during a severe recession, net investment may be negative. For example, in the United States during the depression year of 1933, gross investment totaled only $1.4 billion, and depreciation was $6.9 billion. Therefore, net investment was a negative $5.5 billion. Both the gross investment figure and the net investment figure are meaningful for national income analysis.

Government Spending (G) Included in this category are purchases of finished products by all levels of government—federal, state, and local—and all direct purchases of factors such as labor. Although the government may transfer money from one person to another as in welfare payments, these are not included in GNP, because they do not reflect new production. They merely transfer purchasing power from one set of households to another.

Net Exports (X) In a country with no foreign trade (called a closed economy), exports and imports would not be considered. But clearly, spending by other countries on U.S. goods affects expenditures in the circular flow, just as purchases within the United States do. Thus, foreign purchases must be added to total expenditures. On the other hand, U.S. purchases of foreign goods not manufactured in the United States will have an opposite effect.

Instead of two entries in National Income accounts, however, only one is made, representing net exports. Net exports are exports

The flow of exports from other countries takes money out of the United States. *(Photo by T. D. Lovering, Stock, Boston)*

minus imports. Thus if the United States exported $35 billion worth of goods and imported $33 billion, net exports would be $2 billion. Net exports are negative when imports exceed exports.

GNP from the Income Viewpoint

We have noted that the lower loop of the circular flow (total income) must equal total expenditures (upper loop). Since the production of goods generated $2922 billion in revenue in 1981, how is that income distributed among the factors of production?

Wages This term is broadly defined to include all compensation of employees. Wages, salaries, pensions, fringe benefits, and tips are all included. This is the largest component of GNP, amounting to approximately 60 percent of the total.

Interest This term is a net figure representing the interest paid by the business sector for the use of capital and land, less the interest received by the business sector.

Rent The income earned for allowing the use of real property is rent. This category includes the estimated rental value of owner-occupied homes.

Profit As mentioned earlier, profit is a residual. After all costs except corporate taxes and a few other items have been subtracted from revenue, the amount remaining is profit.

Proprietors' Income One other form of income contains components of both profit and wages— the earnings of unincorporated businesses or proprietorships and partnerships. This category includes net income from small businesses as well as that of suppliers of professional services such as lawyers and doctors. A small part of this income could properly be called profit, but a large share constitutes employee compensation for the self-employed.

If capital did not wear out (depreciate) and there were no government, the various categories of income listed above would equal total expenditures. However, two adjustments are necessary, because part of the expenditures composing GNP are devoted to categories that do not produce income. These are called non-income expenses in the national income accounts.

Capital Consumption Allowance (Depreciation) As discussed in the previous chapter, plant and equipment are used up in the process of producing goods and services. Consequently individual firms estimate the useful life of their equipment and then allocate the cost of the equipment over its predicted lifetime. The annual allowance is called _depreciation._

When an expenditure is made by a consumer, part of the money compensates the firm for the cost of the equipment used in producing the good. From the standpoint of equating expenditure and income, depreciation must be added to the income flow.

Indirect Business Taxes The role of government must also be included in the analysis because indirect taxes are part of our expenditures. These are taxes paid to the government by business firms but not levied directly on the firm. The major categories are sales taxes, excise taxes, and business property taxes. Their effect can best be understood by examining sales taxes. When a merchant sells a $50 item in a state with a 4 percent sales tax, the consumer pays $52. Only $50 is retained by the firm. The other $2 is an indirect business tax that is included in the income side of the ledger to maintain equality between income and expenditures.

These last two categories are nonincome adjustments made to keep expenditure GNP and income GNP equal. This relationship can best be summarized as:

Total expenditures
for goods and services = GNP

                         = Income + Depreciation
                           + Indirect business taxes

ECONOMIC INSTABILITY

The circular flow of income has so far illustrated the interdependence of a modern economy and defined the two views of GNP. It can also be used to show how the level of economic activity can change when the behavior of either households or business is altered. This is because the business firms must depend on the consumption decisions of households for income, while, similarly, households depend on the production and hiring decisions of firms for *their* income. If either one behaves differently than expected, the other will inevitably be affected and will be compelled to change its behavior, too.

Picture a circular flow of income in which households receive $100 million in wages, rent, profit, and interest and spend the entire amount on goods and services produced by the business firms. The flow thus is in equilibrium at $100 million. Now suppose that the households disrupt this equilibrium by saving $10 million, instead of spending it, and depositing the money in banks. Household expenditures on goods and services produced by the business firms now total only $90 million, although the firms' output remains at $100 million.

Does this mean that the circular flow of income is inevitably broken? Not necessarily. Suppose the business firms now decide to increase their inventories by $10 million in order to meet an expected increase in customer demand. They continue to produce $100 million in goods and services, but only $90 million is sold to customers and $10 million is set aside toward future sales.

But how can a business afford to hold $10 million in inventory when they must pay out $100 million to cover the factors of production? Most likely, the banks will loan the business

A decrease in consumer spending may lead to a decrease in production by business. *(Photo by Costa Manos, Magnum)*

firms the needed $10 million. Thus they will receive $90 million from the sale of goods and services and $10 million from bank loans—enough to pay $100 million in wages, profits, interest, and rent, and to increase inventories at the same time.

The new balance in the circular flow of income is shown in Exhibit 5-7. The business sector produces $100 million worth of goods, of which $90 million goes to consumers and $10 million to a planned increase in inventories. House-

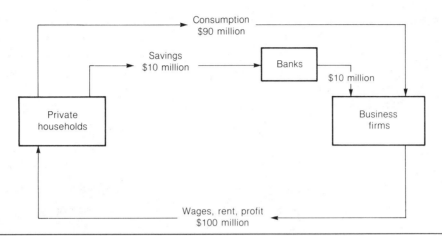

Exhibit 5-7   Circular flow with savings and inventory investments

This diagram shows the circular flow (here monetary payments of the outer loop) in equilibrium. Of the $100 million in payments to households, $90 million is spent on consumption of goods and services and

$10 million is saved. At the same time, businesses plan to build up inventories by $10 million. So long as this behavior remains unchanged, the circular flow of income will remain in equilibrium.

holds receive $100 million in income and they save $10 million. Thus the aggregate demand for consumer goods is $90 million and aggregate supply is $90 million.

Suppose, however, that the households continue to save $10 million and do not increase their demand for goods and services, as the business firms expected. If consumers do not change their spending and saving decisions, the firms will produce $100 million of goods, but sales to consumers will account for only $90 million. The result is an *unplanned* increase in inventories. Consequently, the business firms will want to cut back output, and they will accomplish this by hiring fewer factors of production. Members of some households will then become unemployed, and household income will fall. Now households may become more cautious and reduce their purchases of goods below the previous level of $90 million. The further

result will be an additional decline in production by business firms, and so both business firms and households will be worse off. A recession has begun.

The circular flow of income therefore shows the great interdependence of a modern economy and illustrates that economic instability is easily introduced into the economic system. A more complete description of the processes that determine national income is the subject of the rest of Part II.

SUMMARY

1. The total product available to a society is ultimately what all members of that society have produced (excluding foreign trade for the moment).

2. One person's expenditures are another per-

son's income. This equivalence is demonstrated in the circular flow diagram.

3. The circular flow illustrates the identity between the real flow of goods and productive factors and the monetary payments for these goods and factors.

4. GNP can be measured by either the total flow of expenditures or the total flow of incomes (with depreciation and indirect business taxes added).

KEY CONCEPTS

circular flow of income

factor payments

rent

wages

interest

profit

entrepreneurs

expenditure approach to GNP

income approach to GNP

consumption

investment

government spending

net exports

indirect business taxes

involuntary inventory buildup

QUESTIONS FOR DISCUSSION

1. In an island economy where the only output is coconuts, GNP drops from 1000 coconuts in 1983 to 900 coconuts in 1984. What would happen to individual incomes?

2. Explain the statement, "Your purchases are my income." Is the statement always true?

3. Using the following data, calculate GNP from both the expenditure and income viewpoints.

consumption 612	indirect business taxes 61
gross investment 110	transfer payments 120
gross exports 55	wages 570
gross imports 50	rent, interest, profit, and other
depreciation 65	income 110
net investment 45	government spending 79

4. Which of the following items are actually included in determining GNP? Which category does each fall into?

    a. the wages of a steel worker

    b. dividends received from a utility

_____ **c.** social security retirement paychecks

d. an Army private's pay

_____ **e.** Mr. Jones' purchase of a used car from Mr. Smith

wage **f.** the services of a mechanic working on other people's cars

_____ **g.** the services of a mechanic working on his own car

_____ **h.** the purchase of Mobile Home Industries stock from the company

wage **i.** John Elway's salary

interest **j.** interest received on tax-free government bonds

_____ **k.** the purchase of stolen property by a "fence"

consumption **l.** the purchase of a new pickup truck by a consumer

tax **m.** the sales tax on the purchase of a new oven

5. Suppose that during 1985 gross investment is $130 billion and depreciation is $80 billion. Using an expenditures approach to determine GNP and NNP, how would gross investment and depreciation enter into the calculation? Using an income approach how would they enter the GNP and NNP calculation?

6. Suppose that _inventories increase by $14 billion_ during 1984. How does that affect GNP? _Company invested, increased._

7. Is there any way to determine whether a recorded increase of $14 billion in inventory was desired or whether it was voluntary?

8. Since the expenditures approach and the income approach arrive at the same numbers, is a desirable level of GNP always achieved? _NO_

income approach
but add depreciation to get GNP.

Chapter 6

Classical Economics and the Contributions of Keynes

The ideas of economists and political philosophers, both when they are right and when they are wrong, are more powerful than is commonly understood. Indeed the world is ruled by little else. Practical men, who believe themselves to be quite exempt from any intellectual influences, are usually the slaves of some defunct economist. Madmen in authority, who hear voices in the air, are distilling their frenzy from some academic scribbler of a few years back. I am sure that the power of vested interests is vastly exaggerated compared with the gradual encroachment of ideas.

J. M. Keynes

Keynes used the term "academic scribbler" in the above passage to describe the people who develop the ideas that guide human action. All economic policy is based on some implicit or explicit theory of how the economy works. In the world of macroeconomics these theories of various degrees of sophistication have ruled our efforts to control the key variables of economic growth, inflation, and unemployment.

For centuries, the religious services held to ask for good weather were society's only attempt to control economic activity—that is, agricultural output. Before the nineteenth century, the so-called *business cycles* were viewed as chance misfortunes or the result of panic, error, or fraud. In 1867 an observer suggested, "These periodic collapses are really mental in their nature, depending on variations of despondency, hopefulness, excitement, disappointment, and panic."* In Chapter 1 we saw that some years later William Stanley Jevons blamed sunspots for economic fluctuations, hardly a cause subject to the influence of government. As long as explanations were based on events and troubles outside the economic system, there could be no stabilizing activity by government.

---

* Robert Heilbroner, *The Worldly Philosophers* (New York: Simon and Schuster, 1961), p. 228.

Some scholars believe that a physician, Clement Juglar, who abandoned medicine for economics, was the first to attribute business fluctuations to the economic system itself. In 1862 he pointed out that "the only cause of depression is prosperity." This suggested that the very process of expanding economic activity could cause a downturn. The inevitable conclusion was that a market economy is inherently unstable. While the development of economic theory was to prove the validity of Juglar's basic notion, his contention was long ignored.

Even in the twentieth century, after decades of industrialization, government was not expected to control business cycles. The recurring panics and periods of economic decline did not generate government efforts to eliminate them. Prevailing economic doctrine, called *classical economics*, was largely responsible for this absence of government involvement. Economists of the time thought that the competitive market economy was self-adjusting. Small fluctuations in economic activity might occur, but the markets themselves would make the required adjustments. Since it was believed that the market system would naturally tend to full employment, there was no need for a government stabilization policy.

That unemployment could exist only temporarily was the prevailing economic doctrine until the Great Depression of the 1930s, when the modern industrial economies of the world experienced massive and chronic joblessness. As the depression lingered, U.S. President Franklin D. Roosevelt discarded orthodox economic thinking and responded to the public's demand for government action. Government started its first efforts to stabilize the economy. The government made its role explicit after World War II, when Congress passed the Employment Act of 1946, which made full

Franklin D. Roosevelt responded to the public cry for action, although economic theory did not provide much guidance. *(Wide World Photos)*

employment a national economic goal. The theoretical rationale for these efforts was called "Keynesian economics."

THE CLASSICAL ECONOMISTS

Classical economics, the prevailing economic view during the nineteenth and early twentieth century, was built on the theory of a competitive economic system with a self-adjusting market mechanism that assured full employment. Although, in this thinking, shocks would occasionally disrupt the economic system—wars, political upheavals, and droughts—the disruptions would be short-run phenomena that would be corrected by the forces of demand and supply. The system would always tend to full employment. With this view of the economy, the correct public policy was for government to keep hands off the well-balanced, finely tuned mechanism. *Laissez-faire,* meaning a policy of minimal government involvement in the economy, was the watchword of the day.

The idea of a self-adjusting market economy was based on two assumptions. First, it was believed that there was sufficient demand to sell all output, a relationship called *Say's law.* Second, even when spending was temporarily low, it was believed that there would be adjustments in prices and wages that would bring the economy back to full employment.

Say's Law

Stating that "supply creates its own demand," Say's law was the first pillar of the classical model. It was named for the French economist J.B. Say (1767–1832). Say's law could be interpreted as another way of expressing the identity between income and expenditure as illustrated by the circular flow. Obviously, this simple identity alone does not assure that income level will be either high or low—only that it will be identical to expenditure levels. To the classical economists, Say's law had a deeper significance. They believed it meant that there will always be sufficient purchasing power to demand all of the output produced at the full-employment level.

Their confidence came from the view that households would not provide the factors of production unless they wanted to buy goods and services. If the business sector produced at levels of full employment, there would be sufficient purchasing power to clear the market of all production—at least, if all income were spent. But clearly people don't spend every cent they receive; some earnings are saved. Such a leakage from purchasing power would leave the economy with insufficient demand from households to purchase all the products produced.

Classical economists, however, had considered this possibility. The savings would be loaned to the business sector because of its need for investment goods. The purchase of goods for inventory, as well as plant and equipment, offset the household saving. But if full-employment equilibrium were to be achieved, it was necessary that desired saving by households equal desired investment by business. This left a question: Did any mechanism exist to ensure the equality of saving leakage and investment injection at full employment?

Classical economists argued that saving would always equal investment. The majority of clas-

sical economists believed that the interest rate provided the equilibrating mechanism. People did not really like to save, they said, but the more they were paid for saving, the more they would save. The interest rate is the reward households receive for lending out their savings. On the other hand, classical economists argued, businessmen invested only to make a profit. The higher the interest rate, the higher the cost of investment, and therefore the less profitable the investment. By this logic, the higher the rate of interest, the lower the amount of investment.

Exhibit 6-1 shows the classical saving and investment model in graphical form. Saving increases as the interest rate rises—that is, we have an upward sloping supply of saving. The quantity of funds demanded falls as the interest rate rises. The curves are similar to the demand and supply curves analyzed in Chapter 2. With these functional relationships between saving, investment, and the interest rate, saving and investment would be equal at some interest rate.

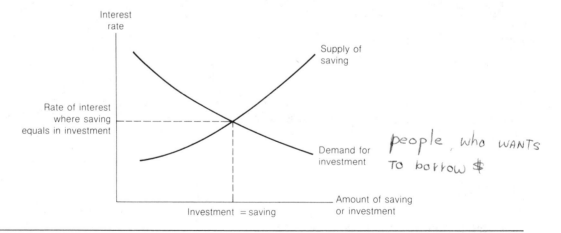

Exhibit 6-1   Classical saving and investment model

This exhibit illustrates the model underlying the classical view of saving and investment. The quantity of saving increases as the interest rate goes up, but the quantity of funds demanded for investment declines as the interest rate increases.

In the minds of classical economists this equality upheld Say's law. Obviously, a sudden shift in the saving or investment curves might cause some temporary excess saving or investment, but the changing interest rate would soon correct the problem.

Price-Wage Flexibility

Price and wage flexibility was the second pillar of classical economics. This mechanism assured that the level of economic activity would remain at a full-employment level of output. At times of unemployment it was believed that wages would fall because unemployed workers would compete for jobs with the employed. As wages fell, the cost of production would also fall, which would increase the producers' profits. Increasing profit would serve as an incentive for the producer to raise output, which would create more jobs until full employment was again achieved.

Of course, lower wages meant lower incomes. But prices of goods were thought to be equally flexible. When demand was insufficient, the competition among producers was supposed to lower prices until goods were sold. Thus, price-wage flexibility provided the mechanism to assure the full-employment level of output, and Say's law assured sufficient demand. Lengthy unemployment was considered voluntary—that is, any worker who desired a job could find it at some wage. Only if the worker expected too high a wage would he remain unemployed. The conclusion followed that there could be no lasting problem of unemployment.

It was an attractive theory for economists of the era, resembling the theories of astronomy that gravitational forces keep a planet on a steady course. The logical steps of the classical model were easy to follow. Cause and effect were clear to the eighteenth century scientist and many scholars assumed that human behavior would be governed by natural laws. In addition, it provided an economic rationale for the doctrine of laissez-faire capitalism. If the free market could keep the economy moving slowly but steadily upward, no government intervention was necessary or desirable. Prosperity was assured.

But the reassuring classical model had some weaknesses. It failed to predict accurately. In astronomy, a theory that cannot predict the correct location of a planet is soon replaced by a more accurate theory. Similarly, in economics a theory that says unemployment will be a minor and transitory problem becomes suspect when unemployment is persistent and serious. However, in the world of ideas an accepted theory is not junked just because it fails to predict accurately. It remains until another theory emerges that does a better job of describing events. The extended depression of the 1930s had prepared the economics profession for a new theory. In 1936 it emerged.

KEYNESIAN THEORY

In 1936 the prominent English economist John Maynard Keynes (1883–1946) published *The General Theory of Employment, Interest, and Money*. This book contained the core of the ideas that are the basis of modern macroeconomic analysis. The ideas have been refined and modified by later economic theorists, but the basic model has not changed. The world described by Keynes in *The General Theory* was not the self-adjusting economy of the classical economists. Keynes argued that nothing in a capitalistic system guaranteed that equilibrium would always occur at full employment. The Keynesian model foresaw periods of extended unemployment and severe inflation.

John Maynard Keynes offered a theoretical basis for government policies to control business cycles. *(Wide World Photos)*

The book received immediate attention from the economics profession, partly due to Keynes' reputation as one of England's foremost economists and partly because the intellectual climate was ready for a change in economic thinking. Six years of deep depression with 10 million unemployed in the United States alone had made the classical theory untenable to many people.

Keynesian View of Saving

But what about Keynes' theory—how did it differ from the classical views? To begin with, Keynes argued that there was no automatic adjustment mechanism. He did not believe that depressions were temporary. He pictured an economy that could languish in the depths of a depression. The key lay in saving and investment behavior. In the classical model, the interest rate was the mechanism that assured equality between investment and saving. When a business slowdown occurred, the interest rate was supposed to fall and businesses therefore would increase investment. But Keynes did not believe in this saving-investment link. He argued that savers and investors are different groups who formulate their saving and investment plans on different criteria. Most importantly, the interest rate plays a very minor role in either of their decisions. .

A major source of saving comes from private households. Why do households save? Do high interest rates affect saving? Research indicates that the interest rate provides relatively little motivation to households to save. Households save for future purchases, for rainy-day accounts, and for retirement. In each case, the level of saving is related more to income than to the interest rate. When incomes are too low, people are required to spend their total income for necessities, leaving nothing for saving. When incomes rise, a larger share of income typically is saved.

Investment decisions are affected by the business cycle. When business profit expectations are low, a small change in interest rates is not sufficient to cause an increase in investment. During an economic boom businesses may invest even at high interest rates. Thus, under many circumstances, future expectations are a much more important determinant of investment than the interest rate.

In summary, the classical assumption that there would always be enough total purchasing power was not warranted. Nor was the second classical assumption, price-wage flexibility, free of criticism.

Price-Wage Inflexibility

The classical economists believed that price-wage flexibility would make corrections when aggregate demand was temporarily too low. Most economists now think that modern economic systems do not have this kind of flexibility. Modern economies have large sectors where competition is not the rule but the exception. Even where flexibility exists, government and labor union actions have limited it severely. Minimum-wage legislation and the power of unions prevent wages from declining regardless of the amount of unemployment. Although inflation may cause real wages in some industries to fall over time, the gradual adjustment process provides more long-term than short-term flexibility in real wages. Without discussing whether inflexibility is desirable, it is sufficient to note that the price-wage flexibility required for the classical adjustment process simply does not exist in modern economies.

Keynes criticized the classical economic system, arguing that the finely tuned self-adjustment process described in classical economics no longer operated. However, Keynes did not stop at criticizing the previous orthodoxy—he supplied an alternative theory of employment and income determination. This model suggested how public policies could be developed to help combat recessions.

Preview of Keynesian Economics

In this chapter and the next we will analyze in detail what determines the level of employment and income. Basically Keynes emphasized the effect of aggregate demand on employment. He emphasized that there was no internal mechanism to assure that sufficient aggregate demand would exist in the economy. This was a rejection of Say's law that supply created its own demand. In the Keynesian model, aggregate demand could be low enough to cause high levels of unemployment. In order to make up for any potential deficiency in aggregate demand, Keynes recommended that government pursue policies to stimulate demand when necessary. The conclusion that government intervention was required for a reasonable level of employment and income was the most startling thesis of *The General Theory*, since it was in direct contrast to the classical economists' laissez-faire philosophy. This emphasis on government intervention in the economy has been a major point of debate on the appropriateness of the Keynesian doctrine.

Controversies Surrounding Keynesian Analysis

Although the intellectual climate in the late 1930s was ready for a new theory, Keynesian analysis was not and has not been totally accepted. There have been two kinds of criticism, or controversy, surrounding Keynesian theory. The first deals with the policy implication of the analysis and its departure from the formerly dominant laissez-faire philosophy. The second persistent criticism is a concern among economists about the weaknesses or shortcomings of the analysis.

Concern about Government Intervention Much of the criticism of Keynesian theory has come from people who object to government intervention, as favored by Keynes. Keynes advocated government spending to increase aggregate demand and preserve free enterprise, but some have interpreted his theory as a threat to the workings of the free market. Some critics of Keynes feel that an expanded government role in the economy would be inefficient and would lead to a reduction in personal freedom. Some of these critics have gone so far as to liken Keynesian theories to those of Karl Marx and to make references to the "takeover" of the government by Keynesians. These critics, however, did not really understand Keynesian theory, which differs radically from Marxian theory. Marx believed that capitalism contained within itself a mechanism that would lead to increasingly savage business cycles, depressions, and unemployment—the seeds of its own destruction. Keynes, on the other hand, firmly believed in capitalism and proposed government action that would limit depressions and thus keep free enterprise viable in the long term.

Theoretical Criticism of Keynes   Although Keynes has provided the basic framework that is used to discuss macroeconomic issues, his theories have not escaped serious criticism from some economists. Much economic research since World War II has been devoted to quantifying the relationships underlying Keynesian analysis and to evaluating competing theories. The following issues have been raised by this research:

1. Keynesian analysis is essentially short run, designed to minimize unemployment or inflation for brief periods. However, economic growth and development are long-run issues and there is no assurance that the Keynesian approach to short-term demand management will yield optimum long-term results. This criticism gained great currency in the popular U.S. press as a result of the poor economic performance of the country during the 1970s. The validity of these "supply-side" critiques of Keynesian theory will be discussed in later chapters.

2. A group of economists called *monetarists* have criticized Keynes because he failed to consider adequately the role of monetary policy

The major spokesman for the monetarist viewpoint, in opposition to the Keynesian viewpoint, is Nobel Prize winner Milton Friedman. *(Wide World Photos)*

in the determination of national income and employment. The importance of the supply of money in the economy is now widely accepted among economists. The nature of money and its role in macroeconomic policy is discussed in Chapters 9 and 10.

3. A final criticism of Keynesian theory is that it assumes that the government is capable of pursuing policies that will stabilize the economy. An increasingly important school of economists argue that political pressures cause Congress to follow macroeconomic policies that destabilize the economy over the long run with the end result being higher unemployment, higher inflation, and slower

Exhibit 6-2 Disposition of personal income for selected years

Year	Amount (in billions) Disposable Income* Y		=	Consumption C	+	Savings S	Percent Allocated To Consumption	Saving
1939	$ 69.2			$ 67.0		$ 2.2	96.8%	3.2%
1949	185.6			178.1		7.5	96.0	4.0
1959	331.9			310.8		21.1	93.6	6.4
1969	622.4			581.8		40.6	93.5	6.5
1979	1597.1			1510.9		86.2	94.6	5.4
1981	1964.7			1858.1		106.6	94.6	5.4

*Excludes interest paid by consumers to business and net personal transfer payments to foreigners.

growth than would have occurred if the government had not pursued a "stabilization" policy. This school of thought does not necessarily criticize Keynesian theory (although many economists of this persuasion also believe Keynesian theory to be incorrect) but instead focuses on the inability of the government to implement this policy. This viewpoint is discussed in detail in Chapter 12, in which we discuss macroeconomic policy.

ELEMENTS OF EMPLOYMENT THEORY

Aggregate demand, the keystone of Keynesian analysis, consists of (1) consumption demand, (2) private investment demand, (3) government demand, and (4) net export demand. Our first concern is with the level of employment that can be maintained by the private economy without the government or foreign sectors playing a role. That is, we are interested in the magnitude of (1) consumer demand for goods and services and (2) the investment demand of the private business sector. The role of government is postponed until Chapter 8. In this section we

will discuss consumption demand and investment demand.

Consumption

Consumption is the major component of aggregate spending. In 1980 it accounted for 64 percent of GNP. Exhibit 6-2 shows how personal disposable income is divided between consumption and savings for selected years.

Many factors affect the level of consumption. But think of your own experience. What really determines how much you spend? If you are like most people, spending is positively related to how much income you receive. That is, the higher your income, the more you consume.

Statistical studies support this conclusion. Exhibit 6-3 shows the relationship between consumption and disposable income in the United States since World War II, illustrating that as income increases, so does consumption. In recent years 93 or 94 percent of disposable income has gone to consumption. This relationship is consistent with Keynes' *General Theory*. Since 1936 a great deal of research has been conducted on the nature of the relationship between income and consumption. This relationship is called the *consumption function*.

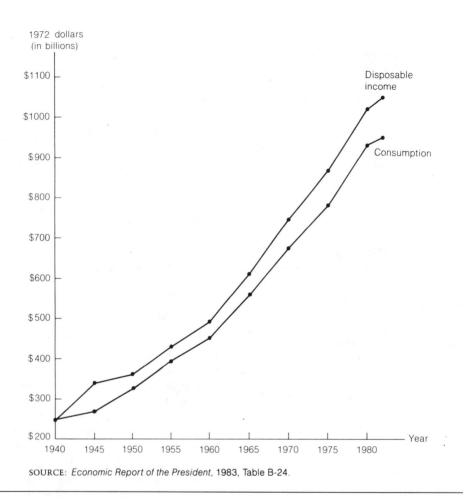

SOURCE: *Economic Report of the President*, 1983, Table B-24.

Exhibit 6-3 Disposable personal income and consumption, 1940–82

This diagram shows disposable personal income and consumption for the period from 1940 through 1982. As disposable income has increased, so has consumption. In most years, the sum shown as being spent on consumption represents 90 to 94 percent of disposable income.

Let us now specify a hypothetical consumption function incorporating the feature we would expect a real one to have. In Exhibit 6-4, line *C* shows the relationship between consumption (*C*) and disposable personal income (*Y*). A straight line at 45 degrees to the origin provides a frame of reference. The significance of the straight line is that it shows equal values of *C* and *Y*, where all income is consumed. For example, point *b* is on the 45-degree line and reflects $500 billion in income and $500 billion in consumption. Point *c* reflects $600 billion in income and $600 billion in consumption.

The figure is a graphic presentation of the data

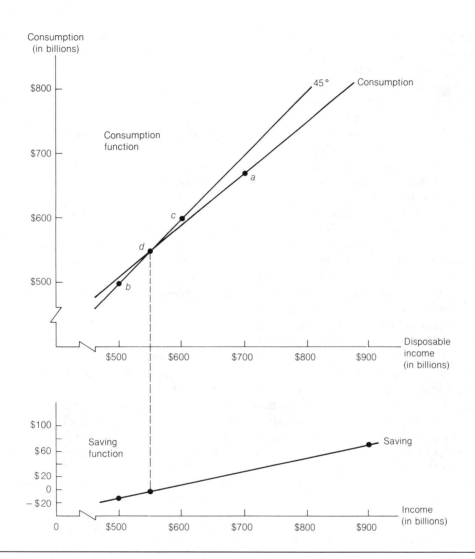

Exhibit 6-4 The consumption and saving functions

A typical consumption function is shown in this exhibit (the data is presented in Exhibit 6-5). The line labeled Consumption *shows the relationship between consumption and disposable income. As disposable income increases, the amount of consumption increases. A straight line at 45 degrees to the origin has been added as a frame of reference; it shows equal values of consumption and disposable income. For example, point* b *on the 45-degree line indicates that point where there is $500 billion in income and*

$500 billion in consumption. Similarly, point c *reflects $600 billion in income and $600 billion in consumption. At point* d, *consumption equals income.*

The lower half of the exhibit shows the saving function below the consumption function. With the level of consumption given, the level of saving can be easily determined. Consumption plus saving equals disposable income. Saving equals zero at point d. *The saving figure illustrates that saving increases as income increases.*

found in Exhibit 6-5. It illustrates what your intuition about consumption told you—as disposable income rises, consumption expenditures also increase. However, the percentage of income consumed changes with the level of income. For instance, at point *d*, *Y* = $550 billion and *C* = $550 billion, indicating that at that level all income is spent on consumption.

To the left of point *d* consumption exceeds income. You might wonder how this is possible. The answer is *dissaving.* Savings from an earlier period or borrowing from future income are used to finance current purchases. Although it is easy to conceive of a family spending more than it earns, it is difficult to conceive of a country doing so. Yet there are examples. Imagine for a moment a developing country that needs foreign aid to grow. Negative saving occurred in the United States at the depths of the Great Depression. In 1933 disposable income was $45.6 billion and personal outlays were $46.5 billion—a negative saving of $.9 billion.

The more relevant part of the consumption function is to the right of point *d.* Here the percentage of income spent on consumption declines as income rises. For example, when income is $550 billion we consume 100 percent; at $600 billion 98.3 percent is consumed; at $700 billion the amount consumed is 95.7

Exhibit 6-5 Hypothetical consumption function (in billions)

Income	Consumption	Saving
$500	$510	$ − 10
550	550	0
600	590	10
650	630	20
700	670	30
750	710	40
800	750	50
850	790	60
900	830	70

percent. To better describe this relationship it is helpful to introduce two additional terms.

Propensities to Consume

An important characteristic of the consumption function is the *average propensity to consume* (APC): the fraction of total income being spent on consumption. In other words, APC equals consumption divided by income, or

$$APC = C \div Y$$

For instance, if income were $100 million and total consumption were $80 million, APC would be 80/100 or 0.8.

Another important measure, called the *marginal propensity to consume* (MPC), is the fraction of additional income the public would devote to consumption if that income were available. Suppose that income increased from $100 million to $110 million. In the past the public spent 80 percent of their income, but that does not guarantee that they would continue to spend 80 percent of the additional $10 million. In fact, an examination of the consumption function in Exhibit 6-4 would indicate that such a rate of expenditure would be unlikely. Typically, the higher the level of income, the lower the percentage spent on consumption.

Symbolically, marginal propensity to consume equals change in consumption (*C*) divided by change in income (*Y*), or

$$MPC = \Delta C \div \Delta Y$$

(The delta symbol [Δ] means "change"; ΔS means "change in saving.") If households spent $7 million out of the $10 million increase, we would say that MPC = 7/10 or 0.7.

With MPC we can answer such questions as, "What would be the effect on consumer spending if our national disposable income grew by $100 billion next year?" If MPC is 0.7, we know that there would be $70 billion more direct demand for consumer goods. In 1981 the marginal propensity to consume in the United States was about 0.87.

Propensities to Save

Having determined the level of consumption, one can easily determine the level of saving. The relationship established earlier for households showed that consumption (C) plus saving (S) equals disposable income (Y). Saving, then, is the amount left after we spend on consumption. That is:

$$S = Y - C$$

The fraction of income that is saved is the *average propensity to save* (APS).

Exhibit 6-4 also illustrates this relationship. It puts the saving function below the consumption function. Examination of the figure reveals that when consumption equals income (at point d), saving is zero. Any point to the left of d indicates negative saving—spending more than income by reducing previous savings or borrowing. Any point to the right of d indicates positive saving. That is, part of income is not consumed, but saved. The complementary nature of saving and consumption is illustrated in Exhibit 6-5. For instance, if total income were $800 billion and consumption were $750 billion, saving would be $50 billion. Saving equals income less consumption.

At higher levels of income a larger fraction of each addition to income will be saved. This fraction, similar to its consumption counterpart, is the *marginal propensity to save* (MPS). The MPS is the change in saving associated with a change in income: MPS equals change in saving divided by change in income, or

$$\text{MPS} = \Delta S \div \Delta Y$$

The higher the level of income, the lower the percentage spent on consumption and the higher the percentage saved. *(Photo by Owen Franken, Stock, Boston)*

The increasing MPS that occurs as income grows is a corollary of the declining marginal propensity to consume.

We know MPS must increase as national income increases because the marginal propensity to consume declines. Just as consumption and saving are related, so are the propensities. All disposable income is either consumed or saved ($Y = C + S$). Hence, the sum of average propensities to save and consume is 1:

$$\frac{C}{Y} + \frac{S}{Y} = \frac{C + S}{Y} = 1$$

The same thing is true for the marginal propensities.

$$\frac{\Delta C}{\Delta Y} + \frac{\Delta S}{\Delta Y} = \frac{\Delta C + \Delta S}{\Delta Y} = 1$$

This means that APC + APS = 1, and MPC + MPS = 1. Hence, if you know one of the average or marginal propensities, you can easily calculate the other.

To illustrate these relationships we use the data from Exhibit 6-5. When total income is $800 billion and consumption is $750 billion, the APC is $750/$800 or 0.94. Saving would be income minus consumption ($800 − $750) or $50 billion. The average propensity to save (APS) would be $50/$800 or 0.06.

$$APC + APS = \frac{\$750}{\$800} + \frac{\$50}{\$800} = \frac{\$800}{\$800} = 1$$

When income rose from $600 billion to $650 billion, consumption rose by $40 billion and saving increased by $10 billion. The marginal propensity to consume ($\Delta C/\Delta Y$) is $40/$50 or 0.8. The MPS ($\Delta S/\Delta Y$) is $10/$50 or 0.2. Again, MPC plus MPS (0.8 + 0.2) equals 1.

Other Determinants of Consumption and Spending

Although income is the primary determinant of consumption, several other factors can also affect spending patterns.

Expectations of Price or Income Changes   If households expect large changes in the price level, or income level, they are likely to change their consumption behavior. For example, when inflation is expected, households commonly save less and spend more on goods and property. This is a natural response, since buyers feel that delaying the purchases will mean paying more

for the goods in the future. If a large increase in income is expected, households may increase their consumption in anticipation of their greater affluence.

Anticipation of Product Shortages   When households expect a war or other event to cut off or reduce available supplies of goods, they tend to hoard the scarce goods. This causes a temporary shift in the consumption function.

Credit   During periods of easy credit, households tend to consume more than in periods of stringent credit. Consumer durables, particularly automobiles and major household appliances, are highly sensitive to the availability of credit. When consumer loans are expensive because of high interest rates, households sometimes postpone purchases.

Exhibit 6-6 shows how consumption expenditures on durable and nondurable goods have grown from 1970 to 1982. As is clear from these data, there have been no serious fluctuations over this period of significant economic instability.

Investment Demand

Investment is the second largest component of aggregate demand. As we have already noted, investment consists of construction, purchases of machinery, and changes in business inventories. In 1982 investment amounted to $453 billion, about 15 percent of GNP. Although investment expenditures account for a small portion of aggregate spending relative to consumption, they account for a lion's share of the instability in the economy. Exhibit 6-7 shows gross private investment expenditures for non-residential purposes, residential construction, and changes in business inventories. The insta-

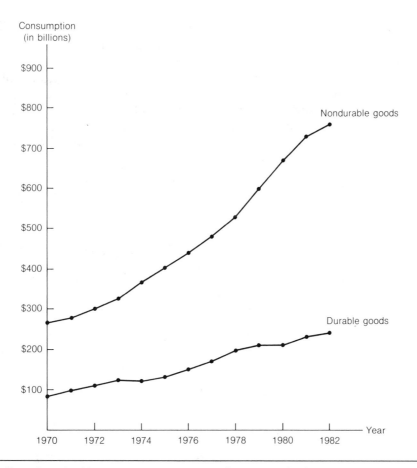

Exhibit 6-6   Durable and nondurable consumption expenditures (in current dollars), 1970–82

bility of these expenditures from 1970 to 1982 is in sharp contrast to the predictability of consumption expenditures shown in Exhibit 6-6.

The reason for this instability of investment spending is not hard to find. The fundamental reason for business investment is that management expects to make a profit. Many factors influence these profit expectations. The firm considering the purchase of a machine must base its decision on *assumptions*, not known facts,

about future economic conditions. For example, the firm must assess whether sales will increase enough to justify the investment, whether the national economy will grow over the life of the machine, whether the machine will soon be technologically obsolete, and what will happen to input costs. All of these estimates of the future will have a major impact on profit expectations and therefore on the amount of investment spending.

The amount of a firm's excess capacity—that is, how much it can increase production without building more plant or buying new machines—will also influence investment spending. Clearly, if its plant is not being used to normal capacity, the firm is likely to postpone expansion of production facilities even if it expects a brisk demand for its output. Thus,

even when profit expectations are high, firms will not invest until they anticipate needing to do so.

The expected rate of profit from a potential investment is called the *real rate of return:* the annual profit in constant dollars (adjusted for inflation) divided by the price of the asset that is assumed to have a very long life. For instance,

SOURCE: *Economic Report of the President*, 1983, Table B-2.

Exhibit 6-7   Gross private domestic investment, 1970–82

if the purchase of new machinery costing $10,000 is expected to increase profits by $2000 every year, the rate of return would be 20 percent.

An individual firm always has a large number of possible projects for investment. Some have a high rate of return while others are less worthwhile. A hypothetical set of possible investment projects for a single firm is given in Exhibit 6-8. The possibilities range from computerization of billing, anticipated to yield a 52 percent rate of return, to plant expansion with a 3 percent return. For simplicity, let us assume that all of these potential investments have the same degree of risk associated with them.

What determines the projects in which the firm will invest and the total amount to be

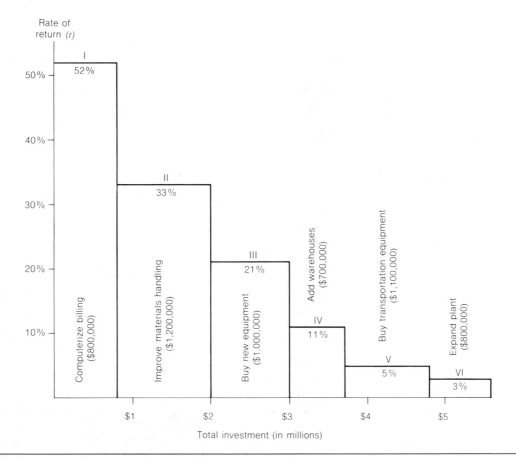

Exhibit 6-8   Hypothetical planned investment schedule for a single firm

This exhibit shows a hypothetical set of potential investments available to a firm. The potential investments are ranked by rate of return (addition to profit divided by the price of the investment). For example, the highest projected rate of return is for the *computerization of the billing system, which costs $800,000 and yields an expected annual savings of $416,000. Economists also refer to the expected rate of return on an investment as the marginal efficiency of investment.*

invested? One answer lies in the cost of borrowing funds. Each point in time carries a cost of borrowing that can be stated in terms of the interest rate. A firm will choose projects whose rate of return is greater than the interest rate paid for the money it uses. It will not undertake projects with payoffs lower than the interest rate. This is true whether the firm borrows the money to finance the investment or the capital is purchased by retained profits. If the firm borrows money at 12 percent to buy a machine that yields a 10 percent rate of return, the firm loses 2 percent on the transaction. Buying the machine with its own funds also means accepting a 10 percent rate of return, when the money could be loaned out at 12 percent. The firm still loses 2 percent because the opportunity cost of using internal funds is the 12 percent market rate of interest.

The problem is illustrated in our hypothetical example in Exhibit 6-8. Suppose the market interest rate is 12 percent. The firm would decide to undertake projects I, II, and III, because these all have returns that exceed the rate of interest (52 percent, 33 percent, and 21 percent respectively). A total investment of $3 million would be undertaken with a 12 percent interest rate. Project IV (adding warehouses) would not be suitable because the interest rate would exceed its projected 11 percent rate of return. If underlying economic conditions were to lower the market interest rate to 9 percent, project IV would now be undertaken and total investment of the firm would increase from $3 million to $3.7 million.

The whole economy also has a planned investment schedule, the sum of all the possible investments of all firms in the economy. Thus, instead of being a discontinuous function as for a single firm, the curve for the total economy is smooth, as shown in Exhibit 6-9.

Exhibit 6-9 illustrates an important feature

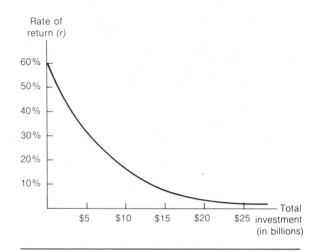

Exhibit 6-9 Hypothetical planned investment schedule for the economy

The planned investment schedule of an economy is the sum of individual firms' investment schedules. Instead of a function as in Exhibit 6-8, it shows a smooth curve. The figure illustrates an important feature of investment demand. It is negatively sloped. The higher the rate of interest, the lower the investment.

of private investment demand. It is negatively sloped. That is, the higher the rate of interest, the lower the investment. At a 20 percent interest rate, $10 billion would be invested. Lowering the interest rate to 10 percent would result in a total investment of $15 billion, an increase of $5 billion.

The planned investment schedule shown in Exhibit 6-9 is an aggregate investment demand curve. It shows the amount firms are willing to invest at various interest rates. Recall that Keynes argued that interest rates were not a very important determinant of investment demand. This is because the planned investment schedule is based on given profit expectations. If expectations about the future change for any reason (e.g., changes in tax laws that affect investments, technological change, onset of recession, or imposition of price controls by the government), the planned investment curve will shift. If profit expectations improve, the curve will shift to the right—there will be more investment demand at any interest rate. If business firms become more pessimistic, the curve will shift to the left—there will be less investment at any interest rate. Keynes believed that these shifts in the planned investment schedule account for far greater changes in the amount of investment than do changes in the interest rate.

SUMMARY

1. The prevailing economic view during the nineteenth and early twentieth century was built on a theory of a competitive economic system with a self-adjusting mechanism that assured full employment. With this view of the economy the correct public policy was for government to keep its hands off the functioning of the finely tuned mechanism. Underlying this mechanism were Say's law and price-wage flexibility.

2. The Great Depression of the 1930s raised doubt about the validity of the classical model. An alternative economic model was presented by John Maynard Keynes; according to his model, there could be long-run unemployment in an economy. In the Keynesian model aggregate demand could be insufficient to assure a reasonable level of employment.

3. The Keynesian view of the income determination process has not been without controversy. It has been questioned by those opposed philosophically to an active government role and by economists who have alternative explanations of the income determination process. Regardless of this controversy, Keynesian analysis has had a tremendous impact on modern economic thought.

4. Aggregate demand is the keystone of the Keynesian analysis. Aggregate demand consists of (1) consumption demand, (2) private investment demand, (3) government demand, and (4) net export demand.

5. An important element in the analysis is the relationship between income and consumption. This relationship is called the consumption function; it specifies the average propensity to consume (APC) and the marginal propensity to consume (MPC).

6. After consumption, the second largest component of aggregate demand is investment. The primary determinant of the level of investment is the profit expectation of business. The anticipated rate of return on investment is compared to the current interest rate to decide whether the investment is worthwhile.

KEY CONCEPTS

classical economics

laissez-faire

Say's law

aggregate demand

consumption function

dissaving

average propensity to consume (APC)

marginal propensity to consume (MPC)

marginal propensity to save (MPS)

average propensity to save (APS)

QUESTIONS FOR DISCUSSION

1. What assumptions of the classical model did Keynes criticize? Do you think these criticisms are valid?
2. If the annual rate of inflation exceeded 30 percent a year, how might households change their consumption and saving habits?
3. Suppose you were considering building an apartment house as an investment. What elements would enter into your decisions? What role would the interest rate play?
4. Suppose Paradise's national income accounts for four years contained this information.

Disposable Income (in millions)	Consumption (in millions)
$300	$320
$400	$400
$500	$480
$600	$560

a. Graph the consumption function and the saving function.
b. Calculate the MPC and the MPS.
c. What are the APC and ther APS when disposable income is $500 million?

Chapter 7

National Income Determination

Determination of national income and employment is at the core of modern macroeconomic theory. The major tools used to understand this process are the consumption function, the saving function, and the investment schedule described in Chapter 6.

The stated goals of U.S. economic policy since 1946 have been economic growth and full employment with reasonably stable prices. Obviously, these goals have not always been achieved. Before we can explain why certain policies have been inadequate, we must specify in some detail the process by which the level of national income and employment is determined.

In Chapter 5 we showed the changes that could occur in the circular flow at equilibrium when either the household or business sector altered its behavior. But there is no guarantee that the level of output associated with the changed behavior is that desired or desirable for a society. For example, the level of output created by decreased consumption might leave many more people unemployed than our society wants. By understanding how the changes in circular flows take place and which components of income are affected, we can develop economic policies better designed to stabilize the economy. In this chapter we will concentrate on using components of income to investigate changes in economic activity.

THE INCOME DETERMINATION PROCESS

An Overview

When we add together the planned spending schedule of all individuals in an economy, we obtain the total demand for goods and services. The planned spending might be for consumer goods (C) or investment goods (I), but together the C and I schedules described in Chapter 6 give us total aggregate demand. (Later, government and the foreign sector will be considered.)

Each level of aggregate output has an associated equilibrium level of aggregate demand. Aggregate demand that is less than national output indicates insufficient demand for the goods produced. Manufacturers do not continue to produce goods that are not demanded; they cut back on production. The reduced output causes a decline in income, because fewer factors of production are utilized. The adjustment process continues until a level of output is reached for which there is sufficient aggregate demand.

In the Keynesian view insufficient aggregate demand is the cause of depression or recession. The combination of consumption spending and investment spending falls short of the level of national income required for full employment. According to this view, inflation is caused by the opposite situation; that is, when planned consumption and investment spending exceed the full-employment output level, inflationary pressures exist.

A Numerical Example

The importance of aggregate demand can be illustrated by a numerical example. Exhibit 7-1 is a hypothetical schedule of planned con-

Exhibit 7-1   Income determination for a hypothetical economy

(1) Aggregate Supply (NNP) (in billions)	(2) Consumption (in billions)	(3) Net Investment (in billions)	(4) Aggregate Demand (in billions) (col. 2 + col. 3)	(5) Tendency of Output
$500	$510	$50	$560	Increase
550	550	50	600	Increase
600	590	50	640	Increase
650	630	50	680	Increase
700	670	50	720	Increase
750	710	50	760	Increase
800	750	50	800	Equilibrium
850	790	50	840	Decrease
900	830	50	880	Decrease

sumption and investment levels associated with various incomes. Columns 1 and 2 show income and consumption figures derived from the consumption function described in Chapter 6. Column 3 (net investment) reflects business community plans to invest $50 billion during the year regardless of the level of national income; that is, the business sector's plan for new buildings and equipment is based not on the present level of the country's income but on the expectation of future profits. (In later sections we shall modify this assumption, but at present, its use simplifies our presentation.) Column 4 shows aggregate demand, which, for the moment, is limited to the sum of planned consumption (column 2) and planned net investment (column 3).

Column 4 is the aggregate demand $(C + I)$ associated with the level of income given in column 1. Column 1, NNP, is both an indication of income and an indication of output, reflecting the identity of the circular flow of income. As a measure of output, column 1 is the aggregate supply schedule. Firms could produce a level of NNP ranging from $500 billion to $900 billion, depending on the expected spending of consumers and businesses. Although various levels of NNP can be produced, there is only one level, $800 billion, at which planned aggregate demand is equal to planned supply. At any other level, forces are at work to change the level of income.

Using Exhibit 7-1 we can analyze the forces driving the system toward equilibrium. Of all the income levels, only one will be a level that can be sustained—the level where aggregate demand is equal to aggregate supply, or the *equilibrium level of income.* An examination of columns 1 and 4 shows that this balanced condition exists when the level of output is $800 billion. Of the $800 billion worth of goods produced, households consume $750 billion and $50 billion are purchased by the business sector.

Each level of aggregate output has an associated equilibrium level of aggregate demand. *(Wide World Photos)*

Let us see why output cannot be sustained at another level. Suppose the business sector produced $900 billion worth of goods and services. Households would then spend $830 billion on goods, and the business sector would plan to invest $50 billion. Therefore, when the country produces $900 billion, demand is not sufficient to clear the shelves of the goods produced. Aggregate supply is $20 billion greater than aggregate demand and represents a level of inventory investment greater than planned. The business sector, seeing that the goods are not selling, will cut back on production to avoid unwanted further growth of inventories.

Suppose that production is reduced to $850 billion. At this level $840 billion is demanded ($790 billion in consumption and $50 billion in net investment), so an additional reduction in output is required. When the $800 billion level is reached, sufficient demand will be present and the involuntary buildup of inventories will cease. Equilibrium will have been reached.

A parallel mechanism occurs when output levels fall below $800 billion. Suppose the business sector is producing goods at an NNP level of $700 billion. Households now purchase $670 billion worth of goods and businesses add to aggregate demand by spending $50 billion on investment goods. Due to the relatively large demand by consumers and investors, business inventories are reduced below desired levels. Because aggregate demand is $720 billion whereas output is $700 billion, a decline in inventories of $20 billion (negative investment) represents a lower-than-planned level of investment. Businesses respond to this happy situation by increasing the level of output, an action that increases the income of factory workers. The consumption function shows that this boost in income in turn increases the level of consumption. Thus, at any output level below $800 billion, keeping inventories at the desired size will cause NNP to increase.

The mechanism that drives the system toward equilibrium allows us to make the following statements:

1. There is a level of income at which planned consumption plus planned investment equals income.

2. When income is below equilibrium, individual firms will expand the level of production until equilibrium has been reached.

3. Similarly, income levels above equilibrium cannot be sustained and the income level will be reduced to the equilibrium figure.

4. Equilibrium is defined as that point where aggregate demand equals aggregate supply.

5. There is nothing inherent in this income determination process that assures that full

employment of resources will be achieved. In fact, equilibrium output could be reached despite a high level of unemployment.

Graphical Analysis

Another method of examining the income determination process is through a graphical analysis, as illustrated in Exhibit 7-2. The 45-degree line and the consumption line were derived from our study of the consumption function in Chapter 6. Because the 45-degree line is equidistant from the horizontal and vertical axes, any point on the line represents equal dollar amounts of NNP and spending. We have already seen that aggregate expenditures and output must be equal when the economy is in equilibrium; thus the 45-degree line is used to determine the equilibrium level of output.

The consumption function is determined by following the pattern developed in Chapter 6. At NNP of $550 billion the consumption function crosses the 45-degree line, indicating that at an output level of $550 billion, households consume all the goods produced. In an economy with no investment, this represents equilibrium. However, the business sector needs goods for investment, too. Exhibit 7-1 shows that investment will be $50 billion at all levels of income. Thus, we must add planned investment to consumption to obtain the aggregate demand function $(C + I)$. This is shown by a line parallel to the consumption function; it lies above the consumption line because it contains planned investment as well as consumption. If planned investment does not change with the level of output, aggregate demand is always parallel to C.

At any NNP level greater than $800 billion, aggregate supply exceeds aggregate demand. When $900 billion in goods is produced, for

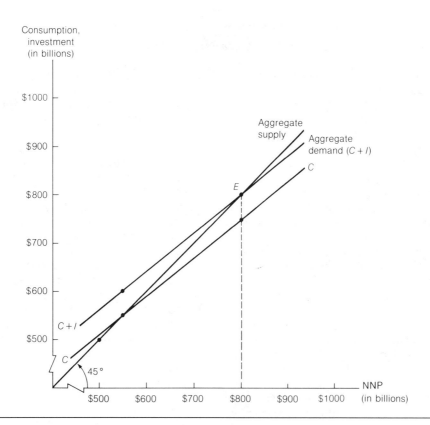

Exhibit 7-2   Income determination process: the aggregate demand approach

This is a graph of the data presented in Exhibit 7-1. The 45-degree line and the consumption function *were shown in Chapter 6. Equilibrium is at point **E**, where aggregate demand crosses the 45-degree line.*

example, only $880 billion in goods is demanded, resulting in an involuntary buildup of inventories. In Exhibit 7-2 aggregate demand is below the 45-degree line, showing that spending is less than output. As we have learned, business firms respond to unplanned increases in inventory by cutting back on production. This cutback would lower NNP (moving left on the horizontal axis) below $900 billion and would continue until production had been cut by $100 billion. At that point, $800 billion, aggregate demand would

equal aggregate supply and equilibrium would be achieved. (To test your understanding of this point you could trace the equilibrating process starting with NNP of $700 billion.)

SAVING-EQUALS-INVESTMENT APPROACH

Examining the relationship between saving and investment is still another way of viewing the income determination process. This approach

---

Econometric Forecasts: Profits to Prophets

A striking example of how apparently abstract theoretical concepts can become useful tools for government and business is the increasing use of large-scale econometric models. Econometrics is a branch of economics concerned with the application of statistical theory to economic problems. National econometric models are mathematical simulations of the economy performed by high-speed electronic computers using large volumes of historical data. Twenty years ago work on these models was considered to be the rather esoteric pursuit of a few academic economists. Today almost no major corporation or governmental agency makes decisions about the future without frequent reference to econometric models.

The basis of these models lies in macroeconomic theory. An equation is created which specifies the relationship among economic variables. For example, the number of automobiles sold in a year could be written as a function of GNP, the price of automobiles, the price of all other goods, the price of gasoline, the availability of auto loans, and the age of existing cars. Similar equations are estimated for other categories of consumer goods (food, housing, clothing, and so forth), investment goods, and government purchases. A total of 120 to 180 equations are estimated. The variables are interrelated so a change in one component will affect the other variables. GNP not only partially determines the number of autos sold, but auto sales are also a component of GNP (due to the circular flow).

Like the wind tunnels used by aircraft manufacturers to simulate the effects of different configurations, econometric models can be used to simulate the effects of different policies. Suppose a tax on energy is being discussed: the econometric model can provide insights as to how that would affect not only GNP but also the consumption of specific goods (for instance, autos). Clients can put different assumptions into the models and estimate the predicted effects upon the different sectors of the economy.

Although not perfect, the models do provide an order and rigor to macroeconomic analysis. Apparently businesses find these models useful. Chase Econometrics, for example, has a client list of over 600, with some firms paying annual fees of over $50,000.

---

is less direct than that of equating aggregate demand and aggregate output. However, it has the advantage of highlighting the actual mechanisms by which equilibrium occurs. It should be emphasized, however, that this method of using saving and investment arrives at the same results as the aggregate demand approach. Recall that income must be either consumed or saved $(Y = C + S)$. We have just shown that the equilibrium level of income equals consumption plus investment $(Y = C + I)$. Since $C + S$ must equal $C + I$, it is also true that saving must equal investment $(S = I)$ when the economy is in equilibrium.

As explained in Chapter 6, consumption plus saving equals income $(C + S = Y)$. From the standpoint of the household, all income is either consumed or saved. Exhibit 7-3 uses data from Exhibit 7-1 to describe this relationship, while Exhibit 7-4 shows these saving and investment data in graph form. The vertical axis represents billions of dollars scheduled to be spent on investment or the amount saved. The horizontal axis shows income. We know it is possible to have negative saving (i.e., dissaving, or spending from past savings), which accounts for the portion of the saving function that is below zero. The saving function reflects the data shown

Exhibit 7-3   Income determination: saving and investment data

(1) Aggregate Supply (NNP) (in billions)	(2) Saving* (in billions)	(3) Desired Investment (in billions)	(4) Tendency of Output
$500	$ – 10	$50	Increase
550	0	50	Increase
600	10	50	Increase
650	20	50	Increase
700	30	50	Increase
750	40	50	Increase
800	50	50	Equilibrium
850	60	50	Decrease
900	70	50	Decrease

* Saving is derived from the "income equals consumption plus investment" relationship.

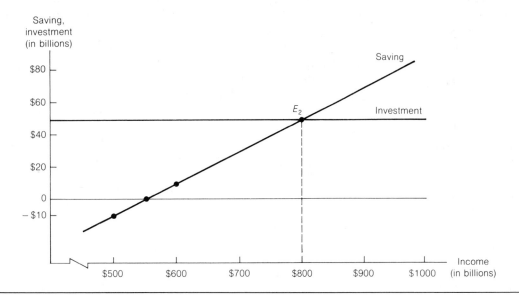

Exhibit 7-4   Income determination process: the saving-equals-investment approach

This is a graph of the data contained in Exhibit 7-3. The investment of $50 billion is autonomous; that is, it remains at the same level regardless of the level of income. Saving increases with the level of income. At point E_2, *saving equals investment and the economy is in equilibrium. At any other income level, the planned levels of saving and investment are unequal and various forces drive the income level to equilibrium.*

in Exhibit 7-3 in column 2. At $550 billion worth of output, no money is saved. Above $550 billion, there is positive saving.

The investment function from Exhibit 7-3 is

also shown on the graph. Earlier we assumed that the business community planned to invest $50 billion regardless of the level of income generated. We called this *autonomous* investment, because investment remains at the same level regardless of income level. In this case, the intersection of the saving and investment functions occurs at $800 billion. At this income level, the planned saving of households is equal to the planned investment of business. At an income level of $800 billion, the economy is at equilibrium, producing sufficient output to generate the saving necessary to satisfy investment plans. This is exactly the same result obtained earlier using the parallel approach, "aggregate demand equals aggregate supply."

At any lower level of income, investment exceeds saving. Consider, for instance, an income level of $700 billion. At this point the planned investment of $50 billion exceeds the planned saving of $30 billion. Therefore, businessmen producing at a $700 billion level of output are unable to build up inventories as planned, because consumers are buying so many goods and services. Thus they increase their level of output, generating more income. Households respond by consuming a large share of the new income, but they also save some of it. When the business community produces at the $800 billion level, the planned saving will be $50 billion, satisfying the investment requirement of business and bringing the system into equilibrium.

There is another way of looking at the relationship between saving and investment. Suppose that there were no saving by households (APS = 0, MPS = 0). Households would spend all the income generated and consumption would equal income. But saving does occur most of the time, pushing consumption lower than output. Whenever business investment is precisely the amount that households save, the economy is in equilibrium. As long as investment is autonomous (that is, does not vary with income), income has to change in order to arrive at a level where household saving equals investment.

INCOME DETERMINATION AND FULL EMPLOYMENT

So far we have discussed the process of income determination but have not mentioned the major criticism Keynes' *General Theory* leveled against classical economists; that is, the economy could be in equilibrium at less than full employment. There is one level of GNP that represents the full employment of productive resources. It is the level of output that an economy can reach when on its production-possibilities curve, as discussed in Chapter 1. This level of output is called *potential GNP*. Potential GNP can be illustrated by a vertical line as shown in Exhibit 7-5.

The full-employment level of GNP in Exhibit 7-5 is $1000 billion (or $1 trillion), higher than the equilibrium level of income shown to be $800 billion. In this situation, the level of aggregate spending $(C + I)$ is too low to realize full employment and potential GNP. Unemployment of workers and idled plant and machines typify this situation. The vertical distance

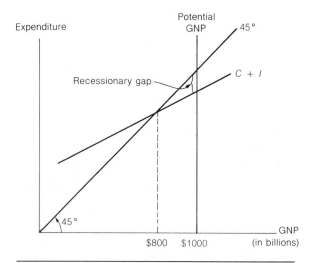

Exhibit 7-5   The recessionary gap

According to Keynes, the economy could be in equilibrium at less than full employment—a situation called a recessionary gap. *(Photo by Owen Franken, Stock, Boston)*

ment spending is very much dependent on expectations of future economic conditions (rather than current interest rates). Low expectations could lead to a less than full-employment equilibrium. Government economic policy would sometimes be required to break the economy out of this recessionary gap to achieve full employment. The nature of these Keynesian policies will be explored in the next chapter.

Aggregate spending can be above the full-employment level of GNP. When this occurs, the level of aggregate demand obviously exceeds the aggregate supply; the result is inflation. This tendency for prices to rise is shown in Exhibit 7-6 and is called the *inflationary gap*. It is the vertical distance between the aggregate demand and the 45-degree line at the full-employment level of income. Keynes and the classical economists have no real argument about inflationary conditions; both agree that rising prices will eventually reduce the level of spending.

Exhibits 7-5 and 7-6 show that unemployment and inflation are caused by very different

between the 45-degree line and aggregate demand at potential GNP is called a *recessionary gap*.

Recall that the classical economists thought that this relatively low level of aggregate demand could not persist because businesses would lower prices and unemployed workers would be willing to lower wages until the *C + I* curve rose to the full-employment level. Rigid wages and prices, said Keynes, prevented such an adjustment. Furthermore, asserted Keynes, invest-

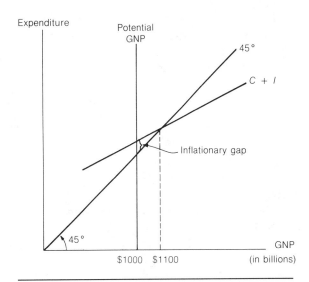

Exhibit 7-6 The inflationary gap

phenomena. Unemployment is the product of aggregate spending crossing the 45-degree line below potential GNP; inflation results when the equilibrium level of spending is above potential GNP. It was generally believed before the 1970s that inflation and unemployment could not increase at the same time, a situation called *stagflation*. Yet stagflation occurred during the 1970s, and is a more complicated situation that will be discussed in subsequent chapters.

THE MULTIPLIER

We have shown how an equilibrium level of income can be derived using both the "aggregate demand" and the "saving equals investment" approaches. Next we will study why a change in aggregate demand, such as a shift in the consumption function or the investment function, can create economic instability. Our discussion will focus on how a change in investment, the most volatile component of demand, affects the level of income.

Exhibit 7-7 illustrates the income determination process with both approaches shown. At the original level of investment (designated as I_1), planned investment is $50 billion (see Exhibit 7-7b). In the saving-equals-investment approach, equilibrium output is at that point where the saving function intersects the investment schedule (E_1). In the aggregate demand approach shown in Exhibit 7-7a, we find the equilibrium level of output at E_1 (that level of output where $C + I$ intersects the 45-degree line). In both cases E_1 occurs where output is $800 billion with an investment level of $50 billion.

Now suppose that some change causes businesses to alter the planned level of investment—a new technology, perhaps, or a change in business expectations about the future. Instead of $50 billion ($I_1$), the new level of planned investment is $90 billion, which we shall des-

ignate as I_2. This change in investment causes new spending, which raises the equilibrium level of income. The new level is shown on the aggregate demand graph (Exhibit 7-7a) as E_2, the intersection of $C + I_2$ and the 45-degree line. The same level of income is shown on the saving-equals-investment graph (Exhibit 7-7b), where I_2 and S intersect at E_2. According to our graphs, the new equilibrium level of income is $1000 billion ($1 trillion).

At first glance a $200 billion increase in income due to a $40 billion increase in investment spending might appear strange, but it is not. It is an example of a process called the *multiplier*

A change in technology (e.g., a change to computer-controlled production) causes an increase in investment, which in turn causes an increase in income. *(Photo by Ellis Herwig, Stock, Boston)*

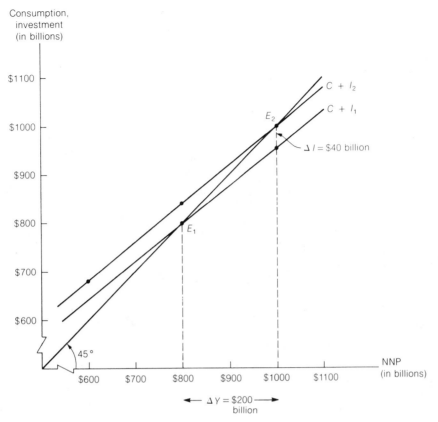

a. Aggregate demand approach

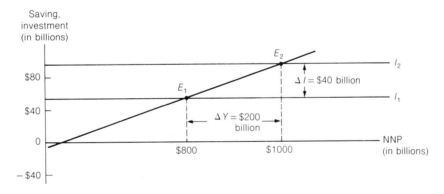

b. Saving – equals – investment approach

Exhibit 7-7 Income determination process

This diagram shows the multiplier effect caused by a change in investment. I_1 is the initial $50-billion autonomous investment that causes an equilibrium level of income at $800 billion ($E_1$). An increase in *planned investment to I_2 ($90 billion) causes new rounds of spending, which raise equilibrium income to $1000 billion. Thus, a $40 billion increase in investment leads to a $200 billion increase in income.*

effect. The multiplier is related to the marginal propensity to consume and is based on the proposition that one person's spending becomes another person's income. The total amount of income generated by increased investment is always a multiple of the amount invested.

An increase in investment is an injection into the circular flow of income. Suppose the marginal propensity to consume is 0.8; the $40 billion increase in investment spending shown in Exhibit 7-7 would immediately increase the income of households by the same amount. These households would spend 80 percent of the total, or $32 billion, and save the other $8 billion. To trace what happens to this spending, let us assume that all $32 billion is spent on automobiles. Workers in the automobile industry would then work more hours and/or new employees would be hired, resulting in higher income for the employees and for the owners of the industry. The autoworkers' households would then spend 0.8 of their $32 billion increase in income—$25.6 billion—on, let us say, clothes and entertainment. Recipients of this income would then similarly spend 0.8 of $25.6 billion—$20.5 billion.

These four rounds of spending can be summarized:

Round	Source of spending	Amount (in billions)
1	Initial investment	$ 40.0
2	Purchase of automobiles	32.0
3	Clothes and entertainment	25.6
4	Assorted goods and services	20.5
Total for four rounds		$118.1

A graph of this process, Exhibit 7-8, shows that each round of spending generates a smaller increment in income. We saw in Exhibit 7-7 that the original $40 billion increase in investment would increase income by $200 billion.

The multiplier is 5. *The multiplier tells us what change in income will result from a change in expenditure.*

Fortunately, one does not have to go through the arithmetic of successive rounds of spending to determine the multiplier. We can borrow a mathematical formula for infinite series that allows us to calculate the multiplier as follows:

$$m = \frac{1}{1 - MPC}$$

where m is the multiplier and MPC is the marginal propensity to consume. For example, if MPC $= 4/5$, the value of m would be:

$$m = \frac{1}{1 - 4/5} = \frac{1}{1/5} = 5$$

If MPC $= 3/4$, then

$$m = \frac{1}{1 - 3/4} = \frac{1}{1/4} = 4$$

Another way of determining the size of the multiplier is to use MPS (marginal propensity to save). As you remember, MPC plus MPS equals 1 and MPS equals 1 minus MPC. Therefore, another way of stating the multiplier is:

$$m = \frac{1}{MPS}$$

For example, if MPS $= 1/3$, $m = 1$ divided by $1/3 = 3$.

Thus, the impact on a nation's income of any change in investment can be calculated as the multiplier times the change in investment. Note that the multiplier shows the change in income resulting from a *change*, not an increase, in investment. The multiplier is a two-edged sword, working to decrease or increase national income.

Suppose, for example, there was a decrease in investment spending of $20 billion and an MPS of one-third. What would be the effect on income? As before, we could calculate the mul-

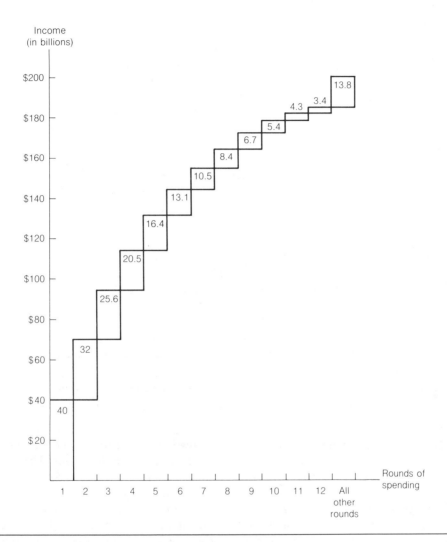

Exhibit 7-8   Rounds of expenditure causing a multiplier effect

tiplier (m) as equal to 1 divided by 1/3, or 3. Since this was a decrease in investment of $20 billion, we would expect a loss of income of three times $20 billion. That is, a reduction in income of $60 billion is caused by the $20 billion decrease in investment. This change in income is shown in Exhibit 7-9.

THE PARADOX OF THRIFT

One application of the multiplier is the potential effect on income of an increase in saving. We can show that in some cases an attempt by a society to increase saving by reducing consumption causes no change in aggregate saving

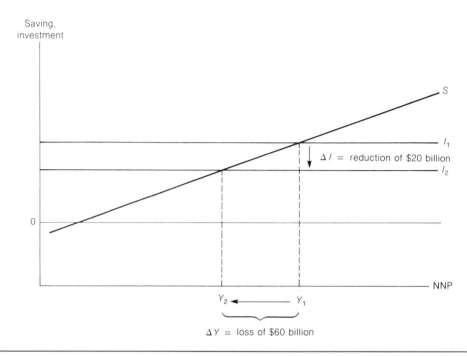

Exhibit 7-9 The multiplier effect with a reduction in investment

The multiplier effect is a two-edged sword. The effect of a reduction in investment is illustrated here.

and may even cause a reduction in income—a phenomenon called the *paradox of thrift*.

Exhibit 7-10 illustrates why a private virtue such as thrift can lead to a lower level of income—without an increase in aggregate saving. Increased saving of $10 billion at each level of income is shown by a shift of the saving function from S_0 to S_1. In other words, at each level of income the saving schedule shows $10 billion more saved. However, with this new saving schedule, income level Y_0 cannot be sustained. At Y_0, saving exceeds autonomous investment $(S_1 > I_0)$. (Remember, autonomous investment does not change with the level of income.) Excess saving causes insufficient aggregate demand. Goods do not sell, because people are saving

instead of consuming. Therefore, producers have to cut back on their output. The lower demand translates into a lower income for workers and stockholders. Consumption decreases further at lower income levels, and the process continues until income is reduced to the point where the new saving level is equal to investment, Y_1 in Exhibit 7-10.

An even more interesting result occurs when investment is not autonomous. Suppose investment is related to output just as consumption is related to output. Then it is called *induced investment*. An induced investment function is illustrated in Exhibit 7-10 by investment function I_1, which increases with the level of income. At the original level of income (Y_0) and saving

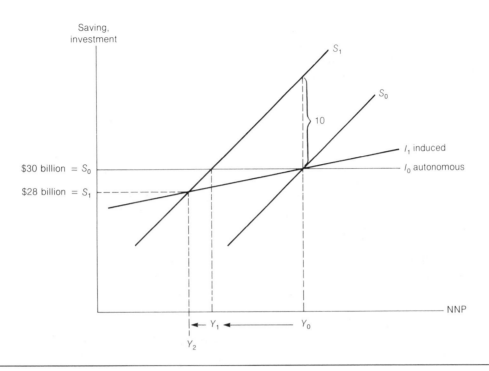

Exhibit 7-10   The paradox of thrift

The diagram shows the effect of a shift of the saving function from S_0 to S_1. If there is an autonomous investment, the impact of the new saving function is to reduce income from Y_0 to Y_1 with no reduction in   *investment. However, if investment is induced, the saving shift causes income to be reduced further to Y_2, and actual saving is reduced from S_0 to S_1—a reduction of $2 billion in this case.*

(S_0), saving equals investment at $30 billion. Now the urge to increase saving occurs, represented by the shift of the saving function from S_0 to S_1. Through the process of diminished aggregate demand and reduced production, income decreases to a new equilibrium level, where the investment function I_1 is equal to the new saving level S_1. The new level of income is represented by Y_2. But note that saving at income level Y_2 is not the $30 billion saved at Y_1 when investment was autonomous, but is now at a lower level of $28 billion.

Thus, we come to a startling "paradox of thrift." If each individual in a society planned to increase his or her level of saving, saving could actually decrease as a result of the impact of aggregate demand and, hence, aggregate supply. A private virtue could become a public vice.

This is an example of the fallacy of composition, discussed in Chapter 1. Saving is certainly beneficial for an individual, but if everyone attempts to increase saving, the results do not necessarily benefit society. The fallacy of composition is a common error but is often difficult to detect. For example, at many campuses student parking is in short supply. An individual who wishes to overcome the parking problem can rise early and be on campus by 6:30 A.M.

However, suppose that every student decided to arrive at the parking lots at 6:30 A.M. Obviously, the best course of action for an individual is not necessarily the best course for society.

LOOKING AHEAD

In this chapter we have discussed the essential elements of consumption and investment in a private economy. Before the model can be applied to public policy, additional aspects of income determination must be included. First, the government's role, with its large expenditures and taxes, must be added; second, the role of money and monetary institutions must be included. Third, the determinants of aggregate supply must be discussed. These topics will be covered in subsequent chapters.

SUMMARY

1. Adding together total consumption expenditures and investment expenditures yields aggregate demand. There are aggregate demand levels associated with every level of income. If aggregate demand is less than national output, there is insufficient demand for the goods produced. Businesses reduce their production of goods when some of their output is not sold. The reduction in output will cause a reduction in employment and hence income. The adjustment process continues until a level of output is reached at which there is sufficient aggregate demand to purchase all of aggregate supply.

2. The adjustment process can be illustrated with either a numerical example or a graph.

The graph uses the aggregate demand line and the 45-degree line, which represents the aggregate supply curve. The intersection of aggregate demand and the 45-degree line indicates the equilibrium level of income. There is no requirement that this equilibrium be at the full-employment level of income.

3. Another way of viewing the income determination process is through the relationship between saving and investment. The alternative method will arrive at the same result as the "aggregate supply equals aggregate demand" approach. Equilibrium output occurs when saving equals investment.

4. Equilibrium need not occur at full employment. A recessionary gap occurs when aggregate demand crosses the 45-degree line below potential GNP; an inflationary gap occurs when aggregate demand is above the 45-degree line at potential GNP.

5. A change in investment spending will bring about a change in income. The total amount of income generated by new investment is a multiple of the change in investment. This is a result of every person's spending being someone else's income. The multiplier is determined by the marginal propensity to consume (MPC). In symbols:

$$m = 1/(1 - MPC) = 1/MPS$$

6. An application of the income determination process is the paradox of thrift. Because of the fallacy of composition, if all individuals raised their saving level, aggregate saving for society may not increase. In fact, with induced investment, the attempt to be more thrifty can result in a lower level of saving for society and a lower equilibrium level of output.

KEY CONCEPTS

recessionary gap	induced investment
inflationary gap	autonomous investment
multiplier	stagflation
paradox of thrift	potential GNP

QUESTIONS FOR DISCUSSION

1. Shown in Exhibit 7-11 are the partially completed income and output schedules for a hypothetical economy.
   a. Fill in the blanks in the exhibit.
   b. Plot the data in the completed exhibit in graph form.
2. Using the data from question 1, find the equilibrium level of national income using the saving equals investment approach.
   a. Determine the equilibrium level of output by numerical analysis.
   b. Determine the equilibrium level of output by a graph of saving and investment.
3. Explain the process by which equilibrium is achieved when the starting point has aggregate demand greater than aggregate supply.
4. What would be the effect upon a nation's income of an increase in investment (I) of 2 billion pesos when the MPC = 1/2? When the MPC = 3/5? When the MPS = 1/5?

Exhibit 7-11 Income and output schedules (in billions) for a hypothetical economy

Aggregate Supply (NNP)	Consumption	Net Investment	Aggregate Demand	Tendency of Output
$270	$ ____	$70	$300	Increase
330	280	____	350	____
390	330	70	____	____
450	380	____	450	____
510	____	70	500	____
570	480	70	____	____

5. Which seems like a more reasonable assumption, autonomous investment or induced investment? Why?
6. The paradox of thrift is one example of the fallacy of composition. Can you think of other examples?
7. Explain how one could have an equilibrium at less than full employment.

Chapter 8

Government and Fiscal Policy

In the last chapter we analyzed national income determination as though there were no government sector. Now we introduce the role of government spending in determining national income. In the modern economy, government expenditures are an important and growing component of aggregate demand. *Fiscal policy* is the use of government expenditures and/or taxes to affect aggregate demand. Its purpose is to stabilize economic activity in order to achieve our macroeconomic goals: full employment, stable prices, and economic growth.

131

COMPONENTS OF FISCAL POLICY

Government Expenditures

In a mixed economy such as that of the United States, the government is a major purchaser of goods and services. Government purchases rose from $251.1 billion in 1970 to $291.2 billion in 1982. In the latter year government expendi-

tures on goods and services accounted for 19.3 percent of GNP. Exhibit 8-1 shows that most of the growth in government purchases was at the state and local level. It also indicates that the government sector is not subject to the great annual fluctuations that typify investment expenditures. These expenditures must be added to consumption (*C*) and investment (*I*) if we are to have a more realistic measure of aggregate

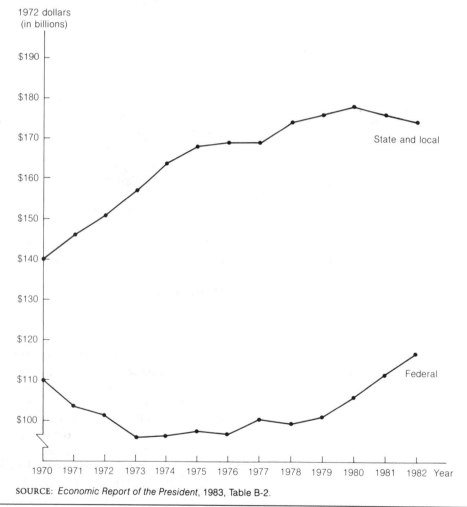

SOURCE: *Economic Report of the President*, 1983, Table B-2.

Exhibit 8-1   Government purchases of goods and services, 1970–82

Government expenditures can play a major role in controlling inflation, keeping unemployment to a minimum, and stimulating economic growth. *(Photo by Peter Menzel, Stock, Boston)*

demand. Government expenditures are designated G. The effect of government spending, G, upon aggregate demand is similar to that of C and I. To a business firm it makes no essential difference whether an electric generator is sold to a government agency or to households. Similarly, when a stockyard sells beef, the effect is identical whether an individual or the army purchases the meat. Thus, aggregate demand consists of the total of $C + I + G$.

Our discussion of the income-consumption decisions of households and the investment decisions of businesses assumed that the decision-making unit would behave in a manner that would further its own self-interest. For example, we showed that a business firm's investment decisions are based upon investment opportunities that are expected to produce a profit. Changes in business expectations

about future profit cause much fluctuation in investment and contribute to economic instability. In contrast, the spending decisions of government are based on national goals as determined by the political process. Among the goals dictated by this process are that government should control inflation, keep unemployment at a minimum, and stimulate economic growth. Because government spending directly affects aggregate demand, it obviously has potential as a tool to stabilize the economy.

The proper fiscal role for the federal government is a matter of constant debate and controversy. On one side of the debate are those who argue that the government should behave as a passive decision-making administrative unit. That is, the government's total expenditures should be limited to its tax revenue. This side contends that a balanced budget for the government will allow the rest of the economy to function efficiently.

The opposite position states that there is no certainty that household and business decisions will automatically lead to full employment and economic growth. This side argues that the government is the proper institution in society to seek the desirable goal of a full-employment equilibrium GNP. Thus, they believe the government should be guided in its taxing and spending role by a desire to maintain the overall health of the economy.

Today most economists would, in varying degrees, agree with the latter position. This is not meant to imply that there is consensus. There are significant differences among economists on which government actions would be most efficient and effective. Furthermore, debate still rages on the relative importance of unemployment, stable prices, and economic growth. Even though economists may disagree on details, however, the vast majority do agree that individual decision making of households and businesses may result in less than optimum levels of employment, growth, and prices. Consequently, some government action is considered appropriate to improve poor macroeconomic conditions. This view has also been adopted by political leaders, both in the United States and elsewhere. Hence, the general policy in the Western world is one in which the government is expected to play a role in macroeconomic policy.

Employment Act of 1946

U.S. public economic policy is based on the *Employment Act of 1946*. The act includes the concept that governmental actions should exert a stabilizing effect on the economy. Passed after World War II because of widespread fear that the

depression of the 1930s might return, the act formalized the government's responsibility and the nation's philosophy in macroeconomic matters. The act stated:

> The Congress hereby declares that it is the continuing policy and responsibility of the Federal Government to use all practicable means consistent with its needs and obligations and other essential considerations of national policy, with assistance and cooperation of industry, agriculture, labor and state and local governments, to coordinate and utilize all its plans, functions, and resources for the purpose of creating and maintaining, in a manner calculated to foster and promote free competitive enterprise and the general welfare, conditions under which there will be afforded useful employment, for those able, willing, and seeking to work and to promote maximum employment, production, and purchasing power.

This act assigned the responsibility for implementing the act to the executive branch of government. As a part of this responsibility the president must submit to Congress the annual *Economic Report of the President* describing the current state of the economy and recommending policies to improve economic conditions. This publication is an important source of information on the status of the U.S. economy.

Adding Government to Our Graph Analysis

In the last chapter the aggregate demand approach showed the equilibrium level of income where $C + I$ intersected the 45-degree line. To include government expenditures in this approach, aggregate demand $(C + I)$ must be modified to include G.

Council of Economic Advisors

The Employment Act of 1946 not only established a national goal of full employment with stable prices, but also established the President's Council of Economic Advisors. The council was given the responsibility of advising and assisting the president in discharging his responsibilities under the act. The council's main activity is the analysis and interpretation of trends and changes in the economy. As part of this activity, members prepare regular reports on current and future economic conditions. A major document, *The Economic Report of the President,* is produced annually. This report reviews economic events during the past year and provides a convenient source of historical data. The effectiveness of the council varies with the interests of the president, the persuasiveness of the council members, and the relative importance of economic issues.

The council has the advantage of injecting economic analysis at a high level in the decision-making process. Of course, political considerations often override economic considerations, but at least the economic aspects are brought into the discussion. The council is not the only source of economic advice to the president. Officials of the Treasury Department, the Office of Management and Budget (OMB), and the Federal Reserve Board also assist in forming economic policy.

The council is a small unit within the federal bureaucracy. Three council members are appointed by the president; one serves as chairman. Their staff consists of 13 senior staff economists, who are experts in specific areas like labor, agriculture, and fiscal policy. The senior staff members are assisted by approximately 20 junior staff, statisticians, and research assistants. The council members and professional staff are drawn primarily from universities and research institutes. They normally serve for one or two years and then return to their positions.

Recent Council Chairmen and Years of Service	Affiliation
Herbert Stein (1969–74)	University of Virginia
Alan Greenspan (1974–77)	President of a large consulting firm
Charles Schultze (1977–81)	Brookings Institution and the University of Maryland
Murray Weidenbaum (1981–82)	Washington University (St. Louis)
Martin Feldstein (1982–)	Harvard University and National Bureau of Economic Research

Exhibit 8-2 illustrates the effect of including G as a component of aggregate demand. The $C + I$ line intersects the aggregate supply schedule at $800 billion. Let us assume that the government will spend $30 billion on goods and services regardless of the level of NNP. The additional planned government spending is added to planned $C + I$ to arrive at the total aggregate demand schedule, which includes household, business, and government demand.

The equilibrium level of NNP is that level where aggregate demand, $C + I + G$, crosses the 45-degree line. In this case, equilibrium NNP is $950 billion. Note that equilibrium NNP has increased from its $800 billion level before government spending by $150 billion, instead of

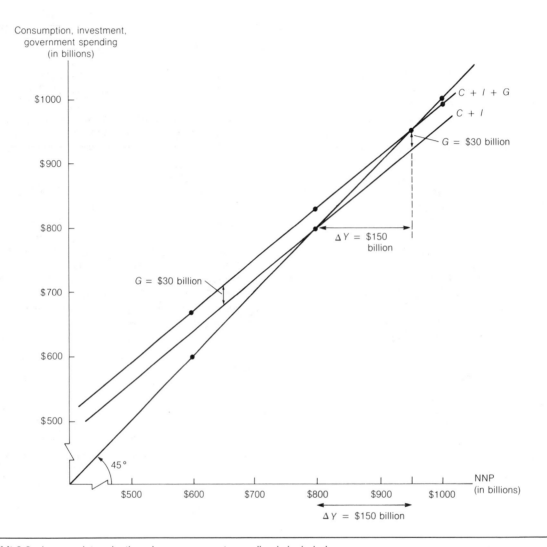

Exhibit 8-2   Income determination when government spending is included

The graph shows the effect of government spending on income. Government spending (G) is shown as an addition to the C + I spending level. An increase in G *of $30 billion causes a change in national income (Y) of $150 billion. This change demonstrates the multiplier effect associated with government spending.*

the $30 billion of government expenditures. This demonstrates that changes in government spending are subject to the multiplier effect in a manner similar to investment multipliers.

(Recall in the last chapter we assumed the MPC to be 4/5.) Equilibrium NNP has increased by the $30 billion change in government spending times the multiplier of 5—that is, $150 billion.

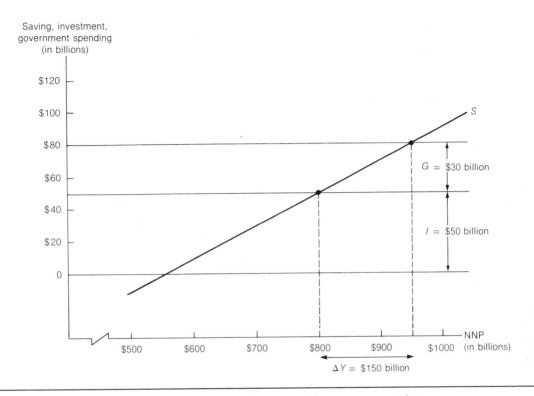

Exhibit 8-3 The addition of government spending to the saving-equals-investment approach

The graph shows the effect of government spending on income. Equilibrium NNP is $800 billion when only private savings and investment are considered. However, government spending is an injection into

the circular flow just as investment is. If $30 billion of government spending is added to the planned investment, there is a resulting $150 billion increase in NNP. Compare this result with that of Exhibit 8-2.

As with investment, it is clear that the size of the multiplier is related to the consumption function. The multiplier is determined by the rounds of spending caused by the initial injection. The now familiar formula for the multiplier is:

$$m_g = \frac{1}{1 - \text{MPC}} = \frac{1}{\text{MPS}}$$

where m is the *multiplier*, MPC is the marginal propensity to consume, and MPS is the marginal propensity to save.

In Chapter 7 we learned from the slope of the consumption function that MPC = 4/5 in our sample economy. Thus, the multiplier is:

$$m = \frac{1}{1 - \text{MPC}} = \frac{1}{1 - 4/5} = \frac{1}{1/5} = 5$$

The effect of government spending can also be shown by the saving-equals-investment approach. Exhibit 8-3 shows an equilibrium NNP of $800 billion when only saving and investment are considered. However, government spending is an injection into the circular flow just as investment is. If $30 billion is added to the planned investment function, there is a resulting increase in NNP to $950 billion.

Government Taxation

The government not only spends but also takes in revenue. Its tax revenues are designated as T. Assume for a moment that the tax comes entirely from households (in practice the government also collects business taxes but here we assume these would eventually be passed on to households). Such a tax on households would obviously affect aggregate demand. Our previous assumption had been that households would either spend or save all income. We now need to distinguish between national income and disposable income. In this case, as in our national accounts, national income less taxes equals disposable income. Households spend or save all their disposable income, which is an after-tax figure.

The effect of taxes on equilibrium NNP can be seen in Exhibit 8-4. Assume that households pay taxes of $30 billion regardless of the level of NNP. Thus, at each level of NNP the households have $30 billion less to spend. How does this affect the aggregate demand schedule? First, we must remember that with MPC equaling 4/5, the household would not have consumed all $30 billion now allocated to taxes; $6 billion would have been saved. Therefore, the effect of taxes will be to reduce aggregate demand by $24 billion at each NNP level, with an accompanying reduction in planned savings of $6 billion. Exhibit 8-4 shows the aggregate demand line shifted down by $24 billion to take into account the effects of taxation. Since C at all income levels is reduced by $24 billion, the planned $C + I + G$ (with tax) schedule is shifted down $24 billion. The equilibrium NNP is

shifted left $120 billion from $950 billion back to $830 billion. Here the two-edged quality of the multiplier becomes evident. NNP is reduced by a multiple of a tax increase just as it is increased by a multiple of an increase in investment.

Using the saving-equals-investment approach illustrates the same phenomenon from a different viewpoint. Exhibit 8-5 shows the original equilibrium, E_1, at $950 billion. Since the $30 billion in taxes caused a $6 billion reduction of saving (due to the MPC of 4/5), we must subtract this $6 billion from the scheduled saving function. This is shown by the saving curve shifting from S_1 to S_2. That is, at each level of income, households will be saving less because some of their income is now allocated to taxes. The total amount of these taxes is added to the saving schedule since both are reductions of funds from the circular flow.

If the government spends these tax monies, the effect of government spending (G) must be added to investment spending (I) to determine the total injection in the system. The total injection now consists of I plus G. Equilibrium will be at a level of NNP where the total injection can be satisfied by saving and tax revenue. Hence, the new equilibrium is where I plus G equals S plus T and is at E_2, which is $830 billion in our economy. This is shown in Exhibit 8-5.

Balanced Budget Effects

In Exhibit 8-2 we showed that increasing government spending by $30 billion would raise net national product by $150 billion; the equilibrium level of income rose from $800 billion to $950 billion. The impact of paying for these expenditures with $30 billion in taxes was then analyzed in Exhibit 8-4. The net result was a decline in national income from $950 billion to $830 billion. This shows the NNP rose by $30 billion simply by raising government expen-ditures and taxes by an identical $30 billion. This paradoxical result is known as the *balanced budget multiplier.*

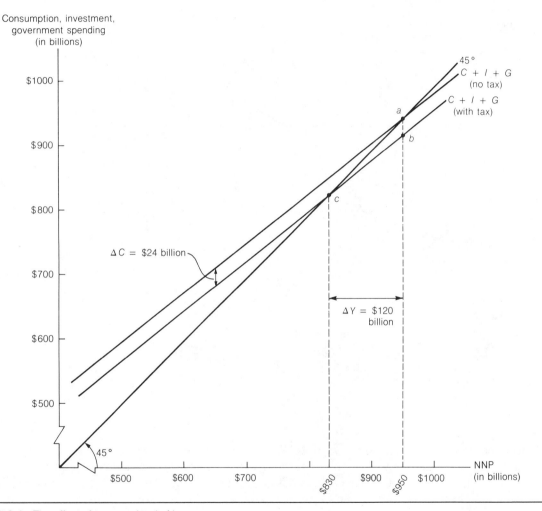

Exhibit 8-4 The effect of taxes on level of income

This exhibit illustrates the effect of taxes on income. We assume that households are taxed $30 billion regardless of the level of NNP. This means that at each level of NNP the households have $30 billion less to spend. With an MPC of 0.80 the household would have consumed $24 billion more if they had not had the taxes to pay. Thus, the effect of taxes (with this MPC) is to reduce aggregate demand by $24 billion. This is shown as a reduction from point a to point b. With the reduction, the new equilibrium is point c—a reduction in NNP of $120 billion. This illustrates the two-sided quality of the multiplier.

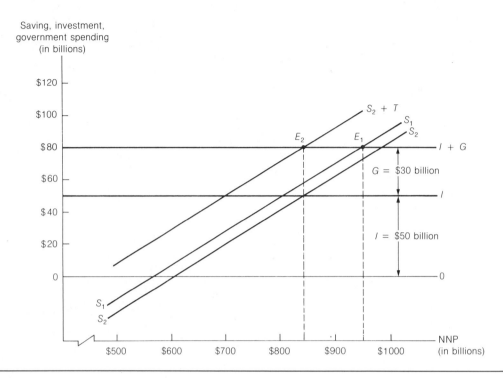

Exhibit 8-5   The effect of taxes on income determination

The effect of taxes on income is shown in this exhibit. We assume that households are taxed $30 billion regardless of the level of NNP. With MPC at 0.80, this means that households will consume $24 billion less but they will also save $6 billion less. Initial

equilibrium is at E_1, $950 billion. After the tax is applied and causes the shift in the saving schedule from S_1 to S_2, the new equilibrium is at E_2, $830 billion. This demonstrates the same result achieved in Exhibit 8-4.

The explanation is a straightforward application of the marginal propensity to consume and the multiplier. The increase in NNP of $30 billion occurs because the government removes $30 billion in household income but then spends the full $30 billion. There is no "leakage" of any of the $30 billion, whereas if households had not paid the $30 billion in taxes, they would have saved $6 billion and spent only $24 billion. The additional $6 billion that stems from gov-

ernment spending goes through rounds of spending and finally increases equilibrium NNP by $30 billion ($6 billion times the multiplier, which is 1 ÷ 1/5, or 5). Thus, a balanced increase in taxes and government spending can make a significant difference in the level of income. Increasing government spending and balancing the budget with an equal amount of tax revenue can increase aggregate demand by an amount equal to the increase in government spending.

ECONOMIC STABILIZATION

Discretionary Fiscal Policy

One of the major economic goals of government is to keep the economy on a steady growth path. Periods of depression or recession as well as periods of rapid inflation are harmful to the stability of a country and can cause much individual suffering. *Discretionary fiscal policy*, the changing of government taxing and spending, is a major tool used to stabilize the economy.

Exhibit 8-6 shows an economy in recession; aggregate demand, $C + I + G$, crosses the 45-degree line at less than potential output. The vertical distance between aggregate demand and the 45-degree line at potential output is called a *recessionary gap*. Faced with such a situation, the government may choose to use fiscal policy to increase aggregate demand in order to move the economy to the full-employment level of income (potential NNP). This can be done in one or more of the following ways:

1. The government can simply increase its purchases of goods and services. The increase in government spending will cause an increase in income much larger than the expenditures themselves because of the multiplier effect. To increase expenditures without new taxes, the government would typically borrow the money. The significance of the national debt is discussed in the appendix to this chapter.

2. The government could stimulate consumption (C) by lowering taxes on households. This would leave individuals with higher disposable income, which in turn would lead to higher expenditures by households on goods and services.

3. The government could use fiscal policy to stimulate investment. A cut in business taxes

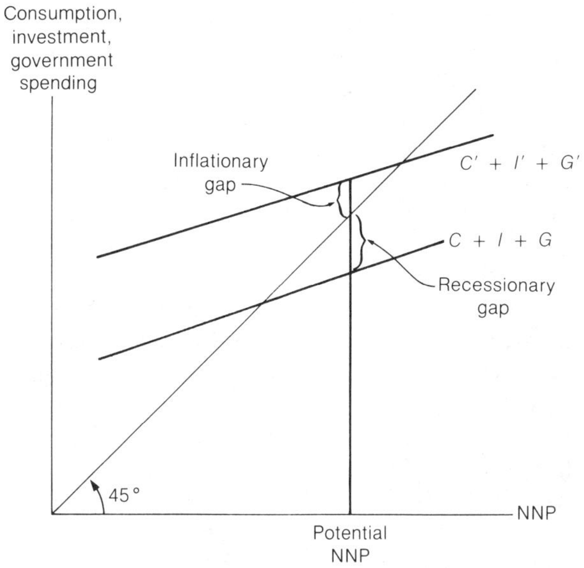

Exhibit 8-6 Inflation resulting from excess demand

Swedish Economic Policy

During a recent recession, Sweden was concerned about high unemployment. In order to stimulate the economy, several laws were passed. One called for payment of a 20 percent subsidy for any increase in inventory above a firm's normal level. As you remember, an increase in inventory is an increase in investment. Hence, the increase in investment would cause an increase in income of a size to be determined by the size of the multiplier. In the United States, inventories are usually taxed by local governments. Which policy should cause the larger increase in national income?

would increase the profitability of invest-ments. To the extent that some projects not previously profitable become feasible, a cut in business taxes can increase investment spending. These cuts in taxes may come in the form of reduced corporate income tax, more liberal depreciation allowances (which allow firms to deduct a larger portion of investment expenses from their income), and /or tax credits for investment spending. An investment tax credit allows some portion of investment outlays (e.g., 10 percent) to be deducted from the normally required tax payment.

When the economy is suffering from infla-tion as the result of excess demand, fiscal policy again offers a possible remedy. This situation is also shown in Exhibit 8-6, where the aggregate demand curve $C' + I' + G'$ crosses the 45-degree line to the right of potential NNP. It is an example of the inflationary gap described in the preceding chapter. Under this circumstance the government would use fiscal policy to lower aggregate demand. Possible methods include cutting government spending, raising taxes on consumers to reduce their expenditures, and/or increasing taxes paid by business firms.

Problems with Discretionary Fiscal Policy There are, however, difficulties to using discretionary changes in government spending as a tool of stabilization policy. One is the political prob-lem of obtaining congressional approval for new funding. Projects that would visibly aid employment in one section of the country lack appeal to congressmen from other districts. Often a compromise package is put together, with public works projects included from various areas in order to overcome congressional parochial-ism. But compromise does not assure that the most efficient set of projects is chosen.

An even more difficult problem occurs when an economy is overheated, with full employ-ment and excess demand, and a reduction in government spending is desirable. Then we see an example of *one-way fiscal policy*. A member of Congress from South Carolina who speaks strongly against inflation is often the one who will vigorously fight a cut in defense spending that closes a base in his or her district. Simi-larly, increases in taxes may be difficult or impossible to pass, but tax cuts are very popu-lar. A broad tax, such as an income tax, is opposed by the population in general, and a narrow-based tax, or loophole, is usually protected by special interests. Thus, senators from tobacco-produc-ing areas are loath to stop tobacco subsidies even when they object to inflation and know that a spending cut would be generally worthwhile.

Another problem with the discretionary use of government expenditures is one of timing. The establishment of the Tennessee Valley Authority (TVA) provides an illustration. TVA was set up in 1932 during the depths of the depres-sion to build a series of hydroelectric dams on the Tennessee River. Although it provided important flood control, irrigation, and electri-cal generation capabilities, the major purpose of TVA was to inject government spending into a severely depressed region.

For the first two years after approval of the project very little spending occurred in the area because extensive project planning was required. Finally, in 1934, actual construction began, and workers, suppliers, and engineers began to receive income from the project. In any but the most severe and prolonged depression such a time lag would have made the increased spend-ing of little value for stabilization purposes. In fact, such a lag could make the spending coun-terstabilizing. Suppose that in a recession year a vast public works project with a two-year lag had been started. Two years later an expansion

The timing of government expenditures can be crucial to their effectiveness in achieving macroeconomic goals. *(Photo by Richard Upton Pickman, Stock, Boston)*

expenditures makes them more acceptable to Congress.

The last problem is that increases in government expenditures often are subject to a ratchet effect in that public spending is more likely to rise than to fall. Once government spending begins, special-interest groups spring up with a strong incentive to keep the spending going. Each proposed cut in spending then draws the ire of the interested groups. Thus, although on our graph we can shift G and T, in practice reducing G can be as difficult as increasing T. This means fiscal policy has a bias for actions that increase government spending.

Automatic Stabilizers

In addition to the fiscal policies described above, automatic fiscal stabilizers also are built into our taxing and spending programs. These programs automatically change government revenue and expenditures when the level of economic activity changes. Some of the more important automatic stabilizers are discussed below.

The Income Tax Structure Both personal and corporate income taxes have a progressive rate structure. As income increases, tax payments to the government increase faster than income. When income drops, payments fall at a faster rate than income does. The effect of such a tax structure is shown in the numerical example in Exhibit 8-7.

Year 1 is a full-employment year followed by an economic slowdown in year 2. In year 1 high taxes are advantageous because they help to keep aggregate demand within limits. But in year 2 high taxes would act as a drag on aggregate demand when the need is to stimulate demand. The progressive nature of the tax structure ensures that a decrease in income will yield a

could be well under way. The expenditures would have come at a time when an overheated economy was already moving toward an unacceptable level of inflation.

Several methods have been suggested to overcome the lag in benefits of government spending. One is to keep a standby list of projects ready to go on short notice. Another proposal is to expand employment in public-service jobs when unemployment rises above a certain minimal percentage. The wage and salary expenditures allow a more rapid startup than construction projects, and the general nature of the

Exhibit 8-7   A hypothetical case to show the stabilizing effect of a progressive tax structure

	Year 1	Year 2
National income	$1000	$900 (10% reduction in income)
Average tax rate	30%	26%
Taxes collected	$ 300	$234 (22% reduction in taxes)

With a tax structure that taxes higher incomes at a higher rate than lower incomes, a stabilizing effect is built into the tax receipts. In this hypothetical example, a 10 percent reduction in national income brings about a 22 percent reduction in taxes.

greater decrease in taxes. Year 2 taxes not only are smaller in absolute amounts, but also are a smaller percentage of income. If the budget is balanced in year 1, a deficit would be likely in year 2, since government spending is not based on tax receipts.

Government Transfers and Subsidies   When NNP decreases, business firms reduce the number of their employees. The employees who are laid off begin to draw unemployment compensation. Families with low incomes find themselves impoverished by the slump and begin to

---

Transfer Payments

The relative size of U.S. government spending has increased during the last 20 years. Although some of the increase has been accounted for by inflation, much of it has been associated with a steady rise in transfer payments. The U.S. government has played an ever-increasing role as a provider of benefits to the poor, aged, and disabled. These benefits come from a wide variety of programs, including Social Security, unemployment insurance, veterans compensation, welfare, food stamps, public housing, Medicare, and Medicaid. As recently as 1965, transfer payments amounted to a relatively modest $28 billion, whereas in 1980 they were over $235 billion. The following table shows the increasing size of transfer payments compared to wages and salaries.

The rapid increase in transfer payments has occurred primarily because of increases in the size of payments and increased coverage. Larger and larger payments have been granted by Congress, and the eligibility requirements have been lowered. The expenditures raise important questions about economic policy. One issue is the effect of these transfer payments on economic incentives and productivity. Another is the fact that individuals receiving transfers from the government expect them to be continued, making an increasing proportion of government expenditures difficult to control.

Year	Government Transfer Payments (billions)	Wages and Salaries (billions)	Transfers as a Percentage of Wages and Salaries
1960	$ 20.6	$ 272	7.6%
1965	28.4	362	7.8
1970	55.0	549	10.0
1975	131.4	806	16.3
1980	234.7	1344	17.5

receive welfare payments. Prices for farm products decrease and so farmers increase their applications for farm subsidies. All these government payments to individuals increase when national income declines. As NNP increases, the payments tend to decrease, thus automatically working to smooth out economic fluctuations.

STAGFLATION

After a successful run through the 1960s, government policymakers faced the awkward combination of rising inflation *and* rising unemployment. The new phenomenon was called *stagflation*. As we have seen, the policy decision rules stemming from Keynesian economics are clear-cut when the goal to be achieved is lower inflation *or* lower employment. As we will see in greater detail in Chapter 11, the prevailing doctrine of the 1960s was that inflation and unemployent would not rise unless the economy was operating beyond the potential level of GNP. Yet the prevailing doctrine was apparently mistaken when, during the 1970s, both inflation and unemployment rose although many resources were obviously underutilized.

The possibility of stagflation was not considered in the conventional view before the 1970s because the phenomenon had never occurred. After the fact, it was not hard to explain. The problem, according to a significant number of economists, was that the economy suffered a series of supply shocks that caused the price level to rise even though many people were out of work. In particular, the first bout of stagflation in 1973–75 was the result of crop failures that raised food prices, at the same time that the Organization of Petroleum Exporting Countries (OPEC) quadrupled the price of oil. Rising oil costs forced business firms to raise prices. Since consumers use both food and gasoline,

The rise in oil prices was a cause of the stagflation felt in 1973–75. *(Photo by Terry Zabala)*

they sought to increase their wages through the collective bargaining process. These supply shocks were magnified by the fact that a policy of mandatory wage and price controls came to an end in 1974. The controls had postponed many price increases until controls were lifted, and the delayed increases magnified the effect of the supply shocks.

We can analyze stagflation with the basic tools of supply and demand. In Exhibit 8-8 we have a downward sloping demand curve similar to the one described in Chapter 3. However, this aggregate demand curve shows that people will purchase fewer goods and services as the price level rises. The aggregate supply curve shows

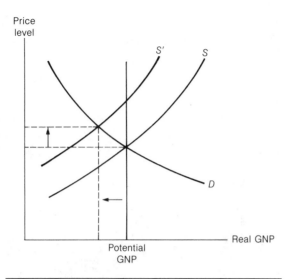

Exhibit 8-8 Movement of the supply curve when there is a major supply shock

that business firms are willing to sell more output when prices are higher. The equilibrium output is where the quantity demanded equals the quantity supplied. In Exhibit 8-8 this is shown to be at the full-employment level of output.

If the economy suffers a major supply shock—in the agricultural and energy sectors, for example—the supply curve shifts to the left to S'. This is because the agricultural and energy products that firms use to produce output now cost more and firms will supply less at any given price level. The result is an equilibrium level of output below the potential GNP, a rise in the price level, and a rise in unemployment—in short, stagflation. In 1978–80, food and energy shortages repeated the 1973–74 circumstances. The inflation rate rose from 9 percent in 1978 to 12.4 percent in 1980. During the same period unemployment rose from 6.1 percent to 7.1 percent.

The Political Economy of Fiscal Policy

Although most economists agree that supply shocks were an important factor in the poor performance of the economy during the 1973–1982 decade, a substantial number believe that other and more important factors contributed to the economic malaise. These broader issues of macroeconomic policy are discussed in Chapter 11. It is also important to recognize that fiscal policy has limitations even when the policy rules are clear because the policy is focused on inflation *or* unemployment. Among these problems are:

1. Congress appears unwilling or unable to respond quickly even when a short response time is essential. Fluctuations in the economy are usually relatively short, and a tax cut or spending increase delayed too long can actually be destabilizing. One suggestion for overcoming this problem is to allow the president a limited flexibility in the tax rate. For example, the president might have the power to raise taxes by up to 2 percent when economic conditions warrant it. Opponents of this plan usually rest their arguments on the basis of the potential shift in political power between the legislative and executive branches. It is also true, however, that the best timing of fiscal policy is not always known until after the business cycle has been completed. As always, hindsight is better than foresight.

2. Political considerations can interfere with economic efficiency. Even when there is general agreement among economists that a tax increase is desirable, special-interest groups will contest the type and form of the tax. Not only is the debate inevitable, but also the resulting delays aggravate the timing problem.

3. State and local taxes are an important and growing part of the total tax burden. But state and local government typically behave like households; that is, they increase spending during prosperity and cut back spending during economic slowdowns. Their behavior is often imposed by state constitutional provisions requiring a balanced budget. It may also be due to the inability of the state or city to borrow additional funds during a recession.

SUMMARY

1. Fiscal policy is the use of government expenditures and taxes to achieve macroeconomic goals.

2. The effect of government expenditures upon aggregate demand is similar to that of personal consumption (C) and investment (I). Hence, including government in aggregate demand means that aggregate demand is the total of $C + I + G$. In a graph analysis, equilibrium is that point where $C + I + G$ crosses the 45-degree line.

3. As with investment, a change in G creates an even larger change in income. The size of the change in Y relative to the changes in G is determined by the *multiplier*. The size of the multiplier is determined by the consumption function. The multiplier can be expressed as:

$$m = \frac{1}{1 - \text{MPC}} = \frac{1}{\text{MPS}}$$

4. The inclusion of government spending in our consideration means that taxes must also be considered. Taxes reduce the amount of income that families have to spend on goods and services. Thus, taxes can be viewed as a reduction in aggregate demand. An increase in taxes shifts the aggregate demand curve downward because a reduction in private spending on goods and services occurs. The change in taxes also has a multiplier effect, which is determined by the MPC of households.

5. One of the chief economic goals of government is to keep the economy on a steady growth path. Two types of fiscal policy can help achieve stability: discretionary policy and automatic stabilizers. Discretionary fiscal policy is the manipulation of taxes and government spending to help adjust equilibrium NNP to a full-employment level. Automatic stabilizers include those fiscal programs that will automatically increase government spending in a recession and increase government taxes in an economic recovery.

6. Stagflation, the simultaneous rising of inflation and unemployment, occurred in the 1970s. Supply shocks affecting food and fuel prices contributed to this new macroeconomic problem.

7. Although fiscal policy could be an effective tool in stabilizing policy, its effectiveness and efficiency is reduced by the political decision-making process.

KEY CONCEPTS

Employment Act of 1946   automatic stabilizers
balanced budget multiplier   supply shocks
discretionary fiscal policy   recessionary gap
one-way fiscal policy   inflationary gap

QUESTIONS FOR DISCUSSION

1. Suppose the federal government increases spending on goods and ser-
    vices by $1 billion and MPC is 3/4. How much will NNP increase?
    How would your answer change if the increased expenditures were
    spent for transfer payments?
2. What are the problems associated with using discretionary fiscal pol-
    icy for stabilization? Which problem do you think is most important?
    What is the proper role for politicians in the making of economic
    policy?
3. Using the data shown in Exhibit 8-2, include taxes of $40 billion with
    no change in government spending. What effect does this budget sur-
    plus have on the equilibrium level of output? What is the new equi-
    librium level of NNP?
4. What would happen to the equilibrium level of Net National Product
    in question 3 if taxes were raised by another $10 billion and G were
    also increased by $10 billion?
5. Why is the progressive income tax considered an automatic stabilizer?

Appendix: THE NATIONAL DEBT

In a 1972 survey, a random sample of the population was asked to identify the major economic problem of the United States. Over 70 percent of those questioned mentioned the national debt, funds borrowed by the U.S. government. A similar poll of professional economists at that time revealed that very few agreed. Such a difference in the perception of problems illustrates a deep underlying difference in understanding and attitude. However, by 1982, many professional economists shared the public's concern over the national debt. In this appendix we will investigate the nature of the national debt and analyze the factors that account for the increasing concern over the size of the debt.

First, we must establish some facts about the national debt. It is not like a private person's debt. An individual debtor owes money to a particular lender or lenders. A parallel situation internationally would be a debt owed by one country to another. However, most of the U.S. national debt is owed to persons and institutions within the United States. Anyone who owns government bonds is a direct holder of that debt. Most people are indirect debtholders through pension funds, mutual funds, or insurance companies. In many cases the payers of taxes and the holders of the debt are the same people. (The 14 percent in foreign hands is an exception, of course.) Thus, to a large extent we owe the debt to ourselves. This kind of "internal debt" is unlikely to occur in a household, but is common for an entire economy.

A second point obscured by the absolute size of the national debt is its relationship to national output. Federal debt as a share of national income has been declining steadily since the end of World War II. (See Exhibit 8A-1.) On the other hand, corporate debt has been rising steadily since 1945, not only in absolute terms but as a share of GNP as well. Yet the growth of corporate debt has not caused nearly as much concern as has the public debt. This may be because investors realize that corporate debt has been used to finance investment—buildings, apartments, machinery, and so forth—necessary for the production of income. Similarly, some of the government debt has been used to invest in important government projects. Just as a corporation's investment in plant produces income, an investment in government projects yields social benefits. A highway, school, airfield, or national park are examples. People are not charged directly for those services, but they are still extremely valuable to society.

A third point is concern over debt repayment. The public worries about the day the national debt must be repaid. However, in practice, every week the Treasury must pay off some maturing bond. But it makes the payment on the national debt by issuing a new bond that other investors are willing to purchase. The national debt is never paid off in the same sense as private debts, like mortgages.

The last argument is that the national debt transfers obligations to future generations. As one senator stated, "The debt of today is the debt incurred by this generation, but tomorrow it will be the debt of our children and grandchildren." Obviously, he disagrees with transferring debt to our future generations. The question is, however, whether society can shift a burden to future generations by means of internal debts. For a society, the cost of a program is its claim on current resources. The

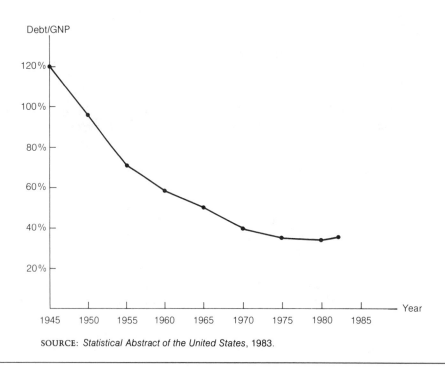

SOURCE: *Statistical Abstract of the United States*, 1983.

Exhibit 8A-1 National debt as a proportion of GNP, 1945–82

greatest increase in the national debt occurred during World War II. During that time people had no new cars to drive, little gasoline, less food, and so on. That was the material cost of the war. (Obviously, the cost in human life was huge, but that is not part of the government debt figure.) If the war debt had been owed to foreign bondholders, we would pay interest today by using current resources to send products abroad to the debtholders. Instead, interest payments are paid to our own citizens, who spend them on further consumption to increase our national output. This is a transfer of purchasing power from taxpayers to bondholders. A fully employed society must give up a part of current consumption to gain future benefits. That is what the United States did during the war.

As we have seen, many widely held concerns about the national debt are not valid. Recent events have caused some economists to believe the burden of additions to the debt has grown too large. Additions to the debt caused by current budget deficits (spending in excess of receipts) have almost doubled between 1981 and 1982, as shown in Exhibit 8A-2. The government borrows money by issuing bonds to pay for expenditures that exceed revenues. If there is a fixed amount of loanable funds, government borrowing must compete with private borrowers. This increased demand for loanable funds will drive up interest rates, and higher rates may discourage some private borrowing for investment. This is called the *crowding-out effect* because private borrowers are crowded out by government borrowing.

Crowding out can occur only under certain

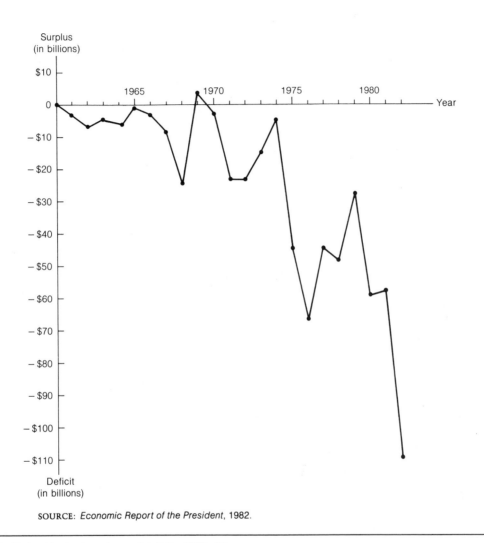

SOURCE: *Economic Report of the President*, 1982.

Exhibit 8A-2   Federal budget surplus and deficits, 1960–82

circumstances. If there is ample excess capacity in the economy, an increase in government spending will increase aggregate demand, raise income, and increase the supply of saving. Greater saving coupled with higher aggregate demand could mean that private investment increases rather than decreases as a result of the deficit. The fact that the U.S. economy has had much unused capacity in recent years and that investment expenditures are more sensitive to business expectations about profits than about interest rates also suggests the crowding-out effect has not yet had a significant impact on the economy.

Chapter 9

Money and the Structure of U.S. Banking

An important element of macroeconomics has not yet been discussed: money. The omission has been deliberate, due to the complexity of the monetary system and to confusion surrounding the topic. However, no discussion of macroeconomics would be complete without the mention of money. Money is much more than a tool used to facilitate the operation of the economy. If the monetary system is working properly, it can improve production and employment opportunities. On the other hand, when the monetary system is out of balance, it can increase fluctuations in an economy's output, employment, and prices.

A realistic and meaningful analysis of income determination must include the monetary system and monetary policy. The following two chapters will cover various aspects of money. In this chapter we will define and explore how money is created.

Money should be an interesting topic. Most people work for it—some people even kill for it. Looking at paper currency, we see nothing more than a small rectangle of paper containing some rather routine-quality printing. A $20 bill has little inherent worth. It does not taste good and provides little heat when burned. Obviously, its value lies in what it represents: claims on the goods or services that people desire. But what gives the paper value? In this section we explore the common elements in all items that have at some time been used as money. The list includes gold, wampum, paper currency, credit cards, traveler's checks, and beaver pelts. The second section is devoted to the structure of the U.S. banking system and how this system affects the supply of money.

WHAT IS MONEY?

Like many complex subjects, money can best be described by the role it plays in economic relationships. In fact, money is desired not for its intrinsic worth but rather for what it does. Although the physical characteristics of money may vary from one country or culture to another, the functions of money remain the same.

Money is a social invention, the purpose of which is to facilitate the workings of an economy in a number of ways. Economists have distinguished three separate functions that money performs. Money serves as (1) a unit of value, (2) a medium of exchange, and (3) a store of value.

Before we discuss each function individually, it is important to note that money is not absolutely necessary in order for trade and commerce to take place. If there is no money, then the trading of goods is accomplished by bartering one good for another on a person-to-person basis. Marty, who is willing to trade 12 tomatoes for 3 yards of cloth, must find someone with 3 yards of cloth who also wants tomatoes. Obviously, barter is difficult except in small transactions and can be time-consuming. Money is usually so superior to barter as a means of carrying out transactions that even the most primitive societies have some sort of monetary system.

The physical characteristics of money have varied greatly from time to time and culture to culture. Money has taken the form of white pebbles, beads, gold and silver, cigarettes, shells, cattle, and even whale teeth. Whatever money looks and feels like, however, it must be easily transportable, generally accepted, and relatively scarce in order to be successful.

Money as a Unit of Value

Money serves as a unit of value—the unit by which the value of all goods and services is measured. This concept becomes familiar when we remember that the unit of weight is the gram or pound, the unit of temperature is the degree (Centigrade or Fahrenheit), and the unit of length

On the island of Yap in Micronesia, large stone wheels serve as money—even though they are not so easily transported as some other forms of money. *(Wide World Photos)*

is the meter or inch. When we measure the value (or price) of any good or service, we use dollars (or francs, or rubles, or another designation of currency) to express the price. Money prices tell us the relative value of one good compared to another and thus serve as the measuring rod by which the value of goods can be placed on a common scale.

For example, the measuring rod for the following items' value is the dollar:

price of oranges = $.90/pound
price of apples = $.30/pound
price of automobiles = $9000/car

If we had chosen oranges as our unit of value instead of dollars, then these items could be priced in terms of oranges:

price of apples = 1/3 pound of oranges/pound of apples
price of automobiles = 10,000 pounds of oranges/car

Although oranges might be useful as a unit of value, we will see that they would be "bad money" because they do not perform the other functions of money as well.

Money as a Medium of Exchange

A medium of exchange is an item that is generally accepted by people in exchange for goods and services. Having a medium of exchange frees a society from barter. Imagine how difficult the functioning of an economy would be without a medium of exchange. For example, in a barter economy workers for steel companies would have to be paid in the steel items they produced. These items would then have to be used to barter for food and housing. By freeing society from barter or direct exchange of goods, money oils the wheels of commerce.

Money as a Store of Value

Money also serves as a store of value, because it allows one to accumulate wealth to be used for later purchases. People hold wealth in different forms of assets, only one of which is money. As a store of value, money's chief advantage is that its "price" never changes: one dollar is always worth exactly a dollar. That's true of no other asset. (This is not to say that its purchasing power remains constant.) For example, oranges are clearly not a good store of value, since they rot in a week or two. An orange today has more intrinsic value than the same orange six months from now. Hence, its "price" or value does change during a time period.

Money is obviously not the only store of value. Once people have accumulated a certain amount of money, they tend to hold their additional accumulated wealth in other asseets that pay some interest, such as government bonds, certificates of deposit, or corporate bonds.

TYPES OF MONEY

Various definitions of the money supply are used in official statistics. That is because assets vary in their degree of "moneyness" and therefore vary in the extent to which they perform money functions. The most obvious form of money is *currency*, the pieces of paper supplied by the government that we use to buy things. A *demand deposit* (more popularly known as a checking account) operates as an almost perfect substitute for currency in that checks are widely accepted as a medium of exchange. The deposit stores value and is obviously a unit of account. Government securities are not commonly thought of as money in the same way as currency but nevertheless have some similar properties. For example, U.S. government bonds are easily converted into currency and hence stand as a unit of account and a store of value. In fact, as a store of value, government bonds are superior to currency since they earn interest *and* retain value. However, bonds are not a good medium of exchange; storekeepers do not typically accept them as payment for a bag of groceries.

To reflect the varying degrees of moneyness among assets, the Federal Reserve System publishes data on four definitions of the money supply. These measures are designated M_1, M_2, M_3, and L, and are shown in Exhibit 9-1. The division is somewhat arbitrary according to the degree of *liquidity*, or ease with which the asset can be converted into a medium of exchange. Thus the assets included in M_3 and L are less liquid than those included in M_1 and M_2. Economists most commonly use M_1 and M_2 when discussing the role of money in the economy.

The most basic definition of the money supply, M_1, includes currency, demand deposits of all sorts, and traveler's checks that are not issued by banks. As is plain from Exhibit 9-1, currency makes up only a fraction, about 27 percent, of this most limited definition of the money supply. As the definition of the money supply is expanded to include "near monies," the degree to which they may be substituted for currency falls. M_2 includes M_1 plus time deposits—savings accounts and other deposits that cannot be withdrawn by check but can easily be transferred to a checking account. They are very liquid, but less so than demand deposits. M_3 represents M_2, large denomination time deposits and money market funds, and L encompasses liquid Treasury obligations.

In January 1982 the money supply measured by M_1 was $453 billion, far smaller than the $1848 billion included in M_2. Thus time deposits are a major source of liquidity in the economy. Assets of lesser liquidity, M_3 and L, do not have such a dramatic effect on the money supply. Exhibit 9-1 shows that in January 1982 M_3 was $2217 billion and L was $2682 billion.

MONEY AND THE PRICE LEVEL

We have previously learned that money is valuable because people accept it in exchange for goods. It buys things. But the amount of money required for transactions varies with the price

Exhibit 9-1 Measure of the money supply, January 1982

Definition	Components		Seasonally Adjusted Dollars (in billions)
M_1			$ 453.4
	Currency	$123.2	
	Demand deposits	243.6	
	Other checkable deposits[a]	82.5	
	Traveler's checks	4.1	
M_2			1848.1
	M_1	453.4	
	Savings deposits	346.8	
	Other small time deposits[b]	856.8	
	Other[c]	191.1	
M_3			2216.7
	M_2	1848.1	
	Large denomination time deposits[d]	308.1	
	Other[e]	60.5	
L			2682.3
	M_3	2216.7	
	Liquid Treasury obligations	465.6	

[a]Includes automatic transfer service (ATS) and negotiable order of withdrawal (NOW) accounts, credit union draft (CUSO) accounts, and demand deposits at mutual savings banks.
[b]Other small denomination time deposits are issued in amounts smaller than $100,000; large in excess of $100,000.
[c]Includes broker/dealer and general-purpose balances of money market mutual funds, overnight security repurchase agreements, and Eurodollars.
[d]Includes term repurchase agreements at commercial banks and savings and loans and institutional balances in money market mutual funds.
[e]Includes Eurodollars held by U.S. residents, banker acceptances, and commercial paper.
SOURCE: *Federal Reserve Bulletin*, March 1982.

level of all items. Obviously, if the national price level doubled, the amount of goods and services that could be purchased with a country's money supply would be cut in half. On the other hand, a decrease of 50 percent in the price level would double the amount of goods and services people could buy. The value of money, then, is inversely related to the price level.

Over time, the value of our money supply has varied considerably. The total money supply rose from approximately $141 billion in 1959 to more than $470 billion by 1982. Exhibit 9-2 shows the increase in the money supply M_1 held by the public over this period. It is clear from the graph that, although the money supply has increased during this time, it has not increased

by the same amount each year. (The amount of money used by the public varies from winter to summer, from the December holidays to the middle of May, according to seasonal needs. In order to present an average money supply, instead of one that is artificially high or low because it measures December's or May's money use, the figures in the exhibit are seasonally adjusted.)

Since Exhibit 9-2 shows the value of the money supply in dollar terms, the M_1 increases reflect inflation (rises in the national price level) as well as changes in the amount of money available to buy goods and services. As pointed out in Chapter 4, the price level has changed considerably over the 1959–82 period. But the value of money is also inversely related to the price

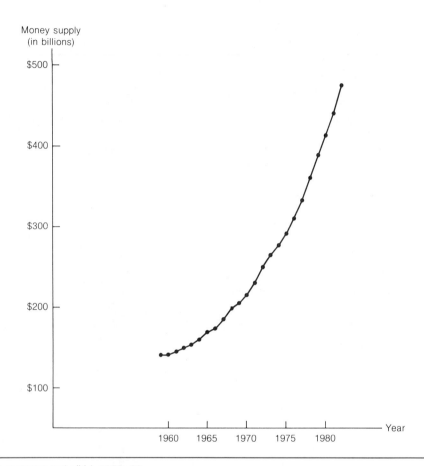

Exhibit 9-2 U.S. money supply (M₁), 1959–82

This exhibit illustrates the increase in the money supply M₁ held by the public from 1959 to 1982.

level. If we choose a base year in which to measure the value of money, we can adjust all other years to a value in terms of base-year dollars. Hence, if a bag of groceries cost $1 in 1972 but $2 in 1980, we would say the 1980 dollar was worth half the 1972 dollar. In the same way we can adjust the money supply to reflect its purchasing power. This is accomplished by dividing the year's price level into the dollar value of the money supply to determine how many base-year dollars are in today's money supply. This amount is called the "real" value of the money

supply and enables us to see how the real supply of money has changed over time.

Exhibit 9-3 shows the real money supply from 1959 to 1982. Note that the 1972 money supply is the same in both Exhibits 9-2 and 9-3 since 1972 is the base year. You will also note that the real money supply generally rose from 1959 to 1973 and generally declined from 1973 to 1982. As we will see in the next chapter, many economists attach great importance to these changes.

We have not yet discussed the mechanism in the economy that causes these variations. You

The money supply varies and is highest in December and May. *(Photo by Terry Zabala)*

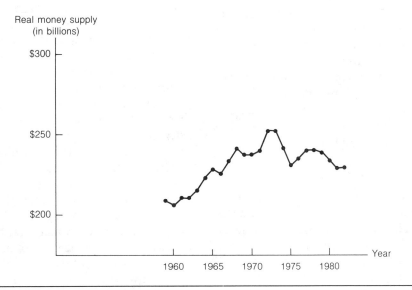

Exhibit 9-3   U.S. real money supply (M₁), 1959–82 (adjusted to 1972 prices)

The "real" money supply is determined by dividing the money supply by the price index to compensate *for the effect of inflation. The growth of money in real terms has fluctuated significantly over the periods shown.*

will recall that M_1 is composed of currency and various demand deposits. The amount of currency in circulation comprised about 27 percent of M_1 in 1982 and has remained within this range or slightly lower throughout the last 60 years. When the United States was on a "gold standard," the amount of money in circulation depended on the amount of monetary gold in the country. When the gold supply was large, the amount of money in circulation was large, and vice versa. However, no major nation currently operates on a gold standard, and so the amount of gold no longer regulates the amount of money in circulation. In the United States, changes in the money supply are in large part determined by the actions of the Federal Reserve System.

THE FEDERAL RESERVE SYSTEM

The Federal Reserve System (often referred to as "the Fed") was established in 1913 and is composed of the Board of Governors, the Federal Reserve district banks, and the commercial banks that are members of the system. The Fed regulates the activities of member banks as well as nonmember commercial banks, branches of foreign banks, mutual savings banks, savings and loan associations, and credit unions.

Board of Governors

Policy for the Federal Reserve System is determined by its Board of Governors, located in Washington. The board is composed of seven members appointed by the president for 14-year terms. The terms are staggered so that one position becomes vacant every two years. The long, staggered terms were designed to insulate the board from short-run political considerations.

The goal was to have an independent monetary authority that would not be influenced by partisan politics.

The board has both administrative responsibilities and the duty of setting national monetary policy. The monetary policy function requires the board to manage the nation's money supply. Administrative duties primarily involve supervision of the nation's banking system. For example, the board's staff reviews merger applications between large banks and lends assistance to banks in financial difficulty so that potential or actual failures do not disrupt the banking system.

Two bodies advise the Board of Governors on policy matters. The Federal Advisory Council (FAC), as its name indicates, is an advisory group that plays no direct role in making policy. The FAC is composed of 12 prominent commercial bankers, each representing one of the 12 Federal Reserve districts. The FAC meets with the board to express opinions on current problems. The Federal Open Market Committee (FOMC) is made up of the seven members of the Board of Governors plus presidents of five of the Federal Reserve district banks. The function of the FOMC is to set policy regarding the buying and selling of government bonds on the market. Through these open market operations, the Fed attempts to control the money supply. How and why the Federal Open Market Committee operates is explained in the next chapter.

The nation is divided into 12 Federal Reserve districts, each with a Federal Reserve bank. Exhibit 9-4 shows the geographic distribution. The district banks represent a compromise between the need for a central bank and a fear of excessive centralization of power. When the Federal Reserve was established in 1913, it was felt that a single central bank might be unresponsive to the specialized needs of the various regions. Agricultural interests, for instance,

Exhibit 9-4 Boundaries of Federal Reserve districts and their branch territories

This map shows the location of the Federal Reserve district banks and their branches within the *continental United States. Alaska and Hawaii are part of District 12.*

feared that a central bank would be controlled by Eastern bankers who would follow "tight money" policies that could hurt farmers, who regularly must borrow money. So instead of a central bank, regional banks were created under the general direction of the Board of Governors.

Originally, the 12 banks had quite a bit of autonomy, but gradually power was transferred from the districts to the Board of Governors. The banks now tend to follow similar policies. They are not of equal size; over half of the system's assets are held in the New York, Chicago, and San Francisco banks. New York, in particular, occupies a key role, with responsibility for monitoring international monetary activity.

The banks are an interesting mixture of public and private control. The Federal Reserve banks are owned by the commercial banks in their district. When a commercial bank joins the system, it is required to buy shares of Federal Reserve bank stock. The role of the Federal Reserve banks is not to make a profit but to carry out the goal of monetary stability. Federal Reserve banks have earned profits—but after a

The Federal Reserve Bank in New York is more influential than some of the others—it has responsibility, for example, for monitoring international monetary activity. *(Wide World Photos)*

6 percent dividend is paid to stockholders, the balance of the profit is turned over to the U.S. Treasury, so there is no incentive to be profitable.

Commercial Banks

The segment of the banking system with which most of us are familiar is the commercial bank—the bank where individuals have checking accounts and savings deposits and where they can borrow money. There are approximately 14,700 commercial banks in the United States, but only 38 percent of these institutions are members of the Federal Reserve System. Commercial banks may be chartered by federal authorities or by state authorities. By law, all nationally chartered banks must be members of the FRS. Membership for state-chartered banks is optional. Exhibit 9-5 shows the composition of the FRS. However, the number of member banks does not indicate the importance of the Federal Reserve in commercial banking. Over 70 percent of bank deposits in the United States are in FRS member banks.

Activities of the Federal Reserve System

The Federal Reserve banks perform major services for financial institutions. Among these are (1) holding reserves or deposits, (2) clearing

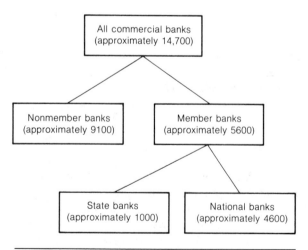

Exhibit 9-5   Commercial banks

By law national banks must be members of the Federal Reserve System. State-chartered banks have the option, and many have chosen to be FRS members. The number of member banks does not indicate the importance of the Federal Reserve for commercial banking. Over 70 percent of the deposits in the United States are in FRS member banks.

checks, and (3) granting occasional loans to financial institutions.

Holding Reserves   Financial institutions are required to keep a stipulated fraction of their deposits in the form of reserves. Part of these reserves are held on deposit by Federal Reserve banks. The amount that must be held in reserve varies by type of deposit and the degree of liquidity. Reserve requirements will be discussed in detail later in this chapter.

Check-Clearing Service   When a person writes a check on the First National Bank of Deadwood (FNBD), South Dakota, to another person with an account in the same bank, the money is simply subtracted from the first account and added to the second; the entire transaction takes place within the bank. But when a check is written on FNBD and deposited in the Second National Bank of Sopchoppy, Florida, the Florida bank must transfer the check to FNBD in order for its customer to receive payment. This process of transferring checks among banks is called *check-clearing*. The Federal Reserve System performs this function for all banks wishing to use the service. Check-clearing was free until passage of the Monetary Control Act of 1980, but now the Fed is required to charge for the service.

Loans to Financial Institutions   Occasionally, an institution experiences a reserve shortage—having more deposits than allowed, given their reserves. To help the bank through such a period, the Federal Reserve bank may grant a loan. This is not a common practice, and if a bank or savings and loan association were to borrow frequently, it would be thought to be following imprudent financial practices. Still, the capability of making these loans is an important feature of the FRS.

Bank Supervision and Regulation

Members of the FRS are subject to regulation and audits, which come under the general supervision of the Board of Governors. The board shares the responsibility with two other federal agencies—the Comptroller of the Currency and the Federal Deposit Insurance Corporation (FDIC). Banks that do not follow prudent financial practices are subject to sanctions by the Board of Governors, one of which is suspension of borrowing rights. The Board of Governors also issues regulations covering various aspects of commercial banking. For example, board regulations establish a maximum rate of interest that can be paid on savings and checking accounts. These regulations are to be phased out by 1986.

The Federal Government's Fiscal Agent

The federal government is a large organization with revenues coming in and expenditures going out continuously. The government enlists the Federal Reserve banks to help with these fiscal responsibilities. For instance, the Fed sells and redeems government bonds. In order that the huge sums collected by taxation do not cause liquidity problems at a specific bank, the Fed spreads the Treasury's funds among several commercial banks and prepares for large disbursements to be made in an orderly fashion.

REGULATING THE MONEY SUPPLY

All of the FRS functions discussed previously fit into the administrative category. We have saved the most important function of the Fed until last: the responsibility for determining the size of the money supply. Whether the money supply *should* be changed is a matter of monetary policy to be discussed in the next chapter. In this chapter we discuss the method by which the policy is carried out. The easiest way to visualize this process is to go back in time to the start of fractional reserve banking.

The Banking System and Money

Long ago, in a less interdependent economy, goldsmiths held gold for making jewelry, dishes, and art objects. When they had a surplus of gold, they sometimes lent it to people they trusted, in return for a small charge. By these loans, the goldsmiths increased their own earnings, increased the borrower's liquidity (or amount of cash), and increased the country's money supply.

Occasionally, other people who held large supplies of gold would ask goldsmiths to store part of their surplus, because goldsmiths had better and safer storage facilities. The goldsmiths might charge for this service, or they might act as bankers, paying depositors a small amount for the right to loan their gold to other persons, so long as gold was available when the depositors wanted it back. They could continue lending excess gold to trustworthy patrons and increasing their own income, while, at the same time, returning uncirculated gold into the economy. In that way purchases or investments could be made that would otherwise have been impossible.

Today, banks operate with the same constraints as the prudent goldsmith of the past. Funds for the bank come from individuals and firms with surplus cash who either want it readily available but safe—as in a checking account—or want their cash safe but also productive (producing additional income), as in a savings account. The tradeoff for the depositor is between availability and productivity. On the other hand, banks must balance desire for a profit with the requirement that their loans be safe and easily convertible to cash.

Fractional Reserves

The early goldsmith recognized that not all depositors would demand their gold on one particular day. Similarly, banks recognize that they need to hold only a portion of the claims that are payable on demand. In a very conservative bank all demand deposits would be available at all times. Only long-term deposits would furnish funds for loans. However, the loss of earnings suffered by failing to recognize that most of the demand deposits would not be withdrawn at the same time would be too great to allow continuation of that policy. As profit-maximizing business firms, banks hold only a fraction of the cash needed to cover the balances they must eventually pay to depositors. This is known as *fractional reserve banking.* Reserves are the unloaned deposits that assure the availability of cash for depositors on demand.

Of course, fractional reserve banking is subject to controls, or some banks might loan more than seems reasonably safe. In addition, reserve controls can be used to regulate the money supply. The Federal Reserve System requires all depository institutions to hold a percentage of deposits as reserves. The reserve requirements after implementation of the Monetary Control Act of 1980 are shown in Exhibit 9-6.

CHANGING THE NATIONAL MONEY SUPPLY

Let us examine further the impact of the fractional reserve system on individual banks and on the nation's money supply.

Exhibit 9-6 Reserve requirements for depository institutions,* 1982

Type of Deposit	Reserve Requirement
Demand deposits	
0–$26 million	3%
Over $26 million	12
Nonpersonal time deposits by original maturity	
Less than 4 years	3
4 years or more	0

*Includes commercial banks, savings and loan associations, mutual savings banks, credit unions, and branches of foreign banks.

Individual Banks

Suppose that a bank received $10,000 in deposits and had $50,000 in capital equipment and cash, which was the bank's net worth. Without a fractional reserve system, the bank would hold $10,000 in reserves against $10,000 in deposits and $50,000 in loans against $50,000 net worth. Both deposits and net worth are payable to others (depositors and owners) and are considered bank liabilities. However, loans and reserves are collected by the bank (if the loans are "safe") and are considered bank assets. The balance sheet looks like Exhibit 9-7a.

Exhibit 9-7 Hypothetical bank balance sheet under two reserve policies

a. Full reserves			
Assets		Liabilities	
Reserves	$10,000	Deposits	$10,000
Loans	50,000	Net worth	50,000
	$60,000		$60,000

b. 20 percent reserves, fully loaned			
Assets		Liabilities	
Reserves	$ 2,000	Deposits	$10,000
Loans	58,000	Net worth	50,000
	$60,000		$60,000

Suppose, however, that the bank decided to hold only legally required reserves, which comprised 20 percent of deposits. Then deposits of $10,000 would require only $2000 in reserves, freeing $8000 for possible loans. If the bank loaned to capacity, its balance sheet would be as shown in Exhibit 9-7b. This financial position allows the bank to make maximum profit on its deposits and to meet all three goals of profitability, safety, and liquidity, if the loans are properly chosen.

This picture of portfolio management is accurate only for one bank and does not demonstrate what really happens to the nation's money supply as loans and deposits occur. Let us investigate further, still with the assumption that the bank holds more reserves than are legally required. These are called *excess reserves*. Excess reserves equal total reserves minus legally required reserves.

Suppose that a bank (let's call it First Copper and Paper Bank—FCPB) with an assumed 20 percent required reserve ratio needs only $2000 in reserves but holds $1000 in excess reserves, as shown in Exhibit 9-8a. Suppose that FCPB then decides to make a loan of $1000 to you for a down payment on a car. (Probably the loan will be made only if you have an account at FCPB, so that the borrowed money can be placed directly in your account.) On the balance sheet FCPB appears to have created $1000 of new money by increasing loans and deposits simultaneously (see Exhibit 9-8b). Note that the required reserve on $11,000 of deposits is $2200, and so FCPB still has excess reserves available for other loans.

Now suppose you write a check for the down payment on the car (decreasing FCPB's deposit total) and the auto dealer puts the check in an account at Second Copper and Paper Bank (SCPB). Of course, SCPB requests from FCPB payment of $1000, which First must pay either

Exhibit 9-8   Balance sheet for First Copper and
Paper Bank at three different times

a. Initial position: $1000 excess reserves

Assets		Liabilities	
Legal reserves	$ 3,000	Deposits	$10,000
Loans	57,000	Net worth	50,000
	$60,000		$60,000

b. After your $1000 loan has been approved but
before you spend it

Assets		Liabilities	
Legal reserves	$ 3,000	Deposits	$11,000
Loans	58,000	Net worth	50,000
	$61,000		$61,000

c. After loan has been spent: no excess reserves

Assets		Liabilities	
Reserves	$ 2,000	Deposits	$10,000
Loans	58,000	Net worth	50,000
	$60,000		$60,000

from reduced loans or from reserves. Since a
function of reserves is to pay checks, FCPB's
reserves are reduced to $2000 (see Exhibit 9-8c).
Hence, FCPB has not created any money at all
and was able to lend no more money than it had
in excess reserves.

The Whole Banking System

Whereas First Copper and Paper Bank could not
actually create new deposits, or money, because
other banks called for payment (hence reducing
reserves), FCPB could have increased the money
supply if it were the Only Copper and Paper
Bank—that is, if no other banks existed. In that
case, the loan of $1000 would increase deposits
to $11,000 and there would be only a $200 additional reserve requirement, leaving $800 in
excess reserves to be lent. Lending $800 would
increase deposits to $11,800 and increase
required reserves to $2360. Hence, $640 of excess
reserves could be lent. In tabular form the Only
Copper and Paper Bank's loans and transactions
are shown in Exhibit 9-9.

Of course, the United States does not have
only a single commercial bank. However, as we
shall see in the next section, First Copper and
Paper Bank's initial loan will provide the same
amount of deposit expansion (or increase in the
money supply) if it is followed through the entire
banking system.

You will recall that First Copper and Paper
Bank, having $1000 worth of excess reserves,

Exhibit 9-9   Only Copper and Paper Bank's transactions when an initial $1000 was held in excess reserves

Initial or New Deposits (Loans)	20% Required Reserves	Excess Reserves	Cumulative Deposits
$1000	$ 200	$ 800	$1000
800	160	640	1800
640	128	512	2440
512	102	410	2952
410	82	328	3362
328	66	262	3690
262	52	210	3952
210	42	168	4162
168	34	134	4330
134	27	107	4464
Collecting the last small series of loans together:			
536	107	429	$5000
$5000	$1000	$4000	

made a $1000 loan to you, which was deposited in Second Copper and Paper Bank. FCPB has increased its loans, decreased its reserves, and not changed deposits. However, SCPB, because of your deposit, has increased both its deposits and its reserves by $1000. Since a reserve ratio of 20 percent means that SCPB's reserve requirement has increased by only $200, SCPB has acquired $800 of lending power in the form of excess reserves. It makes an $800 loan to a friend of yours to invest in a flower stand, and the friend deposits the loan in Third Copper and Paper Bank. Now the changes in each bank's position can be summarized as in Exhibit 9-10.

It is clear that, although First Copper and Paper lost reserves, Second Copper and Paper *increased* its reserves. After Second's loan lowered its reserves by a smaller amount, Third Copper and Paper experienced an increase in its reserves. Now Third Copper and Paper will want to loan $640, the amount of its excess reserves. Another bank, where this new loan causes an increase in deposits, will have increased its deposits and excess reserves, and so it goes. This sequence of events in the banking system is the same as if all the transactions were conducted within Only Copper and Paper. The net result is a total increase in deposits of $5000 if $1000 were initially deposited in First Copper and Paper. The amount of the increase in deposits is clearly related to the required reserve rate. For every

$1000 received, under our assumption of a 20 percent rate, $200 must be saved in reserves and the rest may be lent and subsequently deposited. Hence, a 5 to 1 ratio exists between total increase in deposits and the initial deposit.

The Money Multiplier

You have probably noted by this time that two factors determine the multiple of deposit expansion. The first is the size of the initial deposit or change in reserves. The second is the required reserve ratio. Hence, if the money supply is affected through the banking system's deposit expansion, the Board of Governors must either change reserves or change the required reserve ratio.

The multiple of deposit expansion—or money multiplier—is defined as the reciprocal of the reserve ratio. That is:

$$\text{Money multiplier} = \frac{1}{\text{Required reserve ratio}}$$

In our example, the banking multiplier is the reciprocal of 1/5 (20 percent = 1/5) or 5/1 = 5. Put another way, the value of the total deposit expansion was five times the value of the initial deposit. In a reverse of this action, the money supply can be decreased by lowering excess reserves by $1000. This action will lower the money supply by $5000 (at most) as banks continue to reduce the amount of loans outstanding.

Exhibit 9-10 Changes in balances after three transactions

Bank	Increase in Loans	Change in Reserves	Increase in Deposits	Increase in Required Reserves
First C & P	$1000	−$1000	—	—
Second C & P				
a.		1000	$1000	$200
b.	800	−800		
Third C & P		800	800	160

Institutional Complications

With this knowledge and understanding, you and the Fed should have little difficulty regulating the money supply by means of deposit expansion and contraction. Right? Wrong. In fact, neither banking institutions nor people always behave as we have hypothesized. There are three major areas of complication for the smooth operation of money supply controls.

Bank Reserve Policy   We have assumed that banks want to lend all of their excess reserves and operate normally with only the required reserves. In fact, however, many banks prefer a "safety margin" in the reserve account; they hold excess reserves for a possible run on bank funds or for some future superior investment. The amount of excess reserves varies not only from bank to bank but also from time to time in the same bank. During periods of recession, when people are lowering their personal bank reserves, the bank may keep larger reserves to guard against large withdrawals. If banks hold 25 percent of their deposits in reserve instead of the minimum requirement of 20 percent, then the banking multiplier drops from 5 to 4, and less money can be created by the infusion of a $1000 initial deposit.

Demand for Loans   We assumed in our discussion of money expansion that someone is always willing to borrow the money banks are able to lend. However, during an economic decline or anticipated recession potential borrowers may be less interested in expanding their firms, entering new business ventures, or purchasing large consumer durables. Instead, people adopt a "holding" position and do not apply for loans. The remaining prospective borrowers may be such poor risks that banks will not lend to them. An increase in deposits or excess reserves will have little or no effect on total money supply unless banks have qualified customers who want loans.

Cash Leakage   We have assumed that the proceeds of new loans took the form of increases in deposit liabilities and that all transactions took place by check. But if some of the deposits are reduced by cash withdrawals, the total money supply would increase by a smaller multiple, because cash can be thought of as 100 percent reserves. This is called cash leakage.

These factors cause the actual money multiplier to be smaller than the theoretical limit defined by the reciprocal of the reserve ratio (1/reserve ratio). Thus, if the Federal Reserve System changes reserves, the money supply will change by a multiple that can vary over time as economic conditions change. Changing the amount of reserves in the banking system is the principal vehicle for the operation of monetary policy. This policy is discussed in the next chapter.

SUMMARY

1. Money can be best described by the functions it performs. It serves as a unit of value, a medium of exchange, and a store of value.

2. In modern economies these three functions are performed by coins, currency, and demand deposits (checking accounts). In addition, several other items perform some, but not all, of the functions of money. These are called near money. The most important is savings accounts.

3. The present system of banking in the United States consists of the Board of Governors of the Federal Reserve System, the 12 Federal Reserve banks, and approximately 14,700 commercial banks.

4. The Federal Reserve banks perform numerous service functions for commercial banks, including check-clearing and providing occasional loans to member banks. In addition, the Board of Governors regulates and supervises commercial bank activity. The Fed also serves as the fiscal agent for the Treasury and is responsible for the purchase and sale of U.S. bonds.

5. The above activities are auxiliary to the major macroeconomic activity of the Fed—the control of the money supply, usually called the setting of monetary policy. Since demand deposits are the largest component of the money supply, an understanding of the process of deposit creation is integral to understanding monetary policy.

6. Banks need to keep only a small fraction of total deposits available for withdrawal. The rest of the money can be loaned to individuals. Taking the banking system as a whole, the loan given to Ms. *X* becomes the income of Mr. *Y*. When Mr. *Y* puts the money in another bank, that bank is now able to loan money to Ms. *Z*.

7. The money system reflects the core of macroeconomics discussed in Chapter 5 as the circular flow of income. One person's deposits become another person's loans. All deposits above the reserve requirement can be loaned out. The injection into the money system means that an initial increase in reserves causes a series of rounds of deposits and loans. Thus, an increase in reserves brings about a multiple expansion in the money supply.

8. The size of this money expansion is determined by the size of the increase in reserves and the reserve requirement. Its maximum effect is reduced by three factors—excess reserves, the demand for loans, and cash withdrawals.

KEY CONCEPTS

unit of value	Federal Reserve System
medium of exchange	Federal Open Market Committee
store of value	fractional reserves
near money	excess reserves
demand deposit	money multiplier
money supply	reserve requirement or ratio
M_1	barter
M_2	

QUESTIONS FOR DISCUSSION

1. Cigarettes were used as currency in World War II prisoner of war camps. Can cigarettes perform all the functions of money? What potential problems could you foresee with the use of cigarettes?

2. Suppose you were sure that the United States would experience a 20 percent annual rate of inflation for the next 10 years. What actions could you take to protect yourself against the loss of purchasing power? What are the implications of such inflation for the use of money as a store of value?

3. "Modern money is merely an IOU from somebody you trust." Evaluate this comment. Is it accurate for a personal check given to a store owner? A $10 bill given to a store owner? An American Express traveler's check? A 1980 half-dollar coin? Gold coins?

4. "I can't create money—all I can do is lend the money that people deposit in my bank." Evaluate this statement made by a small town banker. To what extent is it true? To what extent is it false?

5. Why are fractional reserves a key to the profitability of banking? How would bank profitability change if 100 percent reserves were required? Would you prefer that your banker kept excess reserves to assure the safety of your checking account?

6. If the Federal Reserve System were to deposit $1 million into the banking system, with the reserve ratio at 10 percent, what would happen to the money supply? What if required reserves were 3 percent?

Chapter 10

Keynesians, Monetarists and Monetary Policy

In Chapter 9 we discussed money and how the banking system can increase or decrease the supply of money. This chapter describes how the Federal Reserve System can affect the money supply; presents two interpretations of how changes in the money supply can affect national income, employment, and prices; and evaluates the relative merits of the two views. The first view presented is "Keynesian" and is rooted in the national income determination model used in previous chapters. An alternative view is that of the "monetarists," who believe that a proper monetary policy is more effective than fiscal policy in promoting economic growth and stability. But before defining the positions in this debate, let us explain how the Fed can change the supply of money.

TOOLS OF MONETARY POLICY

The previous chapter explained how changes in reserves can affect the money supply through the money multiplier. The supply of money (S_0) is shown in Exhibit 10-1, indicating that the amount of money in the economy rises as the price of using money—the interest rate—increases. This is because banks are willing to make more loans when a higher interest rate makes loans more profitable. Hence, as the interest rate rises, banks maintain smaller excess reserves and the money supply increases.

Monetary policy is the process of changing the supply of money available at any given interest rate—that is, shifting the curve shown in Exhibit 10-1. If the Fed increases the money supply, the curve shifts to the right, from S_0 to S_1. A decrease in supply moves the curve from S_0 to S_2. The Federal Reserve System has three mechanisms by which it can directly influence the amount of money in the economy. These are open market operations, reserve requirements, and discount rate. Each of these controls can influence the supply of money by affecting the size of bank reserves. We begin by explaining the most important of these tools, open market operations.

Open Market Operations

Open market operations are the purchase and sale of U.S. government securities by the Fed. The huge, well-developed market for govern-

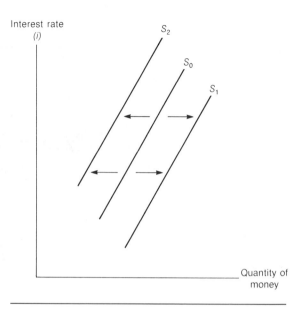

Exhibit 10-1   Increasing and decreasing the money supply

An increase in the money supply is shown by the shift from S_0 to S_1. A decrease in the money supply is indicated by the shift from S_0 to S_2.

ment securities has many participants: state and local government, banks, investment houses, business firms, pension funds, and individuals. The Fed also participates in this market, buying and selling government securities according to policies set by the Board of Governors and implemented in New York by the Federal Open Market Committee.

Increasing the Money Supply   Suppose the Board of Governors has decided to increase the supply of money. To accomplish this goal, the Fed would somehow have to increase bank reserves in order to allow the banks to increase loans by a factor of the money multiplier. One method would be to buy government securities with funds that are not part of the money supply. For example, suppose the Fed buys $1 million worth of government securities from General Motors. The Federal Reserve must write a check for $1 million, which General Motors will deposit in its bank. This deposit raises the bank's excess reserves and the amount of loans the bank can provide to customers.

In terms of the bank balance sheet shown in the previous chapter (Exhibit 9-7), the $1 million enters the bank as both an asset and a liability. If the bank had no excess reserves before the receipt of this $1 million, it would need only $120,000 more reserves (assuming a reserve ratio of 12 percent) and could lend as much as $880,000. The amount of money available for use in the economy has now increased; in Exhibit 10-1 the supply of money has shifted from S_0 to S_1. If the actual multiplier is 8, the Fed's open market operation has increased the money supply by about $8 million.

Decreasing the Money Supply   When the Board of Governors decides that the appropriate monetary policy requires a decreasing money supply the Fed will sell government securities. The Federal Open Market Committee may then sell $1 million worth of government securities to, say, Prudential Insurance Company, which pays for them by a check written against its demand deposits in a bank. The bank's deposits and reserves thus are reduced by $1 million. Now, if the bank has no excess reserves, it must reduce its loans. Once again, through the money multiplier the Fed has influenced the supply of money available by a multiple of the change in reserves. The supply curve in Exhibit 10-1 has shifted from S_0 to S_2.

In summary, when the FOMC is buying government securities, the banking system's reserves and the potential money supply are increased. When it sells securities, the banking reserves and money supply are decreased.

The Discount Rate

Federal Reserve banks can lend money to financial institutions that need to increase their reserves temporarily. Originally, the purpose was to eliminate bank panics by making the system a lender of last resort for banks in trouble, but loans to banks now also play a role in the regular operation of monetary policy. The interest rate charged on loans to financial institutions is called the "discount rate." An increase in the discount rate lowers borrowing by financial institutions, which has the effect of reducing bank reserves, and, of course, the money supply. Similarly, a decrease in the discount rate encourages bank borrowing, thereby raising reserves and the potential money supply. Long-term borrowing is discouraged by the Fed and loans to banks are primarily granted when reserves temporarily fall below requirements.

A reduction in the discount rate is generally regarded as a sign of easier credit, which in turn can contribute to an increase in the construction of homes and buildings. (*Photo by Terry Zabala*)

The discount rate has another role in monetary policy. It is an important indicator of Federal Reserve policy. An increase in the discount rate is generally interpreted as a sign that the Fed is tightening credit and reducing the supply of money. A reduction in the discount rate is generally regarded as a sign of easier credit or an increasing money supply. In 1973, for example, when the Fed increased the discount rate in successive steps from 4 1/2 percent early in the year to 7 1/2 percent by August, people believed that the Fed was going to reduce the money supply or at least curb its rate of increase, reducing the availability of credit. Similarly, reductions in the discount rate in 1982 were widely interpreted as a sign the Fed would for a time follow an expansionary monetary policy that would contribute to a recovery from the worst economic conditions since the Great Depression.

Reserve Requirements

In 1934 Congress gave the Federal Reserve System the power to set the legally required reserve ratio within broad limits. The Fed can increase the reserve requirement for a class of banks, forcing them to draw down excess reserves, reduce loans, or increase demand deposits. The Fed can likewise lower the legal reserve ratio, providing banks with excess reserves and potentially increasing the total money supply.

During the 1960s and 1970s there was a substantial reduction in the proportion of all deposits held in Federal Reserve member banks. As nonmember bank deposits grew, the Fed's control over the money supply was weakened. As a consequence, the Monetary Control Act of 1980 made all depository institutions subject to the same reserve requirements on demand and time deposits.

This act also simplified the structure of reserve requirements. The schedule of reserve requirements in effect since December 30, 1976, was graduated, requiring reserves of 7 percent on the first $2 million in deposits, and rising to 16.25 percent on demand deposits in excess of $400 million. The Monetary Control Act changed reserve requirements to 3 percent for the first $26 million in deposits, and gave the Fed authority to set reserve requirements between 8 and 14 percent on all other deposits. Actual reserve requirements have initially been set at 12 percent for deposits over $26 million. The Fed was also authorized to impose an additional 4 percent requirement on demand deposits but must pay interest on these additional reserves.

The Monetary Control Act reforms were intended not to change the money supply but to increase the Fed's control in exercising monetary policy. Although changing reserve requirements is a powerful tool, it is rarely used because open market operations and the discount rate are usually adequate.

HOW MONETARY POLICY WORKS

We have outlined the tools of monetary policy but have said nothing about the specific mechanism by which monetary policy affects levels of employment and income. That is because economists disagree about the exact nature of the money-income relationship. Almost every economist would agree that monetary policy is important. The area of disagreement is the mechanism through which income and employment are affected by monetary actions. For the purposes of this book we will compress the range of views into two extreme positions. Admittedly, this is an oversimplification; the vast majority of economists would take a position somewhere between the two. For convenience we shall call the positions the Keynesian view and the monetarist view.

Before turning to the details of how monetary policy works, we must briefly describe the demand for money. People demand money, a highly liquid (easily spendable) asset, for three reasons: for transactions, for precaution, and for speculation. The transaction demand for money is obvious in that we need money as a medium of exchange to buy the things we use. Precaution means keeping some money on hand in case of an emergency or sudden need to buy

something. The third reason, speculative demand, arises when people anticipate a change in the price of other assets (for example, stocks and bonds). Holding money enables them to take quick advantage of an opportunity for profit.

People demand money in the same way they demand any other good or service. (See Chapter 2 if you need a review of the basic properties of demand and supply curves.) The higher the price of an item, the less of it people will buy during a period of time. So it is with money. The price of money (its opportunity cost) is the interest rate. If a person holds $100 in cash or in a regular demand deposit when the interest rate is

---

Monetary Policy, Lending, and Borrowing

A continuing conflict has raged throughout U.S. history between two groups—people who lend money (debtholders) and people who borrow it (debtors). This conflict has usually centered on sound or "tight" money policies and institutions. The differences between the two views went like this: sound money meant that prices would remain stable or actually decline. Declining prices cause a redistribution of purchasing power from debtors to holders of debt—people who lend money gain in purchasing power. On the other hand, inflation causes a redistribution of purchasing power from the debtholder to the debtors. Let's illustrate with a simple example.

Suppose that in 1960 I borrow $100,000 for 10 years to buy an apartment house. The rent pays the interest on the loan but does not reduce the principal. However, during the period 1960–70 the prices of all goods and services rise by 100 percent. In 1970 I can sell the apartment for the inflated price of $200,000. After paying off the $100,000 note I still have $100,000. Although the $100,000 will not buy as much in 1970 as in 1960 (due to the 100 percent inflation), I am still ahead. In contrast the person who lent me the $100,000 in 1960 and was repaid in

1970 has only one-half the purchasing power that he had in 1960. (What would have happened if prices had declined over the period?)

Historically, people have believed that increasing the money supply by, for example, issuing paper money would cause prices to rise. Since gold supplies could increase only by new mining, gold was viewed as a much sounder money than paper. Generally, then, debtors preferred paper currency or other forms of expanded money supply because it would cause inflation and lessen their debt in real terms; debtholders usually favored gold or other "hard" money.

It was interest in an expanded money supply that led William Jennings Bryan to give his famous "Cross of Gold" speech during the presidential election campaign of 1896. In this speech Bryan said: "If they care to come out in the open field and defend the gold standard as a good thing, we will fight them to the uttermost. . . . We shall answer their demand for a gold standard by saying to them: You shall not press down upon the brow of labor this crown of thorns, you shall not crucify mankind upon a cross of gold."

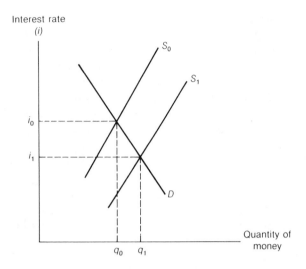

Exhibit 10-2 Effect of an expansionary monetary policy on the money market

This exhibit shows the money market in equilibrium with the quantity demanded equal to the quantity supplied (q_0) at interest rate i_0. An expansionary monetary policy shifts the money supply to S_1 and lowers the interest rate to i_1.

12 percent, it costs that person $12 per year to hold the money. When the interest rate is 6 percent, the cost is $6 per year. As the opportunity cost of holding money rises, the cost of holding idle balances rises, too. Speculative and precautionary balances are most easily reduced in the face of an increased cost of money. Hence in Exhibit 10-2 we see a downward sloping demand for money.

The Keynesian View

The Keynesian view of monetary policy is that changes in the supply of money interact with the demand for money to affect interest rates. Changes in the interest rate in turn affect investment spending and therefore national income and employment. Keynesians explain the workings of monetary policy in terms of the income determination model described in Chapter 7.

We must begin by showing a change in monetary policy. In Exhibit 10-2 we have the money market in equilibrium, with the quantity of money demanded equal to the quantity supplied (q_0) at interest rate i_0. If the Fed raises the money supply from S_0 to S_1 through an expansionary monetary policy, the interest rate will fall to i_1. The lower interest rate reduces the cost of borrowing by firms for new investment, resulting in increased investment spending. Increased investment and subsequent multiplier effects [$1/(1-\text{MPC})$] raise the level of national income. This is shown in Exhibit 10-3. Expansionary monetary policy shown in Exhibit 10-2 raises investment demand from I to I', raising aggregate demand to $C + I' + G$.

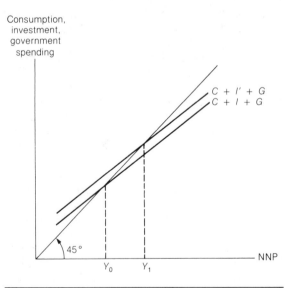

Exhibit 10-3 Increased investment spending due to an expansionary monetary policy

A lower rate of interest will stimulate investment demand to I' in the Keynesian view, raising national income by a multiple of the change in investment.

National income rises by a multiple for the change in investment, from Y_0 to Y_1.

The effect on prices of an expansionary monetary policy depends on how close the economy is to full employment. If the economy is at full employment and the Fed follows an expansionary monetary policy, the price level must rise because output cannot rise. At the other extreme, if there is much unused capacity in the economy, an increased money supply will have little impact on prices. Between these extremes, an expansionary monetary policy would be likely to increase both output and prices. Consider the aggregate demand and aggregate supply curves shown in Exhibit 10-4. If a Fed expansion of the money supply shifts aggregate demand from D_1 to D_2, GNP rises with little or no increase in the price level. Increasing aggregate demand from D_2 to D_3, however, will cause both output and prices to rise, and an expansion of the money supply that shifts the aggregate demand curve from D_3 to D_4 will raise primarily the price level because the economy already is producing near capacity.

A reduction of the money supply due to a tighter monetary policy has the opposite effect on the economy. The transmission mechanism, according to Keynesians, remains the same. Reducing the money supply increases the interest rate, which in turn lowers investment spending. Aggregate demand is reduced and national income falls by a multiple of the changed investment spending. The magnitude of the impact on output and prices depends on the amount of excess capacity in the economy. As shown in Exhibit 10-4, a reduction in the money supply that lowers aggregate demand from D_4 to D_3 will lower the price level, but output is little affected. Under this circumstance a tighter monetary policy will reduce inflationary pressures without affecting income. A contraction of the money supply that causes

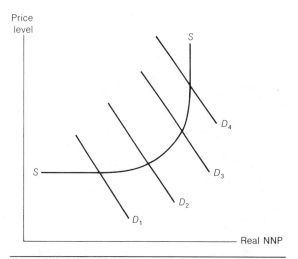

Exhibit 10-4   Effect of an expansionary monetary policy on output and prices

Expansionary monetary policy will lead to inflation with little effect on output if the economy is near full employment. This is shown by the shift in aggregate demand from D_3 to D_4. If there is significant excess capacity, raising aggregate demand (from D_1 to D_2) through monetary policy will cause an increase in output with little pressure on the price level.

a shift from D_2 to D_1 will have little effect on prices but has a devastating effect on output. This occurred during the Great Depression, which started in 1929 and did not really end until the beginning of World War II. After a dramatic decline in national income and employment from 1929 to 1933, the economy was making a gradual recovery through 1937 when, with unemployment at 14.3 percent, the money supply was reduced. The result was a predictable move from D_2 to D_1, the recovery was derailed, and unemployment rose to 19.0 percent in 1938.

In summary, the Keynesian view holds that monetary policy works by changing the interest rate, which in turn affects investment spending. The effect of monetary policy on output

In 1937, the economy was making a gradual recovery when the money supply was reduced and unemployment rose again. (*Wide World Photos*)

and prices will depend on the amount of unused capacity in the economy.

The Monetarist View

Monetarists believe that changes in the money supply have a direct impact on aggregate demand. This view does not accept the Keynesian notion that changes in the money supply are transmitted to national income through interest rates and investment behavior.

The monetarist view is usually shown by an equation derived from national income accounts. The equation is based on the fact that the amount spent on goods and services is equal to the amount received through production of goods and services and transfer payments. Sometimes the equation is referred to as a truism, or identity.

Let M be the money supply and V the velocity, or the number of times the dollars are used during a year. The product MV then represents the total amount of money spent during a year for the nation's output. MV serves as one side of the equation. The other side represents the price and quantity of goods and services sold. Let Q represent the total physical quantity of services produced and P the average price of these products. PQ then represents the value of the nation's output (or national income). This should be equal to the amount spent on those goods, MV. Consequently, the equation of exchange is

$$MV = PQ$$

where M is money supply, V is velocity or turnover, P is average price, and Q is quantity of goods and services.

As noted above, the equation reflects that the total amount spent on goods is equal to the amount received for the goods. A simplified example can illustrate the point. Suppose the money supply is $250 and each dollar is spent, or turns over (velocity), four times a year. Then $M = \$250$, $V = 4$, and spending on output is 4 times $250, or $1000 per year. On the other side, P stands for the average price per unit of output sold and Q stands for the number of units sold in the economy during the year. If the average price is $1 and 1000 units are produced, then $P = \$1$, $Q = 1000$, and the value of national output will be $1 times 1000, or $1000 per year. The equation of exchange is true by definition. The amount spent on output must be equal to the value of goods sold. The two amounts are the two sides of the same coin.

Classical economists of the nineteenth century developed a theory now referred to as the crude quantity theory of money. Starting with the equation of exchange $MV = PQ$, they argued that both V (the turnover or velocity of money) and Q (real output) changed very little in the short run. The constancy of output is a product of the classical assumption of full employment. Hence, any increase in M causes a proportional increase in prices. That is, a doubling of money causes a doubling of the price level.

Monetarists today recognize that V is not fixed but believe that it is relatively stable and more easily predicted than most macroeconomic variables. They also recognize that Q is not always

at full-employment level. At the core of the modern monetarist view is that the demand for money is a key determinant of national income and that variations in the money supply are a major cause of economic instability.

The direct link between changes in the money supply and aggregate demand is illustrated in Exhibits 10-5 and 10-6. Suppose the money market in Exhibit 10-5 is in equilibrium at i_0, where the supply of money (S_0) crosses the demand for money (D_0). If the Fed increases the money supply to S_1, there is an excess supply of money at i_0; that is, people are holding $0q_1$ balances when they want only $0q_0$ at interest rate i_0. Monetarists argue that these unwanted balances are spent on many goods and services, directly raising aggregate demand. In Exhibit 10-

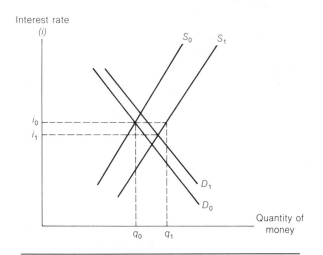

Exhibit 10-5 Changes in equilibrium due to increased money supply

The demand (D_0) and supply (S_0) of money yields an equilibrium interest rate of i_0. Monetarists hold that an excess quantity of money $(q_1–q_0)$ at i_0 due to a shift in the money supply to S_1 will increase aggregate demand. The higher income will raise the demand for money to D_1 and the new equilibrium interest will settle at i_1.

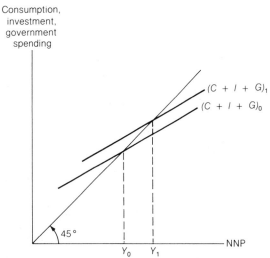

Exhibit 10-6 Rising aggregate demand due to an increased supply of money

Monetarists believe that aggregate demand will increase when the supply of money shifts to the right (see Exhibit 10-5), because people spend unwanted or excess money balances.

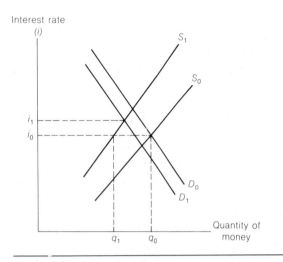

Exhibit 10-7   Effect of a reduction in the money supply

The initial equilibrium for demand (D$_0$) and supply (S$_0$) is disturbed by a reduction in the supply of money to S$_1$. People now hold less money than they want and so they reduce spending, thereby lowering aggregate demand. Lower income reduces the demand for money (to D$_1$) and the new equilibrium interest rate is i$_1$.

6, we see the aggregate demand rising from $(C + I + G)_0$ to $(C + I + G)_1$, with the accompanying increase in NNP from Y_0 to Y_1. The higher level of income, of course, means that people have need for more money to use for the increased number of transactions. Hence the demand for money in Exhibit 10-5 will rise somewhat, from D_0 to D_1. A new equilibrium is established at interest rate i_1.

Reducing the money supply causes the reverse chain of events. In Exhibit 10-7 a decline in the money supply from S_0 to S_1 means that people are holding $0q_1$ money balances when they desire to hold $0q_0$ at interest rate i_0. Since people want to hold higher money balances, they reduce their expenditures on goods and services, thereby reducing aggregate demand and lowering the level of GNP. At the lower level of income, the demand for money shifts downward, resulting in a new equilibrium interest rate at i_1.

Fiscal Policy from a Monetarist Viewpoint

We have already seen how the Keynesian viewpoint can explain the effects of monetary policy. We still must show how the monetarist position can incorporate fiscal policy. Because the equation of exchange $MV = PQ$ does not explicitly include either taxation or government spending, the impact of fiscal policy on GNP (i.e., PQ) must work through either M or V. Any expansionary fiscal policy, such as a tax decrease or an increase in government spending, will increase income. Increasing income shifts the demand for money upward, because households have more transactions. The increased demand for money causes the interest rate to rise. Since a rising interest rate represents an increase in the cost of holding money, the velocity of money (V) rises because people want to hold less money so that they can earn interest on other assets. Thus, with a constant M, we can see that the impact of an expansionary fiscal policy is to increase V, which necessarily means that GNP will rise.

A tightening fiscal policy (i.e., cuts in government spending or increases in taxes) will lower income, decrease the demand for money, lower interest rates, and cause a decline in velocity. Given a money supply, the product M times V (GNP) is smaller than before the restrictive fiscal policy.

Thus we can see that both the monetarists and Keynesian viewpoints can account for the effects of monetary and fiscal policy. The relationships shown in Exhibit 10-4 apply to both Keynesians and monetarists. Similarly, both point to the fact that the state of the economy is a key determinant of whether a policy affects primarily output or prices or both. To concentrate on the differences of opinion over how monetary policy is transmitted in the economy is to ignore substantial areas of agreement between monetarists and Keynesians. Nevertheless, policy prescriptions offered by these two schools of thought are often widely divergent.

DETERMINING MONETARY POLICY

Monetary policy is determined largely by the Board of Governors of the Federal Reserve System. However, as our previous chapter indicated, certain groups and individuals within the banking system have a strong influence on monetary decisions. The chairman of the board is often a spokesman for the Federal Reserve System and is very influential in policy decisions. The Federal Open Market Committee (composed of seven board members and five regional bank presidents) can oppose or approve proposed policies of the Board of Governors that deal with market operations in government bonds. In addition, the Federal Advisory Council, composed of bank presidents, can make suggestions that may influence monetary policy, as can Congress through hearings. To the extent that the president appoints members of the board, the executive branch also influences general policies.

The U.S. Treasury probably has the greatest influence on monetary policy among groups outside the banking system. During the 1940s, when two-thirds of World War II expenditures were financed by the sale of government bonds, the Fed was, in fact, primarily an instrument of the Treasury. Even today, as old bonds are retired, the $1.3 trillion national debt is maintained by selling new securities, which the Fed may then buy (along with other bank and nonbank purchasers). During World War II, money was obtained by selling securities in the open market, which the Fed then bought at the Treasury's asking price. These securities were added to bank reserves and, via our fractional reserve system, the money supply was increased by a multiple of the original value of the securities.

At the end of the war, however, the money supply was large enough to provide great excess demand for goods not yet readily produced. Consequently, prices of most goods rose rapidly. To control inflation, the Fed's best policy tool would have been to sell U.S. securities and reduce reserves. But selling securities would have lowered their price in the open market and increased the interest rate the U.S. government had to pay. The Treasury was opposed to this type of anti-inflationary monetary action. Until 1951 the Federal Open Market Committee supported Treasury bond prices, but in March 1951 an accord was worked out to relieve the Fed of this support requirement. Today FOMC and board policy is made in the light of the Treasury's problems but not because of them.

Independence of the Fed

The independence of the Federal Reserve System is subject to periodic attacks in Congress. Usually these attacks arise when the Fed is following policies that are not politically popular. In 1982, while unemployment was hovering around 10 percent for the first time in three decades, the Fed maintained a tight monetary policy to "wring out" inflation from the economy. Some members of Congress saw that the rate of inflation had fallen and that constituents had shifted their concern to the rising threat of unemployment. Always worried about the upcoming election, Congressmen blamed the Fed for the high unemployment rate and pro-

President Reagan and Federal Reserve Chairman Paul Volcker—the Federal Reserve System was intended by its founders to be independent of the reelection pressures that influence politicians. (*Wide World Photos*)

posed legislation to force the Fed to expand the money supply. In light of such periodic pressures, the forces that allow the Fed to maintain its autonomy provide an interesting study of our political institutions.

The Fed's unique status results from a conscious effort by its founders in 1913. These original efforts were reinforced and strengthened by provisions of the Banking Act of 1935. The goal of the founders was to keep the U.S. central bank free from domination by politicians who would pursue "popular but unsound" (read

"inflationary") policies in their pursuit of reelection. This was an explicit recognition of short-run policies incumbents would follow to aid them in their next election—followed by the next election and the next. Often they would favor continuing expansionist policies, which would cause inflation.

In order to insulate the makers of monetary policy from such political pressure, the governors of the Federal Reserve were given 14-year terms and the funding of the Fed was kept free of congressional review. The nine governors' terms were staggered, one expiring every two years so that no president could appoint a majority of the board during a four-year term. The chairman of the board, although clearly sensitive to the desires of the president, is not under the direct pressures that confront the heads of other independent commissions.

Freedom from budget review has been a major source of Fed autonomy. As a quasi-public corporation, the Fed has full control over the interest from a portfolio of over $130 billion in bonds. This interest is used to pay expenses and salaries of Federal Reserve employees and a 6 percent dividend to the commercial banks that own stock in the Federal Reserve banks. After these disbursements are paid, the remaining interest is turned over to the Treasury in a reversal of the usual practice for government agencies. The Federal Reserve System turns back billions of dollars to the Treasury each year.

Why does Congress allow such autonomy? One possibility is the fear—even among congressmen—that their ever-present concern for the next election might really overstimulate the economy just as the Fed founders said. Another possible reason is the realization that Congress is unable to react to economic changes quickly.

A somewhat cynical political reason, mentioned off the record by congressmen, lies in the value of an independent Fed. When the economy is doing well, incumbents can claim credit regardless of Fed autonomy. However, when things go wrong, they can criticize the autonomous Fed. The incumbent congressional majority can hardly criticize its own fiscal policy, but it can blame the "misguided or incorrect policies of the Fed" for the economic woes of the country. If Congress were to participate actively in Fed decision making, it would lose the opportunity of "passing the buck" for economic problems.

FORMULATING MONETARY POLICY

In Chapter 8 we saw that the process of implementing a stabilizing fiscal policy was entangled in political pressures and delays in implementation due to the budget process. The time required to recognize the need for a policy and put it into action can be so long that conditions may change before the fiscal policy becomes effective. Fiscal policy can thus actually be destabilizing. Monetarists agree with this assessment of fiscal policy. More important, they argue that the money supply is the key to economic stability; in particular, they believe that *erratic fluctuations in the money supply have caused much of the instability in the economy.* The equation of exchange, $MV = PQ$, makes it clear that if V is stable and there are no erratic shifts in M, national income (PQ) will be relatively stable. Thus monetarists believe that the economy likewise will be relatively stable if it is not subject to shifts in aggregate demand caused by variations in the money supply.

Nobel Prize winner Milton Friedman stated the monetarist position very clearly in an address to the American Economic Association in 1967:

> Every major contraction in this country has been either produced by monetary disorder or greatly exacerbated by monetary disorder. Every major inflation has been produced by monetary expansion.

The Great Depression of the 1930s spawned the work of John Maynard Keynes and the subsequent development of the Keynesian viewpoint. It is somewhat ironic that monetarists look to this same period as evidence that erratic monetary policy causes economic instability. A severe contraction of the money supply from 1929 to 1933 reduced the money supply by one-

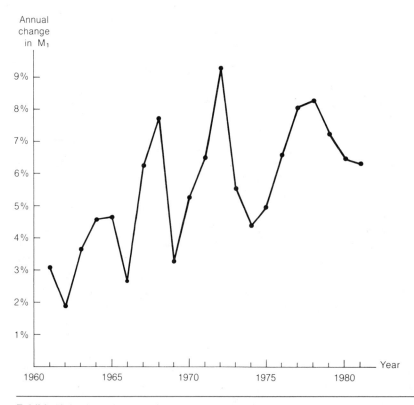

Exhibit 10-8 Annual change in the money supply (m₁) 1960–1982

third. Monetarists believe the sharp reduction caused the massive decline in GNP and the rise in the unemployment rate to 25 percent.

Exhibit 10-8 shows that from 1960 to 1982 the rate of growth of the money supply varied between 1.84 percent (in 1962) to 9.26 percent (in 1972). It is also apparent that the growth of the money supply generally accelerated during this period. Exhibit 10-9 shows the growth in the money supply and increase in the price level for four 5-year periods. These data are consistent with the monetarist position: more rapid increases in the money supply are reflected in increased inflation.

Conducting monetary policy is a straightforward task if one accepts the monetarist interpretation of how the economy works. The goal is simply to avoid erratic shocks to the money

Exhibit 10-9 Growth in the money supply and price level

Period	Percentage Change in Money Supply (M₁)	Percentage Change in Price Level (GNP Deflator)
1960–64	13.9%	6.0%
1965–69	21.4	16.7
1970–74	28.2	25.7
1975–79	33.8	29.7

supply. Expanding the money supply at a steady rate—for example, 4 percent per year—would provide the best environment for steady growth of the economy. Investment spending will still be a source of instability, but the monetarists believe that monetary and fiscal policy designed to correct swings in investment spending will only aggravate the situation. Monetarists feel that although the business cycle will remain, economic stability will be enhanced with this kind of nondiscretionary policy. Since 1979 the Fed has adopted a monetarist position, announcing its intention of allowing a moderate and steady growth of the money supply over a period of several years. Performance, however, has fallen short of this monetarist ideal.

SUMMARY

1. The Federal Reserve System has the responsibility for the control of the money supply. This control is designed to promote the general economic welfare of the country and is called "monetary policy." The Fed attempts to maintain full employment and a stable price level. It "eases credit" when the economy needs stimulating and "tightens credit" when prices are being forced up.

2. The Fed has three direct controls that can be used to control the money supply: open market operations, reserve ratio requirements, and discount rates.

3. There is disagreement over the mechanism by which changes in the money supply affect the level of income and employment. Monetarists believe in a direct link to income through the demand for money. Keynesians argue that the link is indirect and operates primarily through changing the interest rate, which in turn affects investment spending.

4. Monetarists believe that erratic fluctuations in the money supply are the primary cause of economic instability. These economists claim that the proper monetary policy would be to expand the money supply at a constant rate, forgoing a discretionary policy.

KEY CONCEPTS

open market operations

discount rate

demand for money

equation of exchange

monetarists

velocity

QUESTIONS FOR DISCUSSION

1. Keynesian economists typically favor a more "activist" stabilization policy than do the monetarists. To what extent are these tendencies inherent in the Keynesian and monetarist viewpoints?

2. In Germany during the hyperinflation following World War I, the money supply increased 100-fold in one week. Using the equation of exchange, what effect would this have? What assumptions are you making?

3. It has been claimed that expansionary fiscal policy is more effective than monetary policy because it does not depend on the banking community's ability to find customers for its loans. How do you assess this claim?

Chapter 11

Macroeconomic Policy

During the 1960s, textbook discussions of macroeconomics and appropriate government economic policy were easier for students to understand. The textbooks, reflecting contemporary professional opinion, spoke confidently of government ability to control the economy. Not only was there general confidence that major recessions could be avoided, but some held the opinion that government policies could "fine-tune" the economy. However, the experience of the 1970s has made economists more humble about their knowledge of macroeconomic functions. Stagflation, with simultaneous unacceptable levels of both unemployment and inflation, was not supposed to happen, according to the orthodox view of most textbooks used during the 1960s.

The proliferating economic woes of recent years have caused more people to be aware of economists' lack of knowledge about certain economic processes. What was taught in the 1960s was not wrong, but it understandably did not consider events that had not yet occurred. As we shall see in this chapter, the combination of bad economic policy, bad luck, and inevitable economic and social trends transformed a rapidly growing economy with low unemployment and stable prices into one in which none of these goals was realized. Macroeconomic conditions for 1960–1982 are summarized in Exhibit 11-1. In this chapter we shall analyze the conditions that led to a decade in which rising unemployment, unacceptable inflation, and slow growth were the rule rather than the exception. From this experience we shall draw some lessons about stabilization policy for the future.

MACROECONOMIC GOALS REVISITED

In Chapter 4 we described the goals of the economy as economic growth with minimum unemployment and relatively stable prices. The national unemployment rate is composed of many unemployment rates for various population groups and (as we saw in Exhibit 4-7) geo-

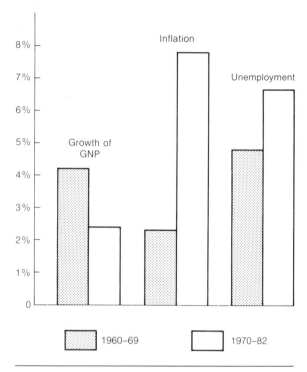

Exhibit 11-1 Economic growth, inflation, and unemployment—average annual rates for 1960–69 and 1970–82

graphic areas. In 1981 the overall unemployment rate was 7.4 percent while the black teenage unemployment rate was more than 37 percent and the unemployment rate in Detroit was 14.4 percent. A given national unemployment rate can be caused by different factors. The same is true for inflation. Thus, before turning to the primary task of this chapter, we need to discuss the various types (and causes) of unemployment and inflation.

Unemployment

Joblessness has many dimensions. From the perspective of public policy, the *structure* of unemployment is very important. By structure of unemployment, we mean the duration of unemployment among those workers counted as unemployed. For example, suppose we have an economy with a labor force of 100 people and an unemployment rate of 8 percent. Unemployment could be distributed among the population in various ways. At one extreme, each of the 100 workers could be unemployed for 4.16 weeks sometime during the year. With this structure of unemployment, no one is out of work for a very long period of time. At the other extreme, eight workers could be unemployed all year while the other 92 workers have no spells without work. A policy that might be effective in reducing unemployment that is evenly distributed among the population might have little effect on a similar level of unemployment that is concentrated on a small segment of the population. Hence, the effectiveness of various macroeconomic policies designed to lower the unemployment rate will vary with the type of unemployment. Here we consider three basic types of unemployment: frictional, cyclical, and structural.

Frictional Unemployment   Frictional unemployment is associated with labor turnover due to the natural workings of the labor market. Estimates are that 20 to 30 percent of U.S. workers change jobs during the course of a year. If workers require an average of two weeks to move from one job to another, frictional unemployment accounts for an average of over 1 percent unemployment. If these workers remained between jobs for an average of 12 weeks, a typical duration of unemployment over the past 20 years, frictional changes would account for about 6 percent unemployment. Frictional unemployment could be reduced somewhat by improving job information, but in a society that emphasizes freedom of choice it cannot be eliminated.

Cyclical Unemployment   Cyclical unemployment is caused by business cycles. When aggre-

gate demand is insufficient, people are laid off and unemployment rises. This type of unemployment is most amenable to correction by the use of monetary and fiscal policies. Limiting this type of unemployment is one of the major goals of economic stabilization policies.

Structural Unemployment   Finally, there is a type of unemployment that reflects joblessness due to mismatches in employment markets. There are geographic mismatches—jobs are available in one area but job seekers reside in another area. There are skill mismatches, brought on by technological change, where positions requiring high-skilled workers are available but low-skilled workers are abundant. Untrained workers or persons whose skills are no longer required by modern technology are typical victims of structural unemployment. Often structural mismatches compound each other. A high school dropout in an economically declining Appalachian coal-mining town is an example of a multiple mismatch.

Agreement on just what constitutes structural unemployment is difficult to reach. Clearly, some unemployment can be attributed to structural imbalances between available skills and the demand for labor. However, when aggregate demand is sufficiently high, workers who might otherwise remain unemployed are drawn back into employment. The exact nature of this relationship and its contribution to unemployment figures is uncertain.

The Natural Rate of Unemployment

Frictional unemployment is unavoidable and the measured unemployment rate will always be greater than zero. From the perspective of stabilization policy, it is necessary to identify the unemployment rate that satisfies the goal of minimum, or "acceptable," joblessness in the economy. Most economists assume that a "nat-

Changes in the production process can change the types of skills required of workers and thus contribute to structural unemployment. (*Photo by Terry Zabala*)

ural" rate of unemployment provides the appropriate target for macroeconomic policy. Some economists equate the natural rate with minimum frictional unemployment. A more general definition is that the natural rate of unemployment is the lowest level that can be achieved without accelerating the rate of inflation.

The latter definition of the natural rate could include structural unemployment—for example, an individual who for 20 years has worked in the Detroit auto industry but has none of the skills demanded by the growing sectors of the economy. Such a person has the wrong skills in the wrong location. If an economy is undergoing major structural changes involving large industries, such workers are likely to be unemployed for an extended period of time. Increasing aggregate demand enough so that firms would retrain these workers would lead to upward pressure on prices; this effect suggests that such workers could be included in the natural rate of unemployment.

It is important to note that this definition of the natural rate of unemployment implies that

Some Social Costs of Unemployment

A study prepared for the Joint Congressional Economic Committee estimated some of the indirect costs of a decline in economic activity. Among the costs considered were increased family conflict, marital instability, physical illness, mental illness, and crime. The average unemployment rate was 1.6 percentage points higher in the 1975–79 period than it was during the preceding five years. The Joint Economic Committee study suggests that the indirect costs of the increase in unemployment over the five-year period was $10.1 billion in 1981 prices.

Direct government costs of unemployment are reflected by increased unemployment compensation expenditures. Increased unemployment over the five-year period raised direct costs by approximately $16 billion. Thus the direct and indirect outlays associated with the increased unemployment in the 1975–79 period totaled about $26 billion.

Exhibit 11-2 Percentage of labor force unemployed, by reason, 1967 and 1982.

Reason	1967	1982
Job leavers	0.6%	0.8%
Reentrants	1.2	2.2
New entrants	0.5	1.1
Total	2.3	4.1

the natural rate may change over time. The natural rate is not the "immutable" rate. In the early 1960s, for example, the natural rate of unemployment was about 4 percent. By 1980 it was estimated to be almost 6 percent. One important reason for the increase was a change in the composition of the labor force. Because of demographic and labor-force trends, the groups that generally have a higher-than-average rate of unemployment had become a growing portion of the labor force. The teenage unemployment rate typically is more than double the aggregate rate; teenagers accounted for 6.9 percent of the labor force in 1960, but 8.47 percent in 1982. Women over age 20 have historically had an unemployment rate 1 to 2 percentage points higher than men. Women over 20 accounted for 30.4 percent of the work force in

1960, a figure that rose to 44.7 percent in 1982. These two groups are more heavily represented in the voluntary unemployed (job leavers) and the unemployed new workers (new entrants and reentrants into the labor force) than are men over 20. Exhibit 11-2 shows that between 1967 and 1982 these demographic and labor-force trends have produced more new entrants, more reentrants, and more job leavers, and thus have caused an increasing percentage of the labor force to be unemployed. The result has been a higher natural rate of unemployment.

A second major category of economic or social changes that can raise the natural rate of unemployment are those that lower the cost of being unemployed. Chief among these are unemployment insurance programs. If living off savings, imposing on friends, or starvation are the consequences of losing a job, a worker is going to be very eager to find a new job, even if it pays less or is less desirable than the old job. Unemployment insurance reduces this desperation by providing the worker with some income during the time between layoff and recall (or when a new job is found). If unemployment insurance becomes more widespread and/or the level of benefits rises, the cost of searching for a new job is on average lower. Hence we would expect workers with unemployment insurance to make a more thorough (or more leisurely) search for a new job. Exhibit 11-3 shows that the percentage of workers covered by unemployment

Exhibit 11-3 Unemployment insurance programs

Year	Covered Employment as a Percentage of Labor Force	Average Weekly Check (in 1980 dollars)
1950	55.2%	$ 77.45
1960	66.6	99.69
1970	71.9	116.53
1980	86.7	107.82

insurance rose dramatically during the 1960–80 period. The average weekly compensation check increased in real terms over most of this period. Although unemployment insurance programs may improve the fit between workers and jobs by allowing a more extensive job search and thus may raise economic efficiency, they also contribute to a higher natural rate of unemployment.

Inflation

Given the magnitude and continuity of inflation during the post–World War II era, serious questions have been raised about whether a modern economy can enjoy the blessings of full employment and price stability simultaneously. Put another way, does a long period of full employment bring into play forces that cause an accelerating rate of inflation? Is the only cure for inflation a deliberate slowdown or recession? Unfortunately, these are very new questions for most economists. Before the 1960s, recessions were considered an integral part of the business cycle. As long as we accepted the inevitability of a business cycle, the question of inflation took care of itself. The developed world is now in a new era where there are no easy answers or direct experiences to draw upon. Here are some types of inflation that economists have identified.

Demand-Pull Inflation When the aggregate demand for products exceeds the capacity of the economy to produce them, excess demand results. Prices for the scarce goods are bid up causing the price level to rise. Keynesians would say that this process occurs when $C + I + G$ (aggregate demand) exceeds full-employment supply. Monetarists would emphasize that M (money supply) is too large in the $MV = PQ$ exchange equation. However, both schools would agree that the sequence starts with excess demand and moves toward inflation.

Certain hyperinflations have been classic cases of this phenomenon. Governments unable or unwilling to tax their citizens have financed their activities by printing money or by creating demand deposits. These actions stimulated demand beyond productive capacity, and inflation resulted. We should certainly note that in periods of excess demand, labor is also a scarce resource, and so wages increase just as prices do. But this type of wage increase is the result of inflation caused by excess demand, not the cause of it.

Cost-Push Inflation Those who believe increased costs push us into an inflationary period argue that the problem begins when the cost of factors of production increases more than the value of the products these factors produce. Because of increases in factor costs, the final product costs are higher; these costs are passed on to consumers in the form of increased prices. The resulting spiral thrusts the economy into a state of inflation. Several versions of cost-push theories are offered to explain why.

Union Push Only. Advocates of this view blame wages as the initiator of inflation. Powerful unions demand wage increases greater than productivity increases warrant. Employers agree to these demands and product costs increase. The higher costs are passed on to consumers in the form of higher prices and inflation results. Thus, wage increases are said to be the cause of inflation.

Industry Push Only.   Also known as the price-push view of inflation, this is a form of cost push in which inflation starts because large corporations selling in noncompetitive markets are determining product prices. For example, in some industries, one firm may serve as a price leader. When it raises prices, the others follow. In this view, certain key industries (such as steel, chemicals, and automobiles) are relatively immune from the pressures of the marketplace. Even in times of excess capacity, they continue to raise prices.

These price increases cause prices to rise in other industries, especially those that use the goods of noncompetitive industries in production. A frequently cited example is the steel industry, which raised prices although demand for steel was dropping. Because steel is used in many other products, the effect of the price increase spread to other industries and furthered the spread of inflation.

Sellers' Push.   A generalized form of cost-push inflation is referred to as a sellers' inflation. In this view the sellers of labor and of goods determine prices that will account for more than 100 percent of total national product. They act as if government will keep demand high enough to buy the higher cost output. If the government does not do so, a recession follows. Since recessions are politically unpopular, the government is always tempted to stimulate the economy by increasing aggregate demand to the level anticipated by sellers, bringing about more inflation.

By demanding wage increases greater than productivity increases warrant, unions help push up the cost of producing goods and, in turn, their prices. (*Photo by Terry Zabala*)

Expectations and Inflation

One version of cost-push inflation shows that the rate of inflation depends on expectations of future price increases as well as actual economic circumstances at any point in time. Consider a union that is renegotiating its contract for a three-year period. The union's goal is to achieve an increase in real wages for its members equal to the increase in worker productivity, here assumed to be 2 percent per year. The contract for the 1979–81 period is negotiated

---

Rational Expectations

Adaptive expectations are formed on the basis of experience in the recent past. For example, a person's expectations about inflation this year could be formed by assuming that this year's rate will be equal to last year's rate. Many economists argue that expectations are formed by considering the future as well as the past. The *rational expectations* hypothesis assumes that decision makers use all available information when predicting the economic future. Among other things, the rational expectations hypothesis suggests that changes in government policy will affect economic decisions because those changes provide information about the future.

Some economists extend the rational expectations hypothesis and argue that government policy will not be able to affect national output even in the short run. In effect, they argue, rational expectations will allow decision makers to anticipate the effect of policy, thereby reducing its effectiveness. For example, suppose the Fed increases the growth of the money supply to increase aggregate demand in order to increase output. In response to this policy change, workers raise wages and firms increase prices because they *expect* more inflation. Prices rise but there is no change in output. If rational expectations were exactly correct (no one argues they would be), policy would be totally ineffective. Only random, unanticipated policies could influence output in the short run.

Most economists accept the idea that economic decision makers anticipate the future, including the future course of public policy. In this regard, the rational expectations hypothesis is widely accepted. The stronger statement that public policy cannot affect output in the short run does not enjoy widespread acceptance.

---

on January 1, 1979. The union believes that the price level will increase over the life of the contract at the same rate it did during the previous contract (6.7 percent per year from 1976 to 1978). This procedure of using recent experience to predict the future is called *adaptive expectations*. A contract is signed in which the union accepts a 2 percent annual increase in wages for expected increases in productivity and 6.7 percent to maintain real wages—a total wage increase of 8.7 percent.

Actual inflation from 1979 to 1981 averaged 11.7 percent per year. This means that the union workers' real income declined by 3 percent per year (11.7 rate of inflation minus the 8.7 percent wage increase). In the next contract (for the 1982–84 period) adaptive expectations will cause the union to demand a 13.7 percent annual increase in wages—2 percent for the productivity increase and 11.7 percent to offset expected inflation. The increase in wages will be reflected in the price of the final product, thereby contributing to a higher price level in the next period even if the actual inflation is less than expected. In this way, inflation in one year may be transmitted to the price level of subsequent years.

The impact of adaptive expectations on the price level is also reflected in financial markets. The interest rate, as we have already learned, is the price of using money for a year. The *nominal interest rate* is the one written on a loan contract whereas the *real interest rate* takes into account inflation's deteriorating effect on the purchasing power of money. To find the real interest rate, we subtract the rate of inflation from the nominal interest rate. That is:

$$\text{Real interest rate} = \text{Nominal interest rate} - \text{Rate of inflation}$$

Since 1960 the real interest rate has usually been between 1 and 3 percent, as shown in Exhibit 11-4. Unexpected inflation in 1974 and 1975 resulted in the rate of inflation exceeding the nominal interest rate. Adaptive expectations would lead the banks to protect themselves against such losses in subsequent periods of inflation. During the 1979–80 period the rate of inflation rose each year, and so did the prime interest rate charged by banks. In 1981 the rate of inflation fell from its 1980 level, but the banking community, having built in long-term inflationary expectations, did not believe that the decrease represented a trend and *increased* the lending rate by more than 3 percentage points. The resulting real interst rate was an unprecedented 8.47 percent. In 1982 the inflation rate fell faster than the nominal interest rate, resulting in a still higher real interest rate.

Inflation is a complex phenomenon. It can be started by forces of cost push or demand pull and sustained through inflationary expectations. Since expectations do not necessarily change when macroeconomic policy is changed, an anti-inflationary policy that works in one circumstance might not be effective in a situation that appears identical except that inflationary expectations differ. Economic condi-

tions, for the purposes of economic policy, cannot be entirely described by measures of output, unemployment rates, or changes in the price level. Expectations about the future matter, too.

A TRADEOFF BETWEEN INFLATION AND UNEMPLOYMENT

Throughout the 1960s economists believed that fiscal and monetary policy could achieve the desired level of either unemployment or inflation. But they also recognized a tradeoff between the two goals. The relationship between inflation and unemployment came to be known as the *Phillips curve,* in honor of Professor A. W. Phillips of the Australian National University, who made the pioneering attempts at quantifying the tradeoff relationship. Exhibit 11-5 shows a hypothetical Phillips curve; it provides a picture of the possible combinations of unemployment and inflation that policymakers may choose in the short run. Suppose that the unemployment rate is 5 percent and the infla-

Exhibit 11-4 Real interest rates, 1960–82

Year	Nominal Interest Rate*	−	Inflation Rate	=	Real Interest Rate
1960	4.82%		1.6%		3.22%
1965	4.54		1.7		2.84
1970	7.91		5.9		2.01
71	5.72		4.3		1.42
72	5.25		3.3		1.95
73	8.03		6.2		1.83
74	10.81		11.0		−0.19
1975	7.86		9.1		−1.24
76	6.84		5.8		1.04
77	6.83		6.5		0.33
78	9.06		7.7		1.36
79	12.67		11.3		1.37
1980	15.27		13.5		1.77
81	18.87		10.4		8.47
82	14.86		6.1		8.76

*Prime rate charged by banks

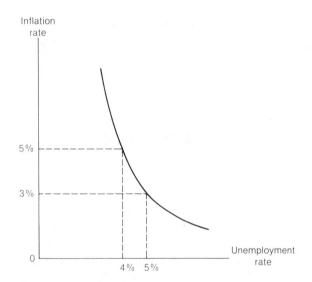

Exhibit 11-5   The Phillips curve

The Phillips curve shows the short-run tradeoff between inflation and unemployment.

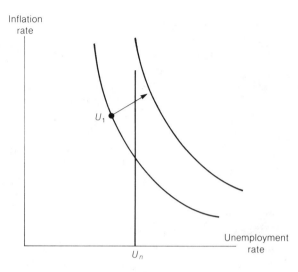

Exhibit 11-6   The short-run and long-run Phillips curve

The long-run Phillips curve is a vertical line at the natural rate of unemployment. Using macroeconomic policy to lower unemployment below its natural rate is likely to shift the Phillips curve to a less favorable short-run tradeoff.

tion rate 3 percent. Policymakers desire to lower the unemployment rate to 4 percent. In an ideal world it would be possible to keep the rate of inflation at 3 percent while the unemployment rate was reduced. The Phillips curve shows that the world is not ideal. In this specific case, the Phillips curve shows that we must accept a 2-percentage-point increase in inflation, from 3 to 5 percent, if we lower the unemployment rate from 5 to 4 percent.

The tradeoff between unemployment and inflation depicted by the Phillips curve is true only in the short run. In the long run, the economy tends toward its natural rate of unemployment. More important, attempts to lower the unemployment rate below its natural rate will result in the acceleration of inflationary pressures. Hence in Exhibit 11-6 we show the long-run Phillips curve as a vertical line at the natural rate of unemployment (U_n). If the unemployment rate is pushed to U_1 on the short-

run Phillips curve, which is below U_n, inflationary pressures of the demand-pull type begin because we are trying to produce more output than is possible with stable prices. This means a higher level of inflation for any given level of unemployment; the short-run Phillips curve shifts to the right, as the arrow shows in Exhibit 11-6. Thus the short-run Phillips curve can shift. Changing demographics, government programs, and other factors can, as we saw earlier in this chapter, change the natural rate of unemployment. Thus the long-run natural rate of unemployment is also subject to change, although it is much more stable than the short-run Phillips curve.

EXPLAINING STAGFLATION

Stagflation, the combination of rising unemployment and accelerating inflation, is inconsistent with the short-run Phillips curve. In the short run, prices will rise if unemployment falls. Stagflation therefore necessarily involves shifting short-run Phillips curves. In what follows we will see that the stagflation that gripped the U.S. economy for much of the 1970s is the product of many forces: demand-pull inflation,

inflationary expectations, a changing natural rate of unemployment, and supply shocks.

Unemployment and inflation data for the 1960–69 period trace out a clear, short-run Phillips curve, shown in Exhibit 11-7. In the early 1960s the natural rate of unemployment (U_n) was approximately 4 percent. Beginning in

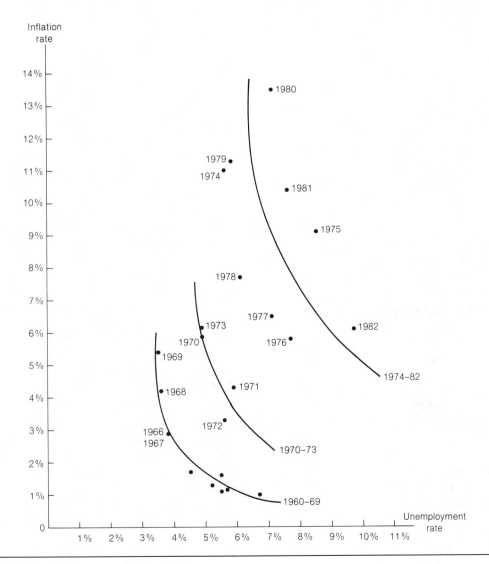

Exhibit 11-7   Three Phillips curves for 1960–82

1966, spending for the Vietnam War accelerated with no offsetting taxes or reduction in nondefense government spending. In the State of the Union message of that year, President Johnson declared that the United States could fight the war without giving up private spending or the Great Society programs he had begun. War spending stimulated aggregate demand enough to push the actual rate of unemployment below the natural rate from 1966 through 1969.

By definition, unemployment below the natural rate causes inflationary pressures and, in this circumstance, apparently caused a shift in inflationary expectations. These changed expectations are reflected in the fact that the unemployment and inflation data for the 1970–73 period trace out a short-run Phillips curve that is to the right of the 1960–69 curve.

The new Phillips curve was abruptly shifted to the right by supply shocks in 1973–74: oil prices quadrupled and crop failures raised food prices. These supply shocks reinforced the earlier inflationary expectations, resulting in a still higher Phillips curve for the 1974–82 period. The inflation-unemployment tradeoff for the 1974–82 period indicates that prices rise very rapidly as the unemployment rate approaches 6 percent. This is indicative of the shift of the natural rate of unemployment from 4 to 6 percent during the 20 years covered in Exhibit 11-7.

We have seen that stagflation has been the product of bad policy (the decision to generate demand-pull inflation during the Vietnam War), bad luck (supply shocks), and inevitable trends (an increase in the natural rate of unemployment). The shift in the natural rate of unemployment means that the unemployment rates that were routinely achieved during the 1960s are now unattainable. Macroeconomic policy goals must stay within the limits of the attainable. It is important to understand how we got

into the situation in which we face the undesirable choices required by the 1974–82 Phillips curve, but it is more interesting to figure out how we can improve macroeconomic conditions. In short, we must determine how we can shift the Phillips curve downward, toward a more acceptable tradeoff between inflation and unemployment.

MACROECONOMIC POLICY FOR THE 1980s

In the previous chapters we have emphasized that the appropriate macroeconomic policies vary with economic conditions. Highest priority for the 1980s is to improve the tradeoff between inflation and unemployment. Given a natural rate of unemployment at 6 percent in Exhibit 11-7, the desired goal is to lower the Phillips curve from that prevailing in 1974–82 to a tradeoff that makes possible lower levels of inflation and unemployment. Among the strategies that have been proposed to achieve this goal are (1) wringing out inflationary expectations via recession, (2) regulating inflation with wage-price controls, and (3) improving the efficiency of labor markets.

Wringing Out Inflationary Expectations

Herbert Stein, chairman of the President's Council of Economic Advisors under President Nixon, called the policy of using recession to wring out inflationary expectations the "old-time religion." This analogy is apt because unemployment with its accompanying hardships is the traditional remedy for rising prices. As demand slackens, upward pressure on prices lessens; some prices may actually fall. Wage demands by labor become lower as inflation is reduced below expectations and because of the fear of unemployment. Fiscal policy can contribute to recession by cutting expenditures and/or raising taxes, thereby reducing aggregate demand. Monetary authorities can lower the rate of growth of the money supply. These policies will lower aggregate demand and eventually reduce inflationary expectations, allowing a downward shift in the Phillips curve.

The cure is distasteful. The higher the Phillips curve, the greater the recessions required to ease the inflationary spiral. This is clear from Exhibit 11-7. Along the Phillips curve that prevailed in 1960–69, an unemployment rate of 6 percent was regarded as a severe recession that would reduce the rate of inflation to less than 2 percent. The inflation-unemployment trade-off from 1974 to 1982 shows that an inflation rate of 2 percent can be obtained only by a rate of unemployment far in excess of the highest shown in the exhibit. In 1982 the underlying forces in the economy, coupled with a relatively tight monetary policy, produced an unemployment rate of 9.7 percent. Inflation fell to 6.1 percent. High unemployment and low inflation is the first step in reducing inflationary expectations and shifting the Phillips curve. During 1983, unemployment fell and the rate of inflation fell to an annual rate of 3 percent. The "old-time religion" seemed to work. The problem for public policy is to promote continued growth that will lower unemployment without setting off a new wave of inflation. Macroeconomic policy, therefore, has to walk a fine line if it is to succeed at wringing out inflationary expectations by raising unemployment.

High unemployment is used in macroeconomic policy to wring out inflationary expectations. (*Photo by Eugene Richards, Magnum Photos, Inc.*)

Incomes Policy

Some economists feel that when the economy is caught in a vicious cycle of inflationary expectations, raising the unemployment rate is too high a price to pay for improved price stability. Indeed, these observers look to the 1982 unemployment rate, the highest since the Great Depression, as evidence. These economists advocate what is called *incomes policy*, an effort to regulate the rate of inflation with some type of wage and price controls.

Politicians are often attracted to an incomes policy because it gives the appearance that the problem is being solved. After all, it seems easy to eliminate price and wage increases simply by making them illegal. Wage and price controls have been instituted by many societies since the third century B.C. and have usually failed. They have been tried in the United States during wars and emergencies; they were tried during the early 1970s. Most economists feel that wage-price controls work well during a short period of emergency, but that they create more and more distortion the longer they remain in effect. During a war, when patriotic fervor is high and the economy is making a transition to mobilization, abandoning the market in favor of rationing and controls is feasible and perhaps even helpful. Adopting the same methods during normal times is an invitation to waste and distortion because the allocation rules are not as obvious. In time of war, military needs obviously take top priority. During normal times, priorities are less easy to determine.

The longer controls are retained, the higher the cost. Holding prices constant is an invitation to lower quality, a technique frequently adopted by producers. With the profit incentive removed, businesses do not increase capacity. This results in shortages of goods for which demand has grown rapidly. For products like paper, which require years to build capacity, controls enforced during one year can mean shortages and price hikes several years later. Hence, the total cost of controls does not show up in the short run.

One of the major costs is that much of the talent of the business community is devoted to circumventing controls instead of increasing production. As people become familiar with controls they discover ways to avoid them. In turn, a huge bureaucracy must be developed to counter the schemes. The minute detail required for effective economic control during World War II sounds like a horror story. For example, an Office of Price Administration order required six pages of small type to specify what was meant, for pricing purposes, by "fruitcakes." Imagine the difficulty of defining an automobile or a house!

Some proponents of incomes policy argue that controls are a good weapon to keep in reserve. Opponents feel that even standby authority is destabilizing, because when inflation begins, business firms will start raising prices to establish a higher figure ahead of the anticipated price freeze. Labor unions will behave in a similar fashion. Thus, the mere threat of controls can turn a mild inflation into a series of price increases.

Economists who favor an incomes policy generally propose the use of economic incentives rather than outright bans to control prices. One such policy is called the *tax-based incomes policy* (TIP). This strategy discourages wage increases by imposing a tax on firms (or employees) that rises with the wage increases. Hence a firm (or its employees) will pay higher taxes if a wage settlement exceeds some guideline; e.g., 5 percent. While most economists are skeptical of putting some form of TIP in practice, failure of more traditional remedies for inflation may lead to greater interest in incomes policy.

Improving the Efficiency of Labor Markets

Using a recession to wring out inflation or following incomes policies are methods that focus on lowering the rate of inflation associated with a given unemployment rate. A reverse approach is to try to lower the unemployment rate associated with a given level of inflation. Programs that accomplish this increase the efficiency of the labor market, thereby reducing the time required to search for a new job and in the process lowering the unemployment rate. Any improvement that can accomplish this will shift the Phillips curve to the left, indicating that there will be a lower unemployment rate at any given level of inflation. Four types of programs may facilitate the matching of workers and jobs that would lower the unemployment rate.

Establishing Employment Training Programs Employment training programs can play a particularly important role for groups with a higher-than-average rate of unemployment—the young, the unskilled, and members of racial and ethnic minorities. Retraining experienced workers can also play an important role in reducing structural unemployment in a dynamic economy. Required job skills are constantly changing. The automobile, steel, and textile industries have all suffered from substantial foreign competition that has lowered domestic employment. Restoring competitiveness has meant increasing automation, which has further reduced employment. Such transitions, inevitable in a vibrant competitive economy, will force workers to seek new employment even though they have gained considerable experience in a par-

In the United States, labor unions tend to resist the use of robots, because they view the robots as reducing the jobs available. But in Japan labor unions have accepted the use of robots, because they view the robots as freeing workers from assembly line tedium. (*Wide World Photos*)

ticular occupation or industry. Most victims are middle aged, suggesting that worker retraining will be an ongoing problem as the rate of technological advance quickens. European countries have allocated more resources and efforts to this problem than has the United States.

Establishing Centers to Distribute Employment Information Some authorities have suggested a national job data base in order to improve the employment information available to the unemployed. Searching for a job is a costly process, especially outside one's home area. A job data base, with a roster of all jobs available, would presumably cut down the search costs. The problem is that the most valuable job information appears to come from informal sources, most commonly from people who already work for a company. Thus, the information available in a data base is not necessarily suited to an applicant's wants or needs. This raises the question of whether the benefits of such a program can justify the cost.

Encouraging Employment in Depressed Areas

A policy that has been popular in Europe and has been tried in a limited way in the United States encourages industry to move to areas of high unemployment. Instead of having unemployed workers leave their friends, families, and public facilities that are already completed and move to other areas, programs were created to provide incentives for employers to come to areas that have high unemployment. In Europe such programs have existed since the early 1950s. Great Britain has provided low-interest loans and salary subsidies for new plants built in the depressed areas of Scotland and Wales. The Economic Development Administration (EDA) of the U.S. Department of Commerce has worked with small budgets in attempting similar programs. Generally, EDA has not influenced much relocation, but given the minimal budget and large number of target areas mandated by Congress, clear success would not have been possible. As a general solution to unemployment, area development does not appear to be workable. As a supplement to other policies, it may be effective in helping reduce geographically based structural unemployment.

Eliminating Legal Barriers

Legal barriers limit the mobility of some human resources. State regulation plays a role in keeping unemployment high in some occupations and fields by requiring licenses to practice certain skills. Some states may require licensing not only for doctors, dentists, and lawyers but also for such fields as barbering, surveying, and giving massages. One state requires licenses for 152 occupations. How much of this regulation is necessary to protect citizens and how much is meant to restrict the migration of human resources is not clear.

Another legal barrier to employment is the federal minimum wage. Some local jurisdictions, such as the District of Columbia and New York City, set minimum wages that are even higher than the federal figure. Many young workers do not have the skills to command such a wage. The minimum wage also narrows the wage difference between skilled and unskilled labor, thus encouraging employers to hire skilled workers or to mechanize their operations. Thus, the effect of a minimum wage is to increase unemployment among unskilled workers. For these reasons, some experts feel that the minimum wage, particularly for young workers, should be eliminated.

Eliminating the minimum wage for young people is opposed on various grounds. One argument is that young families have pressing needs like everyone else. Trade unionists also are concerned that, without a minimum wage, "cheap" young labor will displace older workers, who will then be unemployed. Removing the minimum wage for young people, the unionists contend, would provide cheaper labor to business firms without significantly lowering the total level of unemployment.

Although these claims have some merit, policies of the Netherlands, which exclude all workers under 23 from the minimum-income plan, suggest that such a regulation is not callous toward the needs of the young and does not contribute to the unemployment of older persons. The Dutch have very progressive social programs with a generally lower rate of unemployment than the United States.

SUPPLY-SIDE ECONOMICS

Keynesian and monetarist approaches to economic stabilization offer essentially short-run policies to moderate the business cycle. But neither addresses the issues of long-run economic growth. Indeed, the very success of Keynesian policies through the 1960s led some observers to declare the business cycle obsolete and to predict uninterrupted growth for the future. In this environment, President Johnson can be forgiven the excessive hopes embodied in a series of government programs that would create the Great Society. In short, growth came to be taken for granted.

The declining economic fortunes of the 1970s revived interest in the sources of long-term economic growth. This movement was called "supply-side economics" because it focused on the traditional economic factors that account for increasing the supply of output, rather than the monetarist and Keynesian emphasis on demand. The importance of this long-term perspective in macroeconomics is exemplified by the United Kingdom's decline from the richest country in the world to a relatively poor European country by growing more slowly than other countries. Supply-side economics is the important long-term perspective on macroeconomic policy that is not addressed by the stabilization orientation of the Keynesian and monetarist perspectives.

Sources of economic growth in the past provide an indication of the policies that might augment the rate of economic growth in the future. Economist Edward Denison has analyzed in detail the sources of the rapid economic growth that characterized the 1948–69 period. Technological change was the most important factor, followed by increased labor supply, increased quantity of capital, a better educated workforce, and other factors. The relative importance of these factors is shown in Exhibit 11-8. A program of economic growth would seem to require policies that stimulate people to work, encourage savings that will be invested in plant and equipment, and education and training programs that prepare workers for the jobs required in a dynamic technological economy.

Increasing the Labor Supply

Some public policies discourage people from working. One example is unemployment insurance, because it is likely to prolong job searches. Longer job searches mean a loss of output that could have been produced during the search period. On the other hand, if a lengthier search results in a maximum use of the worker's skills, it may actually raise output. So it is with many

Exhibit 11-8 Estimated sources of U.S. economic growth, 1948–69

Source	Percentage of Growth
Technological change	34.1%
Increase in quantity of labor	23.9
Increase in quantity of capital	21.6
Better educated workforce	11.9
Other factors	8.5
Total	100.0

SOURCE: Edward F. Denison, *Accounting for United States Economic Growth 1929–1969* (Washington, D.C.: The Brookings Institute, 1974).

programs. The costs and benefits must be weighed in order to decide whether a program on net contributes or detracts from growth. It is also important to remember that other goals must be considered as well as economic growth.

Decreasing taxes on individuals and corporations is an integral part of fiscal policy when an increase in aggregate demand is desired. Lowering taxes is also an important part of long-term supply-side economics. Reducing taxes on individual incomes raises the after-tax price of leisure. An example will clarify this point. If a person earning $10 per hour has a 20 percent marginal tax rate, take-home pay for the last hour of work is $8. That amount represents the opportunity cost of leisure because this person must give up $8 to obtain another hour of leisure. If the tax rate is lowered to 15 percent, the price of leisure rises to $8.50. As with many other goods, we are likely to purchase less leisure as its price rises. The impact is likely to be most pronounced among those workers who are relatively free to choose the amount of work they do—second workers in households, younger and older workers. A higher price of leisure helps increase the quantity of labor—a source of economic growth.

Increasing the Quantity of Capital

Under the progressive income tax, persons who earn the highest income pay the highest marginal tax rates. Because wealthy people are the ones most likely to save, high tax rates encourage investment in activities that yield gains in forms that are not taxed or are taxed at a lower rate. A long-term capital gain—the increased price of an asset—is taxed at a much lower rate than income from investing, which includes dividends on stocks and interest earned on various forms of savings accounts. Capital-gain tax provisions, coupled with high marginal tax rates, have caused much capital to be invested in real estate, which provides little income and high capital gains. The attractiveness of investing in business firms through the stock market—a way to increase productive plant and equipment—has less appeal.

The disincentive to invest in plant and equipment is compounded by the fact that corporate income is taxed twice. The corporation pays a corporate income tax on profits; when these profits are distributed as dividends, the individual stockholder is taxed, too. Since the corporate tax rate is 46 percent and the highest personal income tax rate is 50 percent, the government takes 46 cents of an extra dollar of corporate profits and 26 cents (0.5 times 54 cents) if these profits are distributed to high-income stockholders. Thus the government can take a total of 72 percent of additional corporate profits in the form of taxes.

In recent years corporate taxes have been lowered without changing corporate tax rates. This has been accomplished by the Tax Recovery Act of 1981, which allowed for more rapid depreciation of investment in plant and equipment. Now when a firm buys a machine, it can deduct a larger portion of its cost against current income, thus reducing its tax liability. Although such efforts increase the incentive to invest, many economists still advocate eliminating the double taxation of corporate income.

Better Education

Improving the quality of workers through education and training is called investment in *human capital*. Because technological change is also a product of our human capital investments, education plays a very important role in

As more and more jobs apply advanced technology, education is essential to improving the workforce. (*Erich Hartmann, Magnum Photos, Inc.*)

the growth of the economy. Previously we have discussed the importance of worker training and retraining programs that increase the efficiency of the labor market, thereby lowering the unemployment rate. In the long run, however, U.S. economic growth is going to depend on how well we can compete with other advanced nations in the application of advanced technologies. Success in this area is likely to depend on a strengthened scientific and engineering curriculum in U.S. schools. Creating a highly

skilled and educated member of the workforce takes a long time; investment in human capital is an integral part of a supply-side program for long-term growth.

Other Factors

Some observers feel that the decline in U.S. economic growth has been due to the increasing importance of "other" factors. Most frequently mentioned is the rise of government regulation. Federal measures, designed to improve product safety, protect the environment, ensure worker safety, or for many other purposes have proliferated in recent years. Many of the regulations and the accompanying enforcement efforts contribute little to the intended purpose, but can significantly increase the costs to the business firm required to comply with them. Many regulations, for instance, determine *how* a firm will keep its workers safe or the production process it will use to ensure environmental protection. This "regulation by rule" approach puts the agency in the role of deciding the best way to produce, for example, a product in a safe worker environment. Government employees, even when engaged in the most socially useful regulatory activity, simply do not have the expertise to make efficient rules. To minimize the adverse economic effects of government regulatory activity, many economists have suggested that we move from a "regulation by rule" approach to a "regulation by incentive" approach, which would give the firm a financial incentive to achieve the desired result without telling it how to do so. The firm can choose the least-cost method. Once a lower-cost method of regulation is put in place, it is imperative that the social benefits of the regulation be worth the cost. Supply-side economics does not reject the idea of government regulation per se, but its long-term orientation suggests that disruptive aspects of government intervention in the economy should be minimized.

MICROECONOMIC FOUNDATIONS OF ECONOMIC GROWTH

The Keynesian and monetarist views presented in this part of the book have dominated macroeconomic thinking for many years. In recent years economists have been looking at specific markets and incentives that play an important role in the performance of the economy. These are the microeconomic aspects of macroeconomic problems. Supply-side economics focuses on the microeconomic foundations of long-term economic growth. Microeconomics is the subject of Part III of this book.

SUMMARY

1. This chapter describes the various types of unemployment and inflation. Aggregate unemployment figures include frictional, cyclical, and structural unemployment. Inflation can be caused by excessive demand, cost push, and/or inflationary expectations.

2. The rate of inflation depends on expectations of future price increases as well as the actual economic circumstances at any point in time.

3. A short-run tradeoff between inflation and unemployment is depicted by the Phillips curve. The long-run Phillips curve is vertical at the natural rate of unemployment, indicating there is no tradeoff between these goals in the long run.

4. Both the short-run and the natural rate of unemployment can shift over time. Stagflation during the 1970s was caused by an outward shift of the short-run Phillips curve and an increase in the natural rate of unemployment.

5. Reducing inflation and unemployment requires a backward shift of the Phillips curve. The traditional way to lower inflation and inflationary expectations is to "wring them out" via recession. Rising unemployment is the price of the strategy.

6. An incomes policy, the use of some type of wage and price controls, is sometimes advocated by people who feel the unemployment costs of traditional anti-inflationary policy are too high.

7. Keynesian and monetarist approaches to economic stabilization offer short-run policies to moderate the business cycle. Supply-side economics focuses on the factors that will stimulate long-term economic growth.

KEY CONCEPTS

frictional unemployment

cyclical unemployment

structural unemployment

natural rate of unemployment

demand-pull inflation

cost-push inflation

inflationary expectations

real rate of interest

Phillips curve

incomes policy

supply-side economics

human capital

QUESTIONS FOR DISCUSSION

1. Teenage unemployment rates are five times higher than the rate for married males aged 25–55. Married women have a higher unemployment rate than married men. Why do these differences exist? Are they inevitable?

2. Suppose that jobs are available in the Southwest for unskilled laborers. Should an unskilled laborer in Appalachia be paid unemployment compensation?

3. Recessions can purge inflation from the economy at the price of higher unemployment. How high a "price" do you think is reasonable to pay? At what price should we consider an incomes policy rather than recession to reduce inflation?

4. Wages, the major incentive to work, are reduced by income taxes. How would you change your work effort (in terms of hours of work and effort on the job) if taxes were changed? Does your answer change if you are head of a household?

5. Elimination of corporate income taxes is a way to prevent double taxation of dividends and provide greater incentives for increased investment in plant and equipment. Is it "fair" that as individuals we pay taxes while big corporations pay none? Who really pays corporate taxes?

6. If everything remains the same except that the natural rate of unemployment increases, attempts to keep the unemployment rate at its previous level will cause increased inflation. Under what circumstances is this statement true? When is it false?

Chapter 12

International Economics

International trade is the aspect of economics concerned with how economic activity is distributed around the world. Economists have long argued that if trade *among* nations were as "free" as trade *within* nations, international specialization would maximize total world production. And material well-being would be distribted in an equitable way, according to each nation's productivity. This is called the classical theory of international trade. This theory and the mechanics of its operation are the subject of this chapter. We also will discuss conflicts inherent in international economic relations and the attempts to mediate the conflicting interests of nations.

THE ADVANTAGES OF INTERNATIONAL TRADE

Specialization is a fundamental characteristic of modern economies. Within nations, this division of labor makes it possible to achieve a high level of material well-being. Medical doctors, auto mechanics, and bricklayers specialize; their earnings enable them to buy a full range of goods and services. In a modern economy we depend on many people for basic services—food, clothing, heat, transportation, and medical care. Any attempt to reduce this interdependence could be accomplished only at the cost of a decline in material well-being. Material wealth is a product of mutual interdependence, not individual hard work.

Just as individuals specialize to their advantage within a society, regions within nations specialize. In the United States, Texas produces oil, Florida produces oranges, Iowa and Nebraska grow corn, and Michigan manufactures automobiles. No state expects to be self-sufficient—each sells to other states those items it can produce efficiently. Residents then use their earnings from "export" sales to purchase items from other states. Michigan sells autos to Florida; with their earnings auto workers buy oil from Texas, corn from Iowa, and Florida oranges. So it is with nations. They, like regions within countries, have varied resource endowments. Nature has blessed some nations with enormous resources. Saudi Arabia has great quantities of oil, Brazil has an ideal climate for growing coffee, and Chile has large nitrate deposits. Other nations have few resources.

International specialization rests on the relative quantity of factor endowments as well as on their quality. Two nations have resources of similar quantity, but varying proportions will cause different kinds of specialization. Australia has vast amounts of land suitable for growing wheat, which is exported to the rest of the world. A smaller nation may have land equally suitable for growing wheat, but the land might be used differently if it is relatively scarce. When land is plentiful relative to capital and other resources, activities that use large areas of land (called land-intensive activities) will be pursued. When land is scarce relative to other factors, it will be used to take advantage of the more plentiful resources. Thus, independent of the inherent quality of resources, *specialization will vary according to the relative proportions of the factors of production.*

Patterns of U.S. Trade

The volume of international trade as a percentage of GNP varies dramatically among nations. U.S. exports and imports in 1981 were valued at about $234 billion and account for 8 percent of GNP. In Western Europe this percentage tends to be much higher, because smaller nations are of necessity less self-sufficient than large nations. France's exports account for about 21 percent of GNP; West Germany's, about 22 percent; the

Exhibit 12-1 U.S. imports and exports by selected commodity groups, 1981

Commodity	Exports		Imports	
	(in millions)	(percentage)	(in millions)	(percentage)
Machinery	$ 62,946	30.9%	$ 38,212	16.8%
Transportation equipment	32,791	16.1	31,415	13.8
Food and live animals	30,291	14.9	15,238	6.7
Chemicals	21,187	10.4	9,446	4.1
Crude materials except fuels	20,992	10.3	11,193	4.9
Mineral fuels and related products	10,279	5.0	81,417	35.7
Beverages and tobacco	2,915	1.4	3,138	1.4
Oils and fats, animal and vegetable	1,750	0.9	480	0.2
Other manufactured goods	20,633	10.1	37,292	16.4
Total	203,784	100.0	227,831	100.0

SOURCE: U.S. Department of Commerce, *Survey of Current Business*, November 1982.

United Kingdom's, 30 percent; the Netherlands', over 45 percent. Smaller nations specialize more than larger nations and hence engage in more international trade relative to total economic activity.

The pattern of U.S. trade is shown in Exhibit 12-1. The bulk of U.S. trade, both import and export, is with other developed nations. Although the volume of trade is modest as a portion of GNP when compared to that of other industrial nations, it is nevertheless very important. Export sales are crucial to many industries. In 1980 agricultural exports from the United States amounted to $41.3 billion, over 30 percent of total agricultural sales for that year. Exports accounted for almost 16 percent of nonelectrical machinery output. In more narrowly defined industries, such as coin-operated machines and milled rice, exports accounted for more than half of the industry's output.

Imports are equally important. Mineral fuels and related products account for almost 36 percent of the imports shown in Exhibit 12-1 and 31 percent of imports of all commodities. Of the $81.4 billion of fuel imports, $75.6 billion, or 93 percent, is for the importation of petroleum products. Put another way, in 1981 the United States paid approximately 2.6 percent of

GNP for imported petroleum. The United States obtains its entire supply of certain other raw materials and minerals from foreign sources. Among them are coffee, silk, chromium, diamonds, and crude rubber. Three-quarters of the bauxites, aluminum ores, manganese, and asbestos and over half the uranium ores and concentrates used come from foreign suppliers.

Taken together, exports and imports play an important role in the determination of national income. Aggregate demand is composed of all purchases of goods and services. In Chapter 7 it was said that aggregate demand is made up of consumption, investment, and government expenditures $(C + I + G)$. Net exports (defined as exports minus imports) are another component of aggregate demand. If residents of foreign countries buy more from the United States than U.S. residents buy from the rest of the world, our export sales exceed our import purchases—net exports are positive and aggregate demand rises. Conversely, if imports exceed exports, aggregate demand will fall. The effect of net exports on national income and the price level is exactly like any other change in aggregate demand. The overall impact of the foreign sector on national income obviously depends on the size of imports and exports relative to GNP.

National income in the Netherlands, in which almost half of GNP goes to the foreign sector, is much more sensitive to fluctuations in net exports than GNP in the United States.

ABSOLUTE AND COMPARATIVE ADVANTAGE

Absolute Advantage

Trade between two nations is obviously beneficial when each has an *absolute advantage* in the production of a particular commodity. A nation has an absolute advantage if it can produce and transport a commodity to another country cheaper than the recipient nation can produce it. This absolute advantage may result from differences in the quality of resource endowment, from the relative proportions of resources, or from cultural factors. Because the United States cannot grow coffee, Brazil clearly has an absolute advantage in its production. Because of its superior technical base, the United States may be able to produce precision scientific instruments, ship them to Brazil, and sell them there cheaper than it would cost Brazilians to produce them. Hence, the absolute advantage Brazil has in coffee and the absolute advantage the United States has in scientific instruments make clear the benefits of trade.

Comparative Advantage

The advantages of international trade are not limited to nations with an absolute advantage in the production of some commodity. A nation that can produce every commodity more efficiently than every other nation can still benefit from international trade! This rather startling result is explained by the principle of *comparative advantage*. Comparative advantage shows

Brazil has an absolute advantage in the production of coffee. (*Wide World Photos*)

that if nations specialize in what they produce *relatively* more cheaply than other nations, all nations can be better off.*

Let us assume the world is composed of two nations, the United States and Brazil. Each pro-

---

* An intuitive idea of comparative advantage is given by the following example. A surgeon who can type faster than a secretary has an absolute advantage in both surgery and typing. Because the surgeon can't see patients while typing, the secretary is employed to type. The opportunity cost of an hour of the surgeon's time to type is an hour of time as a surgeon—a high opportunity cost. This high cost for typing gives the relatively slow-typing secretary a comparative advantage at the typewriter.

duces cloth and wheat. At the outset we assume that in both countries (1) there are no transportation costs, (2) the economy is perfectly competitive, and (3) labor is the only factor of production, with worker-days the appropriate measure of production costs. In the United States, it takes one day of labor to produce a bushel of wheat or a yard of cloth $(1C = 1W)$. In Brazil, it takes one day to produce a bushel of wheat, but two days to produce a yard of cloth $(.5C = 1W)$; a yard of cloth requires twice as much labor as a bushel of wheat (see Exhibit 12-2). The United States has an absolute advantage over Brazil in cloth, because it can produce cloth more cheaply. If Brazil chooses to shift laborers out of cloth production and into wheat production, instead of a yard of cloth it could produce two bushels of wheat. (In other words, the opportunity cost of producing a yard of cloth is two bushels of wheat.)

If Brazil did choose to produce two bushels of wheat instead of a yard of cloth, it could, theoretically, trade one of the two bushels to the United States for a yard of cloth, profiting by the trade. Conversely, the United States could profit by trade with Brazil, in theory, by trading a yard of cloth for two bushels of wheat (the cost of cloth within Brazil). But obviously, for both countries to profit by the trade, there would have to be a compromise. The United States must receive more than a bushel of wheat to make a profit on a yard of cloth; Brazil must pay less than two bushels of wheat for the cloth to make the trade worthwhile. In other words, for the trade to be profitable to both countries,

the exchange ratio for these two commodities, called the *terms of trade*, must fall between $1C = 1W$ and $.5C = 1W$. For example, if the terms of trade are $.6C = 1W$, both countries will profit. Because of comparative advantage, Brazil can make a profit by trade even though it does not have an absolute advantage in either cloth or wheat.

Specialization If the United States is able to make a profit by producing cloth and Brazil is able to make a profit by producing wheat, the countries might specialize, the United States producing only cloth and Brazil producing only wheat. For this to happen, the costs of production would have to remain the same, regardless of how much wheat or cloth is produced, because if the costs changed, specialization might not be profitable. When the costs per unit of production remain constant (the same) regardless of the quantity produced, the result is called *constant returns to scale*.

Assuming that production costs do not change (that there are constant returns to scale), complete specialization might occur (the United States might produce only cloth and Brazil might produce only wheat). What actually happens when both countries specialize to make a profit by trade? Looking at Exhibit 12-3, we see that

Exhibit 12-2 Comparative costs of production

Commodity	Cost in Worker-Days	
	United States	Brazil
Wheat (1 bushel)	1	1
Cloth (1 yard)	1	2

Exhibit 12-3 Output before and after trade (Assuming complete specialization with trade)

Commodity by Area	Before Trade		After Trade	
	Worker	Output	Worker	Output
United States				
Wheat	50	50	0	0
Cloth	50	50	100	100
Brazil				
Wheat	50	50	100	100
Cloth	50	25	0	0
World				
Wheat	100	100	100	100
Cloth	100	75	100	100

if 100 workers in each country were divided evenly between wheat and cloth production, world output would be 100 bushels of wheat and 75 yards of cloth per day; after specialization, however, with the United States producing only cloth and Brazil producing only wheat, world output is 100 bushels of wheat and 100 yards of cloth. There has been a gain in trade of 25 yards of cloth.

Complete specialization depends, as noted above, on the presence of constant returns to scale. This assumption fixes the relative costs in each country: one bushel of wheat for one yard of cloth in the United States and a ratio of 1 to 2 in Brazil. Given that resources cannot be perfectly substituted for each other, it is likely that resources best suited for the production of wheat will eventually be needed to produce cloth in the United States. This means that the opportunity cost of producing cloth will tend to rise in terms of the amount of wheat forgone. And in Brazil, specialization in wheat will require that resources best adapted to making cloth will be employed in the production of wheat—and its cost will rise. Rather than constant returns to scale, we would expect *decreasing returns to scale*. This means that cost per unit rises as output increases.

The initial wheat/cloth cost ratio in the United States (1 wheat/1 cloth) will fall, because it now costs more to produce cloth. In Brazil the ratio (1 wheat/2 cloth) will rise, because cloth production costs less. As long as the wheat/cloth cost ratios differ, trade can be profitable for both countries. Yet decreasing returns to scale in both countries will tend to reduce the differences in relative costs as trade takes place. An equilibrium volume of trade will result when the cost ratios are equal because neither country can benefit from further trade. This is summarized in Exhibit 12-4. (Adding transportation costs to this analysis, of course, would reduce cost dif-

Exhibit 12-4 The effect of decreasing returns to scale on relative costs

| | Wheat/Cloth Cost Ratio | |
Condition	United States	Brazil
Before trade	1/1	1/2
After trade begins	Falls	Rises
In a hypothetical equilibrium	.67 (2/3)	.67 (2/3)

ferences and the potential gains from trade.) Although decreasing returns eventually reduce cost differentials between nations, the doctrine of comparative advantage shows that all nations can gain from trade.

FOREIGN EXCHANGE MARKETS

Although foreign trade is in principle an extension of internal trade, the fact that nations use different currencies complicates matters. The British use the pound; there are Japanese yen, Dutch guilders, Greek drachmas, and West German marks. These are *foreign exchange*. When you buy a car from a French manufacturer, the firm must receive francs, the domestic currency. Your dollars must somehow be converted into francs. Foreign exchange markets are used to convert one currency into another.

The market for national currencies works like any other market. The price of a foreign currency is called the *exchange rate*. If one dollar will purchase five francs, the franc/dollar exchange rate is 5 to 1; that is, one franc can be purchased for 20 cents. The foreign exchange market is conducted in the large international banking centers of New York, London, Paris, Zurich, Brussels, Frankfurt, Tokyo, and others.

The market in international currencies works like this. If a French firm imports U.S. machin-

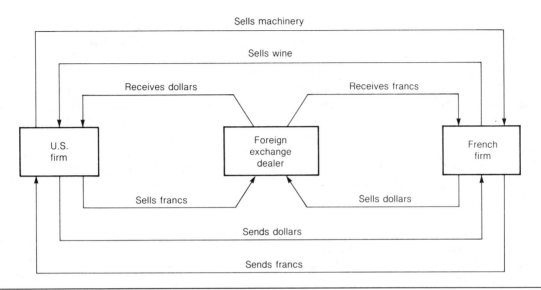

Exhibit 12-5 A simple view of foreign trade

Exports provide foreign exchange earnings, which permit a nation to import commodities from other nations.

ery, it pays the seller by obtaining a draft in dollars from a Paris bank, which charges a commission. How many francs the importer must pay for each dollar is determined by the exchange rate. In this case the payment is made directly in dollars from the French importer to the U.S. exporter. Alternatively, the importer might pay for the machinery by writing a check in francs. Since the exporting firm cannot pay bills in francs, it sells the check to a foreign exchange dealer and receives dollars in return. The foreign exchange dealer deposits the money in a Paris bank account. These francs are then sold to French exporters, who have been paid in dollars by U.S. importers of, say, wine. The export of U.S. machinery earned francs, which allowed Americans to import wine. In general, earnings from exports allow nations to import. This process is shown in Exhibit 12-5.

MAINTAINING INTERNATIONAL EQUILIBRIUM

Freely Floating Exchange Rates

The exchange rate is the price of one currency in terms of another. Since any purchase from a foreign nation requires the exchange of currencies, the price of that currency will influence the final purchase price. For example, assume that a bottle of French wine in France costs 10 francs. If the exchange rate is five francs to the dollar, an American can buy a bottle for $2. Should the exchange rate fall to four francs to $1, the same bottle of wine will cost $2.50 in America even though the costs of production have not changed in France! Thus the exchange rate affects the price of foreign commodities.

When exchange rates fluctuate without government interference, they are called *freely floating exchange rates.*

The adjustment process in international markets is similar to that of other markets. Let us assume that the exchange rate between francs and dollars is in equilibrium—there is no tendency for it to change from its current level. In Exhibit 12-6 this is shown by the intersection of the demand (D_1D_1) and supply (S_1S_1) curves at 5 to 1. One franc is valued at 20 cents. If Americans import more French goods than can be offset by some inflow of funds from France, the balance of payments is in disequilibrium. The rising demand for French products in the United States is represented in Exhibit 12-6 by the upward shift in the demand for francs to

D_2D_2. Given the supply of francs, Americans will now purchase more francs (F_2F_1) for a higher price, shown as 25 cents. The franc/dollar exchange rate has fallen from 5 to 1 to 4 to 1.

By this mechanism French products become more expensive to Americans, leading to a reduction in the quantity demanded. At the same time, of course, U.S. goods become cheaper to the French. At an exchange rate of 5 to 1, a French person could buy a $10 U.S. shirt for 50 francs. At 4 to 1, the same shirt could be bought for

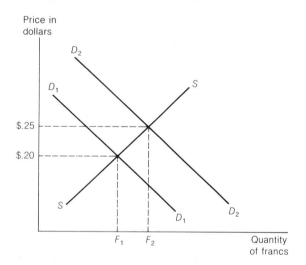

Exhibit 12-6 The foreign exchange market

The demand for and supply of francs determines the dollar price of francs. If Americans were to buy more French products, the demand for francs would increase from D_1D_1 to D_2D_2. The higher exchange rate would make French products more expensive for Americans and U.S. products cheaper for the French. By this process the foreign exchange market can maintain equilibrium.

Exchange rates affect the flow of trade between countries. *(Photo by Frederik D. Bodin, Stock, Boston)*

only 40 francs. The disequilibrium caused by excessive U.S. imports is corrected by the rising cost of francs to Americans, which (1) makes French products more expensive in the United States, thus lowering imports, and (2) raises the export of U.S. goods to France.

This slowing of U.S. imports and stimulation of exports continues until a new equilibrium exchange rate is reached. Freely floating exchange rates are the mechanism by which international markets are kept in equilibrium without the intervention of government.

Factors Affecting Exchange Rates

When the exchange rate for a currency changes, the currency either appreciates or depreciates. When the price of a currency rises relative to another currency, we say it *appreciates*, meaning that its purchasing power over foreign goods has increased. In Exhibit 12-6, increased demand for French output caused the franc to appreciate; one franc could buy more U.S. goods than it could previously (25 cents rather than 20

cents). The flip side of currency appreciation is *depreciation*, meaning that a currency has lost purchasing power over foreign goods. In Exhibit 12-6, the dollar depreciated—that is, one dollar bought fewer francs than previously (four instead of five per dollar).

Exhibit 12-7 shows the rate at which a dollar can be converted to various foreign currencies. Between 1980 and 1982 the dollar appreciated relative to the currencies shown in the exhibit. For example, a dollar could buy almost 242 Japanese yen in 1982—16 more than it could buy only two years earlier.

Several market conditions can have a significant impact on the value of a nation's currency: changes in net exports (as we saw in the example with Exhibit 12-6), the rate of inflation relative to the rate in other nations, and the domestic interest rate relative to the rate in other nations. We will discuss the last two causes in more detail.

Inflation Rate Differentials If the inflation rate in the United States is higher than in Japan, prices in the United States will rise relative to

Exhibit 12-7 Foreign exchange rates

Currency	Units of Foreign Currency per Dollar	
	1980	1982
Austria—schilling	12.94	17.0
Canada—dollar	1.17	1.24
Denmark—krone	5.63	8.53
Federal Republic of Germany—deutsche mark	1.81	2.42
France—franc	4.22	6.85
Italy—lira	856.20	1398.74
Japan—yen	226.63	241.94
Mexico—peso	22.97	147.35
Netherlands—guilder	1.99	2.67
Portugal—escudo	50.08	92.68
Switzerland—franc	1.68	2.06
United Kingdom—pound	0.43	0.62

SOURCE: *Federal Reserve Bulletin*, January 1983.

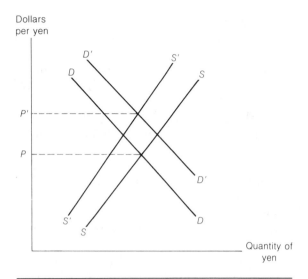

Exhibit 12-8 The effect of inflation on foreign exchange rates

Increasing inflation in the United States can cause Americans to demand more yen to buy Japanese goods (shifting the demand curve from DD to D′D′) while the Japanese buy fewer U.S. goods, reducing the supply of yen from SS to S′S′. The yen appreciates from P to P′.

Japanese prices. These rising prices make U.S. products more expensive relative to Japanese goods, causing (1) Americans to buy more products from Japan, thereby shifting outward the demand for Japanese yen, and (2) Japanese to buy fewer of the now more expensive U.S. goods, lowering the supply of yen in the foreign exchange market. The dollar depreciates while the yen appreciates. The impact of inflation rate differentials is shown in Exhibit 12-8.

Interest Rate Differentials When the real interest rate (the money interest rate adjusted for inflation) is higher in one country than in another, investors will put their loanable funds

in the country with the higher risk-adjusted rate of return. For example, an increase in the real interest rate in France might attract U.S. capital. Since investments would be made in francs, there would be an upward shift in the demand for francs, causing the franc to appreciate. If real interest rates in France fall below those in the United States, loanable funds will move to America, causing the franc to depreciate while the dollar appreciates.

The Evolution of Flexible Exchange Rates

In 1944 at Bretton Woods, New Hampshire, the United Nations Monetary and Financial Conference discussed ways to avoid the difficulties that had previously plagued international economic relations. To provide an institutional framework for the solution of international trade problems, the International Monetary Fund was created. For more than two decades after World War II, the international monetary system was based on some form of fixed exchange rates, in which each country established the price of its currency. As with any price-fixing scheme, if a nation set its currency price too high, the foreign sector would be in constant disequilibrium until the nation "devalued" its currency—that is, lowered the fixed price. Problems of dealing with disequilibria in the foreign sector led to the adoption of flexible exchange rates that restore equilibrium through the price mechanism. Governments nevertheless occasionally intervene in the foreign exchange market. For example, they might purchase large amounts of their own currency to prevent an excessive short-term decline in the value of their currency, leading some observers to describe the current system as one that has "managed" flexible exchange rates.

BARRIERS TO FREE TRADE

Numerous wars throughout history are testimony to the fact that nations do not always act in a way that will maximize national, much less international, economic well-being. Nationalism is an important force in the world. Questions of international policy as debated in most nations focus on national self-interest: Which policies will serve the nation best? Nations seldom consider the adverse effects of their policies on residents of other countries.

Migration of labor between nations illustrates how political reality raises questions about the classical theory of free trade. This doctrine shows that the free movement of all resources in response to productivity differentials will maximize world output. It does not suggest that every nation will benefit. Free migration of people would probably result in a vast migration of labor to the United States, where wages are high. Given the demand for labor, this increase in supply would lower wages in the United States, whereas they would increase in other parts of the world.

American workers clearly are not interested in increasing worldwide efficiency if it implies a loss of material well-being for themselves. Indeed, the idea that a nation can benefit by restricting trade in this and other ways has made the doctrine of free trade very tenuous. Delicate international negotiations are usually required to facilitate freer international trade. The classical prescription of free markets operating without interference from government is an elusive ideal because it overlooks conflicts of interest among nations.

There are two basic ways a nation tries to protect its industry from international economic competition: (1) tariffs and (2) quotas and other forms of regulation.

Nontariff Trade Barriers

France was headed for a $15 billion trade deficit in 1982, causing the French government to impose a series of stiff "administrative" measures designed to cut imports. These measures are examples of trade restraints that are neither tariffs nor quotas. One decree required Japanese videotape recorders to be cleared through customs at Poitiers rather than Le Havre. Because Poitiers is a very small customs point, the move made the machines costlier and delayed their entry. Against Japanese cars the French used complicated customs procedures that were eased once the Japanese "voluntarily" limited their auto exports to France.

Tariffs

A tax on imported items is called a *tariff*. A tariff may be *specific*, that is, a tax on each unit of the commodity, or *ad valorem*, based on the value of the commodity. The United States has imposed tariffs continuously since 1820. A so-called Tariff of Abominations in 1828 levied duties of over 65 percent of the value of imported goods. This rate was almost reached again during the Great Depression after the passage of the Smoot-Hawley Tariff Act in 1930. Since World War II, there has been a consistent trend toward easing tariffs, but they are not likely to be eliminated completely. Recession always generates support for trade restrictions. The arguments advocating tariffs are presented in the next section.

Quotas and Other Trade Restrictions

Whereas tariffs raise the price of imports, import *quotas* limit the amount of a commodity that may be brought into the country. Other barriers to free trade are regulations that specify special requirements for packaging, shipping, and financing, as well as complex or bureaucratic customs procedures.

THE CASE FOR RESTRICTING INTERNATIONAL TRADE

Tariffs and quotas are being used by all nations. Despite the theory of comparative advantage and gains from trade, each nation has reasons to restrain free trade. The case for restraint is always couched in terms of national self-interest. In some cases the national interest may well be served by restraint of free trade; more often, tariffs and quotas are imposed to benefit certain politically powerful groups at the cost of the rest of the population.

Arguments for restraint of trade revolve around three major issues: (1) protecting infant industry, (2) providing for national self-sufficiency, and (3) supporting high wages and employment.

Protecting Infant Industry

An industry is viewed as "infant" when it cannot survive established foreign competition. The infant must be protected until it matures, that is, until it develops economies of scale and sufficient technological know-how. This argument is particularly appropriate in less developed countries, which are most likely to have infant industries. The first secretary of the Treasury in the United States, Alexander Hamilton, proposed the nation's first tariff on just these grounds in his 1791 *Report on Manufactures.*

As the infant matures, the tariff or quota protection is presumably reduced, the trade restraint being held to be a temporary measure. But the

Trade restrictions can be a major political issue for persons who believe that their jobs are threatened by the importation of various goods. (*Photo by Gilles Peress, Magnum Photos, Inc.*)

industry often becomes accustomed to a protected position; reducing the tariff becomes politically difficult. The nation is then saddled with an infant industry; domestic consumers must pay higher prices instead of buying cheaper foreign substitutes. In essence, the tariff remains a hidden subsidy.

Providing for National Self-Sufficiency

National defense considerations cause some people to argue that the United States should be self-sufficient in all industries that are vital in times of war. This argument is weak. In a highly interdependent economy it is almost impossible to distinguish between vital and nonvital industrial capacity. Most industries can be modified to produce items of military significance, and the advantage of having the industrial capacity to fight long conventional wars seems modest in an era of atomic weapons.

Tariff protection for national-security purposes also has disadvantages. Protected industries have less incentive to remain efficient, and inefficiency hardly contributes to national security. Tariffs may also foster the use of scarce resources in peacetime, making us more dependent on foreign suppliers in the long run. Tariff protection is at best an uncertain tool in maintaining national security.

Supporting High Wages and Employment

Wages are higher in the United States than in most other countries, leading many businessmen and labor leaders to argue that tariffs and quotas are required to protect the American worker's standard of living. Cheaper labor abroad gives foreign nations a competitive advantage, they argue; higher-cost U.S. industries thus suffer reduced demand, with unemployment the result.

THE FALLACIES AND APPEAL OF PROTECTIONIST ARGUMENTS

There are a number of fallacies in the arguments of the protectionists. For one, it is obvious that high wages can be sustained by factors other than tariffs or quotas—greater productivity, for example. A laborer in the United States may earn 10 times more than a worker elsewhere, but may be 10 times more productive due to additional capital (tools and machines) to work with. (While this would give the United States

a comparative advantage in capital-intensive production, a low-wage nation would be likely to have a comparative advantage in labor-intensive production—production that requires more labor than capital.) In this regard, it might also be argued that tariffs to protect high wages can lead to inefficiency, higher costs, and inflation, which hurt the general population and undermine the ability to compete internationally. The only beneficiaries are likely to be the workers in the protected industry; tariff protection is then a disguised subsidy to that group. If these workers are deserving of financial relief, the redistribution of income should be made directly and not disguised as a tariff.

Another argument against protectionism is that establishing tariff barriers almost always results in retaliation, with similar barriers raised by trading partners. A tariff reduces a nation's imports; retaliation lowers its exports. The result is diminished international trade, higher prices, and lower output.

Despite the problems associated with limitations of free trade, a long history of trade restraint suggests that its appeal remains strong. Given the fallacies of protectionism, how can we explain its continuing appeal? The answer lies in the way benefits and costs of trade restrictions are distributed among the population.

Let's assume that rising automobile imports from West Germany, Japan, Italy, and Great Britain cause rising unemployment among U.S. automobile workers. As a consequence, auto manufacturers and their suppliers mount a campaign in the U.S. Congress to protect the industry from foreign competition, probably using the third argument for protection: maintaining domestic wages and employment. A tariff on auto imports will clearly hurt auto purchasers who may prefer foreign cars for reasons of price, gas economy, style, or performance.

Frederic Bastiat:
Petition of the Candlemakers (1845)

In this satire Bastiat mocks the arguments for protection accepted by the French government when it protected French manufacturing interests from foreign competition. The candlemakers want the government to eliminate competition from the sun.

To the Honorable Members of the Chamber of Deputies:

We are subjected to the intolerable competition of a foreign rival, who enjoys, it would seem, such superior facilities for the production of light that he is enabled to inundate our national market at so exceedingly reduced a price that, the moment he makes his appearance, he draws off all custom for us; and thus an important branch of French industry, with all its innumerable ramifications, is suddenly reduced to a state of complete stagnation. This rival is no other than the sun.

Our petition is that it would please your honorable body to pass a law whereby shall be directed the shutting up of all windows, dormers, skylights, shutters, curtains—in a word, all openings, holes, chinks, and fissures through which the light of the sun is used to penetrate into our dwellings, to the prejudice of the profitable manufactures that we flatter ourselves we have been enabled to bestow upon the country; which country cannot, therefore, without ingratitude, leave us now to struggle unprotected through so unequal a contest.

We foresee your objections, gentlemen; but there is not one that you can oppose to us which you will not be obliged to gather from the works of the partisans of free trade. We dare challenge you to pronounce one word against our petition, which is not equally opposed to your own practice and the principle that guides your policy.

Do you tell us that if we gain by this protection, France will not gain because the consumer must pay the price of it?

We answer you: You have no longer any right to cite the interest of the consumer. For whenever this has been found to compete with that of the producer, you have invariably sacrificed the first. You have done this to encourage labor, to increase the demand for labor. The same reason should now induce you to act in the same manner.

You have yourselves already answered the objection. When you were told, "The consumer is interested in the free introduction of iron, coal, corn, wheat, cloths, etc.," your answer was, "Yes, but the producer is interested in their exclusion." Thus, also, if the consumer is interested in the admission of light, we, the producers, pray for its interdiction.

Reduced competition after a tariff or quota will probably result in a higher price for domestic automobiles. As shown in Exhibit 12-9, the higher price is the result of a shift in the supply curve from S_1S_1 to S_2S_2 because fewer foreign automobiles can be sold. Each year millions of people will be made somewhat worse off financially. But the tariff may benefit a relatively small group of people—those engaged in auto production—to a significant degree. Workers will enjoy increased employment and perhaps gain higher wages. Profits of the manufacturers may be enhanced, because of fewer competitive pressures. Obviously, both auto unions and producers will lobby in Congress for passage of a tariff. The car buyers each suffer only modest costs from the tariff, although in aggregate their losses may far outweigh the advantages to the auto

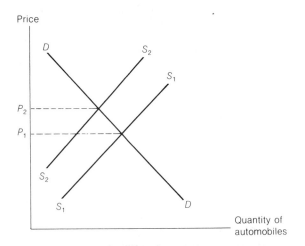

Exhibit 12-9   The effects of a tariff or quota on an industry

A tariff or quota against foreign automakers will shift the supply curve from S_1S_1 to S_2S_2. The rise in price will hurt many consumers slightly, while the makers of automobiles reap substantial benefits.

industry. Consumers are not well-organized politically and will have correspondingly less incentive to advocate free trade in automobiles.

This explains the appeal of tariffs: *While free trade may maximize national economic well-being, restrictions on trade can benefit small groups within an economy.* When these groups are politically powerful, arguments for free trade and the general well-being are cast aside. The allocative efficiency of the harmonious free-trade model can be undermined by the conflicts inherent in the domestic distribution of income.

SUMMARY

1. The volume of international trade as a proportion of GNP varies greatly among developed countries. The United States has a relatively small foreign sector, accounting for 8 percent of GNP. International trade is nevertheless very important because many crucial production inputs are imported and many industries rely on export sales.

2. The principle of comparative advantage shows that if nations specialize in what they produce relatively more cheaply than other nations, all nations can be better off.

3. Foreign trade is complicated by the fact that nations use different currencies. In foreign exchange markets it is possible to convert one currency to another. The exchange rate is the price of one currency in terms of another.

4. Exchange rates are determined by the supply and demand for each nation's currency. Among the important factors affecting a nation's exchange rate are its relative inflation rate and interest rates compared to those of other countries.

5. Despite the case for free trade, the appeal of protectionism remains strong. Tariffs and quotas are the principal weapons used to protect workers and industries from "unfair" foreign competition. Such trade restrictions are often hidden subsidies to the protected group, paid for by consumers in the same country.

KEY CONCEPTS

absolute advantage	freely floating exchange rates
comparative advantage	tariffs
terms of trade	quotas
constant returns to scale	appreciation
decreasing returns to scale	depreciation
foreign exchange	exchange rate

QUESTIONS FOR DISCUSSION

1. Free movement of factors of production and commodities among nations results in a maximization of world output. As a citizen of a developed nation, would you vote for a resolution that bound all nations to this principle? Would you feel the same as a citizen of a less developed nation?

2. If you were on the Council of Economic Advisors, under what circumstances would you propose a quota or tariff?

3. It is sometimes alleged that the U.S. Congress is more prone to impose trade restrictions than the executive branch of government. Can you explain why this might be true? In formulating your answer, consider both the beneficiaries of trade restrictions and the functions of the president.

4. If the United States were exporting more than it imported, the price of the dollar would rise, provided the exchange rate was freely floating. How would this rise correct the disequilibrium and what would the effects be? If you were a member of Congress from an area with many export industries, how would you feel about floating exchange rates under these circumstances?

Part III
MICROECONOMICS

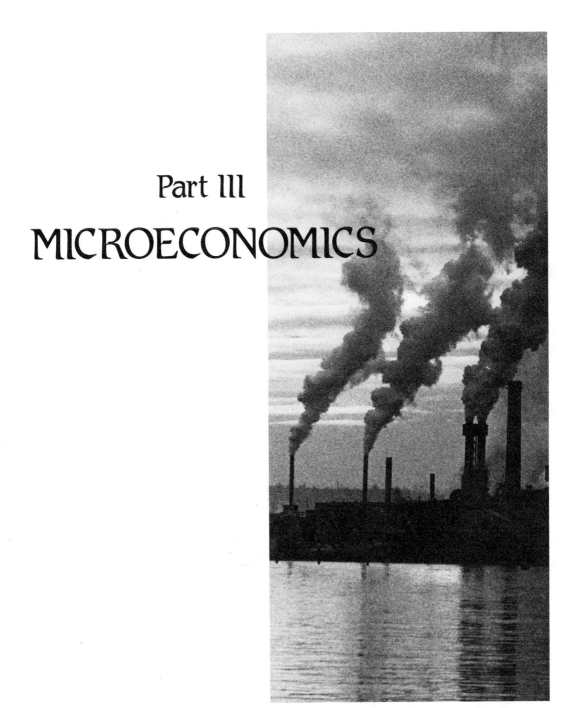

Chapter 13

Demand: The Theory of Consumer Choice

In Chapter 2 we briefly discussed the interaction of demand and supply and the role of price. The purpose of that chapter was to present an overview of the market mechanism. Now, in Part III, we will analyze in detail the components of the market: demand, supply, and market equilibria. In this chapter we look at the demand side of the market. To emphasize that demand is the process of determining which items a consumer will purchase, we have sub-titled this chapter "The Theory of Consumer Choice."

MICROECONOMICS AS A THEORY OF CHOICE

In Western societies, life's necessities plus some comforts are considered a prerequisite for the good life. We say "prerequisite" because although material goods and services are important, most people don't believe that they are the only ingredient in happiness. A minimum level of material well-being is necessary but not all there is to individual satisfaction. Except for the one recorded case of manna falling from heaven, society has had to work and use natural resources to provide for its material needs. Because resources are neither unlimited nor free, any society must allocate them in an efficient way if its citizens are to enjoy a high standard of living.

In this section we study what many econo-mists regard as the center of their discipline—microeconomics, the study of the economic behavior of small economic units. One way to view microeconomics is as a theory of choice. A modern society has literally millions of pos-sible ways to utilize its resources. Each deci-sion-making unit constantly faces choices. The aggregate of these individual choices deter-mines the amount and composition of national output. For example, many of the same mate-rials are used to produce such dissimilar goods as tires, basketballs, rubber bands, and tennis shoes. How many of each should be produced? What should the price be? What combination of machinery and labor should be devoted to produce each good?

Similarly, as a consumer you face numerous daily choices, beginning with what you eat for breakfast. Microeconomics is used in analyzing the system of signals that begins with con-sumer choices and extends back through the production system. The theory of choice is used in all areas of economics.

Marginal Analysis

Economists evaluate alternative courses of action open to individuals, business firms, and governments by considering what will happen if a small change is made in an existing situa-tion. For any problem, the effect of a small change in the initial situation is evaluated: if the ben-efits of a change exceed the costs (i.e., if the change represents a net improvement), the change is made. The process continues until no change will improve the position of the deci-sion maker. Because the changes are measured incrementally, in small steps, the process is called *marginal analysis.*

An example of marginal analysis can be seen in the decision-making process of a small busi-ness firm. A manufacturer of magazine racks, for instance, has to decide how many magazine racks to produce—the optimum level of pro-duction—and the technology to be used. The firm evaluates the effects of small changes in production on profits. For example, an increase in output may require an addition to the plant. If the additional cost is greater than the revenue from the extra output, the firm does not increase production. In this case, the analysis is made to determine how to maximize profits.

Marginal analysis is used to analyze a wide variety of economic problems in many situa-tions. It must be noted that some economists criticize the theory since it works on the basis of an initial situation accepted as a given (for instance, that the production of magazine racks is necessary—the question is only how to pro-duce them). A revolutionary economist would

In determining its optimum level of production, a firm uses marginal analysis—evaluating the effects of small changes in production on profits. *(Photo by Terry Zabala)*

say that the current economic situation needs to be drastically changed, not accepted as the best system to promote individual and collective welfare. But even in the radical's ideal state, marginal analysis is useful in deciding how resources will be allocated. For instance, in an ideal state, some authority must decide whether the existing public transportation is adequate. The initial situation is accepted—that public transportation is desirable. The question is whether society would benefit by having more or less transportation. This is the sort of prob-

lem that the economist's theory of choice is designed to solve.

Marginal analysis cannot operate without a set of social values that determine the magnitude of the costs and the benefits of alternative courses of action. Microeconomics, as a theory of choice, sheds no light on the morality or ethics of outcomes. It does, however, *reflect* the value system of the society, because the relative costs and benefits can be measured only in terms of the values of individual units in the society. Microeconomic tools can be used to facilitate the efficiency of those societies that cultivate humanistic values as well as those that hold them in contempt. It represents the epitome of economic science—the positive economics that we discussed in Chapter 1.

Consumer Choice: The Concept of Utility

As consumers we have an intuitive knowledge about demand. In order to answer certain questions about consumer choice, however, it is helpful to discuss the nature of demand in a more rigorous manner. We will describe a model of the processes by which consumers allocate their purchases among various types of goods.

Economists use the term *utility* to describe the ability of a good to satisfy. Utility is subjective and cannot be measured directly; it depends upon individual taste. But individuals can make comparisons of the satisfaction that various goods bring them. As we consume additional units of a particular good, we get less and less enjoyment (utility) from each successive unit. The phenomenon of diminishing satisfaction from successive units of a good has been experienced by everyone. Food is an excellent example. The first bite of a large steak is delicious; the last bite is usually not so appealing. The first cookie tastes great; the twentieth is not so great. We refer to the total satisfaction of all units of a good purchased as *total utility*—for instance, the total utility of 20 cookies. *Marginal utility* (*MU*) is the utility gained from an additional unit of a good—for instance, one extra cookie. In the cookie example, the twentieth cookie has a smaller marginal utility than the first cookie, but the total utility of 20 cookies is larger than the total utility of one cookie.

Economists call the tendency of succeeding units to yield decreasing satisfaction the *law of diminishing marginal utility*, as illustrated in

Exhibit 13-1 Hypothetical utility schedule

Hamburgers		Lines of Bowling	
Unit	Marginal Utility (in utils)	Unit	Marginal Utility (in utils)
1	20	1	11
2	18	2	8
3	16	3	6
4	10	4	4
5	5	5	2
6	1	6	0
7	0		

Exhibit 13-1. (We have coined an imaginary unit, called a *util*, to represent the quantity of satisfaction an individual subjectively gains from additional amounts of a good.) The exhibit shows two goods whose schedule of marginal utility is consistent with our experience. If these were the only two goods available, how would consumers decide which combination of the two goods to consume? Most individuals do not have the ability to purchase an unlimited quantity of all goods, because they have only a limited amount of funds. We will call this a *budget constraint*. How would a consumer maximize utility—get the most for the money spent?

Start with a situation where a hamburger and a line of bowling each cost $1 and our consumer, Mr. Jones, has $4 to spend. How would he allocate the $4 between the two goods? The allocation process might begin when he spends the first dollar to buy the first hamburger because that purchase yields the highest marginal utility (enjoyment). The second dollar would be spent on a second hamburger, because its marginal utility is still greater than the marginal utility associated with the first line of bowling. His third dollar is spent on a third hamburger—again because of its higher marginal utility. However, if he were to spend his fourth dollar on yet another hamburger, he would get only 10 utils, whereas he could get 11 utils from a

Exhibit 13-2   Hypothetical marginal utility

| | Hamburgers ($1 each) | | | Lines of Bowling ($.50 each) | |
Unit	MU (in utils)	MU/Price (in utils per $1)	Unit	MU (in utils)	MU/Price (in utils per $1)
1	20	20	1	11	22
2	18	18	2	8	16
3	16	16	3	6	12
4	10	10	4	4	8
5	5	5	5	2	4
6	1	1	6	0	0
7	0	0			

purchase of the first line of bowling. Thus with a $4 budget constraint, he would purchase three hamburgers and one line of bowling. His total utility from the $4 expenditure would be 65 utils.

Suppose Mr. Jones' budget constraint is increased to $8. With the additional $4, he would choose a fourth hamburger, a second and third line of bowling, and a fifth hamburger. With hamburgers and bowling priced at $1 each and an $8 budget constraint, Mr. Jones would buy five hamburgers and three lines of bowling and have 94 utils of enjoyment from his purchases. Any other combination of hamburgers and bowling would have provided him with less total utility.

From this example we see that the consumer is said to be in equilibrium when he or she has purchased a set of goods that yields maximum utility. Given a budget constraint, there is no way to rearrange the purchases to yield a higher level of total satisfaction.

As a general rule, *to maximize total utility, arrange your purchases so that the marginal utility of the last good divided by its price is equal for all goods.* In our two-product case, the rule is

$$\frac{\text{MU of Product A}}{\text{Price of A}} = \frac{\text{MU of Product B}}{\text{Price of B}}$$

The applicability of this rule can be shown by lowering the price of a line of bowling to 50 cents. Thus, the utility schedule for lines of bowling must be revised to reflect the additional utils gained per dollar spent (marginal utility/price), as shown in Exhibit 13-2. With a $4 budget constraint, Mr. Jones would compare the marginal utility per unit of hamburgers and bowling to decide how much of each to buy. Because the first line of bowling now provides more utils per dollar spent than the first hamburger, he buys a line of bowling. The second line of bowling, however, provides fewer utils per dollar spent than the first hamburger, and so he buys the first hamburger.

Choices among potential purchases can be made in this fashion until neither good is preferred to the other—that is, until the marginal utils per dollar of all goods are equal. In our example, the second line of bowling and the third hamburger each provide 16 utils per dollar spent. Four lines of bowling and two hamburgers would also consume $4. However, the marginal utility per dollar of the third line of bowling would be only 12 utils, whereas a third hamburger would provide 16 utils per dollar spent. Hence, Mr. Jones would prefer to buy a third hamburger and forgo the third and fourth lines of bowling. Buying three hamburgers and two lines of bowling provides a total of 73 utils

Exhibit 13-3 Buying pattern for achieving consumer equilibrium

Good	Cost	MU (in utils)	MU/Price (in utils per $1)
Bowling line 1	$ .50	11	22
Hamburger 1	1.00	20	20
Hamburger 2	1.00	18	18
Bowling line 2	.50	8	16
Hamburger 3	1.00	16	16
	$4.00	73	

(see Exhibit 13-3), whereas buying four lines of bowling and two hamburgers provides only 67 utils. There is no method of allocating $4 that will yield a higher level of satisfaction than the pattern described.

We can now generalize about the condition for *consumer equilibrium*: It requires that the marginal utility per dollar spent for all purchases be the same.

$$\frac{\text{MU of Product A}}{\text{Price of A}} = \frac{\text{MU of Product B}}{\text{Price of B}}$$
$$= \frac{\text{MU of Product C}}{\text{Price of C}}$$
$$= \cdots \text{ for all goods}$$

At this point, you might be wondering whether this describes the way people really behave. Actually it is a formal statement of common sense. Of course, you don't buy all the goods; you buy only those that give the greatest satisfaction. Ask yourself how you allocate your limited funds over the whole range of potential spending patterns. The general equilibrium rule is also consistent with the increase in quantity demanded caused by a reduction in price, because lowering price increases the marginal utility/price ratio of a good. The formulation shown above is a reasonable description of the behavior of most consumers.

THE NATURE OF DEMAND

The law of demand given in Chapter 2 stated that as the price of a good increases, the quantity purchased decreases. A typical demand curve is shown in Exhibit 13-4. In this figure when the price is increased from P_a to P_b, the quantity demanded drops from Q_a to Q_b. The downward-sloping demand curve reflects the law of diminishing marginal utility. Since marginal utility falls, we will buy additional units only if the price falls. Obviously, the size of the change will vary from good to good. For example, consumption of cigarettes is reduced by a small percentage even when the price of cigarettes increases by a large percentage. On the other hand, a small percentage increase in the price of certain other commodities is sufficient to

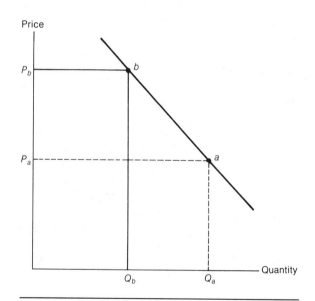

Exhibit 13-4 A typical demand curve

When price is increased from P_a to P_b quantity demanded is reduced from Q_a to Q_b.

cause a large percentage decrease in the quantity purchased. A 5 percent increase in the cost of manufactured logs to burn in fireplaces may cause a 10 percent decrease in purchases; people may instead buy cut wood or even chop their own.

Demand for necessities is price inelastic, whereas a rise in the price of luxuries will decrease the quantity demanded. *(Photo by Terry Zabala)*

Economists have developed the concept of *price elasticity* to describe the response in the quantity demanded of a good to a change in the price of that good. When the change in the price of a good does not cause a proportional change in quantity demanded, we say that the demand is relatively inelastic. This term allows us to rephrase the statement about cigarettes made in the preceding paragraph. Now we can say that the demand for cigarettes is relatively price inelastic. Similarly, when the quantity demanded is sensitive to price change, the good can be described as having elastic demand in that price range.

MEASURING ELASTICITY

The degree of elasticity is measured by the elasticity coefficient, E_d, which is determined by the following formula:

$$E_d = \frac{\text{Percentage change in the quantity demanded}}{\text{Percentage change in price}}$$

Suppose the price of cigarettes went up by 10 percent and this caused a decline in consumption of 5 percent. Then we would say that

$$E_d = \frac{-5\%}{10\%} = -0.5$$

The negative sign in the numerator (-5%) indicates a decrease in quantity.

The use of the elasticity coefficient allows us to state in precise terms the responsiveness of quantity to price. Now we can say that cigarettes have an elasticity of demand of -0.5. This means that a 1 percent change in price results in a less than 1 percent change in the quantity demanded: cigarette demand is relatively inelastic. Any elasticity less than 1 is considered to be inelastic. Our original general statement about the price sensitivity of cigarette consumption was correct. However, with the elasticity formula we can now quantify that relationship.

We know from the law of demand that a price increase is *always* associated with a quantity decrease. Therefore, the negative sign, which always exists in the price elasticity calculation, simply represents this demand relationship. Because it does not add any information about price sensitivity, we discard it. Hence, elasticities will be reported as 1, 7, or 0.3 instead of -1, -7, and -0.3.

The elasticity formula may seem unduly complex; but the complexity results from using percentage change instead of the change itself. Percentages are necessary, beause otherwise we would have to use a number scale that is essentially arbitrary. For example, if a $1 increase in the price of eggs caused a 12-egg decrease in demand, it would appear that a small change in price, 1 unit, caused a 12-unit change in quantity. But this could also have been put another way. We could have said that a 100-unit increase (100 pennies) causes a 1-unit decrease (a dozen eggs). Now an apparently large increase (100 units) decreased demand by only 1 unit. Thus the percentage form is used in describing elasticity. The elasticity formula can be restated as

$$E_d = \frac{\%\Delta Q}{\%\Delta P} = \frac{\Delta Q/Q}{\Delta P/P}$$

where Δ signifies a change. Here is an application of this formula.

When cigarettes are 50 cents per pack, increasing the price by 5 cents means a 5/50 or .10 (10 percent) change in price. Suppose this change in price (P) is associated with a decrease in quantity sold, from 100,000 cartons per day to 98,000 cartons. This means a change of $-2000/100,000$ or a $-.02$ change in quantity.

$$E_d = \frac{-2000/100,000}{5/50} = \frac{-.02}{.10} = -0.2$$

In this formula, the percentage change in price is greater than the percent change in the quantity of goods purchased (.10 is larger than .02). This means that consumers' purchases are affected very little by price. Demand that is insensitive to changes in price is referred to as *inelastic demand.* Inelastic demand is defined by an elasticity of less than 1 (in this case, it was 0.2).

Let's take another example, where demand *does* decrease significantly with an increase in price. If a 1 percent increase in price brings about a 4 percent decrease in quantity purchased, elasticity is 4 (4%/1%). *Elastic demand* is defined as an elasticity of more than 1. Elasticity of exactly 1 is called *unitary elasticity* (the percentage of increase in price equals the percentage of decrease in goods purchased).

Demand curves with different elasticities are shown in Exhibit 13-5. All the constant-elasticity demand schedules appear as curves. A straight-line demand, such as Exhibit 13-4, has different elasticities at different points. Exhibit 13-6 illustrates this phenomenon.

An exercise involving actual calculations with a straight-line demand is presented (see box) so that you can calculate those relationships.

By now, you should have an intuitive feel for the importance of elasticity. Elasticity of demand is a concept that has many important applications.

Revenue and Elasticity

One application of the concept of elasticity is its relationship to total revenue (TR). Total revenue of a firm in a market is simply the total quantity of goods sold multiplied by the price. This is expressed as

$$TR = PQ$$

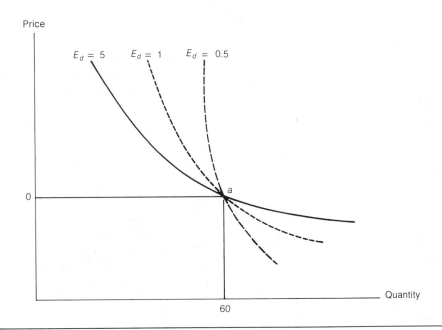

Exhibit 13-5 Demand curves with different elasticities

The same elasticity with various price and quantity combinations creates a demand curve that is not a straight line.

Suppose that when P is $1, Q is 1000. Then TR = $1000. In the special case of unitary elasticity $(E_d = 1)$, a 1 percent increase in price would be associated with a 1 percent decrease in the quantity demanded. In our example, at the new price of $1.01 and quantity 990, TR = PQ = $999.90, which we round off to $1000. Unitary elasticity means there is no change in revenue associated with a price change.

Suppose we consider a segment of the demand curve where demand is inelastic, for example $E_d = \frac{1}{10}$ or 0.1. What would be the revenue effect of a price change? Starting with P = $1 and Q = 1000, an elasticity of $\frac{1}{10}$ or 0.1, means that a 1 percent increase in price would cause a 0.1 percent decrease in quantity. Total revenue increases: the new TR is $1.01 times 999, or

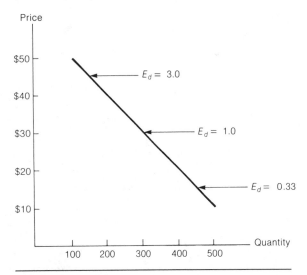

Exhibit 13-6 Elasticities along a straight-line demand curve

Shown above are a straight-line demand curve and elasticities at various points along the demand curve. Although at first the changing elasticities might seem surprising, after working with the elasticity concept the logic of the changes will be clear.

$1009. Demand is inelastic. The $9 additional revenue is the result of consumers' not changing their purchases very much when the price increased.

A similar example with elastic demand illustrates that total revenue can also decrease when price is raised. Assume $E_d = 5$ and

$$\text{old } P = \$1.00$$
$$\text{new } P = \$1.01 \text{ (1 percent increase)}$$
$$\text{old } Q = 1000$$
$$\text{new } Q = 950 \text{ (5 percent decrease)}$$
$$\text{old TR} = (1000 \times \$1.00) = \$1000.00$$
$$\text{new TR} = (950 \times \$1.01) = \$959.50$$

Thus, the total revenue effect of a price change is directly related to the demand elasticities involved.

We can summarize the effect of various elasticities upon total revenue for a price *increase*.

$E_d = 1$ (unit elastic)	TR = no change
$E_d > 1$ (elastic)	TR = decrease
$E_d < 1$ (inelastic)	TR = increase

Can you make a similar summary for price decreases?

It must be emphasized that when economists say demand is inelastic, they do not mean that the quantity of goods purchased does not respond to price. They mean simply that the change in demand is less than proportional to the change in price. The extreme case of inelasticity occurs when there is no change whatever in demand after a change in price. This situation is referred to as *perfectly inelastic demand*. It is shown in Exhibit 13-7a.

There are a few cases where perfectly inelastic demand exists, but they are not significant. An example sometimes used is the demand for insulin by a diabetic: small price increases cause no decrease in demand for this life-sustaining substance. Except for such life-supporting products, it is difficult to imagine products that do not have some sensitivity to price changes.

The other extreme case is that of *perfectly elastic demand*. This is the case where a small

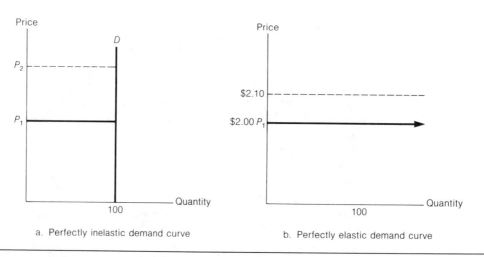

a. Perfectly inelastic demand curve　　　　b. Perfectly elastic demand curve

Exhibit 13-7　Perfectly inelastic and perfectly elastic demand curves

With the perfectly inelastic demand curve, a change in price has no effect upon quantity demanded. With the　　*perfectly elastic demand curve, a small change in price brings about a large change in quantity demanded.*

change in price reduces demand to nothing. Assume the market price of wheat in Chicago is $2 a bushel. At that price farmers can sell all the wheat they can grow. But if one farmer raises the price to $2.10 when everyone else is selling at $2, his sales would be reduced to zero. Exhibit 13-7b is an illustration of the perfectly elastic demand faced by the wheat farmer.

The elasticity of demand for a good is important for businesses and for government policymakers. Suppose a government policy objective is to reduce the consumption of gasoline. If demand for gasoline is very elastic ($E_d > 4$), then a small price increase (e.g., 1 percent) would decrease the quantity demanded by a much larger amount (more than 4 percent). In addition, total revenue to gasoline retailers would decline. On the other hand, if our gasoline demand is highly inelastic ($E_d = 0.2$), then a 1 percent increase in the price per gallon would cause a very small decrease in gasoline consumption, and retailers' total revenue would increase.

Determinants of Elasticity

What determines the elasticity of a good? Several factors are important:

1. *The number of readily available substitutes.* Most decisions by consumers involve alternatives, or choices. Taken as a whole, the demand for food is inelastic. But the decision facing a household is not between food and no food—it is between one type of food and another. The person shopping for a protein source chooses from among beef, pork, beans, chicken, wheat, fish, nuts, and so forth. If the relative price of beef gets too high, the consumer will buy less beef and choose something else instead. The availability of substitutes is an important determinant of the elasticity of demand for a good. Demand for any good is more elastic when there are many good substitutes available.

Does a Dime Make a Difference?

Calls for directory assistance are a problem to phone companies. Most telephone operations have been mechanized to keep labor costs down, but we have not found a substitute for operators who look up telephone numbers. Meanwhile, calls to directory assistance have been doubling every 10 years. In 1980 the costs of directory assistance were estimated to be over $950 million. In order to halt the growth of this labor-intensive activity, companies have spent large amounts on advertising and other techniques to encourage people to look up phone numbers, but their efforts have shown little success. Of course, at least part of the problem stems from the fact that the cost of directory assistance has always been included in the user's fixed monthly charge, and so telephone users correctly perceived that the cost of these calls to them personally was zero.

Recently, in a few areas, the phone companies received permission to charge for information calls. In other jurisdictions the conventional wisdom of politicians and regulators was that the small amount requested (10–20 cents per call) wouldn't make any difference in the use of the directory assistance, and so the charge was not approved. The results of the tests from various areas show a remarkably similar picture. The demand curve for directory assistance does slope downward when a charge is assessed. By charging 10–20 cents for each call beyond a specified number (like six), the volume of calls was reduced by 40 to 60 percent. In Florida a charge of 15 cents per directory assistance call reduced the number by 71 percent.

---

2. *The importance of the item in the total budget.* Goods that account for a small part of the budget can increase in price, and the consumer will still purchase them. For example, if the price of salt were to double, it would not have a large impact upon a household

budget. On the other hand, if the price of automobiles were to double, it would have a profound effect. In general, the smaller the price of a good relative to an individual budget, the more inelastic it is.

3. *The degree of relative necessity associated with the good.* For a person who has to commute to work, transportation expenses would probably be considered a necessity. There-fore, demand for local transportation, at least in the short run, would be more inelastic than, for instance, demand for a European vacation. In general, demand for necessities is more inelastic than demand for luxury goods. (Of course, individuals differ in what they perceive as necessities.)

4. *Role of time.* The adjustment to higher prices often takes time. For example, after the rapid

In the long run, many Americans have adapted to higher gasoline prices by buying small cars that get very good gas mileage. *(Photo by Terry Zabala)*

increase in gasoline prices during 1973–74, a suburban resident without public transit available had few ways to decrease gasoline consumption. Sunday drives might be eliminated, but there might still be a long commute in a big four-door sedan. In the longer run, however, the car could be replaced by one that gets better mileage. Other adjustments could be made if higher gasoline prices continued. For example, a family might move closer to work or to public transportation. Thus, although the demand for gasoline is relatively inelastic in the short run, it becomes more elastic in the long run, as people find other ways to respond to price changes.

Calculating Elasticities

The estimate of elasticities is important in many lines of activity. Exhibit 13-8 gives elasticity estimates for various goods. Are the elasticities estimated there consistent with your intuitive evaluations? Do they seem reasonable? In the next section, we shall discuss how empirical estimates are made.

Midpoint Calculation

A minor problem not yet covered is how one calculates elasticity between two points, one before the price change and one afterward. A numerical example illustrates the problem.

Point	Q	P
a	4000	$5.00
b	6000	$4.00

As you remember, E_d is $\%\Delta Q/\%\Delta P$. However, do we calculate percent of change in quantity using the increase from 4000 to 6000 or the decrease from 6000 to 4000? At first glance we

Exhibit 13-8 Elasticities of various goods and services

Good	Estimated Price Elasticity
Food items	
Cabbage	0.4
White potatoes	0.3
Sweet potatoes	0.8
Green peas, fresh	2.8
Green peas, canned	1.6
Fresh tomatoes	4.6
Durable goods	
Jewelry and watches	0.4
Radio and TV	1.2
Kitchen appliances	0.6
Nondurable goods	
Shoes	0.4
Newspaper	0.1
Services	
Physician services	0.6
Legal services	0.5
Airline travel, short run	0.06
Airline travel, long run	2.4
Foreign travel, short run	0.7
Foreign travel, long run	4.0
Housing	1.0

SOURCE: H.S. Houthakker and Lester D. Taylor, *Consumer Demand in the United States, 1929–70* (Cambridge, Mass.: Harvard University Press, 1970).

might say that it makes little difference—but it does. An increase of quantity from 4000 to 6000 is a percentage change of 2000/4000 or 50 percent. But a decrease from 6000 to 4000 is a percentage change of 2000/6000 or 33 percent. This gives the surprising result that an elasticity viewed as a percentage change going from *a* to *b* is $E_{a \to b} = 50\%/20\% = 2.5$, but viewed the other way as a change from *b* to *a* it is $E_{b \to a} = 33\%/25\% = 1.3$.

The problem is just a quirk of arithmetic due to a change of the base for the calculations. To avoid confusion, economists use a midpoint calculation formula. They take the average price

Elasticity Changes along a Straight-Line Demand Curve

At a price of $6 each, 10 art prints are sold. If the price is lowered to $4, sales rise to 30 prints. The change in quantity is 20 prints and the change in price is $2. The average price over this range is $5—($6 + $4)/2. The average quantity is 20—(10 + 30)/2.

Therefore, the elasticity of demand for prints at a price of $6 is

$$\frac{\dfrac{(10-30)}{20}}{\dfrac{2}{5}} = \frac{\dfrac{20}{20}}{\dfrac{2}{5}} = \frac{20}{20} \times \frac{5}{2} = \frac{100}{40} = 2.5$$

Suppose the price of prints is originally $3 and goes up to $4. Then the elasticity of demand is

Example of elasticity calculations

Quantity of Art Prints Demanded	Price of Art Prints
60	$1
50	$2
40	$3
30	$4
20	$5
10	$6

$$\frac{\dfrac{40-30}{35}}{\dfrac{3-4}{3.50}} = \frac{\dfrac{10}{35}}{\dfrac{1.00}{3.50}} = \frac{10}{35} \times \frac{3.5}{1.0} = \frac{35}{35} = 1.0$$

At this point on the demand curve we have unitary elasticity.

Finally, what happens if the price rises from $1 to $3? Calculate the elasticity of demand for this price range.

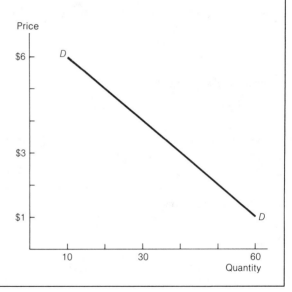

and quantity as the base. The elasticity formula is thus modified to read:

$$E_d = \frac{\dfrac{\Delta Q}{(Q_1 + Q_2)/2}}{\dfrac{\Delta P}{(P_1 + P_2)/2}}$$

In our previous example, the calculation would be

$$E_d = \frac{\dfrac{2000}{(4000 + 6000)/2}}{\dfrac{1}{(4 + 5)/2}} = \frac{\dfrac{2000}{5000}}{\dfrac{1}{4.5}}$$

$$= \frac{0.4}{.22} = 1.8$$

Note that this midpoint calculation falls between $E_{a \to b}$ of 2.5 and $E_{b \to a}$ of 1.3.

OTHER ELASTICITY CONCEPTS

So far we have concentrated on movements along the demand curve. In this section we will discuss factors that cause the entire demand curve to shift. A demand schedule reflects the assumption that other things do not change. When they do, the demand curve often shifts. Obviously, many factors, such as new products or tastes, could shift a demand curve. Two particular factors, however, are so clearly subject to change that we have incorporated terms to describe their impact on demand curves. These factors are personal income and the prices of related products.

Income Elasticity

An increase in income is usually accompanied by an increase in consumption. The increased consumption can take the form of buying more of an item already consumed (e.g., more travel), buying an item never previously purchased (e.g., a swimming pool), or actually reducing the amount of a good that was routinely purchased before in favor of something else (e.g., buying more rice and fewer potatoes). Economists have developed the term *income elasticity* to state this relationship precisely. Income elasticity is usually abbreviated as E_y where Y refers to income.

$$E_y = \frac{\%\Delta Q}{\%\Delta Y}$$

Suppose an individual receives a 10 percent increase in wages and, as a result, purchases 20 percent more steaks. We could then say that the income elasticity of demand for steaks is $E_y = 20\%/10\% = 2$.

A little reflection will show that whenever the elasticity is greater than 1, the percentage of the good consumed changed more than the percentage change in income. On the other hand, an elasticity of less than 1 indicates that the percentage of the good consumed changed less than the percentage of income. $E_y = 1$ indicates a directly proportional rise. These concepts of income elasticity are summarized:

$$
\begin{array}{ll}
E_y = 1 & \text{unit elastic} \\
E_y > 1 & \text{income elastic} \\
E_y < 1 & \text{income inelastic}
\end{array}
$$

To repeat: there is nothing magic about these terms, but they do serve as a shorthand way of describing the sensitivity of goods to changes in income.

This is another concept of value to government policymakers. Suppose the administration wishes to increase demand for durable goods in order to stimulate employment in these industries. One method is to cut personal taxes, increasing disposable income. If the demand for durable goods has a high income elasticity, a small tax decrease will yield a more than proportional increase in the quantity of cars, refrigerators, and other durable goods sold. On the other hand, if the demand is income inelastic, such a policy would not be effective.

Prices of Other Goods

As explained in Chapter 2, the demand for some goods is related to the demand for other goods. For example, if the price of Chevrolets were to rise but the price of Fords did not, we would expect to see more Fords sold—since, for most people, Fords are close *substitutes* for Chevrolets. In economic terms, the demand curve for Fords would shift to the right if the price of a substitute were increased and to the left if its substitute's price were lowered.

Similarly, the demand for some goods is related to the demand for goods associated with them, as *complements*. For example, the use of an automobile is associated with the use of gasoline and tires. Strawberries and shortcake, hot dogs and hot dog buns, baseball gloves and baseballs, refrigerators and electricity are complements. When the price of one complement increases, we would expect the demand for the other one to shift left (decrease). For example, if the price of strawberries were to go up, we would expect the demand for shortcakes to decrease.

As you have probably anticipated, there is a quantitative measure of this relationship called the *cross elasticity of demand*. Without going into the actual problem of calculation we can define cross elasticity as $\%\Delta Q_A/\%\Delta P_B$. Note that if the price of B rises and if A and B are complements, we would expect the sign of the cross elasticity (XE) to be negative. On the other hand, if A and B are substitutes, we would expect a rise in the price of B to cause an increase in the Q_A demanded; the sign is positive. In cross-elasticity calculations we do not discard the sign, because now it gives us additional information about the two goods. What would be the cross elasticity of two goods that are not related—say a hammer and ice cream? In the case of no relationship, XE would be 0. Thus we have the following relationships:

$$\text{XE}_{AB} = 0 \qquad \text{no relationship}$$
$$\text{XE}_{AB} = +\text{ sign} \qquad \text{substitutes}$$
$$\text{XE}_{AB} = -\text{ sign} \qquad \text{complements}$$

One problem students have with elasticity is that they approach it as a mechanical device. Remember to think of it instead as a shorthand way of describing consumer sensitivity in the demand relationship and not as an end in itself.

SUMMARY

1. Elasticity is a measure of the responsiveness of demand to a change in the price of a good. Price elasticity is defined as $E = \%\Delta Q/\%\Delta P$. The elasticity for a good is classified as elastic, unit elastic, or inelastic.

2. The effect of a price change upon total revenue is related to the elasticity of demand for the good. If price is increased for a good in the elastic portion of its demand curve, total revenue will decrease. But if demand is inelastic, total revenue will increase. If demand is unit elastic, a price change will not affect revenue.

3. Elasticity is affected by such factors as (1) the number of readily available substitutes, (2) the importance of the item in the total budget, (3) the degree of necessity of the good, and (4) the time period under consideration.

4. Elasticity calculations should use a midpoint formulation to avoid the arithmetic problem associated with the importance of the base in determining percentage changes.

5. Demand curves can shift when factors such as consumers' incomes, tastes, and the prices of other goods change.

6. Income elasticity is a measure of the responsiveness of demand to changes in income. Cross elasticity of demand is a measure of the responsiveness of the demand for good A to a change in the price of good B.

KEY CONCEPTS

price elasticity	income elasticity
inelastic demand	substitute good
elastic demand	complementary good
unitary elasticity	cross elasticity of demand
midpoint calculation	

QUESTIONS FOR DISCUSSION

1. Explain why price elasticity changes along a straight-line demand curve.
2. What will be the effect upon total revenue if you raise prices with elastic demand? Raise prices with inelastic demand? Lower prices with elastic demand? Lower prices with perfectly inelastic demand? Raise prices with unitary demand? Lower prices with unitary demand?
3. Suppose tuition at your universty were to increase 10 percent. What would the short-run response be? The long-run response? What kind of adjustments might be made?
4. When you eat dinner at a restaurant, how do you decide what to order? Does price enter into your determination?
5. If your income were to double, would you double your consumption of all goods proportionately? If not, which items would be the most income inelastic? Which would be the most income elastic?

Chapter 14

Supply: The Theory of Production and Costs

In Chapter 2 we demonstrated that the interaction of demand and supply in a market determines the price of a product. We are interested in the price of a product because price is the tool used to allocate goods and resources in a market system. If we are to understand how resources are allocated, we need to have a better understanding of the factors that shape and position the supply curve, just as we needed to understand the determinants of demand in Chapter 13.

The most important factor determining the nature and position of a supply curve is the cost of producing the good. At an intuitive level we know that a car that costs $2000 to produce will not be sold for $1000 for very long. In this chapter and the following one, the relationship among the cost curves of an individual firm, the cost curves of a total industry, and the supply curve for the industry are explored. In this chapter we will discuss (1) the nature of costs, (2) the role of diminishing returns in production, and (3) the various types of costs that must be considered. Chapter 15 develops a theory of supply.

THE NATURE OF COSTS

Terms like *cost* and *profit* pose a continual problem in effective communication between economists and other people. Concepts such as elasticity and utility are easily learned, because people seldom have a preconceived notion about their meaning. On the other hand, people use the terms *cost* and *profit* in everyday conversation. However, in economics these concepts are quite different from the popular meaning, with a more narrow and precise definition.

Let us start with the economist's definition of cost and show how it differs from that of accountants or engineers. For the economist, *cost is what one gives up in order to do something or acquire something.* The sacrifice may be tangible or intangible; it may be money, goods, time, security, or whatever. Economists do not consider only out-of-pocket expenses.

Let us illustrate the economist's definition of cost by comparing it to the accounting and engineering definitions.

Explicit (or Accounting) Costs

The most easily identifiable costs are those that involve a direct expenditure—for example, rent for an office, wages, or raw material costs. These types of expenditures have been called either explicit costs, accounting costs, or engineering costs because they can be readily identified and used in accounts. Everyone would agree that such explicit expenditures are properly classified as part of the costs of producing a good.

Economic (or Opportunity) Costs

Economists would argue that, in addition to the explicit costs, other costs exist that are less readily identifiable. These costs consist of what one gives up to get something. For example, a farmer who owns and operates a farm includes in explicit costs the taxes on the farm, maintenance of equipment, and salaries of his help. But the potential rent forgone by not renting the farmland to someone else is not included. The cost of the land is the cost of lost rental opportunity. This type of nonexplicit cost is another form of *opportunity cost.*

Owner-operators often have many costs that are opportunity rather than explicit costs. Take the case of retail-store operators who own the buildings that house their stores, finance the inventory themselves, and manage the stores. By using the buildings they are giving up the opportunity to rent them to someone else; by financing the inventory they give up the opportunity to draw interest, as they might if their

Among the opportunity costs facing an owner-operator are lost rent, lost interest, and lost wages. *(Photo by Terry Zabala)*

funds were in a savings account; by managing the store they yield the opportunity to work for a salary from an employer. In such a case, their accounting costs, or out-of-pocket expenditures, would be dramatically smaller than their total costs, which include opportunity costs (lost rent, lost interest, and lost wages).

Many costs people face are actually opportunity costs and economists include these in any measure of total cost. College students have explicit accounting costs associated with attending college, which include tuition, books, transportation, and supplies. But their accounting costs may be exceeded by the opportunity costs of wages lost by not being employed full-time elsewhere. These forgone wages usually increase as we go up the education ladder. For a college freshman, the usual alternative employment—opportunity cost—is a job traditionally held by a high-school graduate. But for a medical doctor considering a lengthy residency in surgery, each year's opportunity cost will be very large—since he or she could practice medicine in a field with a shorter residency.

THE NATURE OF PROFIT

The concept of profit is also confusing because of its multiple definitions. Accountants usually compute profits as revenue minus accounting costs. But if we define profit as revenue minus economic costs, the remainder will often be much lower than accounting profit.

Wages are the payment to labor, and rent is the payment to land. But what is the payment to the people who combine the factors of production, like labor and land, and take risks? These people, entrepreneurs, require some payment. If they own and operate businesses, they have opportunity costs for their input. These opportunity costs are called *normal profit*—the amount of profit required to keep the entrepreneurs in a particular line of business.

After all economic costs, including normal profit, have been subtracted, the remainder is called *excess profit*.

Excess profit = Revenue − Economic costs (both accounting costs and opportunity costs, including normal profit)

Obviously, these concepts are not used in everyday language. The store-owner/manager who owns the building and works 60 hours a week may believe he is earning a profit. An economist might find, however, that the store-keeper is not counting opportunity costs. By renting the building and working at another job, the owner might earn a higher income. This difference in the use of terms can cause confusion. In this book we will use the terms normal profit or excess profit to distinguish between the two.

THE NATURE OF THE FIRM AND THE PRODUCTION FUNCTION

The Firm

A firm is an institution that combines the factors of production (land, labor, capital, and entrepreneurship) to produce output that ful-fills a need of society. The theory of the firm is based on the simple assumption that firms attempt to maximize profit.

The Production Function

A set of possible inputs and outputs (called a *production function*) is illustrated as a hypothetical example in Exhibit 14-1. Column 1 in this exhibit represents the quantity of variable input used, and column 2 is the total product. For instance, a farmer applies a certain quantity of fertilizer, the variable input, to the land, which is the fixed input, to produce a certain number of bushels of corn, the *total product*. In this function, we could say that 1 unit of fertilizer yields 4 bushels of corn; 2 units of fertilizer yield 10 bushels of corn; and so forth. In column 3 we see the average yield per unit of fertilizer (column 2 divided by column 1), the *average product*. Given that all other inputs are fixed, adding a second unit of fertilizer raises the average product from 4 to 5. Column 4, *marginal product*, represents the change in total product (bushels of corn) caused by the change in the variable input (number of units of fertilizer). For instance, when we move from 1 unit of fertilizer to 2, there is a difference of 6 bushels of corn produced (10 − 4). The 6 bushels of corn over 1 unit of fertilizer equal 6/1—a marginal product of 6. When we add a third bushel of fertilizer, production increases by 8 bushels of corn, so the marginal product of the third unit is 8.

To make the relationship between total product, average product, and marginal product clearer, the data from Exhibit 14-1 is shown in graph form in Exhibit 14-2. The total product curve can be divided into three parts: I, a range showing total product increasing rapidly; II, a range showing total product with less rapid increase; and III, a range showing total product decreasing. Changes in total product are associated with changes in average and marginal

Exhibit 14-1   Hypothetical production function (schedule)

(1) Units of Variable Input	(2) Total Product (TP)	(3) Average Product (col. 2 ÷ col. 1)		(4) Marginal Product $\left(\dfrac{\text{Change in total product}}{\text{Change in amount of variable input}}\right)$
0	0	—	>	
1	4	4.0	>	4
2	10	5.0	>	6
3	18	6.0	>	8
4	25	6.2	>	7
5	29	5.8	>	4
6	31	5.2	>	2
7	32	4.6	>	1
8	30	3.8	>	−2
9	26	2.9		−4

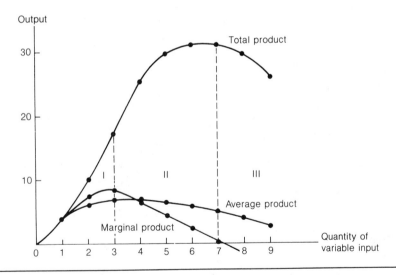

Exhibit 14-2   Hypothetical production function

The data from Exhibit 14-1 is plotted above. The total product curve can be divided into three parts: I, a range where total product increases rapidly; II, a range of less rapid increase; and III, a range where total product decreases. These changes in total product are associated with points on the marginal product curve. These relationships are also seen on the average product curve. As long as the marginal product is greater than the average product (lies above it on the graph), average product increases; but when marginal product is less than average product, average product decreases. In stage I marginal product is increasing, in II it is declining, and in III it is negative.

product. We can see that as long as the marginal product is greater than average product (lies above it on the graph), average product increases, but when marginal product is less than average product, average product decreases. In stage I, marginal product is increasing, in II it is declining, and in III it is negative.

Let's take another example of a production function, a machine shop. In the machine shop, labor is the variable input. An initial increase in the number of workers yields increasing marginal products because people can specialize and perform their tasks more efficiently. After a certain number of workers are added, however, specialization reaches maximum advantage. Further increases in the number of workers only cause coordination and scheduling problems. This illustrates the *law of diminishing marginal returns*, which was intuitively introduced when we discussed the law of supply in Chapter 2. This law says that the amount of additional output obtained from each additional unit of input eventually begins to decrease, because the proportion of fixed factors relative to variable factors becomes too small for efficient production. This is not to say that the additional workers are less efficient than the earlier ones, but that the changed mix of inputs—fixed and variable—is not as efficient a mix as the earlier one.

SHORT-RUN COSTS AND THE PRODUCTION FUNCTION

So far we have discussed production in terms of physical units. The question producers face is how cost and the production function are related. This relationship is easiest to see over the short run. The *short run* refers to the time period when certain inputs are fixed and others are variable. For example, owners of a machine shop can produce additional output in the short run by hiring additional labor and adding more

shifts, but they cannot build another shop in the short run.

Let us show in a general way how costs are related to productivity in the short run. Exhibit 14-3 provides a numerical example of diminishing returns and labor costs. Columns 1, 2, and 3 are from Exhibit 14-1 and are used to illustrate a production function in the context of a machine shop in which the variable unit is labor. Column 4 represents average labor productivity (the average product of labor). Assuming that each worker is paid $10 per day, we can arrive at a total labor cost, column 5, by multiplying the number of workers by their daily wage. Since we know the total product per day and the total labor cost for a day, we can determine the amount of labor cost per unit associated with various numbers of workers. For example, with only one worker, the labor cost per unit of production is $2.50. But if we have four workers and increase their efficiency by allowing them to specialize in what they do best, the labor cost per unit of output drops to $1.60. As we continue to add workers, holding the other factors fixed, we exhaust the advantage of specialization and run into diminishing returns: with eight workers, labor costs have again risen to $2.66 per unit of production.

As we continue to increase inputs by one factor, the marginal productivity of the factor will eventually decrease and unit cost of production will rise. This technological relationship, diminishing returns, underlies the cost curve you will be using in the next section.

Cost Schedules

In the short run, some costs of production do not vary with the level of output. In the machine shop, certain expenses do not change, whatever the amount of output. For example, property taxes, interest on the loan to buy the machinery, cost of the five-year lease, and the salary of

Exhibit 14-3 Diminishing marginal returns and labor costs

(1)	(2)	(3)	(4)	(5)	(6)
			Average Labor		Labor Costs per
		Marginal	Productivity	Total Labor Costs	Unit of Output
Unit of Labor	Total Product	Product	(col. 2 ÷ col. 1)	(col. 1 × $10)	(col. 5 ÷ col. 2)
0	0			$ 0	
		> 4			
1	4		4.0	10	$2.50
		> 6			
2	10		5.0	20	2.00
		> 8			
3	18		6.0	30	1.67
		> 7			
4	25		6.2	40	1.60
		> 4			
5	29		5.8	50	1.72
		> 2			
6	31		5.2	60	1.93
		> 1			
7	32		4.6	70	2.18
		> −2			
8	30		3.8	80	2.66
		> −4			
9	26		2.9	90	3.46

the manager who has a two-year contract remain the same. If the machine shop stopped production, these expenses would continue; they are called *fixed costs*. Some inputs, however, do vary with the level of output—e.g., labor hired by the day. If the shop shut down, these *variable costs* would cease. At *any* level of production, the *total cost* (TC) of operation includes the total fixed cost (TFC) plus the total variable cost (TVC) associated with various levels of output.

Exhibit 14-4 shows a schedule of costs associated with each level of output. Note that there

Exhibit 14-4 Short-run cost structure of a firm

(1) Quantity of Output	(2) Total Fixed Cost	(3) Total Variable Cost	(4) Total Cost	(5) Average Fixed Cost (col. 2 ÷ col. 1)	(6) Average Variable Cost (col. 3 ÷ col. 1)	(7) Average Total Cost (col. 4 ÷ col. 1)	(8) Marginal Cost (Δ col. 4)
0	$100	$ 0	$100				
							> 50
1	100	50	150	$100.00	$50.00	$150.00	
							> 30
2	100	80	180	50.00	40.00	90.00	
							> 25
3	100	105	205	33.33	35.00	68.33	
							> 23
4	100	128	228	25.00	32.00	57.00	
							> 22
5	100	150	250	20.00	30.00	50.00	
							> 24
6	100	174	274	16.67	29.00	45.67	
							> 36
7	100	210	310	14.30	30.00	44.30	
							> 54
8	100	264	364	12.50	33.00	45.50	
							> 69
9	100	333	433	11.11	37.00	48.11	

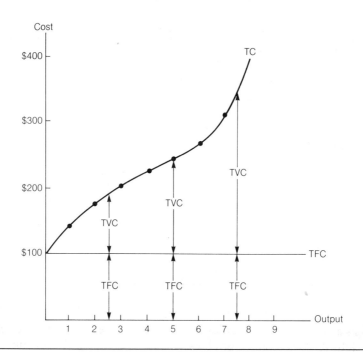

Exhibit 14-5   Hypothetical total short-run costs

At any level of production, total cost can be divided
into the total fixed cost (TFC) and total variable cost

(TVC). Notice that total fixed cost does not change
with the level of production.

is a fixed cost even at 0 output, which remains
the same at each level. This includes the lease
and all long-run contracts. The total variable
cost (TVC) includes raw materials and labor,
which vary with the amount produced. Note
that at 0 output, TVC is 0 and that it increases
with the level of output. The total cost (TC) is
the sum of TFC and TVC.

Exhibit 14-5 shows total fixed costs, total variable costs, and total cost. It shows in graph
form how the total cost at any level of production consists of the fixed and variable
components.

Average and Marginal Costs

Another important type of cost is the average,
or per-unit, cost. Certain relationships that are
important to the firm are made clearer when
using average and marginal costs.

Average Fixed Cost (AFC) In our example fixed
cost is $100. Thus if the firm produces 1 unit,
the average fixed cost of that unit is $100/1, or
$100. But when it produces 2 units, the total
fixed cost is spread over 2 units. Average fixed
cost for each of 2 units is $100/2 or $50. The

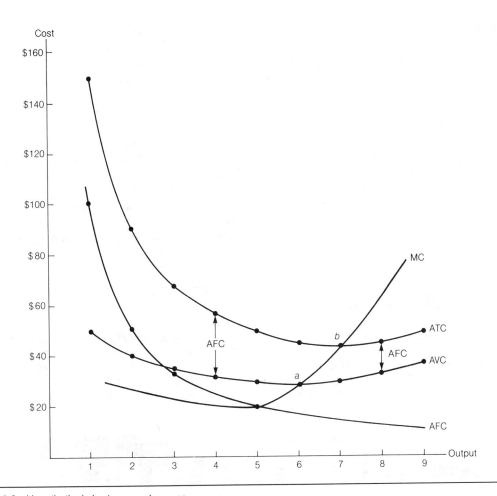

Exhibit 14-6 Hypothetical short-run cost curves

This figure shows the various average-cost curves as well as the marginal-cost curve, all derived from Exhibit 14-4. The shape and position of the latter curve demonstrate the influence of the law of

diminishing marginal returns. Point a is the minimum point of the AVC curve. Point b is the minimum point on the ATC curve and is the technically efficient point for the firm to produce.

more units produced, the smaller the amount of fixed costs per unit. This relationship is shown in Exhibit 14-6 and labeled AFC. It can also be seen as the distance between ATC and AVC, since ATC − AVC = AFC.

Average Variable Cost (AVC) As the level of output is increased, more inputs like labor, raw material, and electricity are required. However, there is no requirement that the cost increase be at a constant rate. In fact, the law of diminishing returns and the production function imply that the average-variable-cost curve should vary. Exhibit 14-6 shows this relationship between average variable cost and the quantity produced.

Average Total Cost (ATC) Average total cost can be determined by either of two methods: by dividing total cost by the quantity produced (ATC = TC/quantity produced) or by adding average variable cost and average fixed cost (ATC = AVC + AFC). The diagram demonstrates the latter method as well as showing ATC calculated from Exhibit 14-4.

Marginal Cost (MC) One other cost curve must be described—marginal cost, the additional cost of producing an additional unit of output. It is the change in total cost divided by the change in output (MC = ΔTC/Δoutput). Since total fixed cost does not change with the level of output, marginal cost reflects the change in the variable cost associated with the increase in output. As you will remember, the average-variable-cost curve reflects the eventual effect of diminishing returns. The marginal-cost curve must eventually increase as additional variable inputs become successively less productive. Its typical shape is shown in Exhibit 14-6 also.

Costs of Operating an Automobile

Given below are average costs for operating a four-year-old auto in 1982. Can you separate the components into average fixed costs (AFC) and average variable costs (AVC)? If someone borrowed your car and paid for the gasoline used, how much would you have "lost" by letting the person use the car?

Are you including AFC as part of your losses? If someone offered to reimburse you for running errands with your four-year-old Volkswagen, how much would you charge? How long is the short run when making cost decisions with a four-year-old car?

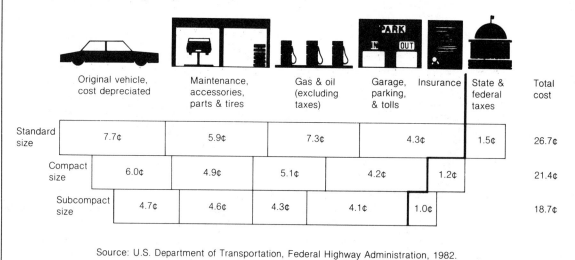

	Original vehicle, cost depreciated	Maintenance, accessories, parts & tires	Gas & oil (excluding taxes)	Garage, parking, & tolls	Insurance	State & federal taxes	Total cost
Standard size	7.7¢	5.9¢	7.3¢	4.3¢		1.5¢	26.7¢
Compact size	6.0¢	4.9¢	5.1¢	4.2¢		1.2¢	21.4¢
Subcompact size	4.7¢	4.6¢	4.3¢	4.1¢	1.0¢		18.7¢

Source: U.S. Department of Transportation, Federal Highway Administration, 1982.

Relationships between Total Costs and Marginal Costs

The stage is now set to point out some geometric relationships that reflect important economic functional relationships. Careful study of Exhibit 14-6 indicates that the marginal-cost curve passes through the average-total-cost and average-variable-cost curves at the minimum points *a* and *b*. This is no accident—it is a definitive relationship that has important implications for economic behavior of the firm. When the marginal-cost curve is above an average-cost curve, that average cost is rising; when the marginal-cost curve is below an average-cost curve, that average cost is declining. Where MC intersects an average-cost curve, either ATC or AVC, the average cost is as small as possible (and exactly equal to marginal cost). At this point average cost does not go up or down since the cost of the marginal unit is not changing it.

The reason for this relationship is not high-powered economics or even mathematics. It is true by definition. We can use student test scores to illustrate: If you have had five exams with an average score of 80 and you take an additional exam (marginal) and score 90, your average test score will rise. On the other hand, if your score on the marginal (additional) exam is 60, it will lower your average. When the marginal score is 80, your average does not change.

Application of Cost Curves to Firms' Decision Making

Minimum-Cost Point The point where MC intersects ATC from below is the minimum point on the ATC curve (point *b*) in Exhibit 14-6. This is a *technically efficient* point of operation for a firm in the short run (when fixed resources are already committed) because it is the lowest per-unit cost. It is sometimes referred to as the point of the least-cost combination of inputs.

Shutdown Point The minimum point on the average variable-cost curve for the firm (point *a*) is also significant. This point, where the marginal cost curve intersects from below, is called the *shutdown point*. Since variable cost inputs can be stopped at any point, the firm needs to know when it is best to shut down. The answer is that the firm should shut down when it cannot cover its out-of-pocket or variable expenses. In our example, minimum average variable cost is $29 per unit and the average fixed cost at that

The shutdown point for a firm should be when it can no longer cover its variable expenses. *(Photo by Peter Southwick, Stock, Boston)*

production level is $16.67 (Exhibit 14-4 output level 6). Although the firm needs $45.67 per unit to cover all its expenses in the short run, it will operate at any price above $29. The reasoning is that the fixed costs will go on whether the firm shuts down or not. If it continues selling at a price above the average variable cost, the firm will be cutting its losses. On the other hand, if the price received is less than variable expenses, every unit of product increases losses. The rule, in the short run, is that a producer will produce whenever the firm can obtain more than its average variable cost for each unit of product. A firm may continue to produce for a short period when it does not cover AVC if it hopes to do so in the near future and wishes to keep its labor force together and/or maintain its markets. However, this is only a temporary possibility.

An application of this shutdown point can be found in the following newspaper article.

Two Turkey Firms Kill Young Birds over Costs

ATLANTA—Officials at two large turkey hatcheries in the Southeast say they killed thousands of poults (baby turkeys) because the cost of raising them far outstrips what a farmer can get for them.

James E. Thaxton, president of Thaxton Turkeys, Inc., Watkinsville, Ga., says he recently disclosed in a telegram to the Secretary of Agriculture that the concern killed 30,000 poults in May.

Bruce Cuddy, vice president of Cuddy Farms, Inc., Marshville, N.C., says Cuddy slaughtered 200,000 poults so far this year and may kill that many more in the next three months.

"We don't like to do this," Mr. Cuddy says, "but we don't have a choice."

Mr. Cuddy explains that hatcheries simply hatch the turkeys for farmers to buy and raise. But with the cost of turkeys averaging 34 cents a pound and the farmer being able to sell them for 20 cents a pound or less, he adds, farmers have been increasingly reluctant to buy them.

LONG-RUN COSTS

We have seen that the difference between the short run and the long run is that in the short run some factors are fixed. In the long run, however, all resources are variable. If new capacity is needed, it can be built. Long-term leases expire and equipment wears out or can be sold. Therefore, in the long run there are no fixed costs. From the cost curves for a firm in the short run note that average total costs and average variable cost curves decreased and then increased. This characteristic shape of the cost curves was caused by diminishing returns.

Diminishing returns do not affect the shape of the long-run cost curve. Diminishing returns are caused by some factors remaining constant while others increase. In the short run plant size is fixed, so the addition of labor (variable input) to the fixed plant will eventually result in diminishing returns. However, in the long run there are no fixed factors. The underlying forces that shape the long-run cost curve differ from those of the short-run cost curve.

The Nature of Long-Run Costs

The nature of the long-run cost curve is most evident when a firm is planning to enter an industry. Through engineering studies the firm knows the cost curve associated with each of various plant sizes. These hypothetical short-run cost curves are plotted in Exhibit 14-7, where ATC_1 is the smallest possible plant and ATC_{10} is the largest. As one builds larger plants the per-unit cost is reduced at first. That is, the minimum cost for ATC_1 is higher than ATC_2, ATC_2 is higher than ATC_3, and so on. But after ATC_6 plant size, there are no additional savings to be realized. In fact, beyond ATC_6, costs per unit start to rise as plants get larger. In such a situation, the desired level of output for the firm

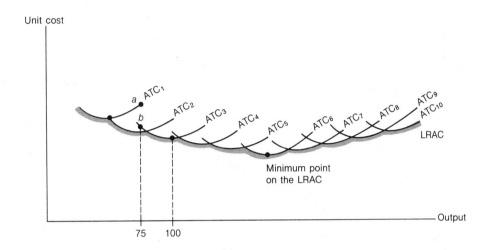

Exhibit 14-7   Hypothetical long-run cost curve with 10 plants of varying sizes

Sizes of plants that could be built range from ATC₁ (the smallest) to ATC₁₀ (the largest). Once a plant has been built, the ATC curve reflects the range of production. The least-cost segment of the short-run ATC curve describes

and comprises the lowest costs of all plant sizes. The least-cost segment forms the LRATC curve. This particular LRATC curve is lumpy because of the limited options shown.

determines the plant size that would minimize per-unit costs.

In our example, if desired output were 75 units per day, minimum cost would be attained by building plant size 2. Plant size 1 or 3 would have a high average cost at a 75-unit output (as shown by points *a* and *b*). However, if the desired capacity were 100 units, ATC₃ would yield the lowest per-unit costs. This illustrates an important characteristic of long-run costs. The long-run average-total-cost curve includes segments of the short-run average-total-cost curves that describe the lowest costs for all feasible size plants. The curve described in these points is the *long-run average-total-cost curve (LRATC)*, or, as it is sometimes called, the *planning curve*.

Exhibit 14-7 shows a situation with only a limited number of options on plant size. This might be true in some industries, but the more

likely situation is that it is possible to build almost any size plant. Then there would be a large number of possible plant sizes, and instead of a lumpy curve, as in Exhibit 14-7, we would get a smooth long-run average-total-cost curve. Exhibit 14-8 illustrates such a situation. Instead of segments of short-run ATC curves (SRATC curves), the LRATC curve now is made up of points of tangency for an infinite number of potential SRATC curves. This yields the smooth LRATC curve shown in Exhibit 14-8, which we will use in later discussions.

Economies and Diseconomies of Scale

We have shown the LRATC as decreasing and then increasing. This shape has important implications for much economic theory, as well

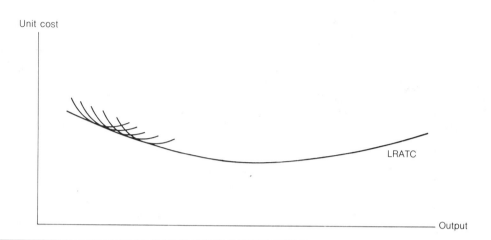

Exhibit 14-8   Long-run cost curve with many plants of varying sizes

This figure shows the smooth LRATC composed of the points of tangency of an infinite number of plant sizes.

as public policy. But we have not explained the reason for this shape. *It is important to note that the shape of the LRATC curve is not caused by the same forces that shape the SRATC curve.* The SRATC curve turns upward because of the law of diminishing returns. In the short run some factors, like capacity, are fixed, and eventually diminishing returns to these variable inputs will increase per-unit costs. But in the long run no resources are fixed, so diminishing returns from capacity limitations are not applicable. The shape of long-run cost curves is explained by the phenomenon economists call economies of large-scale production and diseconomies of large-scale production.

Economies of Scale   As plant size increases, there are methods and techniques that lower per-unit costs. Three important economies of scale are the following:

1. *Specialization in the use of factors.* As workers specialize in one task or machines are

built to accomplish one job, they often become more efficient. Instead of using a general tool, such as a hammer, for several operations, a machine in a large-scale operation can be designed to accomplish a specific task in a shorter time. This reduces time spent between jobs, makes training easier, and usually allows a producer to substitute labor-saving machines for expensive labor.

2. *Fuller utilization of indivisible factors.* Some operations require a factor that cannot be purchased on a divisible basis. For example, a remote plant might require a physician in the plant to treat injuries. Since it is difficult to purchase one-quarter or one-half of a physician, it may be necessary to hire one full-time, even if he is not fully utilized. Increasing the size of the plant makes it possible to use the indivisible factors better, thus lowering per-unit costs (until, of course, the firm gets so large that it will require another physician).

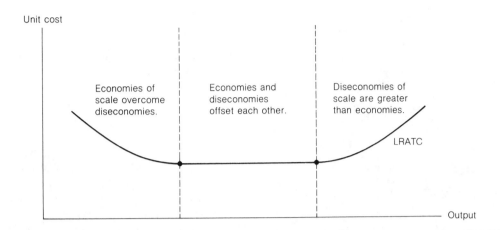

Exhibit 14-9 Hypothetical long-run average cost curve

The shape of the LRATC curve is determined by the phenomenon of economies of scale.

3. *Better utilization of by-products.* Many processes create by-products. For example, in large-scale gold refining, small quantities of silver are recovered. For a small producer, the silver is not worth recovering, but in large-scale operations it can become a valuable addition to revenue. Similarly, large-scale meat-processing plants can produce commercially valuable chemicals and fertilizers. Such recovery operations make costs per unit decrease with scale.

Diseconomies of Scale Although there are often some savings from producing more output, costs can also increase. These higher costs are called diseconomies of scale.

The major diseconomy of any organization is the increase in administrative costs associated with coordinating and controlling the organization. Most studies show that administrative costs increase with size, more than proportionately. Everyone has had experience with the inflexibility of large organizations. Operating procedures become standardized and managers become clerks who use the "book" to guide their decisions. Inflexibility and inefficiency go hand-in-hand. Anyone dealing with the post office or the army will probably understand this. Many of the largest corporations that have lost market share or lost large amounts of revenue have been described as inflexible and bureaucratic. Examples include A & P, Braniff Airlines, Swift, and Montgomery Ward.

For a limited range of output, the economies caused by expansion are greater than the diseconomies; but eventually as the firm grows beyond a certain size, the diseconomies outweigh any cost savings and the LRATC starts to rise. Exhibit 14-9 illustrates this phenomenon. Naturally, the point at which the LRATC curve begins to rise varies with technology. The lowest point on the LRATC is reached at a higher level of output in some industries than in others. In the automobile industry the output that represents minimum cost is at a higher level than in shoe manufacturing.

By developing robots to insert tiny parts into circuit boards for color television sets, this company cut its workforce from 2000 to 800. (Wide World Photos)

Cost and Production

Using both long- and short-run concepts, we have analyzed the factors that influence cost. Not surprisingly, both the amount a firm produces and the industry supply curve are influenced by cost structures.

In the following chapters we discuss how the shape of short- and long-run cost curves can influence pricing and output decisions of firms.

SUMMARY

1. Terms like *cost* and *profit* have specific meanings when used in economic analysis that are different from their meanings in general conversation. The major difference is that economic analysis includes opportunity costs.

2. The firm is an organization that combines the factors of production in order to produce a product that satisfies some need of society. How this activity is accomplished is described by the production function, which specifies the combination of inputs that yields a certain output.

3. With all inputs but one held constant, the relationship between total product and a variable input can be established. The usual pattern is that the first few units of variable input cause a marked increase in total product. As more units of the variable inputs are combined with the fixed factor, the marginal product per variable input declines. This decline is caused by the law of diminishing marginal returns.

4. The costs of production are related to the production function. As the average output associated with each input falls, the variable cost per unit of output must increase. This relationship is specified in the short-run cost function.

5. The factors that cannot be changed are called fixed costs because they do not vary with level of output. Variable inputs are variable costs because they do vary with output level. For the decision maker, the marginal cost of producing an additional unit is vitally important.

6. In the long run no costs are fixed. The significant cost consideration for a decision maker is the engineering- or planning-cost curves for potential plants of various sizes. These costs reflect economies and diseconomies of scale.

KEY CONCEPTS

explicit costs

accounting costs

normal profit

excess profit

production function

total product

average product

marginal product

law of diminishing marginal returns

short run

fixed costs

variable costs

total cost

average fixed cost

average variable cost

average total cost

marginal cost

minimum-cost point

shutdown point

long-run average-total-cost curve

economies of scale

diseconomies of scale

QUESTIONS FOR DISCUSSION

1. Would it be possible to have positive accounting profits and negative economic profits? What is the difference between these two types of profits?
2. What are the opportunity costs for a college freshman? A senior? A graduate student? A postdoctoral fellow? Are the opportunity costs of a history professor different from those of a medical school professor?
3. Develop a list of fixed or variable costs for a business. Would such items as salaries, insurance, and fuel be included in the list? Why is time important in preparing your list? How long would it take until there were no fixed costs?
4. Why does a firm's ATC curve always have a U shape?
5. Following is a schedule of workers and total output of a hypothetical firm, the David Manufacturing Corporation, a swimming-equipment producer.

Number of workers	Output of swim fins
1	50
2	110
3	160
4	200
5	230
6	250
7	260
8	265
9	270
10	268
11	265
12	255

From this schedule draw a total-product curve, average-product curve, and marginal-product curve. Is it possible for an input to have negative marginal productivity?

6. Suppose the David Manufacturing Corporation has the following costs schedule.

Number of swim fins produced per day	Total cost of production
0	$100
10	140
20	170
30	190
40	200
50	220
60	250
70	290

From this data draw the fixed-, variable-, and total-cost curves. Draw the marginal-cost curve on the same curves. Are these short-run or long-run cost curves?

7. Using a university as an example, what would happen if the size of the organization doubled? What would be the sources of economies of scale? What would be the sources of diseconomies? How do you measure the output?

Chapter 15

Supply in Perfect Competition

Chapter 2 presented an overview of the market using industry supply and demand curves. In this chapter we view the workings of the market from the standpoint of the individual firm, since it is the aggregate results of individual decisions by firms that form supply curves for an industry. We will show that under specific conditions, the unregulated decisions of private firms can lead to the best allocation of resources from a social point of view. We will also show that under more common conditions, the decisions of firms do not assure an optimum allocation of resources.

CHARACTERISTICS OF PERFECT COMPETITION

As a starting point we use an idealized version of the world called *perfect competition*. Perfect competition is the name given a market structure where (1) there is a large number of buyers and sellers, (2) there is a homogeneous product, (3) producers may enter or leave the market with relative ease, and (4) knowledge of price is readily available to all parties. These four conditions require further elaboration.

1. *Large number of buyers and sellers.* Originally, a market was a place to which commodities were brought for display and sale. In current usage, the term refers to the set of transactions among buyers and sellers of a given commodity. But in defining a large number of participants, the question is, how large is large? In this case *large* is not an absolute number like 20 or 500, but it has a functional definition. The number of participants required for a competitive market is large enough to assure that the action of any single buyer or seller has no significant impact upon the market. An example of a large number of suppliers can be found in the market for corn. If the largest grower of corn were to withhold corn from the market, its absence would not even be noted, nor would it affect the market price. In a perfectly competitive market the participants are "price takers":

There are so many firms that no one's presence or absence will affect the market price.

The other extreme can be found in the auto industry; if General Motors withheld cars from the market, chaos would result. A slight problem of definition is involved here. We commonly think of the auto companies as competing with one another. A more accurate description is that the auto companies are rivals who recognize a high degree of interdependence. Individual firms in this type of market affect price sufficiently so that they are called "price makers" rather than price takers. In a market with only a few producers, the conditions of perfect competition are clearly not present even though rivalry may exist.

2. *A homogeneous product.* In order to have a homogeneous product, potential buyers must perceive various goods as being identical or perfect substitutes. They need not be identical physically, but buyers must perceive them to be similar. Suppose all aspirin were identical chemically, but buyers were willing to pay more for Brand X than Brand Y. The price differential would imply that buyers *thought* there was a difference. Examples of homogeneous products would be major commodities like wheat, corn, and carrots, as well as many finished products like rolled steel, chemicals, and lumber.

3. *Ease of entry to, and exit from, the market.* The key here is whether obstacles exist that prevent entry to, or exit from, a market. Easy entry and exit require a high level of mobility of resources among alternative markets. Obstacles to mobility can take various forms—legal, technological, or economic. Legal barriers include licenses or patents. Technological barriers are such features as

trade secrets and the size of the operation. Lags in production, perceived risk, economies of scale, and a limited availability of crucial inputs are all included in economic barriers.

An example of an obstacle to market entry can be demonstrated by comparing corn production with production of oranges. When farmers perceive corn as more profitable than some other farm product, they can switch to corn in the following growing season, using the same equipment and land previously devoted to rye or wheat. A rise in the price of oranges might trigger a similar desire to enter orange production, but in addition to climatic restrictions there is a lag of five to seven years before an orange tree can reach maturity. In this case, the major barriers to entry are the time lag and climate. In an industry like manufacturing television sets, barriers to entry include large capital requirement, marketing organization, and patents.

4. *Knowledge of prices.* This requirement simply assures that buyers know if prices of one seller are lower than the prices of others. In a market where prices change rapidly, this means that price information must be disseminated quickly. For example, the New York Stock Exchange ticker tape fulfills this requirement in the stock market.

Stockbrokers must have access to the latest stock price information. *(Photo by Barbara Alper, Stock, Boston)*

Perfect Competition: Fact or Fiction?

Clearly, no industry meets all the requirements of perfect competition. Does that mean it is a useless theoretical fiction? The answer is emphatically no. There are two very good reasons for studying perfect competition: first, we gain insight into the workings of important industries that approximate perfect competition, such as textiles and lumber. Second, and more important, the results achieved under perfect competition can serve as the norm by which to judge other market results. Under certain assumptions, perfect competition yields the most efficient allocation of resources. It provides a yardstick to measure how far other markets vary from the optimum resource allocation. An analysis of a theoretical situation, perfect competition, provides a useful tool in studying other markets just as physicists' study of "perfect vacuums" enables them to make predictions about the real world based on this theoretical concept.

THE FIRM IN PERFECT COMPETITION

We have previously defined the firm as the institution where inputs are brought together to produce output. In order to describe how a firm makes decisions, it is necessary to analyze the motivations and the constraints upon its actions. These vary with the structure of the industry. In perfect competition, as noted earlier, a large number of firms compete for customers on the basis of price, service, maintenance, and other considerations. In order to simplify economic analysis, economists usually focus on the pricing aspects of competition. In perfect competition, individual firms can sell all they produce at the market price. This makes the firm's decision-making process relatively simple. The firm maximizes profits by choosing the optimum level of production without concern for whether all the goods can be sold.

Total Revenue/Total Cost Approach

How is this optimum level of production arrived at? Several methods can be used. One of the easiest conceptually is the total revenue/total cost approach. Exhibit 15-1 illustrates the process with a numerical example and a graph.

We know that profit (π) is equal to total revenue minus total cost. (In symbols, π = TR − TC.) Since the firm desires to maximize profits, it will choose to produce at that level of output where total revenue minus total cost is greatest. Total revenue is calculated by multiplying the price received by the number of units sold. At the price of $10, in Exhibit 15-1, the first unit yields a total revenue of $10, the second unit $20, and so on. The total cost is derived from the hypothetical cost curve. Total profit is found by subtracting total cost from total revenue. In the first unit produced, total cost is greater than total revenue (due to the large fixed costs). This yields a total profit that has a negative sign and should be interpreted as a loss. At the fourth unit, total cost equals total revenue, so there is zero profit, while the fifth to eighth units yield a profit. The entrepreneur can see that the greatest profit comes when the firm produces six units.

The graph in Exhibit 15-1 illustrates the same phenomenon. Because the firm is receiving the same revenue from each unit sold, the TR curve is a straight line. Each time another unit is sold, TR increases by the same amount—the price of the product. The total-cost curve starts above TR due to fixed costs that must be met even if no goods are produced. This means that losses are incurred in the production of units 1, 2, and 3. When TC crosses the TR line, the firm is breaking even. Points *a* and *b* are called *breakeven points*. Production of six units yields the greatest profit. A breakeven point is reached between the eighth and ninth unit, and at nine units losses are again incurred.

Let us review what we have just done. We have noted that a firm will attempt to maximize profits by producing at an optimum level—one that maximizes the difference between total revenue and total cost. By knowing the cost curves and the product's price, we have determined the level of production of the firm.

Exhibit 15-1   Total revenue/total cost approach to profit maximization

Unit	Price (P)	Quantity (Q)	Total Revenue (TR = (P × Q))	Total Cost (TC)	Total Profit (π = TR − TC)
1	$10	1	$10	$30	− $20
2	10	2	20	34	− 14
3	10	3	30	37	− 7
4	10	4	40	40	0
5	10	5	50	44	6
6	10	6	60	49	11
7	10	7	70	60	10
8	10	8	80	75	5
9	10	9	90	95	− 5

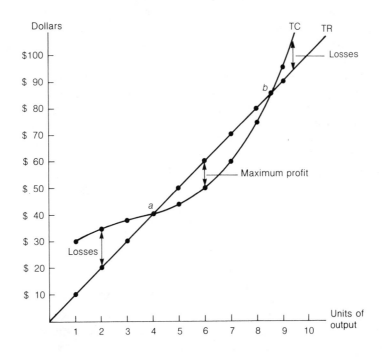

The table shown above illustrates the approach of a firm in perfect competition to profit maximization. Total revenue is derived by multiplying the price of the product times the quantity produced. The costs are determined by the technical aspects of the production function. Profit maximization is achieved after the sixth unit of production, where total profit is greatest. The graph derived from the table shows profit maximization at that point where there is the largest difference between TR and TC (the sixth unit).

Marginal Cost and Marginal Revenue

We can reach the same solution by use of marginal analysis. Exhibit 15-2 uses the same revenue and cost schedule as Exhibit 15-1. However, marginal-cost (MC) and marginal-revenue (MR) figures are derived from the total columns. At this point we will state a rule, which will be explained shortly. *Profit is at a maximum (or losses the smallest) at that level of output where marginal cost equals marginal revenue.*

Why does this rule hold? It follows from the definition of marginal costs and revenue. In our example, we know that for each unit sold we gain an additional $10. If we can produce that unit for $8, we would make a profit of $2 on the good. On the other hand, if it costs $14 to produce the good, there would be a loss of $4. If it costs $10 to produce and yields $10 in additional revenue, we are indifferent whether to produce or not. Whenever marginal cost is greater than marginal revenue, total cost is going up faster than total revenue. Similarly, if the marginal cost is less than marginal revenue, then total revenue is going up faster than total cost and profits are increasing. Hence, we continue to increase the level of production (and our profits) whenever marginal revenue is greater than marginal cost. As soon as they become equal, we have reached the optimum production level. Remember that the marginal analysis is derived from the total analysis, and so the solution is the same.

In Exhibit 15-2 we can look at possible decisions that could be based on this table. For the first unit marginal revenue is $10 and marginal cost is $4 so we would produce the unit. A similar analysis results in producing the second to sixth units. However, the seventh unit would cost more to produce than it would return in revenue. Thus the firm arrives at the same decision by marginal analysis as by the total revenue/total cost approach.

The graph in Exhibit 15-2 illustrates the same point. The MR curve is a straight horizontal line at the unit price level of $10. The MR line has this shape and position because the firm can sell all the product it wishes at the same price (in this case $10 per unit). Price equals marginal revenue. The MR = P line represents the demand curve for the competitive firm's output. This means that P = MR = the demand curve for the firm. The marginal-cost curve is derived from the total-cost curve given in Exhibit 15-1. The MC and MR curves cross at a level of output slightly beyond 6 units. At that point MC = MR = $10. At any point to the left of this intersection MR is greater than MC, and more profit can be made by producing more units. At any point to the right, MC is greater than MR, and production beyond that level would bring a reduction in profits. The profit-maximizing level of output is where MC = MR.

In the following discussion of resource allocation in competitive markets, the concepts can be demonstrated by tabular analysis or by graphical analysis. Because tables are unwieldy, we shall concentrate on graphs. Remember, however, that these graphs have underlying numerical schedules.

The Firm's Adjustment in the Short Run

In this section we investigate how firms adjust to changes in price when they are maximizing profits. As a starting point, Exhibit 15-3 illustrates the three possible conditions that can occur. In all three, price and marginal-revenue curves are identical since the firm can sell all its products at the going price in a perfectly competitive market. For instance, any one of these cases could represent a Kansas wheat

Exhibit 15-2 Marginal revenue = marginal cost approach to profit maximization

Unit	TR	MR	TC	MC	AVC	ATC
			FC = $20			
1	$10		$30		$10.00	$30.00
		> $10		> $ 4		
2	20		34		7.00	17.00
		> 10		> 3		
3	30		37		5.60	12.30
		> 10		> 3		
4	40		40		5.00	10.00
		> 10		> 4		
5	50		44		4.80	8.80
		> 10		> 6		
6	60		49		4.83	8.17
		> 10		> 11		
7	70		60		5.70	8.60
		> 10		> 15		
8	80		75		6.90	9.40
		> 10		> 20		
9	90		95		8.30	10.60

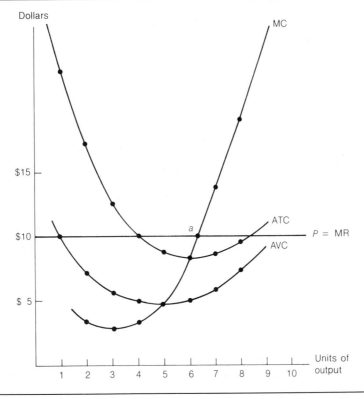

The table demonstrates the approach to profit maximization where firms will produce until the marginal revenue derived from a good exceeds (or equals) the cost of producing it. Since MR equals $10, the firm should increase production until MC exceeds $10—between the sixth and the seventh unit.

Therefore, the firm should produce 6 units to maximize product. (Note that this is the same result achieved with the approach that equates total revenue and total cost.) The graph shows the same information. Here the point where the MC and MR curves cross is the point where MC and MR are equal.

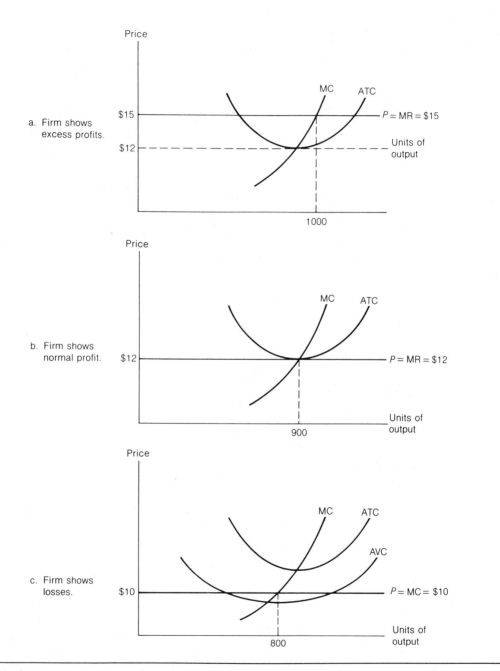

Exhibit 15-3   Short-run costs and price (perfect competition)

This exhibit shows three cost and revenue conditions: (a) the firm is making excess profits that will attract new entrants; (b) the firm is making normal profits; (c) the firm is making losses and will leave the industry.

farmer who can sell the entire crop produced on the farm at the same price.

Excess Profits The firm's profit-maximizing output (where MC = MR) occurs at 1000 units. At this level of output the average total cost per unit is slightly higher than $12. Revenue per unit (average revenue) is $15, which means the firm is making an excess profit of almost $3 per unit. (Total excess profit would be 1000 units × $3 = $3000.) We call this excess profit because, as you remember, the ATC curve already includes a normal rate of return to the entrepreneur. Thus the firm's profit is in excess of that required to keep it in the market. Put another way, this is the type of profit that will attract other firms into this competitive market.

Normal Profits In Exhibit 15-3b the ATC is $12 per unit, but the price received for the good is $12. In such a case, TC = TR. There is no excess profit, but a return for the opportunity cost of the entrepreneur is included in the ATC curve. This is an equilibrium situation in a competitive market. No excess profits exist to attract other firms, yet there is a normal profit to keep each firm in the industry.

This important condition deserves additional comment. Note that the profit-maximizing output where MC = MR indicates a level of output that is also the minimum point on the ATC curve. This minimum point is where the firm produces at the most efficient level of output. Profit maximization and efficiency can both be achieved at the same level of output. In addition, when price is equal to marginal cost, the buyer is paying a price equal to the marginal effort (in dollar terms) needed to produce the good. Society is receiving output at the lowest possible price; the costs of resources used are reflected in the prices of the good sold. This is why perfect competition is used as the standard by which we judge other market structures.

Losses The third possible condition is shown in Exhibit 15-3c, where price is below cost. In this case the optimum level of output is still where MC = MR because at this point losses are minimized. Should the firm produce at all? The answer lies in our discussion of the shutdown point in Chapter 14. In the short run the firm will continue to produce as long as the price exceeds its out-of-pocket expenses of production, as shown by the AVC. In this example, this condition is met and so the firm produces even though it loses money. Obviously, this is not an equilibrium level since no firm can continually accept losses. Eventually the firm will not renew leases or replace equipment, thus removing fixed costs, and will leave the industry.

In the short run under perfect competition, a firm makes adjustments by changing the level of output to arrive at that level of production where MC = MR. If the firm makes a normal profit, it will remain in business. Excess profits serve to encourage new firms to enter the industry. These new firms will increase supply by shifting the supply curve right, which will lower the market price and decrease the excess profits.

Price, Marginal Cost, and Consumer Choice

At this point let us put our understanding of a profit-maximizing firm into the context of consumer choices and resource allocation. What is the consequence of the fact that, at equilibrium, price equals marginal cost? We can answer the question better if we keep in mind that the price of a good in the market is the relative value society places on that good. It is the price we are willing to pay to buy it.

At the same time, the marginal cost of a product is the value we place on the factors that produce additional units of the product—the value to society of another hour of our time, or

The price of a good in the market is the relative value society places on that good. *(Photo by Terry Zabala)*

another stick of wood, or any other factor. When $P = MC$, the value we place on the product exactly equals the value we place on the factors necessary to produce it. The market is allocating resources the way consumers and producers have expressed their choices.

Consider the situation in which price is greater than marginal cost. The value of the product is greater than the value society puts on the inputs necessary to produce it. Additional resources should be allocated to produce more of the good. If they were, the price would decline and, eventually, would equal the good's marginal cost. Conversely, when the price is less than the mar-

ginal cost, consumers want fewer units of the product and would rather allocate the input resources to other products. Obviously, the lack of profit will convince the producers to allocate resources elsewhere.

In thinking about consumer choices and resource allocation, it is helpful to think of prices and costs as the mechanisms that carry information about society's preferences in the use of resources.

SHORT-RUN SUPPLY

We are now ready to show the relationship between cost and supply. We will first derive the supply curve for an individual firm, then aggregate the firms' supply curves to develop an industry supply curve.

The Firm's Short-Run Supply Curve

In Chapter 2 we stated that a supply curve is a schedule of the quantity of goods forthcoming at various prices. How would the supply schedule for a competitive firm look in the short run? Exhibit 15-4a illustrates the AVC, ATC, and MC curves for a firm producing one good. On the same graph five price levels are shown. We know from previous study that a firm will produce at a level of output where MC = MR. The cost curves allow us to build a short-run supply curve. At a price of $10, what quantity would be produced? The answer is that when MC = MR, the firm would produce 1090 units at $10 each, as shown on the supply schedule. Similarly, the schedule shows that at $8, the firm would produce 1000 units. At $6, 880 units would be

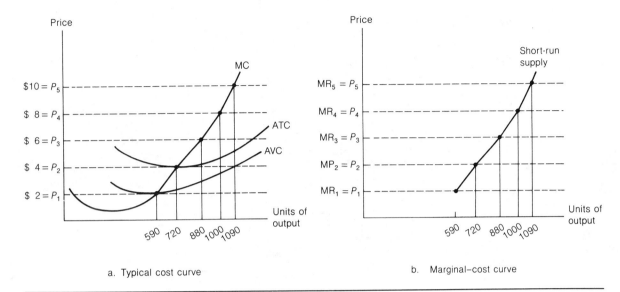

Exhibit 15-4   Short-run supply of a firm

On the left is a typical cost curve. At various prices the firm will maximize profit by producing where MC and MR are equal. The higher the price, the greater the level

of output. In the short run, the firm's supply schedule (above the shutdown point, where MC equals AVC) is the MC curve. On the right is a plot of the MC curve.

forthcoming and at $4, 720 units would be the profit-maximizing output. But at $2, how much would be produced? The answer: no production, because at $2, the firm is not covering its out-of-pocket expenses, as indicated by the AVC curve.

We can restate the firm's short-run supply curve as follows: *The short-run supply curve of a firm is the marginal-cost curve for all prices greater than the shutdown price on the AVC curve, the shutdown point being the level of production at which out-of-pocket expenses exceed the price.*

For convenience, the points from Exhibit 15-4a are plotted on Exhibit 15-4b so that the supply curve can be seen more clearly.

The Industry's Short-Run Supply Curve

Having established the competitive firm's short-run supply curve, we can easily derive the industry's supply curve, for the *industry's short-run supply curve* is the sum of all firms' short-run supply curves. The process is illustrated in Exhibit 15-5. To simplify the graph, only three firms' short-run supply (SRS) curves are used, but any number could have been included.

In Exhibit 15-5a, Firms *A*, *B*, and *C* have different SRS curves, which reflect, among other things, differences in their technology and in the age of their production facilities. This difference can be seen most clearly in the potential

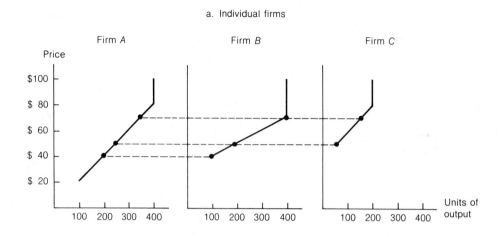

a. Individual firms

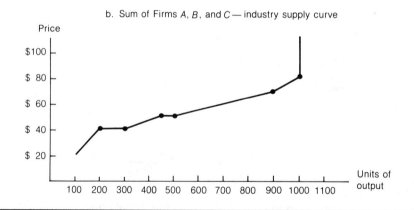

b. Sum of Firms A, B, and C — industry supply curve

Exhibit 15-5   Short-run supply of an industry

Firms A, B, and C have different short-run supply curves, which reflect their underlying cost curves. In order to find the industry supply curve, we add the supply curves of the individual firms. Although this example uses only three firms, the same process could be used for numerous firms (and the curve would be smoother). Note that the total industry curve has the characteristic upward slope.

supply of the good at a price of $20. Then Firm A would be willing to supply 100 units, whereas Firms B and C would not supply any units because the price is below their shutdown points. At $20 the total industry supply comes from Firm A; in fact at any price between $20 and

$40, Firm A remains the only producer. This is shown in Exhibit 15-5b, where the segment of industry supply from $20 to $40 is identical to Firm A's SRS curve. However, when the price reaches $40, Firm B is also willing to supply 100 units. Now the industry supply is 300 units

(200 from Firm A and 100 from Firm B). Between $40 and $50, the industry supply curve consists of the output from Firms A and B. Finally, at $50, Firm C is also willing to supply output, and above that figure all three firms are contributing to supply. But when the price reaches $80, all have reached maximum capacity and in the short run cannot produce more output no matter how high the price rises. This is illustrated by a perfectly inelastic supply curve at $80 with a total industry output of 1000.

We have started with the cost curves for an individual firm, which are determined by technology and the age of their production facilities. By using the assumption of profit-maximizing behavior we derived the firm's short-run supply curves. The competitive industry's SRS is the horizontal summation of the firms' short-run supply curves. All of these industry SRS curves should slope upward, as the law of supply suggests, because individual SRS consists of marginal-cost curves that increase as production levels rise.

The Short-Run Adjustment Process

The industry short-run supply curve can be used to illustrate the market adjustment process. Exhibit 15-6a shows an industry short-run supply curve labeled S_1 and a total demand curve D_1. The market for the good is in equilibrium at a price of P_1 and quantity of Q_1. This is an equilibrium price because the producers are willing to supply the quantity demanded by consumers.

Assume that the demand curve shifts to the right, because people's preferences or incomes have changed. The demand curve shift is shown by the new demand curve D_2. The short-run

a. Market

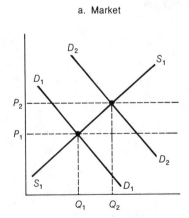

b. Firm

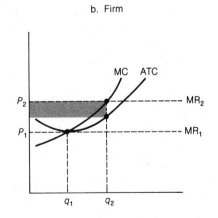

Exhibit 15-6 Short-run adjustment process

This exhibit shows the relationship between the industry and firm adjustment to changes in demand. On the left is an industry equilibrium at Q_1 and P_1. A shift in demand is shown by D_2. With the new demand, equilibrium price rises to P_2 for the industry. On the right is the firm's response to the shift in demand. At P_2 the firm's marginal revenue has risen to MR_2. The firm increases production to equate MC with MR_2. The new profit-maximizing level of production for the firm is now q_2. At q_2 excess profits are made; because of these profits, eventually new firms will enter the industry.

response is for prices to rise in order to bring the market back to equilibrium. The new equilibrium will yield a market price of P_2, and Q_2 units will be produced.

What does this mean to individual producers? Since they can sell all the output they produce at the market price, their marginal-revenue curve shifts upward from MR_1 to MR_2. Each firm immediately responds by increasing its output to the level (q_2) where $MC = MR$.* Rather than realizing normal profits at q_1, each firm now has excess profits at q_2. The magnitude of the excess profits is the difference at q_2 between the average total cost per unit and the average revenue per unit, with this difference then multiplied by the number of units sold to arrive at total profit. The shaded area on the graph illustrates how much excess profit the firm is earning.

The *short-run adjustment process* has brought the market into equilibrium by equating total supply and demand, S_1 and D_2. This equilibrium has created excess profits for the firm. As noted earlier, however, excess profits attract new firms into the industry. Thus, the short-run adjustment process will bring the market into equilibrium by adjusting the output of existing firms. In the long run it will increase supply by attracting new firms into the industry.

LONG-RUN SUPPLY

The Firm's Long-Run Supply Curve

Firms can make adjustments in the long run that are difficult to make in the short run. With

---

* Abbreviations for concepts concerning an industry are uppercase; abbreviations concerning a single firm are lowercase, conventionally. Knowing this distinction is useful in preparing or reading graphs.

excess profits, the capacity of existing plants will be increased and new firms can build new plants. The newcomers will build plants that are the most efficient in size and that can incorporate the latest technology, in order to minimize their costs. *In perfect competition the firms have no choice; unless they build optimum-size plants, they will not survive in the long run.*

What is the optimum-size plant? Let us go back to the long-run average-cost (LRAC) curves.

The short-run adjustment process brings the market into equilibrium by adjusting the output of existing firms.
(Photo by Cary Wolinsky, Stock, Boston)

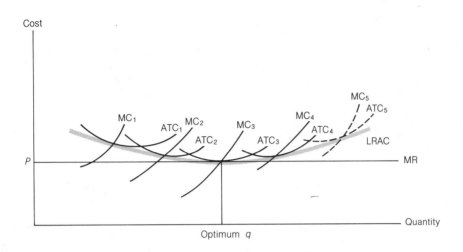

Exhibit 15-7 Long-run average costs and equilibrium

The long-run average-cost (LRAC) curve of a firm is the least-cost combination for all possible firm sizes. If the firm in perfect competition does not build an

optimum-size plant, it will not be able to compete in the long run. In the situation shown above, the plant with ATC_3 curves will be the optimum size.

The LRAC curve shows least-cost combinations for all possible firm sizes and production technologies. For that reason, they are sometimes called planning curves. Exhibit 15-7 shows a typical LRAC curve. If the firm does not build an optimum-size plant, it will not be able to sell its output at a price as low as other producers and will therefore lose its share of the market.

The Industry's Long-Run Supply Curve

What does this constraint imply about the industry long-run supply curve? Exhibit 15-8a shows what happens when the entry of new firms does not bid up the price of resources needed by the industry. This is the case when the industry requires only a small portion of the total supply of a resource. For example, suppose unskilled labor was an input and the industry normally used only 0.1 percent of labor avail-

able in its geographic area. Then new firms could acquire all the unskilled labor necesary without bidding its price up because their additional demand would not significantly shift the labor-market demand curve.

The Long-Run Adjustment Process

The *long-run adjustment process* allows for the changing of fixed factors, like the sizes of plants, as well as variable inputs. Suppose the industry starts in equilibrium at price and quantity levels shown in Exhibit 15-8a at E_1, which is the intersection of S_1 and D_1. A shift in demand occurs, as shown by D_2. The short-run response is increased price and quantity, as shown by the new short-run equilibrium E_S. But excess profits at this equilibrium point attract new firms that build optimum-size plants and increase aggregate supply to SRS_2. The market then set-

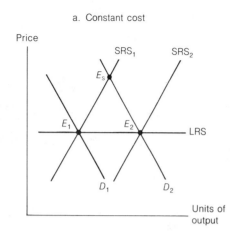

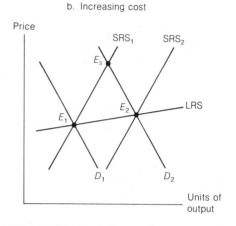

Exhibit 15-8   Long-run supply curves for constant- and increasing-cost industries

These figures illustrate the adjustment process in the long run. On the left is the supply curve of a constant-cost industry. A shift in demand to D_2 is initially met by a rise in price. However, the short-run excess profits attract other firms, which enter with optimum-size plants. The result is the new equilibrium, E_2, at the same price and cost as before the shift in demand. The figure *on the right shows the effect of a similar demand shift in an increasing-cost industry. Here excess profits attract new firms also, which enter with optimum-size plants. However, because of the increased price of an essential factor that is scarce, the new firms have a higher cost; consequently the new equilibrium, E_2, is at a higher price.*

tles at equilibrium E_2 for the new demand D_2 and supply SRS_2. Note that the cost at the new equilibrium is the same as the old cost. The long-run supply curve can be located by drawing a line between E_1 and E_2. This is the long-run supply (LRS) for the industry. Because the long-run price does not increase for the higher levels of output, this is a *constant-cost industry* and the long-run supply curve is flat.

Exhibit 15-8b illustrates an *increasing-cost industry*. In this industry, firms also enter with optimum-size plants. But inputs in this industry are not in unlimited supply. For example, the amount of land suitable for growing certain types of grapes is limited. If the demand for wine made from that grape were to increase, new firms would bid up the price for marginal grape-growing land. In such a case the equilibrium price indicated by E_2 is higher than at E_1.

In theory one might also encounter a *decreasing-cost industry*. Usually, however, this possibility exists only for a limited range of output. The costs finally rise as some important factor becomes scarce.

Firms in a perfectly competitive market must produce at the most efficient point or their excess profits will increase the number of firms, and, therefore, the supply. Consequently, long-run supply curves are either flat—in an industry with constant costs—or rising—in an increasing-cost industry.

SUMMARY

1. The short-run supply curve for a firm is the marginal cost curve above the shutdown point.

2. The industry short-run supply curve is the sum of the short-run supply curves for all firms that make up the industry.

3. Excess profits in an industry in the long run attract new firms. The new firms increase supply, and this reduces the excess profits.

4. Losses in the short run will eventually cause firms to leave the industry. When they do, the aggregate supply curve will shift left and price will increase until normal profits have been reestablished.

5. The shape of the long-run supply curve is determined by the supply of factors required for the industry. If inputs are plentiful and if the industry does not influence the market price by their need for additional inputs, the cost of additional output will be the same as previous production, indicating a *constant-cost industry*. However, if one or more factors is in limited supply, expanding output will result in increasing unit costs. This case is called an *increasing-cost industry*.

KEY CONCEPTS

perfect competition

homogeneous product

ease of entry and exit

breakeven points

marginal revenue

short-run supply curve of a firm

short-run supply curve of an industry

short-run adjustment process

long-run adjustment process

constant-cost industry

increasing-cost industry

decreasing-cost industry

QUESTIONS FOR DISCUSSION

1. If a store purchased goods for $6 and sold them for $6, how long would it be able to stay in business?

2. Do profits really influence the decisions of a firm? Explain.

3. New York City is the only city in the United States that has had rent controls continuously since 1941. Assume that the construction industry resembles a perfectly competitive industry. What would be the impact of rent controls on incentives of firms considering entry into the apartment rental business? How does this affect the availability of apartments?

4. If the corn-producing industry resembled a perfectly competitive industry, what would be the effect on corn prices when (a) the price of fertilizer increased, (b) a new seed developed at the state university increased the yield per acre with no additional costs, (c) farm laborers

were mandated higher wages by an act of one state legislature, (d) farm
laborers were mandated higher wages by an act of the U.S. Congress?

5. A young woman home for the summer after her first economics course
   told her businessman-father that the equilibrium level of profits in a
   perfectly competitive industry is zero. The father said no one would
   stay in a business where there is no profit. Could you help resolve
   this dispute? How?

6. Why is $P = $ MC a good thing for society?

Chapter 16

Monopoly and Imperfect Competition

In the previous chapter, we discussed the behavior of firms under conditions of perfect competition. Obviously, many industries do not operate under conditions of perfect competition, and for these we must develop other models to explain the behavior of firms. The range of possible market structures can be viewed as a spectrum, as shown in Exhibit 16-1, from those with many competing firms to those with only a few.

Exhibit 16-1   Market structures

	Imperfect Competition			
Perfect Competition	Monopolistic Competition	Oligopoly	Duopoly	Monopoly
Many firms	Many firms	"Few" firms	Two firms	One firm
Homogeneous product	Differentiated products	Mutually recognized interdependence		
No significant barriers to entry				

Looking at Exhibit 16-1, you can see that perfect competition, on one hand, and monopoly, on the other, are the extremes of the spectrum. Perfect competition occurs when there are a large number of firms in an industry and no one firm can control the market. *Monopoly* exists when a single firm supplies the market. Between these extremes is a range of structural conditions referred to as *imperfect competition.*

The general category of imperfect competition includes *duopoly,* where two firms control a market; *oligopoly,* where a small number of firms control a market; and *monopolistic competition,* where there are many firms in a market but the products of the firms are differentiated. (Remember that in perfect competition firms produce homogeneous products.)

In this chapter we shall first analyze the effects of monopoly on supply, then the general nature of imperfect competition, and finally the implications of market structure for resource allocation.

MONOPOLY

In perfect competition, an industry must have enough producers so that no single firm can affect

A patented process essential to the production of a good can create a monopoly for the firm holding the patent. (*Photo by Bob Adelman, Magnum, Photos, Inc.*)

the market. Monopoly, however, exists when there is only one firm producing a product for which there are no reasonable substitutes. For example, the single producer of electricity in a particular region has a monopoly because there is no close substitute for electricity.

Monopolies are achieved in a variety of ways. The most common is through legal restrictions that prevent other firms from entering the market. Examples include television station licenses or patents that control a key process needed to produce a good. Economies of scale can also make it nearly impossible for a second firm to enter a market—for example, the high cost of duplicating telephone lines prohibits the establishment of a second telephone firm in a geographic area.

The Demand Curve for a Monopolist

The crucial distinction between a perfectly competitive firm and a monopolist is related to market demand. In monopoly the demand curve facing a firm and the demand curve for its industry are identical—a monopolist can be thought of as a one-firm industry. The two curves are not identical, however, under perfect competition, as Exhibit 16-2 illustrates. There are two differences between the monopolist and the perfectly competitive firm. First, the monopolist can increase sales only by lowering price. In contrast, the individual firm in perfect competition faces a perfectly elastic demand curve; it can always expect to sell as much as it pro-

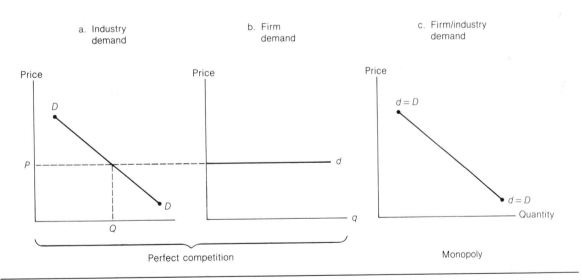

Exhibit 16-2 Demand curves

In perfect competition, the individual firm has a demand curve that is perfectly elastic, even though the demand for the industry slopes downward.

However, the monopolist always faces a downward-sloping demand curve. That is, the monopolist can increase sales only by lowering the price.

Exhibit 16-3 Monopoly solution

(1)	(2)	(3)	(4)	(5)	(6)	(7)	(8)	(9) TR − TC (+) profit or (−) loss
Q	P	TR	MR	Q	TC	ATC	MC	
0	80	0		0	10			−10
			> 72					
1	72	72		1	20	24	10	+52
			> 56					
2	64	128		2	36	18	16	+92
			> 40					
3	56	168		3	60	20	24	+108
			> 24					
4	48	192		4	92	24	32	+100
			> 8					
5	40	200		5	140	28	48	+60
			> −8					
6	32	192		6	192	32	52	0
			> −24					
7	24	168		7	280	40	88	−112
			> −40					
8	16	128		8	352	44	72	−224
			> −56					
9	8	72		9	432	48	80	−360
			> −72					
10	0	0		10				

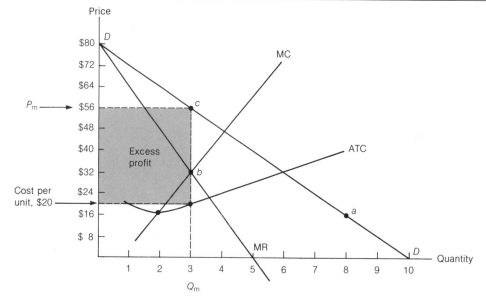

Revenue and cost information for a monopolist are given here in both table and graph form. The monopolist follows the same profit-maximizing rule of firms in perfect competition. It produces at that point where MC equals MR (shown as point b), which is 3 units. With 3 units the demand is sufficient to generate a price, P_m, of $56. Under these conditions there are excess profits. It costs an average of $20 to produce the goods and they can be sold for $56 each—a profit of $36 per unit.

duces at the market price. Second, the monopolist firm can have a conscious price policy, because it can choose the price and output level that will yield the highest level of profit. Put another way, the competitive firm is a price taker whereas the monopolist is a price maker. By choosing the quantity it will produce, the monopolist sets the price of a good.

A hypothetical example of demand for a monopolist's product is given in Exhibit 16-3. Columns 1 and 2, which are also plotted on the graph, describe a conventional downward-sloping demand curve. Column 3, total revenue, is found by multiplying the price the monopolist receives for each good by the quantity demanded.

It is the calculation of marginal revenue, column 4, that shows the nature of monopoly most clearly. The marginal-revenue curve of the monopolist slopes downward even more rapidly than the demand curve. Instead of a horizontal MR curve—the firm's demand curve in perfect competition—in monopoly, we have different curves for MR and for demand.

How can this phenomenon be explained? Looking at the graph in Exhibit 16-3, point *a*, we see that at a price of $16, 8 units could be sold. To sell a ninth unit, the monopolist must lower the price on all units to $8. Potential revenue from the first 8 units will be lost, although revenue from unit 9 is gained. In this case, the marginal revenue of the ninth unit would be negative (8 units at $16 means TR equals $128, and 9 units at $8 means TR equals $72, so MR equals −$56). Each additional unit sold adds to total revenue the price of that unit minus the price reduction on all units that could have been sold at higher prices. This means that the marginal revenue of a monopolist is always less than the price of the additional unit sold, which accounts for the difference between the marginal revenue and demand curves.

Price and Quantity Determination

Since the monopolist faces a downward-sloping demand curve, the quantity produced determines the price of the good. What level of production will be chosen? The answer lies on the cost side of the picture. Although the firm is a monopolist on the product side, it usually purchases its inputs in a more competitive market. The monopolist does not have control over the shape and position of cost curves, which are determined by technology and factor prices.

What rules does a monopolist use to determine the optimum level of output that would maximize profit? The monopolist maximizes profits by producing at that output level where marginal cost equals marginal revenue. The logic that makes MC = MR a profit-maximizing rule for a monopolist is identical to that for a firm in perfect competition. In either case, a firm will make additional profit whenever the revenue from additional output is greater than the cost of producing that output. However, the effect upon resource allocation of the quantity and price solution (MC = MR) is different for a monopolist because the MR curve slopes downward.

Profit-maximizing behavior of the monopolist is illustrated in Exhibit 16-3. Columns 6, 7, and 8 give the total cost, average total cost, and marginal cost curves for a hypothetical firm; the curves are plotted below the table. Looking at the graph, we note that MC = MR at point *b*, where these two curves cross.

The profit-maximizing point in Exhibit 16-3 is at an output level of 3 (labeled Q_m). What price will be charged at that level of output? The price is determined by demand, *D*, which tells us the amount people will be willing to pay at that level of output. The price is determined by the intersection of the quantity (Q_m) and the DD curve. In this case the price charged is $56 (P_m).

We can also calculate the excess profit from the information in the figure. At an output of 3 units, we note that the average total cost is $20 per unit. Since we have 3 units, TC must equal $60, but TR (calculated as $P \times Q$) is 56×3 or $168. Total excess profit (TR − TC) is $168 − $56 or $108. The same information can be derived from the tabular data, in which total profit is shown in column 9. Here we can also see that the average revenue of $56 is $36 more than the $20 average cost. The profit per unit sold is $36, and 36×3 makes $108 total excess profit. Thus a monopolist maximizes profit by charging whatever demand will bear at that level of output where MC = MR.

Monopoly Pricing and Resource Allocation

In perfect competition there is a built-in mechanism that eliminates excess profits—the entry of new profit-seeking firms. In a monopoly the mechanism does not operate because some barrier keeps firms out and sustains the monopoly. A monopolist still has an incentive to be efficient and minimize costs. But these lower costs will not be passed on to the consumer.

Note that the monopolist does not charge "all that the market will bear" for *each* good; the goal is to maximize *total* profit, not the profit made on one unit sold. When a monopoly exists, however, consumers pay higher prices for smaller quantities than would be produced under competitive conditions. Hence economists have argued that perfect competition leads to better resource allocations than monopoly. In a monopoly the price of the good is not equal to the marginal cost; instead the price is higher than the cost of inputs necessary to produce

that unit. As we learned in the previous chapter, when the price of a product is greater than its marginal cost, too little is produced to meet society's demand. Since meeting consumers' needs is a fundamental purpose of our economic system, monopoly has generally been condemned.

IMPERFECT COMPETITION

The economy is not dominated by either perfectly competitive firms or monopolies. Most firms operate under conditions of imperfect competition. Firms in such industries have some control over price, but their power to make prices is constrained by the extent of the competition they face. Generally, a firm in a monopolistic competitive industry—one with many sellers of somewhat differentiated products—will have less control over price than an oligopolist or duopolist. Generally, the more competition a firm faces, the closer the industry will be to the competitive ideal of MC = P; excess profits will be small. As firms gain more control over price, however, consumers must pay higher prices. Recognizing the degrees of imperfect competition makes our analysis more realistic, but it does not alter the basic fact that when firms are price makers rather than price takers consumers generally are worse off.

Monopoly and perfect competition are said to be deterministic—that is, assuming profit maximizing, we are able to determine from a firm's cost curves the price and quantity that will be produced. This is not easily done in imperfect competition. In imperfect competition other assumptions must be added to that of profit maximization, involving the behavior of the other firms in the industry. For example, suppose an oligopolistic firm wishes to increase

A cartel, such as the Organization of Petroleum Exporting Countries (OPEC), limits competition in order to increase the profitability of its members and so is a type of imperfect competition. (*Wide World Photos*)

its prices. It *must* consider how other firms in the oligopoly will respond. Will the other firms also increase their prices? Will they change their levels of output?

The problem is that when we consider all the additional assumptions necessary to cover the market actions and reactions we no longer have a general solution. We now have special cases based on specific assumptions: when we vary the assumptions we change the results. This means that few general statements can be made about imperfect competition. We will divide this section into three segments. The first will describe an oligopoly and the problems that beset all models of imperfect competition. The second will characterize monopolistically competitive industries. The third will introduce a tool that economists hope will lead to more deterministic models in the future.

Oligopoly

Oligopolies tend to set prices and leave them in effect for a long period—a year or more. These prices are "rigid," in contrast to the "flexible" prices in competitive industries such as textiles or lumber. Rigid prices are resistant to changes in demand or costs. What accounts for this behavior on the part of the oligopoly? Let's suppose an oligopolist, which we'll call Firm *A*, is considering a price change. If it increases its prices, it may lose sales, as consumers switch to another firm. If it lowers its prices, it fears

---

Oligopoly Pricing Decisions

The automobile industry is a classic case of oligopoly, with General Motors, Ford, Chrysler, and American Motors accounting for over 98 percent of domestic production. Their recognized mutual interdependence is illustrated by this account of their pricing for the 1976 models, which appeared in the *Wall Street Journal* on December 19, 1975.

Ford Motor May Retract New Price Boost If Buyers Resist or Competitors Stand Pat

Dearborn, Mich.—Ford Motor Company acknowledged that it is leaving the door open for a possible rollback of recently announced price boosts if consumers resist the increase or if competitors fail to follow suit. Ford earlier this week announced its second price increase on 1976-model cars and light trucks.

The executive also indicated that failure of General Motors Corp. to attempt a second 1976 model price increase might cause Ford to reconsider its action. "If GM doesn't follow," Mr. Ford said, "we'll be watching the market very carefully." Chrysler Corp. announced price increases earlier in the week of $25–$70 on selected models.

Are these statements consistent with the behavior described by the kinked demand curve?

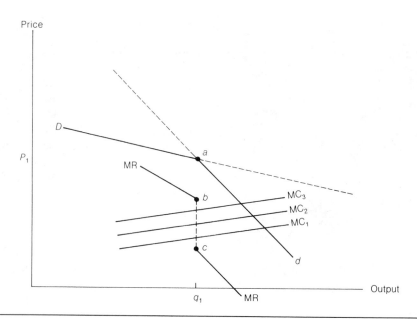

Exhibit 16-4   Kinked demand curve

The kinked demand curve illustrates the options open to an oligopoly. Starting at price P_1 the oligopoly assumes that competitors will not follow a price increase and the firm will face an elastic demand curve, Da. On the other hand, it is assumed that the rivals will follow a price decrease, as shown by the inelastic demand of line segment ad; hence, the kink in the demand curve and the discontinuity in the MR curve. Keeping the price stable seems to be the best solution for the firm.

the other firms will follow, because to do otherwise would mean a significant loss of their sales. So what does Firm *A* do? Nothing. It perceives its rivals' potential reactions and decides not to change prices unless there is a major change in costs.

The Kinked Demand Curve   Exhibit 16-4 shows a graph of a demand curve for the oligopoly, referred to as a *kinked demand curve*. Point *a* is the initial price and quantity. The firm perceives that if it raises its prices, the other firms in the industry will not follow. If the other firms did follow the price increase, the firm would have a demand curve as shown by the dotted line—that is, the demand curve for the total industry. But since the other firms will not follow the price increase, the firm's demand above *a* is very elastic. The solid line shows the firm's actual demand curve if rivals do not raise their prices.

On the other hand, the firm perceives that if it lowers its price below *a*, the other firms will also lower their prices so as not to lose sales. This means the firm will increase sales only slightly in response to a lower price since all firms in the industry will lower prices. The demand curve faced by the firm is not as elastic as it was for price increases. Again, the solid line shows the firm's perceived demand curve, now below *a*.

The firm's demand curve (labeled d) has a "kink" at a. The marginal-revenue curve (MR) for the firm is derived from the demand curve. Starting with the d curve above a, the first line segment of MR is derived in the usual manner. However, due to the change in the slope of d, there is a discontinuity in the MR curve from b to c. It is this discontinuity, shown by the dotted line from b to c, that gives the model its unique characteristics.

An oligopolist maximizes profit, like any other firm does, by producing at that level of output where MR = MC. The difference in this case is that small changes in MC do not change the optimum output level. Note on the diagram that MC_1, MC_2, and MC_3, representing different cost schedules, all cross the MR curve at the same quantity of output, q_1. Only a large shift in costs would make it worthwhile for the firm to change from point a. Thus the model describes behavior consistent with the relatively rigid prices actually observed in oligopolistic industries.

The kinked demand model has several significant weaknesses. It cannot explain how the industry got to the initial price. Nor can it explain what the new price would be if a cost increase moved the industry past the kink. However, our purpose here is not to examine this model in great detail but rather to use it as a vehicle to illustrate the general characteristics of all models of imperfect competition. Note how sensitive the results are to the assumption about the other firms' reactions. There is, however, no clear, unambiguous, or compelling reason to believe that the other firms will behave in the specified manner. It seems equally likely that the other firms in the industry might elect to follow the price rise. This simple change in assumptions drastically changes the results.

Similar statements could be made about any model of imperfect competition. This line of inquiry started in 1838 with the great French mathematician-economist, Antoine Augustin Cournot, and it deserves a great deal more research. Many complications exist in developing models to describe the real world. With various degrees of product differentiation added to the varying sets of behavioral assumptions (including collusion and noncollusion among firms), an almost unlimited number of models becomes possible. Some of these can be helpful in particular situations, but none has yet been developed that is as generally applicable as the model used in perfect competition and monopoly.

Cartels

Sometimes firms in the same industry group together to limit competition in order to increase their joint profitability. These groups are called cartels. They are most effective when supported by governments. The Organization of Petroleum Exporting Countries, OPEC, is the most prominent and successful modern cartel. In the United States such agreements are illegal.

Usually cartels set prices and production levels at mutually agreeable levels. Their purpose is to lessen competition and form a monopoly, which will raise prices and revenue by controlling production and dividing up markets among participants. Of course, cartels succeed only when demand is inelastic and their price increases yield increased total revenue for the sellers.

Obviously, agreement among firms removes uncertainty and helps firms avoid unwanted production. But it also divides the market among participants and requires a stable consumer demand. Unstable demands have broken up some cartels, but others have failed for other reasons. The nitrate cartel in the 1920s and 1930s was offset by the development of synthetic substitutes. As long ago as 1498, the copper cartel was broken by a German banking family, the Fuggers, who sold large amounts of copper outside the cartel in an effort to increase their market share. Political pressure or dissolution by legal means can also break up cartels.

All oligopolies recognize their mutual interdependence and seek ways to reduce uncertainty about their competitors' actions. Economists are still struggling to find a good system for predicting the effect of this interdependence on resource allocation. The kinked demand curve and the experience of cartels suggest the multiplicity of possible reactions. But we have not yet been able to identify the exact price-quantity relationship in oligopoly markets as we have in situations of monopoly or perfect competition.

Monopolistic Competition

Some markets have elements of monopoly and also elements of perfect competition. The firms act as if their competitors set the price (they are price takers) and yet behave as if they face a downward-sloping demand curve. This type of market is called *monopolistic competition*. It is characterized by a large number of firms in the market, each selling a product slightly different from the others.

For example, spaghetti is a fairly uniform product. If many firms produced and sold it, the market for spaghetti would be perfectly competitive, and no one producer would be concerned about the competitors' market actions. However, a firm might wish to establish its own share of the market to avoid having to accept all price changes. To do this, the firm first makes its product distinct—by superficial changes in shape, texture, and color, by packaging, or by advertising. The resulting product now acquires its own demand schedule, with price decreasing as quantities increase. Because the other spaghetti brands are good substitutes, the firm's

In monopolistic competition, there are a large number of firms, each selling a slightly different product. (*Photo by Terry Zabala*)

demand curve is relatively elastic. Some consumers do respond to price changes, but not all switch from one brand to another. Those who stay with the original product form the basis of that product's own demand schedule.

Clearly, in this type of market structure firms do not set a price equal to marginal cost. However, the difference between MC and *P* is not as great as in a monopoly, because the advantages gained by advertising, a patented packaging gimmick, or some other distinguishing characteristic are fairly easily overcome. A firm's demand curve shifts frequently in monopolistic competition, and it is difficult to determine how other firms in the market will behave.

A Fifteenth-Century Cartel

Cartels are not a new phenomenon, nor are the reasons for them. A fifteenth-century example may help illuminate the cartel operation.

Pope Paul II set up a monopoly of the rich alum beds owned by the Church and condemned as unchristian the use of alum from Moslem Turkey. Alum was a key ingredient in leather tanning and cloth dyeing, so it had a steady market demand. Another mine, owned by Ferdinand, king of Naples, however, offered serious competition to the Pope. Each mine tried to increase its market share by increasing production, hoping the other mines would not react. The increased supply caused such a drastic drop in price—with large alum surpluses—that each mine was worse off than before. Consequently, on June 11, 1470, Pope Paul II and King Ferdinand signed a detailed cartel agreement that set alum prices high. They split sales profits, but left production decisions to each mine. If sales were made below the cartel's fixed price, the seller had to make up the partner's loss. This cartel had the support of both church and state and was able to last for 30 years before rivalry and additional supplies eroded its effectiveness.

RESOURCE ALLOCATION

Under perfect competition, a firm pursuing profit-maximizing behavior will make MC equal MR equal *P*. This equilibrium has great benefits for society. The price of the good is equal to the marginal cost of producing the good. Put another way, the value to the consumer of the last unit purchased is equal to the monetary value of the resources used in the production of that good. This means that consumers' demands, as measured in the marketplace, are filled in the best manner possible given the limited resources available to a society.

Let us compare the results expected from perfect competition with those from monopoly:

1. *When a monopolist, or to a lesser extent an imperfect competitor, makes MC equal MR, there is a misallocation of society's resources.* Remember that in a monopoly, the price consumers pay for a good is greater than the cost of the resources needed to produce that good. Thus, a monopoly misallocates resources by restricting output and charging a higher price than that determined by perfect competition.

2. *Monopolists make excess profits, yet there is no resulting entry by other firms.* These long-run excess profits mean that a factor of production is being paid more than its productivity would warrant under competition. This can cause inequality in income distribution, which compounds mistakes in resource allocation.

3. *Monopoly does not assure the rapid adoption of the most efficient technology.* The monopolist has an incentive to lower costs in order to increase profits, but will purchase new equipment featuring new technology only when existing equipment wears out. Compare this with an industry in which new firms are always ready and able to enter if they can adopt a new technology that will give them a cost advantage over existing firms.

Very few definitive statements can be made about industries with imperfect competition. Some oligopoly models yield misallocations of resources that are worse than monopoly, but they are generally based on unrealistic assumptions. Most oligopoly models suggest resource allocation worse than that in perfect competition but better than that in monopoly. As a general rule, we know that a firm that faces a sloping demand curve will not allocate resources as efficiently as will a competitive firm facing a perfectly elastic demand curve.

SUMMARY

1. Monopoly is a situation in which one firm is the only source of supply. Duopoly has two firms as sole suppliers, and oligopoly consists of a small number of suppliers who recognize their mutual interdependence.

2. The marginal-revenue curve for a monopolist slopes downward more rapidly than the demand curve. This occurs because in order to increase sales, a monopolist must lower prices. Each additional unit sold increases total revenue by the price of that unit *less* the price *reduction* on all units that could have been sold at the higher price. The marginal revenue of a monopolist is always less than the actual price paid for the additional unit sold.

3. The monopolist can maximize profits by producing at that level of output where marginal cost equals marginal revenue (MC = MR), in which case price per unit will be higher than the marginal cost for that unit.

4. In a monopoly, price is greater than marginal cost, and so consumers pay higher prices for smaller quantities. This causes an inefficient resource allocation because the social cost of producing goods is less than the value of those goods in the marketplace.

5. In monopolistic competition, there are many sellers with products that are similar, and hence good substitutes, but these products are different enough that they can each claim a small market share. These firms face a downward-sloping demand curve that is highly elastic because many good substitutes are available. These firms produce when MR = MC, but the price they charge is greater than MC. They are not as efficient at resource allocation as perfect competitors. But because their demand curves are highly elastic, the inefficiency is probably not too great.

6. There are innumerable models to explain the behavior of oligopolies. The recognized mutual interdependence within oligopolies leads to a wide variety of assumptions about reactions. An example of an oligopoly demand curve is the kinked demand curve, which is based on the assumption that competitors will follow any price decrease but will not respond to a price increase. Under these assumptions a pattern of behavior emerges that provides a determinant price and quantity. However, under other assumptions a different solution emerges.

KEY CONCEPTS

monopoly
imperfect competition
duopoly
oligopoly

monopolistic competition
kinked demand curve
cartel

QUESTIONS FOR DISCUSSION

1. "A monopolist will never incur losses." Analyze the validity of this statement.
2. "Since every good competes with every other good for the consumer's dollar, there can never be a monopoly." Evaluate this statement.
3. Nothing in the market mechanism keeps price equal to marginal cost for a monopolist. Are there any forces outside the market that could influence the price and marginal cost decision? How about legal or political forces?
4. Why is there a tendency for collusion to occur in oligopolies?
5. Is there any reason to believe that monopolists who charge higher prices will provide better services than firms in competitive industries?

Chapter 17

The Structure of U.S. Industry

Chapter 3 discussed the history of business in the United States, and a brief review of that chapter would be helpful. So far our study of microeconomics has focused on the firm in perfect competition or monopoly, with imperfect competition discussed but not emphasized. However, in the real world, many industries are characterized by imperfect competition. One branch of economics, called industrial organization, applies microeconomics to the subject of the structure and performance of all industries, including those classified as in imperfect competition. Why are industries structured the way they are? How did they get that way? How competitive are they? Is industry organized in a socially desirable manner?

Exhibit 17-1   The largest industrial firms in the United States, 1982

Rank	Company	1982 Sales (in millions)	Number of Employees (in thousands)
1	Exxon	$97,172	173
2	General Motors	60,025	657
3	Mobil Oil	59,946	188
4	Texaco	46,986	60
5	Ford	37,067	380
6	IBM	34,364	364
7	Standard Oil of California	34,362	42
8	DuPont	33,331	165
9	Gulf Oil	28,427	52
10	Standard Oil of Indiana	28,073	58
11	General Electric	26,500	367
12	Atlantic Richfield	26,462	52
13	Shell Oil	20,062	37
14	U.S. Steel	18,375	120
15	Occidental Petroleum	18,212	54
20	United Technologies	13,577	184

Exhibit 17-2   The largest retailing companies, utilities, and nonmanufacturing firms in the United States

Rank	Retailing Company	1982 Sales (in millions)
1	Sears, Roebuck	$30,020
2	Safeway Stores	17,633
3	K-Mart	16,772
4	Kroger	11,902
5	J.C. Penney	11,787
10	Winn-Dixie	6,674

Rank	Utility	1982 Assets (in millions)
1	AT & T	$148,186
2	GTE	22,294
3	Pacific Gas & Electric	13,635
4	Southern Company	12,301
5	American Electric Power	12,224
10	Texas Utilities	8,021

Rank	Bank, Headquarters	1982 Assets (in millions)
1	Citicorp, New York	$129,997
2	Bank of America, San Francisco	122,221
3	Chase Manhattan, New York	80,863
4	Manufacturers Hanover, New York	64,041
5	J. P. Morgan, New York	58,597
10	Security Pacific, Los Angeles	36,991

SOURCE: *Fortune*, July 1983.

PRESENT CONDITIONS

The United States is a very large market. In areas such as manufacturing, utilities, insurance, banking, and retailing, a few very large corporations provide many of the goods and services we use in our daily lives.

Exhibits 17-1 and 17-2 list the largest manufacturing, retailing, utility, and banking corporations in the United States. Most of the manufacturing firms' names are familiar. The importance of the auto industry to the economy is shown by the presence of two automakers and six petroleum companies among the 10 largest industrial firms. A similar picture emerges in retailing where Sears, J. C. Penney, and K-Mart (Kresge) sell to a national market. In utilities, AT&T dwarfed the industry before 1983; however, on January 1, 1984, as part of an antitrust settlement, the former giant was broken into eight separate companies. In banking, California-based Bank of America was the largest U.S. bank for many years; however, in 1982 it was surpassed by Citicorp. It should be noted that four of the six largest banks are located in New York City, the financial center of the United States.

Exhibit 17-3 illustrates that foreign corporations are also large. These large corporations based outside the United States show the importance of petroleum in the world economy.

DEFINING AN INDUSTRY

Some industries are relatively easy to define. Others are more difficult, because it is difficult to establish their boundaries. The cigarette industry is an example of an easily defined industry. There are no close substitutes for cigarettes; the closest are other tobacco products such as cigars, pipe tobacco, and snuff. However, increases in the price of cigarettes do not affect the amount of cigar and pipe tobacco sold. As we know from previous chapters, the price of a substitute good or the quantity produced should change when the related good's price changes, and so it appears that other tobacco products are not good substitutes for cigarettes. We can then say that the cigarette industry is made up of the producers of cigarettes.

The boundaries of other industries are less clear. Take the case of beverages. Is 7-Up a sub-

Exhibit 17-3 The largest industrial corporations outside the United States, 1982

Rank	Company	Country	Industry	Sales (in millions)
1	Royal Dutch Petroleum, Shell Oil	Netherlands/Britain	Petroleum	$82,291
2	British Petroleum	Britain	Petroleum	52,199
3	ENI	Italy	Petroleum	29,444
4	Unilever	Britain/Netherlands	Food products	24,095
5	Française des Petroles	France	Petroleum	22,784
6	Kuwait Petroleum	Kuwait	Petroleum	20,556
7	Elf-Aquitaine	France	Petroleum	19,666
8	Petoleus de Venezuela	Venezuela	Petroleum	19,659
9	Fiat	Italy	Auto	19,608
13	Volkswagenwerke	West Germany	Auto	16,822
14	Daimler-Benz	West Germany	Auto	16,281
15	Nissan Motor	Japan	Auto	16,251

stitute for Coca-Cola or Pepsi-Cola? Is iced tea? What about beer or orange juice? For some functions 7-Up might be a perfect substitute for Coke; for others it might not be. The different functions of a product and its substitutes make it difficult to define an industry's boundaries precisely.

In addition, the problem is complicated by regional and local markets. Suppose you were evaluating the market for cement in Salt Lake City, Utah. Obviously all cement producers in the Salt Lake City area would be potential suppliers. But would you include cement manufacturers in Denver or those farther away—in St. Louis, for example? High-value, lightweight products like diamonds, furs, and watches, can be shipped anywhere at low cost, and so any

producer within a country is a potential supplier. On the other hand, the cost of hauling cement is so high relative to its price that only firms in the immediate vicinity can be considered potential suppliers. The appropriate market for cement in Salt Lake City would probably include only those producers within some limited distance, say 100 miles. By defining the market we have delineated the boundaries of the industry.

The Concentration of Firms within an Industry

Among the most important characteristics of an industry are the *number* and *size* of the firms included. The measure most frequently used to describe these characteristics is the *concentration ratio*. To determine the concentration ratio, all firms in the industry are ranked by size. Various measures of size, such as total sales, total assets, or number of employees, have been used. Exhibit 17-4 illustrates a hypothetical example; the concentration ratio indicates the share of the market held by the largest firms. In the United States, such data is published for the largest four firms in an industry, the largest eight, and the largest twenty. Exhibit 17-5 provides a representative sample of the industry data collected by the U.S. Bureau of the Census.

As the table shows, industry structures differ considerably. The fur goods industry numbers 1591 firms, and the largest four have only 4 percent of the market. This is clearly an unconcentrated industry; the firms in the fur goods industry can take action independent of the actions of other firms. The fur goods industry may not be perfectly competitive, but it has enough firms and a broad size distribution that approximates perfect competition. On the other hand, the cigarette industry is a highly concentrated industry. Only seven firms produce the

High-value, lightweight products like diamonds and watches are not limited to local or regional markets. (*Photo by Richard Kalvar, Magnum Photos, Inc.*)

Exhibit 17-4 Determining concentration ratios in the gidget industry

Rank	Firm	Market Share	
1	General Gidget	21%	
2	United Gidget	15	CR4 = 57%
3	International Gidget	12	
4	U.S. Gidget	9	
5	Royal Gidget	7	CR8 = 79%
6	North West Gidget	6	
7	Southern Gidget	5	
8	Golden Gidget	4	
9	Standard Gidget	3	CR20 = 92%
10–20	Various firms	10	
21–38	Various firms	8	

total output, with the four largest firms having 81 percent of the market. A cigarette firm's decisions regarding pricing and output must take the actions of other firms into account.

A concentration ratio is a summary figure that can give an indication of the competitive conditions in an industry. But it does not provide all the information desired about the distribution of size.

Suppose you had two industries with a concentration ratio for the four largest firms (CR 4) of 60 percent. Industry *A* has four firms of approximately equal size, each with 15 percent of the market. Industry *B*, on the other hand, has a dominant firm with 51 percent of the mar-

ket; the next three largest firms have approximately a 3 percent share each. In this case, the CR 4 figure would make the industries appear to be of similar structure, whereas they are really dramatically different. Despite this potential weakness, the figure remains probably the single most important indication of an industry's structure. A concentration ratio allows us to infer the degree of interdependence among firms, which we cannot measure in other ways.

We have considered concentration in specific markets; a separate but related question is the concentration of economic power in the total economy. We are concerned here primarily with the question of overall economic power and

Exhibit 17-5 Concentration in selected manufacturing industries, 1977

Industry	Total Number of Companies	Percentage Value of Shipment Accounted for by the Four Largest
Fur goods	1591	4%
Handbags and purses	539	11
Brass or bronze castings	535	20
Carpets and rugs	167	26
Canned seafood	345	42
Hand saws	70	55
Elevators	—	63
Chewing gum	20	88
Cigarettes	7	81

SOURCE: U.S. Bureau of the Census.

political influence of the large firm. In order to determine the magnitude of this economic power, we need a measure of the inequality of the distribution of corporate wealth. The presence of excessive concentration of economic power is inconsistent with the ideal of a decentralized market economy.

The trend of general concentration in manufacturing for selected years can be seen in Exhibit 17-6. This table shows sizeable increases from 1919 to 1967 with a stable pattern thereafter. Overall, the share of value added in manufacturing held by the 200 largest corporations increased from less than 17 percent in 1919 to more than 43 percent in 1977. A similar pattern emerges when the share held by the four largest firms and that held by the 20 largest firms is analyzed.

The principal source of growth of large firms has not been internal growth, but acquisition of other firms through mergers. There are three different types of mergers. A *horizontal merger* involves two firms that provide similar goods and services, like two steel companies. A *vertical merger* is the merger of a supplier and user, such as a shoe manufacturer and a shoe retailer. A *conglomerate merger* is a merger of two firms that is neither horizontal nor vertical, such as a steel producer and an airline.

During the 1960s there was a great wave of conglomerate mergers in the United States. These mergers tended to raise general concentration levels without affecting industry concentration measures, since conglomerate mergers do not combine firms in the same industry. Some of the largest U.S. corporations actively pursued a policy of conglomerate mergers during this period. Included were ITT, LTV (Ling-Temco-Vought), Loews, Gulf and Western, Tenneco, Signal Oil, and Occidental Petroleum. The overall impact in general concentration is difficult to define and analyze. Most economists tend to focus on individual markets and not on the economic power that large financial resources can provide. This does not mean that conglomerates do not pose important questions for public policy.

Exhibit 17-6 Aggregate concentration in manufacturing, 1919–77

Year	Percentage Value Added Held by the 200 Largest Firms
1919	17%
1929	25
1947	30
1967	42
1977	43

Rapid Growth through Merger

Among the firms that led the conglomerate merger movement during the 1960s, Ling-Temco-Vought was one of the most prominent. A medium-sized electronics firm in 1961, LTV started its merger movement with Chance-Vought Aircraft ($101 million in assets). Other significant acquisitions included a 1967 merger with Wilson Co. ($196 million), a large meat packer, a sporting goods producer, and a pharmaceutical manufacturer. In 1968 LTV took over Jones & Laughlin Steel Corporation ($1.09 billion). As a result of these mergers and others, in 1969 LTV emerged as one of the largest producers of military aircraft, the third largest meat packer, the largest producer in many lines of athletic equipment, a major airline owner—via its acquisition of Braniff—and the eighth largest steelmaker. LTV thus grew from a small company to the fourteenth largest manufacturing company in the United States by 1969. But LTV had bitten off more than it could chew and sank into a series of losses; by 1975 it had returned to a smaller size. This story, however, illustrates how mergers create a more centralized economy, with fewer participating firms making decisions about resource allocations.

Product Differentiation

Another important structural characteristic of an industry is *product differentiation*. Product differentiation exists when consumers perceive differences between the products of firms that make up an industry. The behavior of firms in an industry is influenced by the degree of difference perceived. In some industries products are homogeneous, with no differentiation—including most agricultural commodities (for example, wheat or corn), raw materials (for example, iron ore and lumber), and some finished products (for example, steel and zinc). In those industries one firm cannot charge significantly more for its products than another firm. The grade and quality of the product is often determined by an outside agency, government or private, to help consumers know what they are purchasing. This category includes eggs, meat, lumber, and cement.

On the other hand, automobiles, clothing, fur goods, jewelry, and cosmetics are characterized by a high degree of product differentiation. Even if the products are not truly different but advertising has convinced people there is a difference, higher prices can be charged for the products perceived as of "higher quality." The power of advertising can be seen when identical products are sold under a nationally advertised brandname or under a chain-store brandname. Often the national brand sells for 20 or 30 percent more than the identical product carrying the store name. If consumers *perceive* a difference, even where none exists, then product differentiation becomes significant.

Industries with a high degree of product differentiation often engage in heavy advertising expenditures and market "new improved models." Their products are usually sold directly to consumers, not for use in other production, since purchasing agents are unlikely to be swayed by artificial product differentiation.

Automobiles, clothing, jewelry, and cosmetics are characterized by a high degree of product differentiation. (*Photo by Owen Franken, Stock, Boston*)

Barriers to Entry into an Industry

In some cases potential competition can have as great an impact on market equilibrium as actual competition. Imagine a firm that is the sole producer of a good. The owner of the monopoly knows that if he charges an excessive price, other firms will be attracted to the industry. If there are no *barriers to entry*, the monopolist will either make excess profits in the short run and attract competition or charge low prices, make little or no excess profit, and keep competition out. In either case the consumer receives the advantage of reasonable prices. Conversely, when barriers to entry are present, the monopolist can charge higher prices and receive excess profits without concern for the effects of potential competition.

Economies of Scale When a firm cannot achieve minimum costs of production until it produces a significant share of the national market, there is a barrier to entry.

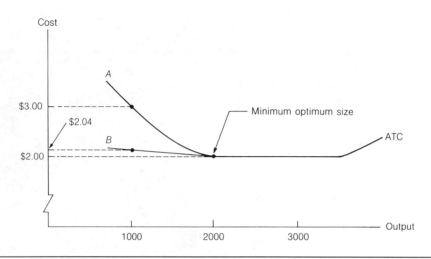

Exhibit 17-7   Role of scale economies

In industry A there is a heavy penalty for suboptimum size, whereas in industry B there is little penalty.

Hence industry B would be likely to attract many suboptimum-size firms.

Exhibit 17-7 shows diagramatically the relationship between level of output and per-unit cost (average cost) for two industries, A and B. In each industry the minimum per-unit cost is achieved at an output of 2000 units. No additional savings occur beyond that point. A firm in industry A producing 2000 units per week has costs of $2 per unit. Producing at half that level—1000 units per week—the firm's costs rise to $3 per unit. To enter industry A at that level, half the minimum optimum scale, results in a cost disadvantage of 50 percent, or $1 per unit. Therefore, it would be impractical for a firm to enter industry A unless it could achieve a volume of 2000 units per week.

The importance of this scale economy is a function of the size of the national market relative to the minimum optimum scale. With a total national market of only 2000 units per week, there would be room for only one firm of optimum size. If the national market is 10,000

units, five optimum-size firms could operate. With a demand of 100,000 units per week, as many as 50 optimum-size firms could participate in the market.

A different situation is illustrated with industry B. Here, too, minimum optimum scale is 2000 units. But in industry B the cost disadvantage of producing below the minimum optimum scale is much less severe. A firm entering the industry at half minimum optimum scale, 1000 units, would have per-unit costs of $2.04— only 2 percent more than the costs of a firm producing at minimum optimum size. We would expect industry B to attract many suboptimum-size firms.

In summary, the role of scale economies as a barrier to entry depends on two factors: (1) output of a minimum optimum firm relative to the national market, and (2) the cost disadvantage faced by a potential entrant who produces at less than minimum optimum scale. In such activities as agriculture, construction, and retail sales, scale economies play no role since the minimum optimum is a tiny portion of the national market.

Legal Barriers   Entry into some industries is precluded by legal sanctions. Television broadcasting over the open airwaves is an example. The number of TV stations broadcasting within a geographical area must be limited to prevent interference with one another. A potential broadcaster requires a frequency grant from the Federal Communications Commission, but the desirable very high frequency (VHF) channels have already been assigned in all major cities. Entry into VHF broadcasting is completely blocked. Existing firms need not worry that excess profits will attract competition, because potential entrants cannot respond.

Other types of legal barriers to entering an industry include license requirements to practice a profession or provide services, as for a lawyer, certified public accountant, liquor stores in some states, or horse racetracks. In some geographic areas, exclusive franchises are granted for cable television, electric utilities, taxi service, and air-transport service.

Probably the most widespread legal barriers are patents. Patents give an inventor the exclusive right to a product or a process for 17 years, effectively keeping potential entrants from an industry.

Absolute Cost Advantage   This barrier occurs when the costs facing a new firm are higher than those of existing firms producing at the same level of output. This situation is shown in Exhibit 17-8. When old Firm *B* produces 4000 units, its costs are $1 per unit, while at the same output level new Firm *A* faces costs of $1.40 per unit.

Television broadcasting is an industry with legal barriers to entry. (*Photo by Jerry Berndt, Stock, Boston*)

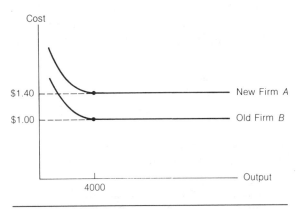

Exhibit 17-8 Hypothetical example of absolute cost advantages

With an absolute cost advantage, the established Firm B faces lower costs at every level of production than does Firm A.

Such an absolute cost difference can arise from several causes. Most commonly, the old firm controls some essential input at cost lower than that available to a new entrant. Perhaps the old firm holds a long-term contract for cheap electric power, or controls a source of high-grade raw materials. Another source of absolute cost advantage is a trade secret essential to the product. A famous example of such a secret is the formula for Coca-Cola, which is not patented; however, any potential entrant would have to spend considerable funds on research to establish itself in the market. A third absolute cost advantage can be the cost of capital. This cost advantage exists only if new entrants are considered a greater risk than existing firms and therefore must pay more for their capital.

Additional Elements of Market Structure

Concentration, product differentiation, and barriers to entry are not the only possible structural characteristics that affect an industry. Others include the growth in demand, the elasticity of demand, and changes in concentration. These factors can have an important impact on pricing and quantity decisions.

OVERALL EFFECT OF STRUCTURAL ELEMENTS

In general, evidence shows that the more highly concentrated an industry, the higher its profit rate. And generally the highly concentrated industries are those with high barriers to entry and/or a high degree of product differentiation. The question of which comes first is like that of the chicken and the egg. The high profit levels of concentrated industries may be due to the blocked entry that keeps out potential competitors. But high profits also allow massive expenditures on advertising to promote and perpetuate product differentiation.

The large expenditures associated with product differentiation can be seen in the cigarette industry. Advertising expenditures for a single brand can exceed $12 million per year. It is highly unlikely that a new small firm could enter these big leagues of product differentiation.

Also, industries often change in structure as they mature. Although auto production was not homogeneous, before 1920 there had been low barriers to entry and low levels of concentration. Then Henry Ford achieved a dominant market position by producing a good product at a low price. The price of a Model T dropped from $950 in 1909 to $290 by 1925. There were 84 firms in the industry in 1920, when well-financed General Motors entered with heavy advertising, a well-developed dealer system, and emphasis on styling. The structure of the industry changed rapidly and soon there were substantial barriers to entry. It was no longer enough to produce a superior car—all the ancillary attributes, such as a well-financed dealer system, became necessary. Firms began to fold, and the industry became more concentrated. Today the three largest auto manufacturers account for more than 92 percent of domestic output.

OVERVIEW OF INDUSTRY STRUCTURE IN THE UNITED STATES

Several U.S. industrial sectors approximate the conditions necessary for workable competition. That is, while not perfectly competitive, they have no structural characteristics to preclude relatively satisfactory performance. This category includes much of retail trade, agriculture, service trades, construction, forestry, and mining. Industries that appear not to have the structural characteristics for unregulated competition are local utilities, transportation, and communications. However, these sectors are usually regulated by a state agency or a federal agency. The competitive picture in finance and manufacturing is not clear. Some manufacturing has a high degree of concentration and barriers to entry, which would seem incompatible with a competitive industry. Structures of other manufacturing industries seem more consistent with competitive conditions.

SUMMARY

1. The U.S. industrial structure is continually changing. Some sectors expand rapidly while others decline. Within industries firms change in importance and size.

2. Some industries are relatively easy to define whereas others are more difficult. The presence of substitutes makes it hard to define the limits of an industry. In addition, if the cost per unit of value of shipping the good is high, there are geographic limits to the market.

3. By structure we mean those characteristics of an industry that influence the way it behaves. Among the most important are the number and size distribution of the firms in an industry, the degree of product differentiation, and the barriers to entry.

4. Barriers to entry are particularly important characteristics of an industry. Barriers to entry include economies of scale, legal barriers, and absolute cost advantage.

KEY CONCEPTS

concentration ratio
horizontal merger
vertical merger
conglomerate merger

product differentiation
barriers to entry
legal barriers

QUESTIONS FOR DISCUSSION

1. What industries have declined in importance over the past 10 years? Why? What industries do you think will decline in the future? Why?
2. How large an impact does advertising have on a consumer? Can advertising induce consumers to change brands of a particular commodity they normally buy? Can advertising change consumers' expenditure patterns? If there were no media advertisement, would people change their consumption patterns? In what way?
3. In agriculture the largest producers still produce less than 1 percent of the national supply. Is there some reason that giant firms have not

been able to gain dominant market shares in agriculture as they have in manufacturing?

4. How many of the largest 20 firms are you familiar with? Do you know what they produce? What percentage of the civilian labor force works for the five largest companies? The 10 largest? The 20 largest?

5. Every year *Fortune* magazine publishes a list of the 500 largest manufacturing companies, 50 largest banks, 50 largest transportation firms, 50 largest retailers, and 50 largest insurance companies. Go back a decade and compare the largest manufacturing companies of that time with the list today. Are there any new companies? Which companies are no longer on the list? A similar exercise can be done for banking, transportation, and other sectors. Is there similar stability in these lists?

6. Is it true that U.S. firms are the largest in the world? What is the basis for your opinion?

Chapter 18

Markets for Factors of Production

MARGINAL PRODUCTIVITY THEORY

Income distribution in economic theory is dominated by the idea that the factors of production—land, labor, and capital—earn a portion of the output they help produce. This approach is called *marginal productivity the-*

307

ory. The American economist John Bates Clark (1847–1938) outlined this approach in his book *The Distribution of Wealth.* He sought to find a natural law that explained how the income of society is divided. Assuming the economy was perfectly competitive, Clark showed that the supply and demand for factors of production would interact in such a way that each would receive the amount of wealth that it created. The unstated ethical presumption at the foundation of this approach to income distribution is "from each according to his wish, to each according to his contribution."

Marginal productivity theory explains the behavior of firms in the market for production resources. As such, it is but one blade of the supply-and-demand scissors that determine the income of the factors of production. In this chapter we will first investigate the demand for factors given the supply of factors. Next we will discuss the actual pricing of specific factors—particularly labor and capital—in greater detail.

Demand for farmland is derived from demand for food. (*Photo by Ellis Herwig, Stock, Boston*)

The Demand for Factors

Factors of production generally earn income when they are used by business firms. Business firms, unlike the consumers of final products, get no intrinsic satisfaction from using factors of production; they do so only to make a profit. And they make a profit only if there is a demand for the product.

The firm's demand for factors is derived from the consumer's demand for the output and is therefore called *derived demand.* In this century, for example, the decline in the demand for horsedrawn transportation has greatly reduced the demand for blacksmiths, a factor of production for that form of transportation. Because fewer horses are being used, fewer horseshoes are needed and therefore fewer blacksmiths are required.

Conversely, demand for steel, rubber, and plastics are all derived in part from the widespread use of automobiles. Another example is demand for farmland, derived from the demand for food. Because the demand for every factor of production is derived from its ability to satisfy the desires of consumers, the idea of factor usefulness underlies the marginal productivity approach to income distribution.

Marginal productivity theory explains the behavior of business firms in the factor markets. Presumably if either too much or too little of a given factor is used in production, profits will not be maximized. The business firm

Exhibit 18-1 Determining the demand for labor under competitive conditions, given the quantity of other factors

(1) Units of labor	(2) Total product (TP)	(3) Marginal physical product (MPP, ΔTP)	(4) Price of final product (P)	(5) Total revenue (P × MPP)	(6) Marginal revenue product (ΔTR)
0	0	—	$2	0	—
1	70	70	$2	$140	$140
2	160	90	$2	320	180
3	220	60	$2	440	120
4	270	50	$2	540	100
5	300	30	$2	600	60
6	310	10	$2	620	20

employs marginal analysis to determine the best use of inputs. It investigates the impact of an extra unit of input on output to determine how many units should be employed. *The marginal product of a factor of production is the extra output that results from adding one extra unit of the factor, given that all other factors are held constant. That is, the marginal product is equal to the change in total product divided by the change in the use of a factor, all other things held constant.*

This concept determines a factor's contribution to output. Exhibit 18-1 shows how much a firm's output is increased with an increment of labor in terms of both physical product (column 3) and in terms of dollar value (column 6), when the quantity of all other factors is given. When 1 unit of the variable factor—in this case, labor—is added to the given quantity of other factors, total product is 70 units. This is also shown as the *marginal physical product* (MPP) of labor, because the use of 1 unit of labor raises total output by 70 units. The dollar value of the MPP is called *marginal revenue product* (MRP). If the product can be sold to consumers for $2 per unit, total revenue is $140, and the marginal revenue product of labor is $140.

With 2 units of labor, total output rises to 160 units, and the marginal physical product is 90—that is, the addition of one more worker raised output by 90 units. Total revenue is now $320, and marginal revenue product is $180. But, because of the law of diminishing marginal returns (noted in Chapter 14), further additions of the variable factor, when all other factors are constant, result in smaller and smaller net additions to output. This is shown in column 3 of Exhibit 18-1. After an initial increase, the marginal physical products decline from 90 to 10.

The demand for labor by the business firm is derived directly from its marginal revenue product curve. The marginal revenue product of labor shows how much the last worker contributes to the revenue of the firm. For example, if a firm facing the conditions shown in Exhibit 18-1 were to hire five workers, the fifth worker would contribute $60 to the firm's revenue. If a worker could be paid less than $60, the firm would gain by hiring at least five workers. On the other hand, if a worker costs more than $60, it would not be profitable to employ the fifth worker; this worker would generate less income than cost. Thus, we see that the marginal revenue product is the firm's demand for labor.

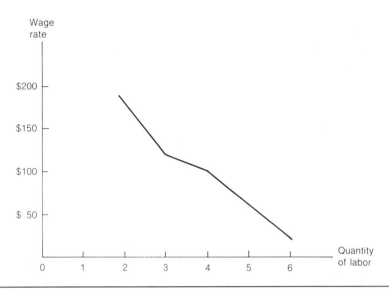

Exhibit 18-2 The derived demand for labor

The demand for a factor is derived from its capacity to produce items that consumers want. It is determined by the factor's marginal physical product, *the price of the final product, and the relative prices of factors and their substitutability. The data for this particular demand curve are given in Exhibit 18-1.*

Exhibit 18-2 shows the demand curve for labor based on Exhibit 18-1.

The demand for a factor is determined by its productivity as reflected by its marginal physical product. A second determinant of factor demand is the price of the product that determines the value of this additional output. There is a third element that affects the demand for factors: their relative prices and the ease with which one factor can be substituted for another.

Cost Minimization

The rational business firm will not hire a factor of production if its contribution to total revenue is less than its cost. However, at this point we have little insight into how many units of the various factors will be employed, because

we investigated the demand for labor *given* the quantity of other factors of production. In order to maximize profits from a certain level of production, the business firm must find the combination of factors that will minimize costs. The cheapest combination is determined by the relative prices of the factors of production. In order to minimize costs, the business firm must be in a situation where a dollar's worth of any factor adds as much to total physical product as a dollar's worth of any other factor of production.

Assume that we have a business firm that purchases two factors of production, labor and capital, in a perfectly competitive market. The marginal physical product of labor is represented by MPP_L and by P_L, the price of labor. Signifying the marginal productivity of capital as MPP_C and the price of capital as P_C, the equa-

Exhibit 18-3   A numerical example of the least-cost combination of inputs

Quantity of Inputs		Marginal Products		Marginal Physical Product Divided by Price (P_L = \$10; P_C = \$5)		
(1)	(2)	(3)	(4)	(5)	(6)	(7)
Labor	Capital	Labor	Capital	Labor	Capital	Total Cost
2	8	60	15	6	3	\$60
3	5	50	25	5	5	55
5	3	30	40	3	8	65
7	1	10	50	1	10	75

tion for minimizing the cost of a given level of output is:

$$(1) \quad \frac{\text{MPP}_L}{P_L} = \frac{\text{MPP}_C}{P_C}$$

In this equation, a dollar expenditure for labor will yield as much physical product as will a dollar expenditure on capital. If the equality does not hold because of a change in price of either capital or labor, the firm will substitute one factor for the other until equalization is reestablished. If, for example, the price of labor rises, equality in equation 1 will become an inequality in equation 2.

$$(2) \quad \frac{\text{MPP}_L}{P_L} < \frac{\text{MPP}_C}{P_C}$$

Given the inequality, the firm is clearly getting more output per dollar expenditure from capital than from labor. Consequently, the cost-minimizing strategy requires the firm to use more capital and less labor until equalization is reestablished.

As long as the firm substitutes capital for labor in this situation, the eventual equalization of the ratios is guaranteed by the law of diminishing marginal returns. As the firm uses more capital, the marginal physical product of capital

will begin to fall, as was shown in Exhibit 18-1. Thus MPP$_C$/P_C will tend to get smaller as more capital is used. Conversely, if less labor is employed, the marginal physical product of labor will tend to rise. Consequently, MPP$_L$/P_L will tend to get larger. In response to altered prices of factors, the business firm will tend to substitute one factor for another until costs are minimized for a given unit of output.

A numerical example of this cost minimization rule is given in Exhibit 18-3. We assume that the price of labor is \$10 per unit and the price of capital is \$5. The various quantities of capital and labor shown in the exhibit yield a constant level of output. The firm wishes to choose a combination of these inputs that will minimize its costs. Should it choose 7 units of labor and 1 of capital, the firm gets more output per dollar from capital than from labor, as shown in columns 5 and 6. The firm can therefore lower cost by using less labor and more capital. This substitution will continue until marginal products and factor prices are equal. Column 7 shows that minimum cost is achieved when this equality is achieved.

This example, of course, shows only two factors of production, but the principle shown in equation 1 can be extended to all relevant inputs. The general case is shown in equation 3.

$$(3) \quad \frac{\text{MPP}_A}{P_A} = \frac{\text{MPP}_B}{P_B} = \cdots = \frac{\text{MPP}_n}{P_n}$$

Whenever the equality among any number of factors is changed, cheaper ones will be substituted for the more expensive ones until equality and cost minimization is reestablished. And the principle of cost minimization shows that the price of any factor of production will affect the demand for other factors of production, depending on the ease of factor substitution.

Profit Maximization

Marginal productivity theory not only clarifies how a firm may minimize its costs given a level of output; it also indicates the level of output that will maximize profits. It is clear from the outset that if the marginal revenue product (MRP) of labor is greater than the wage rate, then the firm can earn more profit by hiring more labor. Since the marginal revenue product is the marginal physical product times the price of the final output (MRP = MPP × P), the law of diminishing marginal returns indicates that the marginal revenue product lessens as more of the factor is employed. Consequently, the firm will continue to hire labor until the marginal revenue product of labor equals its price. That is:

$$(4) \quad \text{MRP}_L = P_L$$

If this equality is achieved and we divide both sides by the price of labor, we get:

$$(5) \quad \frac{\text{MRP}_L}{P_L} = \frac{P_L}{P_L} = 1$$

For capital or any other input we could write a similar equation:

$$(6) \quad \frac{\text{MRP}_C}{P_C} = \frac{P_C}{P_C} = 1$$

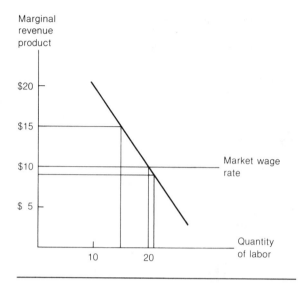

Exhibit 18-4   Marginal productivity and profit maximization

A firm maximizes profit when the marginal revenue product for each factor is equal to its price. In this example, the twenty-first worker costs more than the MRP, but 20 or fewer workers contribute more to revenue than cost.

Note that both ratios in equations 5 and 6 equal 1. In profit maximization, the ratios of the marginal revenue product of all factors to their prices must be equal. That is:

$$(7) \quad \frac{\text{MRP}_L}{P_L} = \frac{\text{MRP}_C}{P_C}$$

This relationship can be clarified with a numerical example, as shown in Exhibit 18-4. Assume the firm is operating where the marginal revenue product (MRP) of labor for an hour of work is $15 while the wage rate is $10 per hour. The last worker generates $15 in income for the firm but costs only $10—contributing $5 in profits. If the firm is buying labor in a competitive market, it is a price taker and can buy all the labor it wants for $10 per hour. But as more labor is hired, the marginal physical product of labor will fall due to the law of diminishing marginal returns. The MRP will also fall. The firm will continue to hire labor as long as the last laborer contributes more to revenue than cost—i.e., so long as MRP exceeds the wage rate. If the firm hires 20 workers, the marginal revenue product will fall to $10. Any more labor will yield less revenue than it cost. The twenty-first worker generates about $9 for the firm but costs $10. The nineteenth worker has a MRP greater than $10. Hence, when MRP = P for all factors, the firm will be maximizing profits.

In summary, the demand for a factor of production within a business firm will depend on three things: (1) the productivity of the factor, (2) the price of the output that the firm produces, and (3) the ratios of factor prices and the degree of substitutability among them. In the extreme case, there is no substitutability when factor inputs must be used in fixed proportions. In such a circumstance, for example, 2 units of capital must be used with 1 unit of labor. In this case, relative prices don't matter because the business firm is not free to vary the ratio of inputs. The firm's factor demand curve is its marginal revenue product schedule, which shows how much of a factor the firm is willing to purchase at various prices. As in any other demand curve, the relationship between price and quantity shifts either up or down according to changes in a determinant of demand. Examples of changes in each of the three determinants of the demand curve follow. (They are summarized in Exhibit 18-5.)

1. *A change in the price of the final product.* If the price of shoes were to rise, the value of the marginal product (MRP) of a shoemaker would also rise, as would the demand for shoemakers. The rise in shoe prices generally causes an increase in demand for the labor, machines, and leather used in shoe production.

2. *A change in factor productivity.* The marginal productivity of a factor is determined by the quantity and quality of the factors

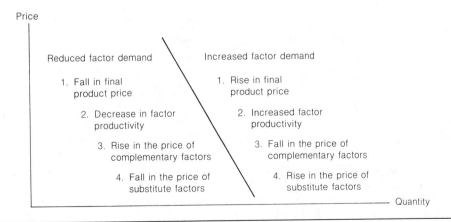

Exhibit 18-5   How the demand for a factor of production can change

---

How Much Was Broadway Joe Worth?

The Los Angeles Rams football team paid 34-year-old Joe Namath between $150,000 and $200,000 for the 1977 season. Season ticket sales to games in which the Rams participated were projected to rise by about 2500 but that was presumed to be a result of a very good schedule and few available seats. The productivity of Namath was expected to show up in the single game tickets for the four exhibitions at home. Curiosity over whether Namath could make a comeback was expected to generate an additional 6000 to 8000 tickets sold. If the Rams sold 6000 extra preseason tickets for each of the four games at the average price of $10, the extra $240,000 revenue would cover Namath's salary. In effect, the Rams were projecting the marginal productivity of their newly acquired quarterback.

---

used in production. If the tools available to workers are improved, worker productivity will rise. Similarly, increased training may increase the output of a worker. Increased marginal physical product will, of course, increase demand for labor.

3. *A change in the prices of substitute or complementary factors.* As noted before, the firm will attempt to employ the combination of resources that minimizes the cost of production. Consequently, any change in the price of a related factor is likely to affect the demand curve for all other factors used in production. If labor and capital are substitutes for each other, an increase in the price of capital will increase demand for labor and reduce the quantity of capital used. If they are complementary, the price increase is likely to diminish the use of labor. If the price of a substitute for labor falls, the demand for labor will decrease. For example, when the price of an automated shoe-making machine

falls, the demand for shoemakers will fall. (A fall in the price of a complement, on the other hand, is likely to increase demand for labor. More shoemakers may be in demand if the price of leather falls.) The demand curve for a factor is influenced by the prices of other factor inputs, as well as the ease with which they can be substituted for one another.

THE MARKET DEMAND FOR A FACTOR

The market demand curve for factors, like that of products, is derived by summing the individual demand curves for all buyers in the market. For each factor of production, the market demand curve is the sum of the marginal revenue product curves of all the firms that use that factor. This is shown in Exhibit 18-6. Given the price of the factor at P_1, the marginal revenue product curve of Firm 1 shows that the firm will purchase 5 units of the factor; Firm 2 will demand 10 units also at P_1. The horizontal summation of these demand curves at price P_1 is 15 units. This represents the market demand for the factor of production at this price.

Under conditions of perfect competition, each business firm is too small to affect the total demand for a factor of production. It has no control over the price, which it then takes as a given, as shown in Exhibit 18-6. Given the market supply and demand curves S_1 and D_1 shown in Exhibit 18-7a, we see that quantity Q_1 is demanded by the business firm. If the firm purchased less than Q_1, it would find that the marginal revenue product would exceed the price of the factor. Therefore, it would have an incentive to expand the use of that factor because it was contributing more to revenue than it cost. Similarly, if the firm bought more than Q_1 of the factor at the equilibrium price, the cost of the factor would exceed its contribution to total

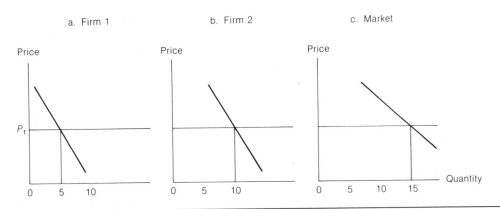

Exhibit 18-6 Market demand for a factor—the horizontal summation of the individual demand of firms

Firm 1 will purchase 5 units of the factor at price P_1; Firm 2 will demand 10 units at the same price. The market demand is found by adding the two marginal *revenue product curves together; assuming that these two firms are the only ones using the factor, the market demand is 15 units at price P_1.*

revenue, and the firm would lose money. Clearly, the rational choice is to equate the marginal revenue product and the wage rate, as shown in Exhibit 18-7.

Any change in the supply of a factor can be shown in this diagram. For example, if the sup-

ply curve S_1 shifts to the supply curve S_2, the market price of the factor will fall. Business firms will purchase more of it—in this case, quantity Q_2. The decrease in factor price results in an increase in quantity, depending, of course, on the elasticity of the firm's demand for the factor.

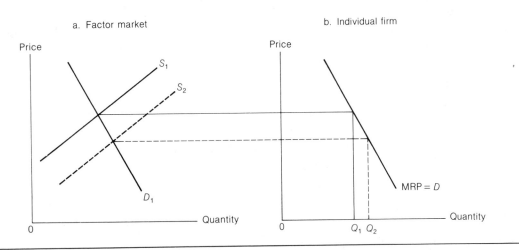

Exhibit 18-7 The factor market combined with the marginal revenue product curve to determine the amount of a factor used by the firm

If the supply curve shifts from S_1 to S_2, the market price of a factor falls. Instead of purchasing Q_1 units *of the factor, businesses now purchase Q_2 units at the lower price.*

THE LABOR FORCE

The labor force consists of all persons over 16 years old who are working or seeking employment. In 1982, 110.2 million persons were in the labor force. All were employed either full time or part time or were unemployed. Whether or not a person is in the labor force depends on many considerations. We expect, for example, fewer people over 65 than under 65 to be seeking work or be employed. Labor-force participation among married females will be lower than that of married men because many are engaged in the care of children at home. Single females are more likely to work than their married counterparts.

The *labor-force participation rate* is the percentage of a classification of people who are in the labor force. These rates are shown in Exhibit 18-8 for various age, sex, and marital status classifications for 1981. In all cases, married men (spouse present) have the highest rate of labor-force participation throughout their lives. The rate falls for the 45–64 age group, due to an increased frequency of ill health and early retirement. After the retirement age of 65, labor-force participation sharply declines. As expected, married females (spouse present) have a lower labor-force participation rate than single females. Nevertheless, the exhibit shows that over half of all married women between ages 20 and 45 are engaged in the labor force. Single persons have a similar pattern of labor-force participation rates to that of married persons but at a lower level for males and a higher level for females.

The Supply of Labor

As suggested in Exhibit 18-8, many factors determine the supply of labor. However, economists typically depict the supply of labor as a relationship between the wage rate and a quantity of labor per unit of time, assuming all other factors are held constant. The supply curve of any commodity is generally assumed to be upward sloping on a graph showing the relationship between price and quantity.

In the case of labor, it is often hypothesized that the supply of labor is "backward bending." The logic behind the *backward-bending supply of labor curve*, shown in Exhibit 18-9, is simple. Below the wage W_1, the supply of labor curve has the normal upward slope, because any

Exhibit 18-8   Labor-force participation rates by age, sex, and marital status, 1981

Marital Status and Sex	Age				
	16–19	20–24	25–44	45–64	65+
Married, spouse present					
Male	92.4%	96.5%	97.2%	83.5%	19.9%
Female	47.2	62.1	61.3	47.4	7.1
Single, never married					
Male	58.2	80.9	87.8	64.6	19.9
Female	52.3	75.4	82.5	64.3	11.9
Widowed, divorced, or married, spouse absent					
Male	80.0	91.9	92.5	73.0	13.0
Female	53.4	69.9	77.7	60.1	8.2

SOURCE: U.S. Department of Commerce, *Statistical Abstract of the United States.*

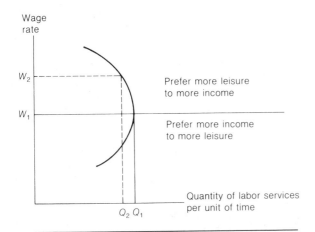

Exhibit 18-9 Backward-bending supply of labor curve

At some point individuals may want to work less even at a higher wage because of the increasing disutility of work and the decreasing marginal utility of income. Since rising wages will attract more workers into the labor force, the supply of labor for the entire economy is upward sloping.

increase in wages induces workers to give up more leisure for work. They prefer more income to more leisure. If wages rise beyond a certain level, a worker might decide that the increased income from more work would not be worth the leisure given up. In fact, if a worker's response to a wage increase beyond W_1 is to prefer more leisure to more income, the supply of labor curve would actually be backward bending.

The technical explanation for this phenomenon can clarify this relationship. Economists generally assume that labor involves disutility; that is, work is something to be avoided. Although the appropriateness of this assumption can be argued, it is clear that work does involve disutility when a lot of it is performed during a given period. In other words, no matter how good one's job is, too much work in a given period of time is likely to involve disutility. Beyond some quantity of labor supplied during

a time period, increasing amounts of labor will involve increasing marginal disutility. Therefore, we have a rationale for the upward-sloping portion of the supply of labor curve. Individuals will not be willing to work longer hours unless they are paid more per hour to offset the increasing marginal disutility.

The increasing marginal disutility of work during a given period, coupled with the parallel concept of falling marginal utility of income received from that work, is the basis of the backward-bending portion of the supply curve shown in Exhibit 18-9. Consider an individual who is being paid wage W_1 and is offering Q_1 units of labor services per unit of time. Let us investigate the reaction to an increase in the market wage from W_1 to W_2. At the higher wage rate the worker chooses to avoid the increasing disutility of another unit of work. In fact, as the curve is drawn in Exhibit 18-9, the number of hours worked can be reduced, yet total income increases because the increase in income (the area W_1 and W_2 times Q_2) is greater than the decline in income from working less (the area between Q_1 and Q_2 times W_1).

It is reasonable to believe that the backward-bending supply of labor curve is valid for most individuals. The most dramatic indication of this is that unions are increasingly demanding voluntary, rather than required, overtime. Regardless of the complexities of the production process, such as the assembly lines of the automobile production plant, the unions claim that the members want the right to say no to increased work even at the premium overtime pay rate. Although the issue of voluntary overtime in labor-management negotiations confers credibility on the backward-bending supply of labor curve for individuals, this curve does not necessarily hold true for the economy as a whole.

An increase in wages may tempt some persons to increase their amount of leisure relative to the amount of work they perform. But the same rising wage rates will tempt others to enter the labor market because the opportunity costs of not working become greater. For example, occasional workers (such as some housewives) will enter the labor market as the price for part-time work increases. Students and retired people may also seek part-time work. In short, an increase in wages is likely to increase the labor-force participation rate. Also, some part-time workers will be induced to work full time. Thus, it would appear that the backward-bending supply of labor curve holds for individuals, whereas a normal upward-sloping supply of labor curve is relevant for the economy as a whole. At *very* high wages, of course, the backward-bending supply curve may even hold for the entire economy.

WAGE DETERMINATION UNDER COMPETITIVE CONDITIONS

Wages paid to labor account for about three-quarters of the U.S. national income. As a factor of production, labor includes all personal services provided by people: wage earners, salaried professional people, and independent businessmen. Their wages are usually expressed in terms of time—so many dollars per hour, day, week, or year. When wages are paid per unit of work accomplished, wages are said to be in the form of piece rates.

Economic explanations of wage determination must account for a great variety of types and levels of compensation paid to human resources. Such a theory must explain why the wages of a relatively unskilled auto assembler are greater than those of a highly skilled auto mechanic. It should also explain why the wages of farmworkers are near the poverty level while

---

Hourly Wages

The variation in individuals' earnings is rather dramatic. David Harop in *World Paychecks: Who Makes What, Where and Why* has converted various annual salaries into hourly rates for comparison purposes. For those occupations not paid by the hour, the hourly salary is determined by dividing the annual salary by 2080 hours. Hence, Dave Winfield's annual salary of $1,500,000 converts to $721.25 per hour. Representative hourly salaries in 1982 are given below:

Dave Winfield, baseball player	$721.15
Tom Brokaw, television journalist	721.00
C. C. Galvin, Jr., chairman of Exxon, America's largest corporation	488.65
Jackie Sherill, football coach, Texas A&M	137.98
Lane Kirkland, president, AFL–CIO	52.88
Anesthesiologist (net)	45.19
Warren Burger, chief justice of the United States	40.70
George Shultz, secretary of state	33.47
Army general (4 stars)	27.64
Plumber, Seattle	16.71
Locomotive engineer	14.86
Carpenter	12.90
CPA, average	12.50
Flight attendant (top salary)	11.79
Coal miner	11.46
Secret Service agent	9.01
Logger	8.81
Corrections officer (Alabama prison guard)	7.71
Supermarket cashier (nonunion)	7.53
Zookeeper	6.47
General duty nurse	5.93
Bartender	5.26
Bank teller	4.90
Ladies' garment worker	4.68
Private first class, U.S. Army	3.81
Priest	1.73

---

the wages of some skilled workers are very high. Furthermore, the fact that many poor people work full time all year round for low wages must be reconciled with the fact that chief officers of some large corporations, athletes, and entertainers receive annual compensation in excess of $500,000. Finally, we must be able to explain why a prizefighter can earn over $1 million in one evening.

When the labor market is competitive, we assume that there are large numbers of both employers and workers. No single employer or employee can influence the market wage rate. Under such circumstances, the wage rate is determined by the intersection of the supply of labor with the demand for labor. In Exhibit 18-10a, the market demand curve for auto mechanics represents the horizontal summation of all the individual marginal revenue product curves of employers. The upward-sloping supply curve indicates that higher wages are required to attract more employees. The market wage rate is shown as $12 an hour.

Wage differentials in competitive labor markets are easily explained. Consider Exhibit 18-10b, where the market for unskilled laborers is presented. Given the supply and demand curves for this factor of production, the equilibrium wage is $4 per hour, a level far below the equilibrium wage for auto mechanics.

This differential is explained by two factors. First, demand for auto mechanics is greater than demand for unskilled workers at any wage rate. The marginal revenue product of the sixth auto mechanic is higher than for the sixth unskilled worker. Second, the supply of auto mechanics is far smaller than that of unskilled workers. The shortage of auto mechanics relative to unskilled workers, coupled with the greater demand for their services, accounts for the relatively high wages of mechanics.

Wage differentials under competitive circumstances vary according to the different skills workers possess. In general, auto mechanics have more skills than manual laborers and are paid a higher wage. This reflects both the higher marginal revenue product of this more skilled factor of production as well as its relative scarc-

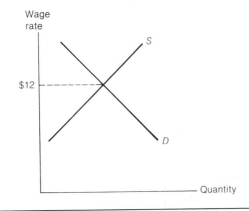

a. Market for auto mechanics

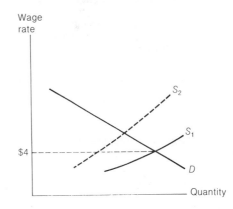

b. Market for unskilled workers

Exhibit 18-10 Determination of wages in competitive labor markets

On the left, the intersection of the supply and demand curves shows a market wage of $12 per hour   *for auto mechanics. On the right is the equilibrium wage for unskilled workers—$4 per hour.*

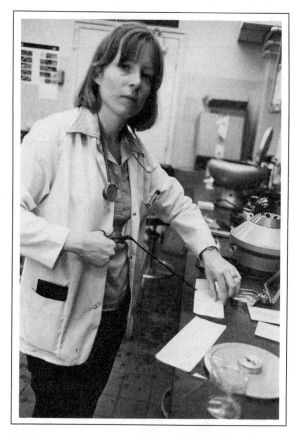

Workers with skills that are in demand but that are possessed by few people generally receive higher wages. (*Photo by Steve Potter*)

ity. Similarly, surgeons receive higher salaries than auto mechanics. Although labor may be relatively homogeneous at birth, people improve their skill levels with investments in both education and on-the-job training (investments in human capital).

The term *human capital* comes from the idea that an individual "invests" in education and training in order to receive a higher income at some time in the future. That education increases earnings for males is clear. Exhibit 18-11 shows the median earnings of males by age and education in 1980. Not only does education increase earning power, earnings also increase with age. The increase is undoubtedly because of the skill acquired from the job training and experience. Earnings of males generally increase until the age category 45–54, then decline in the 55–64 age group. The single exception is the most highly educated group, with 16 or more years of education.

The skill differences created by variations in education, on-the-job training, and other forms of skill acquisition create *noncompeting groups.* Separate markets determine the wages of these various types of labor. The more easily one type of labor can be substituted for another, the less likely it is that there will be sharp distinctions in the salaries of the two groups. An obvious

Exhibit 18-11   Median earnings of males by age and education, 1980

Age	Less than 12	Years of Education 12	13–15	16 or more
18–24	$ 5,412	$ 6,824	$ 6,975	$ 8,271
25–34	11,141	13,996	14,376	20,737
35–44	13,871	18,017	19,733	31,212
45–54	15,122	19,127	23,061	36,241
55–64	14,193	18,213	21,428	39,639

SOURCE: Estimated for 1980 census data.

Is the Economic Value of a College Education Declining?

The fallacy of composition tells us that what is good for the individual may not be socially desirable. Although formal education has been the key to getting a good job, the increasing numbers of college educated people are reducing the economic value of a college degree. According to one study, as many as 27 percent of labor-force members are overqualified for the jobs they hold. This can lead to worker dissatisfaction and, according to some research, lower productivity among overqualified workers.

---

example of noncompeting groups is auto mechanics and surgeons. The amount of training and skill involved in being a surgeon is so great that the barriers facing an auto mechanic who wishes to be a surgeon are almost insurmountable. Consequently, the wage differential between auto mechanics and surgeons is substantial.

On the other hand, we would not expect a great wage differential between auto mechanics and other workers with manual skills and an understanding of machines. Auto mechanics could easily acquire the skills required of the other occupation if the wage differential rose too high. In that event, auto mechanics would be encouraged to move into the other employment. Wage differentials can be explained in terms of the skill differentials and the ease of substitutability between one form of labor and another.

Not all differentials, however, are accounted for by these two factors. There are *compensating wage differentials*, which reward workers for undertaking particularly unpleasant tasks. A job may be undesirable because it involves the possibility of bodily injury, has unpleasant surroundings, requires employment on evening shifts, or may be subject to substantial seasonal unemployment. For example, the "graveyard" shift often receives a wage slightly higher than daytime workers. In such cases the marginal revenue product of the worker does not increase; the firm's demand for labor does not change. On the contrary, because of the job's undesirable characteristics, workers are reluctant to take employment at a given wage. Consequently, the supply curve shifts upward, as shown by the supply curve S_2 in Exhibit 18-10b. The wage rate increases, and a smaller quantity of labor is employed. Thus, under competitive circumstances it is possible for wage differentials to exist for people of equal skill and productivity because of compensation for differences in job desirability.

UNIONS

More than 22 million American workers belong to labor unions. Many more are covered by union agreements even though they are not union members. There are about 200 national unions in the United States.[*] Each is composed of local unions whose members pay dues that are shared by the local and national union. When a unionized industry employs a large number of workers in a small geographic area, locals may be very large. The Ford local of the United Automobile Workers (UAW) numbers over 30,000 members. Most locals have fewer than 1000 members. Some have as few as a dozen members.

When a union attempts to organize the workers in a factory, it petitions the National Labor Relations Board for an election to determine the exclusive bargaining agent for the workers. The

---

[*] Many are called international unions because they have local chapters in Canada.

secret ballot will list any union that has received
signature cards from more than 10 percent of
the workforce requesting such an election. A
"no-union" option also will be listed. A union
receiving a plurality of votes is designated the
sole collective bargaining agent for the workforce. It will bargain for higher wages, fringe
benefits such as medical insurance and paid
vacations, procedures to satisfy worker griev-
ances, and seniority rights. The union will also
try to ensure its own existence. It will bargain
for a union shop, requiring all new workers to
join the union within a month of their employment. Automatic deduction of union dues from
wages—called a checkoff—also strengthens the
union.

Unions in Competitive Industries

Through collective bargaining, unions usually
seek to increase wages and increase their membership by increasing total employment. As we
will see below, the goals of increasing wages and
increasing employment often conflict. This is
particularly true when unions bargain collectively with firms in competitive industries. In
a competitive industry the price of the final
output is fixed by the market. Assuming that
the marginal physical product of labor is not
subject to change by any action of the firm, the
marginal revenue product and the demand for
labor are also fixed. If the demand for labor is
fixed, any increase in wages must necessarily
reduce employment.

In an attempt to increase wages, unions representing skilled workers are likely to control
the supply of workers through some system of
accreditation acquired through the union. For
example, the union may require a long appren-
ticeship with only a limited number of persons
accepted. An example is shown in Exhibit 18-
12 when the supply curve shifts from S_1 to S_2.

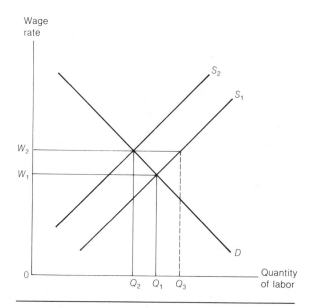

Exhibit 18-12　The effect of unions on wages and
employment

*Unions can raise wages by reducing the supply of
workers from S_1 to S_2 or by fixing a wage (W_2) above
the market equilibrium. In either case, the higher
wages will result in fewer people being employed in
the affected firms or industries. Generally, unions
must trade some employment for increased wages.*

The wage rate rises from W_1 to W_2 while the
quantity of labor employed per unit time falls
from Q_1 to Q_2.

If the union representing workers is less able
to control supply because of little skill differentiation between its workers and others, the
union will negotiate a fixed wage above equilibrium. If the union succeeds, as shown in
Exhibit 18-12 at wage W_2, we see that employment declines from Q_1 to Q_2 and a number of
workers ($Q_2 - Q_3$) seek employment at the new
wage rate but cannot get a job. The net effect
of the policies is similar: wages will be higher
and employment lower. The reduced-supply
approach is more likely to be used by skilled
workers, and the wage-above-equilibrium ap-

proach is more likely to be used by workers with few special skills.

This tradeoff between higher wages and reduced employment might be avoided in the competitive industries with positive profits. In the short run, unions could force the firm off its demand curve. In terms of Exhibit 18-12 the firm might hire Q_1 workers at a wage above W_1 in the short run by reducing its level of profits. In the long run, however, excess profits in a competitive industry are likely to be short-lived due to new entry into the industry. The wage increase gained in the short run is likely to come at the expense of some future smaller increment in salary. And business firms forced off their demand curve in such a way gain an incentive to adopt technical changes that in the long run substitute capital for labor. Such a development, of course, would reinforce the long-run problem facing labor unions—namely, that increased wages for membership generally mean a smaller level of total employment.

Unions Facing a Monopsonist

When labor unions face a monopsonist, that is, a single hirer of labor that has no competition, they can obtain increases in both wages and employment because the union can force the firm closer to a competitive equilibrium. This is, of course, the rather special case of the company town.

The monopsonist's objective is to equate the marginal revenue product of labor with the marginal cost of labor. In this case, however, the marginal cost of labor is greater than the actual supply curve of labor. The reason is that as the firm pays a higher wage to induce more workers into its labor force, it must also pay a higher wage to all previously employed workers. Consequently, in order to hire an additional worker it must increase the wage rate not only for that employee but for all other employees as well.

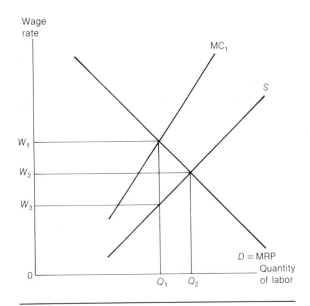

Exhibit 18-13 The wage rate and monopsony

In the special case of a monopsonist, the firm is not a price taker and must induce more workers to seek employment. Since the higher wage must be paid to all workers, the marginal cost of labor lies above the supply curve. When the firm equates MRP with marginal cost it will hire fewer workers than a competitive firm. A union could raise both wages and employment if it could force the monopsonist toward a competitive equilibrium.

The cost of adding another worker, the marginal cost of labor (MC_L), is higher than the average cost of labor as reflected by the supply curve. Of course, a competitive firm doesn't face this situation because it can hire all the workers it wants at the market wage; i.e., it is a price taker.

In Exhibit 18-13 the monopsonist will equate the marginal revenue product of labor with its marginal cost and will hire Q_1 amount of labor. However, in order to hire this much labor, it need pay only wage W_3. This, of course, is beneath both the competitive equilibrium wage and the equilibrium quantity of employment. Consequently, the union may be able through collective bargaining to force the monopsonist toward a competitive equilibrium, thereby increasing both employment and the average wage paid labor. It is important to emphasize that monopsony in labor markets could occur under only unusual circumstances in a modern economy.

Do Unions Raise Wages?

In answering the question of whether unionized workers are in fact better off, it is often noted that the share of national income that has gone to labor and proprietors has been roughly constant for the last 40 years. This leads some observers to conclude that labor unions have not increased the well-being of labor in the aggregate since the Great Depression, even though union power greatly increased.

In one respect, we can definitely say that workers are made better off by unions. This issue, however, deals with job security rather than employment or wages. Before labor unions established grievance procedures, a worker could be fired at the whim of the supervisor or employer. The worker had to take constant care not to offend those in authority. Grievance procedures have given workers recourse in such situations.

As for the wage question, the answer probably is that some union workers are made better off while others are not. As we can easily deduce from the above analysis, unions in noncompetitive industries are likely to realize higher wages because firms can pass the increases on to consumers in the form of higher prices. To a certain extent, this means that union workers in noncompetitive industries are gaining at the expense of consumers as a whole. Thus, the fact that unions are successful in noncompetitive industries raises the cost of living for union members in competitive industries who are not so fortunate as to gain long-run increases. There seems

Because of differences in the way industries pass on their increased costs of doing business, auto workers probably benefit from union-won wage increases more than retail clerks but less than airline pilots. (*Photo by Terry Zabala*)

to be a distributional effect of labor unions within the labor community itself. The true answer as to whether or not unions raise wages seems to come in three parts: one-third of the unionized workers benefit from significantly higher wages (teamsters and airline pilots, for example), one-third benefit from slightly higher wages (auto and steel workers), and one-third do not have their wages increased in the long run at all (textile workers and retail clerks).

THE RISE OF UNIONISM

In the 1790s craftsmen in Philadelphia, New York, and Boston organized the forerunners of modern U.S. unions. These organizations were usually founded to achieve specific objectives, and once the goals were achieved, the organization faded. A *long*-lasting union of this era was that of the Philadelphia cordwainers (leather workers), who maintained a union from 1794 to 1806. Periodic depressions weakened the unions. Emerging craft unions faded in the depression of 1818–20 and again in 1837.

Attempts of workers to organize at this time were often frustrated by court rulings that held societies of workers to be illegal conspiracies under English common law. In 1842 the Massachusetts Supreme Court ruled in *Commonwealth vs. Hunt* that attempts to unionize could not be criminal unless their goals were criminal. And the objective of Hunt and his fellow members of the Boston Bootmakers' Society, which was to strike for union security, was ruled legal.

Despite the ruling in *Commonwealth vs. Hunt*, prospective unions still faced a very hostile climate. Ross M. Robertson has argued that this climate was at least partly related to the American dream of self-reliance and rugged individualism.

Americans were at least half a century behind the times in their failure to realize that the agrarian economy, in which the individual did have some measure of control over his own destiny, was fast disappearing. Business and professional people felt that the working masses would be content if they were not stirred up by a few misguided and power-hungry rabble rousers. If a man worked hard, did what he was told, and saved his money he could always rise to the top, they thought. To grant security to unions in the form of, say, a closed shop was an unconscionable interference with the rights of both employers and those laborers who wanted to remain rugged individualists.[*]

---

[*]Ross M. Robertson, *History of the American Economy* (New York: Harcourt, Brace, and World, 1955), p. 336.

Craft unions gained strength during the 1860s. It is estimated that at that time there were 41 national craft unions with a combined membership of over 300,000. But the labor movement remained weak because so many separate organizations were formed along craft lines. This problem became obvious to many labor leaders after six years of depression in the 1870s. Only eight of the 41 national craft unions survived.

One of the most romantic organizations of workers was called the Knights of Labor. The Noble and Holy Order of the Knights of Labor was founded in 1869. After years of slow growth, its membership rose spectacularly to almost three-quarters of a million members by 1886. The Knights' program had strong progressive overtones, calling for an eight-hour day, equal pay for equal work by women, abolition of child labor, establishment of cooperatives, and public ownership of utilities.

But this very set of ideals caused the Knights of Labor to collapse. Because of its democratic nature the Knights supported the cause of all workers. Skilled workers with high wages did not want to fight for better pay for their less skilled "brothers." The internal conflict coupled with the problems of leadership reduced the organization's influence. The Knights ceased to exist in 1917.

In 1886 several national unions broke with the Knights of Labor to found the American Federation of Labor (AFL). Under the leadership of Samuel Gompers, the AFL enjoyed substantial growth, in part because there were no prolonged periods of unemployment during the first two decades of the twentieth century. Labor leaders had decided that unionism should live in peaceful coexistence with American capitalism. Rather than seeking to destroy capitalism by political action as a labor party, the AFL sought to improve wages and working conditions through evolutionary changes. In politics, organized labor tried to play one major party against the other with a policy designed to defeat labor's enemies while rewarding its friends. This approach probably minimized the number of political losses and maximized the number of legislative bills passed favorable to labor.

Membership in unions reached five million by 1920, but the depression of 1920–21 and subsequent optimism of the late 1920s reduced union strength.

The familiar conflict between the high-wage skilled workers and the relatively unskilled led to dissension within the American Federation of Labor. In the mid-1930s it became clear that the traditional craft union, which organized all persons who did similar work, was unwieldy and ineffective for the needs of workers in modern mass-production industries. It was argued that unions should be organized to include all the workers in a particular industry. The Committee for Industrial Organizations was formed within the AFL in 1935 and broke with the parent organization in 1936. As the independent Congress of Industrial Organizations (CIO), the new group included such organizations as the United Automobile Workers and the United Mine Workers. The split continued until 1955 when the two merged into a new organization called the AFL-CIO.

During the Great Depression of the 1930s significant prolabor legislation was passed by Congress. The Norris-LaGuardia Act of 1932 prohibited federal courts from enforcing efforts of business firms to require an employee to promise, as a condition of employment, that he or she would not join a labor union. Such a requirement was called a *yellow-dog contract* and had greatly impeded the efforts of unions to organize workers. The National Industrial Recovery Act of 1933 stated for the first time that workers had the right to organize and bargain collectively with employers. The NIRA was declared unconstitutional for unrelated rea-

---

Union Mergers

Although mergers between companies make the headlines on financial pages, a rising tide of union mergers remains almost unnoticed. In the last 26 years almost one-third of the existing labor organizations have been affected by a merger.

In many cases the merger merely provides a decent burial for a union that has been overcome by time and technology. For instance, the merger of the Cigar Makers with the Retail, Wholesale and Department Store Workers was important only to labor historians. The Cigar Makers was the base of Samuel Gompers and other union movement leaders at the turn of the century. However, automatic machinery had replaced the skilled workers and membership had declined from 70,000 in the 1920s to fewer than 2500 at the time of the merger.

Other mergers are of greater economic significance. A legacy of the AFL-CIO split of the 1930s was the existence of two or more unions claiming the same jurisdiction. To avoid union competition for members, mergers were encouraged. For example, the Packinghouse Workers and the Amalgamated Meatcutters joined forces.

Other mergers have increased union control over substitute goods. For example, the Steelworkers union has absorbed the Aluminum Workers, the Mine, Mill and Smelter Workers, and the catchall District 50 of the United Mine Workers. This gives the Steelworkers effective jurisdiction over the entire metals industry.

---

sons, but Congress passed the National Labor Relations Act (Wagner Act) in 1935. This act spelled out unfair labor practices prohibited to employers and established the National Labor Relations Board to help determine the legitimate representative of employees.

Prolabor sentiment in Congress diminished after World War II. After many strikes, the Labor-Management Relations Act of 1947 (Taft-Hartley Act) put constraints on labor unions and prevented them from engaging in "unfair labor practices" that were earlier forbidden to management. The old identification of labor unions as subversive once again appeared as the Taft-Hartley Act required union officials to sign affidavits that they were not Communists.

The section of the Taft-Hartley Act most threatening to unions allows states to forbid compulsory union membership. While union shops are legal under federal law, states may outlaw them. Advocates of state "right-to-work" laws argue that individuals should not be forced to join any organization. Union opponents point out that these laws allow workers to benefit from union efforts without paying dues, thus reducing union membership, financial support, and, ultimately, chances for union survival.

THE PRICE OF LONG-LASTING ASSETS

People and institutions with loanable funds can earn interest on their money while taking virtually no risk. By putting the money in a savings account, little of the flexibility of money is given up. The question is, why would someone take these liquid funds and purchase land or capital equipment that has a long life? The usual answer, of course, is to make profits. In this section we investigate how a business firm decides to purchase a long-lived asset instead of holding liquid assets—and how these decisions will ultimately determine the price of long-lasting assets.

One great problem facing a business firm that hopes to reap the benefits of an investment over a long period of time is how to estimate the value of a dollar in the future; a dollar today is not equal to a dollar tomorrow. If I am to choose between $100 today and $100 a year from now I would hardly be indifferent between the two. I would choose the $100 today and put it in the bank to earn 5 percent interest on that money, assuming zero inflation. One year hence I would have $105. In this case, a dollar today is worth more than a dollar tomorrow.

Business investments in capital equipment are likely to reap benefits long into the future. Consequently, a process is required by which the firm can evaluate the benefits that will accrue over this period of time. An alternative to purchasing capital equipment is to invest the money the equipment costs in something else.

Business investments in capital equipment are likely to reap benefits long into the future. (*Photo by Peter Menzel, Stock, Boston*)

This may yield a higher rate of return. Comparing these potential investment earnings with the purchase price of capital equipment is called evaluating the present value of future income or *net present value.*

We know that if the interest rate were 8 percent, $100 today would yield $108 a year from now ($100 + .08 of $100 = $108). This is the same as 1.08 times $100. But what if we know we will have $108 a year from now and want to know the present value of $108? To determine the net present value of $108 a year from now, we divide $108 by 1.08 (1 plus the interest rate of .08) and get $100. Similarly, if we wanted to know the net present value of $100 a year from now, we would divide $100 by 1.08, which is $92.59.

In general, the net present value (NPV) of X dollars one year in the future is the dollar value divided by 1 plus the interest rate.

$$(1) \quad NPV = \frac{X}{(1 + i)}$$

The net present value of $100 two years from now at 8 percent would be:

$$(2) \quad NPV = \frac{100}{(1.08)^2} = \$85.73$$

This result is arrived at because $85.73 must be invested at 8 percent for two years in order to realize $100. In general, the net present value of an income of X dollars per year is equal to:

$$(3) \quad NPV = \frac{X}{(1 + i)} + \frac{X_2}{(1 + i)^2} \cdots \frac{X_n}{(1 + i)^n}$$

Two things become clear from this calculation. First, the value of a dollar becomes progressively smaller in net present value terms as it is promised further and further into the future. The denominator gets larger and larger because of the effects of compound interest. Second, the net present value involves, in effect, a reverse interest rate. An interest rate determines the value of a dollar sometime in the future. When it is applied in the net present value formulation, i is called a *discount rate.* It determines how much money would have to be invested today at that interest rate in order to receive the dollar value cited in the future.

The net present value formulation can be used to determine whether it pays for the firm to purchase a capital good or whether it would be better to invest in something else. This is true if the discount rate accurately reflects the opportunity cost of the funds to the firm—that is, the rate at which it can both borrow and lend. It pays to purchase a capital good (such as a machine) whenever the net present value of the income it produces over the years exceeds its purchase price.

In a competitive economy, the price of a long-lasting asset will tend toward the net present value of its expected future earnings. Assume that all firms have about the same expectations and so the expected benefits from an asset are the same. If the net present value of the future earnings is larger than the price of the asset, the purchaser will make a profit. This profit will encourage other firms to bid a slightly higher price for the asset, since they will be willing to take a smaller profit if necessary. Under conditions of free entry, this competitive process will continue until the price of the asset is equal to its net present value. Then no firm can expect to earn a profit by offering more for the asset. Profits will tend toward zero under competition.

SUMMARY

1. A business firm receives no intrinsic satisfaction from hiring factors of production. Its demand for factors is derived from the consumer's demand for the firm's output.

2. A firm minimizes the cost of producing a given level of output when the last dollar spent on each factor yields the same output. The marginal physical productivity of each factor divided by its price must be equal for all factors when cost is minimized.

3. To maximize profits, the firm must equalize the ratio of marginal revenue product of factors divided by their prices.

4. Three elements determine the demand for a factor: (1) its marginal physical product, (2) the price of the final product that determines the value of this productivity, and (3) the relative prices of factors and the degree of substitutability among them.

5. The labor force consists of all persons over 16 years old who are working or seeking employment. About 110 million people are in the labor force. Labor-force participation varies according to age, sex, and marital status.

6. Diminishing marginal utility of income, coupled with the increasing disutility of additional work during a given period, suggests a backward-bending labor supply curve for individuals.

7. Long-lasting assets are priced according to the net present value of expected future earnings. The process of discounting future benefits is crucial to the evaluation of all investments, both public and private, that extend over time.

KEY CONCEPTS

marginal productivity theory

derived demand

marginal physical product

marginal revenue product

conditions for cost minimization

conditions for profit
    maximization

labor-force participation rate

backward-bending supply of labor
    curve

noncompeting groups

compensating wage differentials

net present value

collective bargaining

discount rate

QUESTIONS FOR DISCUSSION

1. John Bates Clark wanted to develop a "natural law" that explained how income is divided in society. To what extent do you think his marginal productivity theory achieved this objective?

2. Can marginal productivity theory explain why a minimum-wage law is likely to result in an increase in unemployment?

3. Do you believe police personnel should have the right to strike? What about surgeons? If you don't believe they should have the right to strike, how would you prevent a strike called for by a union of doctors or police personnel?

4. "Marginal productivity of labor is more difficult to measure in large firms than in small firms. This theory of distribution therefore was more appropriate in the nineteenth century than it is in the twentieth century. Personnel management policies, not markets, determine wages in large firms." Is this statement true? If it is, does it mean that marginal productivity theory is irrelevant?

5. Many states have legislation called the "right-to-work law." This eliminates the union shop because workers covered by union contracts are not required to join the union. As a labor unionist, how would you feel about this legislation? Would your feelings be different if you owned a large business?

6. Assume the government offers a limited number of licenses that permit firms to repair automobiles. This restricted competition will probably lead to higher repair costs that hurt consumers. From a social point of view, this policy can be considered irrational. Under what circumstances is there an element of unfairness in the elimination of this policy?

Chapter 19

Inequality: Problems of Incentive and Equity

Earlier we discussed the problems of stabilizing economic activity and of resource allocation. When affluence is realized by an efficient allocation of resources and its stability is achieved through macroeconomic policy, knotty economic problems can still remain. Many of these problems relate to income distribution.

Inequality of income is consistent with the idea of justice as long as there is agreement on the rules that generate economic differences. In a track meet we expect the swiftest runner to finish first. The losers do not cry foul because of the inequality; rather, they accept the rules under which the meet is conducted. So it is in economic activity. If people accept the rules that govern the distribution of economic benefits, they will accept the outcome unless inequality is generated by persons violating the rules.

THE ECONOMIC ROLE OF INEQUALITY

Inequalities play an important role in any socioeconomic system. A market economy allocates all its resources on the basis of price differentials. Wages and salaries are the price of labor. Wage differentials are the signals that encourage workers to enter occupations in relatively short supply. When the income of teachers is decreasing compared with that of engineers, many students shift their course of study from education to engineering. Market economies rely on income differentials to allocate labor resources. And these necessarily result in differences in income.

Wage differentials are not the only way to encourage workers to enter occupations where

High government officials are among the people who may be motivated less by a job's salary than by its status or some other aspect. *(Photo by Bill Fitzpatrick, The White House)*

labor is in short supply. Social status may be an equally effective way to influence the occupational choices of people. In the United States, high income itself confers a certain amount of social status. Workers may be motivated by high social status as much as by income per se. Socialist countries typically rely on social motivators as well as income differences to encourage people to select occupations in which they are needed.

That people are motivated by status is best demonstrated by the number of wealthy people willing to take substantial cuts in salary to become high government officials. The relatively low pay in the public sector, for both elective and appointed office, suggests that inequalities other than income (like varying degrees of prestige) can be useful in encouraging the allocation of labor resources. A market economy operates on the basis of income inequality; other economic systems use other forms of inequality. But the allocation of labor and other resources ultimately depends on different evaluations of their importance, measured in terms of income, social status, or by some other means.

Wage inequality in a market economy also provides an incentive for workers to use and improve their skills. In the extreme, when able-bodied workers receive no income if they do not work, they have high incentive to use their skills. The advantages of high income and the insecurity of low income also provide young people with a powerful motivation to develop skills desired in the marketplace.

The Functional Distribution of Income

Economists measure income distribution in two ways. One approach analyzes how national income is divided among the factors of production. It measures the portions of national income that go to the owners of labor, capital, and land. This is called the *functional distribution of income*. When Karl Marx analyzed the workings of the capitalist economy in *Das Kapital*, he built his analytical structure on the *labor theory of value*. According to Marx, all production is ultimately the product of labor, which should therefore receive all national income. Marx's criterion for distributive justice was that those responsible for production should receive the product. Since labor was responsible for all output, any portion of national output going to capitalists was exploitation. The functional distribution of income is particularly useful in analyzing how national income is divided between labor and capital.

Exhibit 19-1 shows the functional distribution of income from 1900 to 1982. These sta-

Exhibit 19-1   The functional distribution of income, by percentage, 1900–82

Payments	1900–09	1930	1950	1970	1976	1982
Compensation of employees	55.0%	62.1%	64.1%	75.6%	76.3%	75.3%
Proprietor income	23.6	15.8	15.6	8.4	7.2	5.2
Rental income of persons	9.1	6.4	3.9	2.9	1.7	1.5
Corporate profits and inventory valuation allowance	6.8	9.2	15.6	8.9	8.7	8.1
Net interest	8.5	6.5	.8	4.2	6.1	9.9
Total	100.0	100.0	100.0	100.0	100.0	100.0

SOURCE: *Long Term Economic Growth 1860–1970*, U.S. Department of Commerce, 1973; D. Gale Johnston, "The Functional Distribution of Income in the United States," *Review of Economics and Statistics* (May 1954); *Statistical Abstract of the United States*.

tistics don't exactly conform to the economist's notions of wages, interest, rent, and profit. Proprietor income is particularly hard to interpret, because part of it is a product of proprietors' labor and part is properly construed as a return on capital. Since landowning farmers are included, it also includes an element of rent. Despite this shortcoming in the data, the functional distribution presented in Exhibit 19-1 provides useful information about how national income is divided among the factors of production.

Two things about the functional distribution of income stand out. First, the share of national income going to labor is large—about 75 percent in recent years. Although it is frequently assumed that all proprietor income should be allocated to labor, historical experience suggests that about one-third of it is a return to property.* If this is correct, the share of national income going to labor is about 80 percent when proprietors' labor earnings are added to wages and salaries. This indicates that 20 percent of national income goes to the owners of property and land, in the form of rent, interest, and profits.

The defenders of the free-enterprise system point to this large share of wages and salaries to disprove Marx's theory, although leftists view the 20 percent as a huge tax placed on workers by the owners of property. As we shall see, most discussions of income distribution are heavily laden with notions of "fairness" and other value judgments.

A second feature of the functional distribution shown in Exhibit 19-1 is that labor's share of aggregate income has been increasing over time. In the decade following 1900, labor's share of national income was only 55 percent. It has

Labor's share of national income has been increasing since 1900 partly because proprietorships have been decreasing. *(Photo by Michael Weisbrot, Stock, Boston)*

risen steadily since, because the share going to proprietors has fallen during the same period. From 1900 to 1982 the proportion of national income paid in the form of wages and salaries increased about 20 percent, while proprietors' share fell over 15 percent. This reflects the increasing concentration of economic activity discussed earlier. The individual who was a small-scale proprietor at the turn of the century is now likely to be employed by a large corporation as a store manager; as a result, this income now counts as wages and salaries rather than proprietors' income.

---

*D. Gale Johnston, "The Functional Distribution of Income in the United States," *Review of Economics and Statistics* (May 1954).

The decline of proprietorships does not entirely explain the increase in labor's share of national income. During the past 80 years, a trend toward labor-intensive activities has also increased labor's share of national income. Labor's share in agricultural activities is quite low, and in this century much of the labor force moved out of farming pursuits into more labor-intensive manufacturing activities. More recently, the fastest-growing sector of the economy is public and private service, which is highly labor-intensive. The increasing importance of labor in the production process during this century partly explains the rising share of national income going to labor. A third explanation is that labor unions have also modestly contributed to the increase.

The Proportional Distribution of Income

The most common method of analyzing the distribution of income is to observe how total income is divided among the population regardless of the factors of production. The distribution of national income among families is shown in Exhibit 19-2. It shows the proportion of fam-

Exhibit 19-2   The proportional distribution of family income, 1981

Income Class	Percentage of Families
Under $5,000	6%
$5,000–$10,000	11
$10,000–$15,000	14
$15,000–$20,000	12
$20,000–$25,000	17
$25,000–$30,000	12
$30,000–$40,000	12
$40,000–$50,000	9
$50,000–$75,000	5
$75,000 and higher	2

SOURCE: U.S. Department of Commerce

ilies in various income classes in 1981: 6 percent of families had an income below $5000 and 40 percent had more than $25,000.

The data in Exhibit 19-2 offends some people's sense of justice. Approximately 6 percent of all families have so little income that their basic nutrition and health needs cannot be met, while other families enjoy incomes exceeding $1 million a year. This poverty amid affluence has raised many challenging questions about the fairness of income distribution. Yet others argue that these differences are needed to motivate workers and reflect individual contributions to national welfare. The determinants of the distribution of income and the policy issues surrounding it are discussed in this chapter.

INCOME DISTRIBUTION: POSITIVE VERSUS NORMATIVE ECONOMICS

Remember from Part I that positive economics is based on the scientific method and the absence of subjective value judgments. Positive economics is used to determine the impact of economic events and policies on income distribution. When practicing normative economics, economists make judgments as the situation requires. Since many issues of income distribution are inherently normative, there is no way for social scientists or society to avoid making value judgments regarding the distribution of income.

In one respect, applying scientific thinking to income distribution leads to a deadend. When a reformer claims that aggregate well-being will rise as a result of some income distribution policy, the positive economist might ask for proof. The reformer, of course, cannot give such proof because the argument is based on plausible outcomes, not proven results. It may be argued, for example, that taking income from families who have earnings exceeding $100,000 and redistributing it to poor families would make society better off. This is based on the theory that the marginal utility of income falls as people get more money. The utility lost by the rich family will be smaller than that gained by the poor family. But this cannot be proven—it is only plausible. The economist who insists on scientific proof that one pattern of income distribution is preferable to another will find only frustration. Just as the reformer cannot provide scientific proof, neither can the positive economist prove that the existing distribution is preferable.

THE EXTREMES OF INCOME DISTRIBUTION

The Poor

The U.S. government defines poverty based upon the cost of a set of goods and services that provide minimal housing, nutrition, clothing, and medical care. Families or individuals with incomes below the poverty line presumably are receiving inadequate amounts of one or all of these basic needs. This poverty line varies with the number of persons in a household. In 1981 a family of four was determined to need a money income of $9287 to live above the poverty line.

If a family of four were to spend approximately 30 percent of its income on food, this budget would allow $2786 for food expenditures during a year. This is $7.63 per day for the family. More than 31.8 million Americans lived at a standard of living equal to or below this level of income in 1981. This amounts to 14 percent of the U.S. population.

Exhibit 19-3 Persons below poverty level, 1981, based on money income

Group	Percentage Classified As in Poverty
All American	14.0%
Whites	11.1
Blacks	34.2
Hispanics	26.5
65 and older	15.3
18 and under	19.8
People on farms	23.0

Some characteristics of the poor are shown in Exhibit 19-3. The poverty profile in the United States is dominated by two kinds of people: those with low productivity because of low skills and those of school age or retirement age.

Poverty statistics lend support to the idea that minority groups and women have not had an equal chance in the marketplace. The incidence of poverty among these groups is very high. More than three out of every 10 black persons live in poverty. An equally alarming statistic deals with households headed by women: over 40 percent of these households live in poverty. High divorce rates raise the prospect that many women will head a household at some point during their lifetimes. It is not a comforting prospect in light of these statistics.

Of course, it is important to remember that some young people are poor because they are training for high-paying jobs. Medical students are a case in point. Their poverty is far different from that of an unemployed laborer with a family to support.

There remains significant disagreement on the appropriate measure of poverty. Although the money income figure of $9287 for a family of four is not seriously challenged, the number of families below this line is questioned. It has

Changing Families

No discussion of family income and poverty problems would be complete without a discussion of changing family structure. The decline in the proportion of husband-wife families during the 1970s has been the most important factor affecting family income data. On the average, families with working wives have higher incomes than other types of families. The shift of the 1970s can be seen in the following data.

Type of Family	White		Black	
	1980	1970	1980	1970
Husband-wife	85.1%	88.3%	53.7%	65.6%
Male household—no wife present	3.0	2.3	4.6	3.8
Female household—no husband present	11.9	9.4	41.7	30.6

The rise of female-headed households, particularly among blacks, has been a significant factor in increasing the number of families below the poverty line. This can be seen in the median family income associated with the different family situations.

Type of Family	1980 Median Income	
	White	Black
Husband-wife	$23,501	$18,593
Wife employed	27,238	22,795
Wife not employed	19,430	12,419
Male household—no wife present	18,731	12,557
Female household—no husband present	11,908	7,425

been pointed out that many programs helping the poor pay off "in kind" rather than in money. For example, poor families often live in public housing where the rents are lower than in comparable private housing markets. Subsidized housing has the effect of lowering the poverty line but the effect is not included in most studies. The importance of noncash subsidies can be seen in a recent Census Bureau study indicating that when the value of food stamps, Medicaid, and subsidized housing is included in family income, the percentage of households living in poverty dropped from 14 percent to 8 percent. Whether the figure is 8 percent or 14 percent or somewhere in between, however, there still remains a group of people at the bottom of the income distribution who are living with minimal material well-being.

The Rich

"Rich" can be defined in two different ways: (1) by income and (2) by wealth. High incomes will usually follow if there is great wealth but the reverse is not necessarily true. For example, a recently certified neurosurgeon might well have a high income but almost no wealth (and in fact be significantly in debt). Also, different observers may perceive the two categories of rich differently. The surgeon whose earnings are at least in part the result of his investment in training, skill, and 60-hour work weeks may evoke a different attitude than an individual not gainfully employed who receives the same earnings through returns on inherited wealth.

Wealth   *Forbes* magazine identified and ranked the 400 richest persons in America. This survey of the "Forbes 400" has provided a valuable source of data on the super-rich of America. (The box provides some information on this group, whose individual wealth ranges from $75 million to $2 billion.) The current 400 appear to vary more than in earlier studies of America's wealthy. Approximately 150 inherited their wealth. These include many with familiar family names: 14 Rockefellers, 30 DuPonts, and five Mellons. However, others have attained the list in a short time without inheritances, by identifying a hot product line (e.g., Steven Jobs, the founder of Apple Computers, became a centi-millionaire at age 27). Philip Knight with Nike athletic shoes and George Lucas of *Star Wars* fame are additional examples of young entrepreneurs who achieved great wealth early.

The impact of great wealth upon income redistribution also must be put into perspective. The richest man in the United States has wealth estimated at approximately $2 billion, certainly a massive fortune. However, if it were confiscated and redistributed to every citizen of the United States it would just about be sufficient to buy each person a steak dinner.

Income   The box "Hourly Wages" in Chapter 18 shows wide variation in individual earnings. The characteristics of those at the bottom of the income distribution have previously been discussed. What about the characteristics of those on the high side? In 1980 approximately four million households had incomes exceeding $50,000. The age distribution of this group shows the importance of training and experience in achieving higher earnings. Among families headed by a man or woman under 30, fewer than 1 percent had incomes exceeding $50,000. Similarly, among families headed by a person over 65 and thus typically no longer in the active labor market, only 2 percent exceeded the $50,000 mark. More than 13 percent of families headed by someone in the prime working years between 45 and 55 had $50,000-plus incomes.

Viewed from an occupational standpoint, the $50,000-plus group is heavily loaded with certain professionals. Virtually all physicians and dentists in private practice fall in this group. Managers and self-employed entrepreneurs also are heavily represented. Virtually absent are laborers, operators, and most individuals employed in organizations except in management positions.

MEASURING INCOME INEQUALITY

In analyzing the distribution of income, it is sometimes difficult to determine when the dis-

The Forbes 400

The September 1982 issue of *Forbes* contains the most current and careful compilation of wealth held by individuals in the United States. In order to qualify for inclusion on the list, an individual needed approximately $75 million in assets. A self-made shipping magnate, Daniel Ludwig, 85, was identified as the wealthiest American, with $2 billion.

Brief autobiographical summaries of the "Forbes 400" contain fascinating insights into the diversity of this group. At one extreme are such individuals as former Governor and Ambassador Averell Harriman and members of the Mellon family who have spent 50 years or more in public service or philanthropy. At the other is Robert Vesco, who is described as a "fugitive from justice" after allegedly looting a mutual fund and whose residence is believed to be a yacht armed with guided missiles.

Of the 400, approximately 150 *essentially* inherited their wealth. The other 250 either are entirely self-made or inherited some wealth and proceeded to expand their holdings into significantly larger fortunes. In this day of high income taxes, it is interesting to note that it is still possible to start with nothing and become among the very wealthiest—David Packard, who started with $500 and a garage workshop in 1939 while a graduate student, became one of the few billionaires on the list through the development of Hewlett-Packard Corporation.

Among the major fortunes, the most numerous method of achieving wealth was real estate (63), of which over half were made in New York City (33).

Oil was the basis of 43, followed by newspapers and publishing (40), computer technology (12), retailing (12), hotels and casinos (7), and entertainment (5). Others were made in such varied and nonexotic areas as potatoes, oranges, wines, grains, Campbell soups, ranching, Johnson's wax, cosmetics, textiles, trucking, and dog and cat food.

Here are sketches of a few recent multimillionaires:

Philip Knight, 44. In 1965, started selling running shoes to college track coaches. Persuaded prominent U.S. runners to test the shoe design in 1972. Has established Nike shoes as one of the premium recreation shoes. Estimated wealth, $275 million.

George Lucas, 38. Indifferent high school student. Directed *American Graffiti*, partner in *Raiders of the Lost Ark*, and principal of *Star Wars*. Estimated wealth, $100 million.

Steven Jobs, 27. College dropout who saw the potential of home computers. With a partner, started production in 1976 in family garage on $1300 received from the sale of VW Microbus. Worth $100 million.

Fredrick Smith, 38. Father left him $3.2 million. He invested in an idea he developed for a Yale economics course: Federal Express. Professor gave him a low grade, said it wouldn't work. Nevertheless he raised $80 million in capital and started business in 1973. Wealth now estimated at $100 million.

---

tribution has become "more equal." Changes in the distribution of income may be ambiguous. The second fifth may receive less income, while the third fifth receives an increasing portion of the aggregate income. What determines whether these changes constitute more equality or less equality?

To answer this question, economists use a device called the *Lorenz curve*. This curve shows how income is divided among the population.

Exhibit 19-4   Percentage of aggregate income received by families, by fifth and by top 5 percent, 1929–81

Income Class	Percentage of Income				
	1929	1947	1970	1976	1981
Lowest fifth ⎫	12.5%	5.0%	5.4%	5.4%	5.0%
Second fifth ⎭		11.8	12.2	11.8	11.3
Third fifth	13.8	17.0	17.6	17.6	17.4
Fourth fifth	19.3	23.1	23.8	24.1	24.4
Highest fifth	54.4	43.0	40.9	41.1	41.9
Top 5 percent	30.0	17.2	15.6	15.6	15.4

SOURCE: U.S. Department of Commerce, *Statistical Abstract of the United States*, 1982.

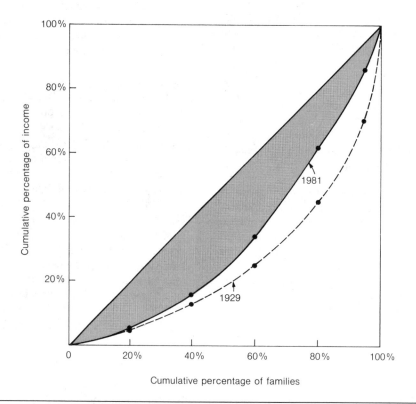

Exhibit 19-5   Lorenz curves showing income inequality in the United States, 1929 and 1981

The Lorenz curve shows how income is divided among the population. The diagonal line represents total equality, whereas the curved line shows the actual distribution. Income inequality can be measured using the gini coefficient: the ratio of the shaded area to the total area under the diagonal. A ratio of zero indicates complete equality. The trend shown here between 1929 and 1981 is toward equality.

The Lorenz curve for the 1981 data presented in Exhibit 19-4 is shown in Exhibit 19-5. The horizontal axis shows the cumulative percentage of families; the vertical axis shows the cumulative percentage of income.

A 45-degree line through the origin represents complete equality. Anywhere along this line the percentage of income is equal to the percentage of the population. The lowest 20 percent of the population would be receiving 20 percent of the income. The lowest 60 percent of the population would be receiving 60 percent of the income. From Exhibit 19-4 we know that the poorest 20 percent of the population received 5.0 percent of the income in 1981. This is one point on the Lorenz curve plotted on the solid line near the 45-degree line. The poorest 40 percent of the population received 16.3 percent of total aggregate income, another point on the Lorenz curve. The cumulative percentages of income and population trace the income distribution. The final point derived from Exhibit 19-4 is that in 1981 the poorest 95 percent of the population received 84.6 percent of aggregate income. Joining all these points gives us the Lorenz curve for 1981, showing the level of inequality.

Inequality as measured by the Lorenz curve is often presented in terms of a single number that captures the extent of inequality. Inequality is measured by comparing the area between the Lorenz curve for 1981 and the line of total equality with the total area beneath the line of equality. That is to say, a measure of inequality is the shaded area in Exhibit 19-5 divided by the entire area beneath the line of complete equality. This ratio is called the *gini coefficient*. As the Lorenz curve moves closer to the line of complete equality, the ratio of the shaded area to the total area will get smaller. This means that a gini coefficient of 0 represents total equality, whereas a ratio of 1 represents total inequality.

The trends in income inequality in the United States from 1929 to 1981 are illustrated in Exhibit 19-5. The dotted curve in that figure represents the income distribution in 1929. It clearly shows that the shaded area between the Lorenz curve and the line of complete equality has gotten smaller since 1929. This implies, of course, that there has been a move toward greater equality. The gini coefficient has gotten smaller in the past 52 years. The data in Exhibit 19-4 shows that income distribution has changed little since World War II.

Economics of Discrimination

It is often argued that luck plays a major role in determining the distribution of income. Yet some

Nursing has been a profession preferred by women because they could enter or leave it as family responsibilities allowed. *(Photo by Terry Zabala)*

a. Skilled labor

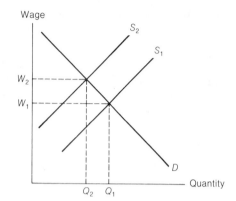

b. Unskilled labor

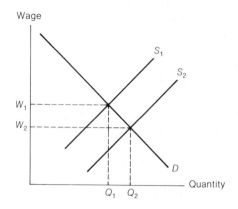

Exhibit 19-6   The effect of employment discrimination on the structure of relative wages

Employment discrimination can increase the differential between skilled and unskilled workers. If some people are excluded from skilled jobs, supply in

these occupations is diminished and wages rise. This also increases the supply of workers for unskilled jobs, diminishing the wage in those occupations.

systematic differences seem unrelated to skill, inheritance, or luck. Discrimination against minority groups and women accounts for some of these differences. A theory of discrimination supplements marginal productivity theory as an explanation of income determination.

The effects of discrimination in the labor market are illustrated in Exhibit 19-6. Assume that minority workers are systematically excluded from skilled employment and are relegated to unskilled employment. Because minorities are not given skilled work, the supply of skilled workers is smaller than it would otherwise be. Wages will be higher (W_2 instead of W_1) for skilled workers because of this reduced supply. Discrimination, of course, will increase the differential between skilled and unskilled workers. The supply of unskilled workers is now expanded (from S_1 to S_2) because the excluded group can seek employment only in that market. Consequently, the wage rate of unskilled workers will be lower than it would otherwise be.

Those who gain from discriminatory behavior are skilled workers who are not discriminated against. Employers of labor may be worse off because they have to pay higher salaries for skilled workers, although they pay lower salaries to unskilled laborers. As long as they use more skilled than unskilled labor, their costs will be higher because of discriminatory behavior in hiring.

Overt discrimination is illegal in the United States. But a related phenomenon also fosters income inequality by limiting the upward mobility of some workers. This is explained by the *dual labor-market theory*, which is based on the idea that there are two labor markets: one that provides employment with possibilities for advancement and a "secondary" market with only deadend jobs. The secondary labor market provides no avenue for the worker to move into jobs that offer upward mobility. Minority males have been relegated to the secondary labor market by discriminatory employment practices and by reduced opportunities for education and training. As a result, older blacks are concentrated in low-wage, unskilled occupations.

Women also have been relegated to a secondary market through a combination of preferences and discrimination. Often women prefer part-time work and jobs that allow them to enter and exit the labor market at will, so that they may fulfill roles in the home. Historically, women have not been career-oriented, and they found jobs in the secondary labor market where it did not matter if they were sporadic members of the labor force. Professions that allowed easy entry and exit became "the female careers"— nursing and teaching being the most prominent.

PUBLIC POLICY TOWARD INCOME REDISTRIBUTION

Public policy toward income redistribution provokes great disagreement and emotional debate. The cause of this emotionalism can be readily understood. Proponents of more equitable income distribution tread on what others consider their inalienable property rights. Egalitarians argue that society can distribute income as it likes because individuals receive income not in isolation but rather as part of a complex interdependent modern society.

Opponents of income redistribution argue that the market allocation of resources distributes income to factors according to their contribution to output and assures allocative efficiency so that aggregate income is maximized. This appeal to the market is not a strong defense of the existing distribution of income. As we saw in Chapter 18, marginal productivity theory takes the initial ownership of the factors of production as given. Once the distribution of factors is given, the distribution of income is largely determined. Consequently, to appeal to the market allocation of resources through marginal productivity theory is essentially to side-step the whole issue of how much equality there should be in the economic system.

Partly because of the issues raised above and partly because of different definitions of equality, there is no political consensus in the United States regarding the "just" distribution of income. But while we cannot identify the best income distribution, the goal of eliminating poverty has considerable support. The existence of grinding poverty among those unable to help themselves is widely condemned. In this section we will explore some of the policy options for eliminating poverty and discuss some issues of inequality.

Social Welfare Programs

In 1979 governments at all levels in the United States spent $428.4 billion, or $1912 per capita, on social welfare programs. This impressive figure, however, exaggerates the expenditures made on behalf of many poor persons. The programs that absorbed these expenditures are shown in Exhibit 19-7. The largest proportion of welfare

Exhibit 19-7 Social welfare expenditures by source of funds (in billions), 1979

Expenditure	Federal	State and Local
Social insurance (old age, survivors, disability, workers' compensation, retirement, and unemployment compensation)	$163,744	$ 29,844
Veterans and other Defense Department programs	20,333	190
Housing	3,802	424
Public aid	43,612	21,037
Civilian medical programs	12,150	12,346
Other social welfare	6,449	4,192
Total	264,186	164,215

SOURCE: U.S. Bureau of the Census, *Statistical Abstract of the United States,* 1983.

expenditures was designed to redistribute income to retired workers and their families. Efforts to ensure retired and aged workers against poverty accounted for $193.6 billion, 45 percent of the total social welfare expenditures reported in Exhibit 19-7.

Welfare Programs

Welfare is a maze of different programs, some of which are financed cooperatively by federal, state, and local governments. The three main programs are Aid to Families with Dependent Children (AFDC), Medicaid, and food stamps.

AFDC made cash payments of $12.8 billion to 10.9 million people in 1981. Most recipient families were headed by women who were divorced, deserted, widowed, or never married.

Medicaid, which helps pay poor people's medical expenses, has been the fastest growing category of welfare in terms of costs.

Unlike the first two programs, food stamp benefits are paid entirely by the federal government. During fiscal year 1981, 22 million Americans received food stamps at some time.

Welfare Program and Year	Recipients (in millions)	Cost (in billions)
AFDC		
1970	7.3	$ 3.9
1975	11.1	8.4
1980	10.5	12.0
1981	10.9	12.8
Medicaid		
1970	14.5	5.0
1975	21.2	12.1
1980	17.7	21.0
1981	18.3	31.0
Food stamps		
1970	4.3	.5
1975	17.1	4.6
1980	21.1	9.2
1981	22.0	9.7

Because these programs are designed to assist productive workers in the event of disability or retirement, the benefits do not filter down to many poor people who never fully enter the labor market. Female heads of household and their children, unemployed school dropouts, and many occasional workers in low-wage industries are not likely to be recipients of welfare expenditures dedicated to retirement and worker insurance.

The nonaged poor and their children who cannot find employment because of a lack of skills, discrimination, a lack of motivation, or some mental or physical disability receive benefits primarily from programs classified as "public aid" and "other social welfare" in Exhibit 19-7. These programs include Job Corps, Neighborhood Youth Corps, Community Action, Vista, surplus food for the needy, food stamps, and child welfare, as well as aid to the aged, blind, and disabled not covered by other social insurance programs. The $75.3 billion spent on these programs accounted for 2.8 percent of GNP. This represents a considerable increase in expenditures to help the poor: in 1950 such efforts took only 1 percent of GNP.

Poverty and Economic Growth

Despite the fact that a relatively small portion of Gross National Product has been used to assist the poor, there has been a dramatic decline in the incidence of economic hardship since World War II. The steady rate of economic growth during most of this era made a significant contribution to this decline in poverty. Economic growth attacks poverty in two ways. First, a high rate of growth means a higher demand for labor relative to supply; because of labor market tightness, the average wage of relatively unskilled workers is higher than in a stagnant economy with a relatively low demand for labor.

Second, the availability of jobs at relatively high wages encourages additional workers in families to seek employment, thereby contributing to family income and reducing the incidence of poverty.

Real Gross National Product increased 143 percent from 1950 to 1982. During the same time, the percentage of families with incomes under $7500 (in 1978 dollars) decreased from 35 percent to 11 percent of the population. Of course, these figures overestimate the impact of economic growth on poverty because a large part of the rapid growth during this time can be attributed to increased education of workers. It is not clear, however, that economic opportunities for highly educated people would be available in the absence of growth. Robert Lampman argues that it is a mistake to underestimate the power of economic growth to reduce poverty because it is closely related to increased levels of education.

Whether the reduction of poverty due to such improved levels of educational attainment should be attributed to economic growth or to social policy is a semantic problem. It is part of the adaptation process to new and higher skilled occupations and hard to separate from the whole process of growth. This process, in turn, pulls people into areas where educational opportunities are greater. This is not to deny that increased educational opportunity will not in itself contribute to the rate of growth. The changes in occupational status referred to above were no doubt facilitated by progress on the educational front.*

The economic growth that has been very effective in raising the economic status of the poor may not eliminate poverty in the future. An increasing portion of the poor appear to be

insulated from the benefits of economic growth because they have either low productivity or are not engaged in the labor force. Four groups appear to be particularly immune to economic growth as a way of eliminating poverty: those with little education, the aged, the disabled, and women heads of household. Workers with little education do not possess the skills that are demanded in a modern economy, and so growth of the modern economy does little to improve their situation. The aged and the disabled are less active in the labor force, and so economic growth does not help them greatly either. Growth has a modest impact on the economic status of women heads of household because of their traditional role in caring for children and their relegation to secondary status in the labor force. If the trend toward increased employment for women continues, growth may be more effective in improving their economic status. Nevertheless, as the proportion of the population in poverty declines, the groups relatively unresponsive to growth are likely to constitute a greater proportion of the poor. Thus, it is clear that a policy of maximizing economic growth will not be sufficient to eliminate poverty.

Earnings and Education

The systematic effect of education upon earnings is demonstrated in the following table.

Head of Family (age 25 or older)	Median Family Income 1981
5 or more years of college	$38,785
Finished college	32,720
1 to 3 years of college	26,873
Finished high school	23,003
1 to 3 years of high school	16,810
Finished grade school	14,568
Did not finish grade school	11,998

---

*Robert J. Lampman, *Ends and Means of Reducing Income Poverty* (New York: Academic Press, 1971), p. 124.

Minimum-Wage Legislation

Many people work full time all year and yet cannot earn enough to keep themselves or their families out of poverty. This is one of the most frustrating forms of indigence. A full-time worker receiving $3.35 per hour cannot earn enough to lift an urban family of four above the poverty level. And many workers who earn significantly more than $3.35 an hour when working remain in poverty because of seasonal layoffs or because they have large families. Many occupations pay low wages or offer intermittent employment during the year. Impersonal market forces can impose a life of poverty on hard-working heads of household who cannot find better employment.

One proposed remedy for this problem has been minimum-wage legislation guaranteeing every employed worker a "living wage." With such a policy the government merely decrees that no worker may be paid a wage below a certain minimum figure. The classical argument against minimum-wage legislation is that many unskilled workers are not productive enough to merit earnings higher than the market wage. In response to a minimum wage, firms would employ fewer unskilled workers.

The effect of a minimum wage is shown graphically in Exhibit 19-8. In the absence of government intervention the market wage (W_1) will be at the intersection of the demand (D) and supply (S) curves with Q_1 workers employed. A minimum-wage rate established at W will reduce the quantity of labor demanded to Q_2 and the number willing to work at that wage will increase to Q_3. Under the new legislation the number of workers $Q_3 - Q_2$ will be unemployed because Q_3 are seeking employment but only Q_2 will actually obtain a job. The increase in income experienced by the unskilled work-

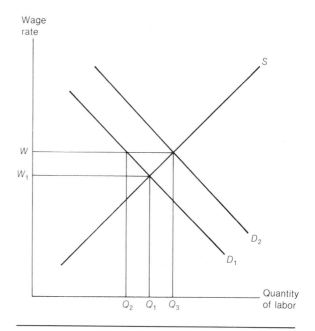

Exhibit 19-8   The effect of minimum-wage legislation on the employment of low-skilled workers

*A minimum-wage law (**W**) reduces the quantity of workers demanded while increasing the quantity supplied. The result is unemployment. Some workers benefit from higher wages (Q_2), but others may lose their jobs ($Q_1 - Q_2$).*

ers who remain employed is clear, although the improvement was at the expense of those workers who lost their jobs, $Q_1 - Q_2$. Some gain but others lose, and the net gain in social welfare is uncertain. To the extent there is a social gain, it is paid for by the poor.

Since passage of the Employment Act of 1946, maximum employment consistent with stable prices has been a national goal. Establishing a minimum wage for all workers is therefore in conflict with the desire to employ all persons seeking work. Economists have traditionally argued that to increase the quantity of labor demanded, like any other commodity, the wage rate must be lowered so that employers find it attractive to hire more workers.

One way to implement a minimum wage without an increase in unemployment is for the government to shift the demand for labor to D_2, as in Exhibit 19-8. In such a circumstance the government guarantees every worker a job at the minimum wage. The government acts as an *employer of last resort,* for it hires the unemployed. A potential problem with this plan is that it may increase public-sector employment in activities that are not in need of expansion. To the extent that these projects are "make-work" and meaningless, they do not increase the worker's sense of economic independence and self-esteem. At the same time they represent an inefficient use of resources.

Government as an employer of last resort may be subject to the first criticism, but the projects need not be "make-work." Properly organized projects could not only provide useful public services but also train unskilled workers for jobs in the private sector. Although such programs require imaginative planning, they are not impossible.

Operating as an employer of last resort, the government can eliminate the conflict between the goals of a guaranteed annual wage and full employment. Such a policy, however, must be supplemented by a system of transfer payments to the poor who do not participate in the labor force for reasons of age, disability, and child-care responsibilities. An alternative approach to eliminating poverty does not rely on the government's intervention in the workings of the labor market. Rather, it is based on income transfers independent of labor-force participation.

It is sometimes said that the problem of poverty is that the poor don't have enough money. The policy conclusion drawn is that the poor

As an employer of last resort, the government could eliminate the unemployment effects of a minimum wage by employing the unemployed. *(Photo by Leonard Freed, Magnum Photos, Inc.)*

should be given more money. This method of redistributing income consists of transfer payments and subsidies—taking income from one person and giving it to another.

One method of transferring income is called the *negative income tax;* the government pays negative income taxes to families in poverty. In 1981 the official poverty line for an urban family of four in the United States was $9287. If every family were raised to this poverty line, the government would have to transfer some $17 billion, or roughly 1.5 percent of GNP.

This very straightforward method of eliminating poverty has, however, a built-in disincentive to work. Consider the family of four that has no income because the head of household has been unemployed for a year. With a negative income-tax program the family would receive $9287 from the government. As labor market conditions improve, let us assume that the head of household can earn $7000 a year by working full time. Since $7000 is $2287 below the poverty line, the household head would receive a $2287 negative income tax payment.

The problem with this simple negative income-tax scheme is readily apparent. When the head of household does not work at all, the family receives an income of $9287. If the head works full time all year, the family's material well-being does not increase—its income is still $9287. This, in effect, is a 100 percent tax on all earnings under the guaranteed annual income. A rational person would probably prefer to continue to receive the annual income, entirely supported by the state, rather than take a low-paying, low-status, and probably unpleasant job.

This work-disincentive effect has been built into many welfare programs, but it can be reduced. A variation of the simple negative income tax has been designed to guarantee each family a certain income and at the same time encourage people to earn as much as they can. Such a work-incentive program could be based on a poverty income for an urban family of four—say, $4000. If the family earns no income, it would receive the negative income tax equal to the designated minimum income. Unlike the simple program described above, not every dollar earned would be subtracted from the negative income-tax payment. Instead, only a por-

tion would be reduced. If earnings were taxed at 50 percent, every $1000 earned would reduce the negative income tax by $500. Families earning up to $8000 would be recipients of some payment from the negative income-tax program.

A principal advantage of the negative income-tax scheme to combat poverty is that it can replace many separate welfare programs, which needlessly increase the costs of administration.

A potential weakness lies in the remaining work-disincentive effects. Consider, for example, a person who works for $4 an hour, or $8000 a year. After a negative income-tax scheme is instituted, annual income remains $8000. In effect, the person now receives $4000 a year from the negative income tax and earns $2 per hour for 2000 hours a year (40 hours a week times 50 weeks). This reduction in the effective wage rate from $4 to $2 an hour may cause the worker to spend more time at leisure and to work less. To claim that the negative income tax has no work-disincentive effects is to assume that workers will choose to maximize their income rather than optimize the work-leisure relationship. Since leisure is generally considered a desirable thing, workers may well substitute leisure for work when the rate of pay is reduced.

The Tax System

Taxes are imposed by government to pay for public services and to redistribute income. How the tax burden is divided among the population is important in any analysis of the distribution of income. The tax burden, or what is called the *tax incidence*, can be of three basic types: progressive, proportional, or regressive.

A *progressive tax* requires people to pay a higher fraction of their income in taxes as income rises. For example, a person making $5000 may pay 10 percent of that income in taxes, whereas someone making $20,000 would pay 20 percent of it in taxes.

A *proportional tax* requires that all people pay the same proportion of their income in taxes. Thus, in our example, people earning $5000 and those earning $20,000 would pay the same percentage of their income. Of course, the higher-income person would pay more taxes in absolute dollar terms.

In contrast, a *regressive tax* takes a larger fraction of low incomes than it does of high incomes. In such a circumstance we may find that the tax takes 10 percent of a $5000 income but only 5 percent of an income of $20,000. Such a tax is regressive because the proportion of the income paid in taxes falls as income rises. A regressive tax does not necessarily mean that low-income people pay more tax dollars than people with high income. In our example, the $20,000 income bracket paid twice as much tax as did the $5000 income bracket. The lower-income group paid $500, whereas the $20,000 group's 5 percent tax was $1000.

Most federal tax receipts come from the personal income tax, which is somewhat progressive. The rate of taxation increases from zero for the lowest-income groups to as high as 50¢ on an extra dollar earned as certain income by the highest-income groups. Income taxes on the profits of corporations are generally thought to be proportional in effect. It is widely believed that corporations pass these taxes on to consumers in the form of higher prices.

An example of a regressive federal tax is the payroll tax used to finance the Social Security system. The Social Security program requires that employees contribute a percentage of their salaries up to a certain figure, after which the tax rate is zero. In 1983 employees and employers each had to contribute 6.7 percent of all wage income below $35,700. Income earned beyond $35,700 and unearned income were not taxed

The Income Tax and How It Grew

Today's federal income tax on individuals bears little resemblance to the tax described by income tax supporters when the income tax amendment was being discussed by state legislatures in 1909. Skeptics were assured that rates would never go above 4 or 5 percent and that only a few people would even pay the tax. After ratification of the amendment, Congress passed the income tax law in 1913. It provided for a 1 percent tax on incomes over $3000 ($4000 for a married couple)—a level exceeded by only 3 percent of U.S. wage earners. A tax of up to 7 percent was levied on very high incomes—from $20,000 to over $500,000.

Rates went up during World War I but soon came down again. As recently as 1941, the federal income tax raised only $41 million annually. During World War II, the rates were again raised with very high marginal rates; however, few individuals were included in the high rates.

In 1947, after the severe inflation of the war years, 80 percent of families in the United States had annual incomes of less than $5000. The effective tax rate was 8.4 percent. A worker making $5000, with a wife and two children, paid $420 in income tax plus $30 in Social Security tax.

Today, due to economic growth and inflation, the average family has an income of $23,000. That means the average worker is paying taxes intended originally for the rich. In addition, Social Security taxes have risen from a maximum of $30 in the 1930s to $2170 in 1982.

at all. Such payroll taxes are regressive because most of the revenue is contributed by low- and middle-income people. Although the distribution of Social Security benefits may make the net effect more proportional than regressive, Social Security has mixed income-redistribution effects. Among the people who pay Social Security taxes, the system is regressive because the percentage of earnings paid into the system falls as income rises. When Social Security benefits are extended to include poor persons who have not contributed to the system, its effect is more progressive.

Redistributing Income

A free enterprise economy can have just about any income distribution it chooses. Far from being unable to redistribute income as some radicals have claimed, a progressive tax structure coupled with various transfer and expenditure programs can increase economic equality. Recent evidence suggests that after the changing age distribution is taken into account, income has become more equally distributed in the past four decades.

Income redistribution in the United States has occurred largely without design. It has been the product of ad hoc and patchwork programs that have become law without a serious discussion of our notion of distributive justice. These pro-

grams, because of their ad hoc quality, have often made income redistribution far more expensive than it need be. For example, concern for the poor has led Congress to control the price of gasoline and natural gas because the poor have limited capacity to purchase these necessities. State utility commissions regularly control the price of electricity for the same reason. The policies are often conceived with compassion for the poor, yet their results are to distort market prices and discourage investment in activities that should be expanded. Rising prices should signal the need for more energy and the development of substitute fuels; yet our concern for the poor causes us to eliminate the signs of need.

We have previously emphasized that income redistribution may dampen the incentive to work. Ad hoc policies that redistribute income through product markets merely compound the problem by adding an unnecessary layer of inefficiency. The problem is that we apparently are unwilling to state our income redistribution goals explicitly and then tax some people and give the receipts to others—the least disruptive way of redistributing income.

From a strictly economic point of view we have accomplished some income redistribution in an inefficient way. This is not too surprising. Neither economists nor politicians really know what disincentive effects accompany a policy of income redistribution. One understandable response to this lack of knowledge is to alleviate the condition of the poor in an ad hoc way, avoiding the basic issue of disincentives. Our frontier heritage of self-help is another reason why our current method has political appeal: it is possible that we cannot agree on a standard of fairness by which to redistribute income. Ad hoc policies probably stem from a lack of political consensus. The price is unnecessary inefficiency.

Economic policy is not made in a vacuum.

Subsidizing Health Hazards

The U.S. government subsidizes tobacco farmers but at the same time tries to discourage smoking because of its adverse effect on health. Stopping the subsidies is unacceptable because the farmers would suffer significant economic damage. In 1977, this concern led President Carter to reject U.S. Department of Health, Education, and Welfare Secretary Joseph Califano's suggestion that the tobacco subsidies be dropped. Whenever public policy is formulated, the income distribution effects are an important consideration.

Political forces are the very essence of policies regarding income redistribution. A representative Congress will consider the well-being of poor people along with other issues. As a result, we expect economic policies to be formulated in light of their impact on the income distribution. Hence Congress deals with energy shortages by keeping the price low so that the poor can still buy even though the supply will not increase. A democratic society will invariably have conflicts over how resources are distributed. Although this problem is an understandable product of our political system and historical experience, a clear specification of our distributive goals may serve the interests of the poor and foster a more efficient use of resources.

SUMMARY

1. All societies use some form of inequality to motivate their members. In market economies, wage differentials play a prominent role in the allocation of labor among occupations.

2. The functional distribution of income describes the shares of income going to the factors of production. The proportional distribution of income shows how income is divided among the population. Most questions of distributive justice are based on this measure.

3. About 14 percent of the United States population lives in poverty. Income inequality fell from 1929 to 1947 but has not changed markedly since then. Recent research suggests that demographic patterns are responsible for this stability since World War II.

4. Inequality of income is illustrated by the Lorenz curve, which compares the cumulative percentage of the population with the cumulative percentage of income. The gini coefficient measures the degree of inequality.

5. Although discrimination is hard to quantify, it appears to have played a significant role in reducing the income of blacks and women compared to white males. Some economists analyze this discrimination in the context of the dual labor-market theory.

6. In 1979 the United States spent 18 percent of GNP on social welfare programs. Most of these expenditures were for worker insurance and retirement and did not benefit many of those in long-term poverty.

7. Economic growth increases employment opportunities for the poor who are members of the labor force. Growth has played a major role in reducing the number of poor people. In the future it may not be as effective because an increasing portion of the poor is not engaged in the labor force.

8. Minimum-wage legislation can be used to guarantee the working poor a "living wage." If the government does not act as an employer of last resort, the costs of this legislation will be borne by the unskilled workers who lose their jobs.

9. A guaranteed annual income is a way of transferring money to the poor without a great number of separate welfare programs. Its work-disincentive effects may be minimized if only a portion of family earnings are subtracted from the negative income-tax payment.

10. In the long run a guaranteed annual income will probably lower the incentive to work among unskilled people. This will raise the cost of many goods and services that require unskilled labor in their production.

11. Taxes can be progressive, proportional, or regressive. The incidence of taxes in the United States is probably somewhat progressive with the portion of income going to taxes rising with the level of income.

12. Significant income redistribution will inevitably affect the allocation of resources. Its desirability depends on our sense of distributive justice and our preferences for material production.

KEY CONCEPTS

economic purpose of inequality

functional distribution of income

proportional distribution of income

poverty

Lorenz curve

gini coefficient

dual labor-market theory

minimum-wage legislation

government as an employer of last resort

negative income tax

tax incidence

progressive tax

proportional tax

regressive tax

QUESTIONS FOR DISCUSSION

1. What do you think about the concept that people should receive income in accordance with their contribution to society? How do you measure contributions?

2. "Discrimination against minorities tends to raise total labor costs. Firms who discriminate therefore sacrifice profits to subsidize majority workers. And nondiscriminatory firms are expected to earn excess profits." Can you verify this statement with a theoretical analysis? How can you explain the practice of discrimination when it seems illogical from an economic point of view?

3. Describe the working conditions, pay, and prospects for advancement for a job you have held. Did your co-workers share any general characteristics—for example, age or education? Would you classify this job as being in the primary or secondary labor market?

4. Do you favor a guaranteed annual income? At what level of income would you favor such a program? In this context, how do you identify the tradeoff between allocative efficiency and equity?

5. Should the overall tax structure of the United States be regressive, proportional, or progressive? In formulating your answer, does it matter how the benefits of government programs are distributed?

Part IV

GOVERNMENT AND RESOURCE ALLOCATION

Chapter 20

Government Allocation of Resources

In the previous chapters we have discussed the method by which the market mechanism allocates resources. Traditionally this has been an area of great interest to economists. Today an area of increasing importance is the *nonmarket allocation of resources*. Here decisions are made without concern for their effects on the profits of the organization. For example, federal, state, and local governments, and such diverse non-profit organizations as universities, churches, and charitable groups (as well as a myriad of groups like Girl Scouts, Masons, American Legion, and Little Leagues) all operate in this manner. The discussion that follows focuses on the role of government in resource allocation, although many of the comments would be equally applicable to other nonmarket institutions.

SIZE OF THE GOVERNMENT SECTOR

One reason we focus on government is its size and recent growth. In 1929, the share of Gross National Product accounted for by all levels of government was less than 11 percent. In 1983 government receipts amounted to over one-third of GNP, and government spending totaled more than $500 billion.

Some of the government receipts and expenditures do not differ markedly from the market activities of private business organizations. For example, the Tennessee Valley Authority (TVA) and the Bonneville Power Administration (BPA) generate and sell hydroelectric power. They buy factors at market-determined prices and sell their product at prices similar to those of private profit-maximizing organizations.

On the other hand, some government activities have no relationship to market activity. The majority of federal government activities

Food stamps, a kind of transfer payment, have no relationship to market activity. *(Photo by George W. Gardner, Stock, Boston)*

fall in this category. Transfer payments—payments to individuals for which no services are performed—are an example. The budget of the Department of Health and Human Services, which dispenses many transfer payments, is the largest of any government agency, having surpassed that of the Defense Department in 1970. The Defense Department also, of course, allocates resources outside the market. In sum, federal nonmarket activity is large and growing.

Every society must have a means of answering basic economic questions: What products are to be produced? How are they to be produced? Who is to receive them (income distribution)?

These questions can be answered by allowing the market mechanism to make the allocations, through demand, costs, and prices. Alternatively, allocations can be decreed by the government or set by custom. In most modern societies, the market mechanism and government combine to allocate resources.

In this chapter we will attempt to answer two questions. First, what are the weaknesses in the private allocation of resources that *could* be improved by government action? Second, is there any way to assure that government *will* allocate resources in a "better" manner than the private sector? (Just because a private market does not allocate resources optimally does not automatically assure that government will do any better.)

PROBLEMS OF MARKET ALLOCATION

Allocation of resources by a private market system has been criticized by many people for a long time. The critics have included early Greek philosophers, medieval churchmen, and some present-day economists. In general, they argue that society should pursue higher goals than those created by private markets. Here is an example of such criticism by a noneconomist (Arthur Schlesinger, Jr.):

And it is also the fact that the unregulated marketplace is patently unable to deal with urgent problems in our day. It has manifestly failed, for example, to control inflation while avoiding mass unemployment. . . . Nor can the unregulated marketplace cope with problems like oil that are essentially political rather than economic in character. Nor can the unregulated marketplace bring about the reconstruction and expansion of our mass transit system, which would be both helpful in reemployment and essential in the conservation of energy. Nor can the unregulated marketplace

meet the nation's needs for health care, education, housing, welfare, solvent cities, and environmental protection.*

From the standpoint of economic analysis, two major criticisms in this statement must be considered:

1. Private markets may be inefficient in their allocation of scarce *resources.*
2. Private markets may distribute *goods and services* in an inequitable, unjust, unsafe, or inefficient manner.

To the extent that these criticisms are valid, the government, acting as the agent for society, may enter the market to try to correct them.

SOCIAL VS. PRIVATE COSTS AND BENEFITS

A major source of inefficiency is the divergence between *social costs and benefits* and *private costs and benefits.* To survive, a private firm must do a reasonable job of making profits. To make profits, the firm maximizes the difference between its total private revenue and its total private costs. Under competitive conditions, when private benefits and costs are identical to social benefits and costs, the firm that maximizes profits also maximizes net benefits for society. Under these conditions, private firms are efficient allocators of resources.

What if private costs and benefits are not identical to social ones? Then the firm responding to market incentives is no longer necessarily working for society's benefits, as in the following cases.

---

* "Laissez-Faire, Planning and Reality," *Wall Street Journal* (July 30, 1975). Arthur Schlesinger, Jr. is professor of humanities at the City Universty of New York and Pulitzer Prize winner in history and biography.

Monopoly and Imperfect Competition

As we know from earlier chapters, in perfect competition the firm produces at a level of output where the price equals marginal cost. Price and quantity accurately reflect the benefit to society (shown by consumers' willingness to pay for the good) and the costs to society (measured by the marginal cost of producing the good).

That relationship no longer necessarily holds in cases of imperfect competition or restrictive agreements. A noncompetitive firm will produce a quantity of goods that maximizes profits—when marginal cost is less than price. The difference between price and cost is inefficiency from the standpoint of society. Consumers are willing to pay more for the good than the actual cost of producing it. To maximize profits, the noncompetitive firm produces less than the quantity society desires.

External Costs and Benefits

A private market may fail to register total costs and benefits when a transaction affects someone external to it. For example, if your neighbor buys a goat and sells the milk, the private cost and benefit are limited to the neighbor and the buyers. But if the goat's odors or bleating offend you, nothing in the private market will register your annoyance. *Externalities* are present when the actions of one group or individual in a market affect the well-being of others without their consent.

A common example of an externality is a factory that emits smoke and pollutes the air. Pollution does not cost the firm anything, and so it has no incentive to spend a large amount on pollution control equipment. If no one were affected, the private cost of using the air to dump the emissions—zero—and the social cost—zero—should be equal. But if persons living downwind are bothered by the pollutants, the cost to society is no longer zero, but an amount that reflects the reduced quality of the environment for downwind residents. This is a case of negative externalities—when a firm is producing more of the good than is optimal.

Public Goods

Sometimes, social benefits and private benefits diverge. The products bring benefits to the public, rather than only to private users. Because the firm equates private costs and private benefits, it is likely to underproduce the product despite its positive external benefits.

An extreme example is the product that does not lose value if its rate of use increases—sometimes referred to as a public good. A lighthouse built to warn ships off dangerous shoals is a public good. It does not matter whether one ship, 20 ships, or 100 ships see the light; its value remains the same. Yet there is no feasible way to charge each ship for the use of the light. Without potential profits no private firm would go into the lighthouse business. Public goods are always underprovided by the private market because private benefits (profits) are not as high as the social benefits. Many other products have public aspects although few can be classified as pure public goods. Common examples are public health facilities and roads.

CAN GOVERNMENT POLICIES AFFECT RESOURCE ALLOCATION?

Monopolies

In brief, the stated government policy has been to break up or prevent monopolies and restrictive agreements through legislation—an objective that has not always been achieved. When

The social benefits from a public good such as a lighthouse are higher than the potential profits to a private owner. *(Photo by Peter Menzel, Stock, Boston)*

such policies do not seem feasible, public regulation or public ownership has been tried. When externalities exist, government can intervene in one of four ways.

1. *Establish public enterprise.* The government can establish a public enterprise to provide the goods and services, including in its mission the task of equating social cost and benefits. A public enterprise usually prices its product at less than marginal cost, because the social benefits are greater than the private benefits. An example is education, which has always been thought to provide positive externalities to a community. Public education customarily has been provided free to children and more has been potentially available than the quantity children's parents are willing to pay for directly.

2. *Eliminate negative externalities.* The government can prohibit negative (harmful) externalities, eliminating them entirely. However, this course of action must be considered carefully, since the costs of prohibition may be excessive from the standpoint of society as a whole. For example, a plant creating noise pollution in the middle of the Nevada desert might not harm many people, but the same plant in downtown Manhattan might disturb millions. How strictly should noise pollution standards be enforced? An absolute action in this case might cost more than the social gains are worth.

3. *Have the firms provide compensation to injured parties.* Instead of attempting to prohibit negative externalities, society might simply force the firms in question to compensate the injured parties. For instance, a noise polluter could have the option of paying each nearby resident financial compensation instead of installing noise control equipment. In such a case disturbing nearby residents is no longer free; it has a price that reflects the approximate cost of harm to society. The government has now caused the externality to be "internalized" within the firm. Private decision makers must now consider social costs, because they are equal to private costs. This approach avoids the inefficiency of outright prohibition. Rather than spend millions of dollars to stop the noise at a plant in Nevada where only 10 prospectors are affected, the firm would probably pay the prospectors a compensation. In New York City, the firm would probably choose noise abatement equipment, since the cost of compensation would be very large.

4. *Tax the firms responsible.* Another way of "internalizing" externalities is by taxation—the government establishes a tax on externalities that approximates their social cost. A firm can continue to operate at that level where marginal private cost equals marginal gains. But marginal private cost now includes social cost, or taxes.

Suppose a plant emits 1000 pounds of pollutants per month. The cost of removing the first 900 pounds, using primary recovery methods, would be $100,000 per month. To eliminate the next 70 pounds, with secondary methods, would be $130,000 per month, and the cost to remove the last 30 pounds, using tertiary methods, would be $90,000. Now suppose the government finds that $2000 per pound per month reflects the social cost of the emissions in a particular geographic area. If the firm does nothing, it will pay a pollution tax of $2 million per month. Clearly the firm will choose to install primary recovery equipment. If the firm does no more, it will still pay a pollution tax of 100 pounds times $2000, or $200,000 per month. The private cost of secondary recovery equipment is only $130,000 per month, so the firm would still maximize profits by installing it. But the tax on the remaining 30 pounds of pollution will be $60,000, and tertiary recovery costs $90,000, so the firm will not install it.

Thus, we have a case where the marginal social cost of stopping all pollution is less than the marginal social gain. We have "internalized the externality." In practice, however, such taxes can be difficult to administer. How accurately can the government set a tax to reflect the social costs of pollution? How accurately can it judge the public perception of benefits?

In the Love Canal disaster, government had to deal with both immediate evacuation of the residents and longer-term cleanup of the former chemical dumpsite. *(Wide World Photos)*

Public Goods

As noted earlier, a private market will underproduce a public good. One method to assure a socially desirable level of output is public ownership of roads, parks, lighthouses, public health programs, and other products with aspects of a public good. Another method is to subsidize private firms that produce "public good" products.

Subsidies have traditionally been used, for example, to assure air and rail transportation to areas that generate insufficient travel revenues.

Equity and the Price System

A primary criticism of private markets, as you remember, is that they may be inefficient in allocating scarce resources. We have seen that, under certain conditions, this criticism is valid. Governments typically try to correct the misallocations through traditional means—taxes, subsidies, regulation, and ownership.

The second criticism is that the price system does not yield equitable results. But this is less the fault of the price system than of the political system for failing to respond to equity problems. For example, most people would agree that something is wrong when children suffer from lack of food. The problem in this case is not the price of food, which comes close to reflecting the costs of production to society, but the distribution of income. Equity can be separated from efficiency; the price system is independent of income distribution.

GOVERNMENT ALLOCATION OF RESOURCES IN PRACTICE

In the previous section we discussed some methods government *could* use to allocate resources and to improve the efficiency of the overall allocation system by equating social costs and social benefits. In this section we will briefly examine whether government actions are likely to improve efficiency. The mere presence of a market imperfection does not mean that government intervention will improve matters.

The question of how and why governments allocate resources is just beginning to receive attention from economists. Therefore we have only limited research to report. Considering the size and importance of government spending in the modern economy, it is surprising that more research into the government allocation mechanisms has not been conducted.

The fundamental tenet of economics is that individuals respond to incentives. In the private sector, individuals seek to maximize utility, which translates into firms seeking to maximize profits. Individual employees in government presumably also wish to maximize personal utility. How is this translated into the actions of government? What are the goals of government?

To begin with, government is not a homogeneous activity. There are federal, state, and local authorities; there are elected officials; there are bureaucracies, regulatory agencies, the judiciary. Quite possibly each group responds to different incentives and has a different time horizon. Any attempt to develop a comprehensive model of behavior would be difficult if not impossible. We can, however, investigate the incentives of certain decision-making units and see whether these incentives would lead to government behavior that might reduce inefficiencies in market-determined allocation of resources.

FRAMEWORK OF GOVERNMENT DECISION MAKING

Rational Ignorance of Voters

In the private market an individual must make purchasing decisions and directly bear the responsibility for them. If you buy a bad product, you must put up with it. Thus there is a strong incentive for a prospective purchaser in a private market to gather information bearing on a potential decision.

By contrast, the political decision-making process is collective. No single voter has much to say about the outcome of an election. In addition, a complex set of issues is frequently reduced to single alternative choices. There is little incentive for a voter to gain all the information available on each issue, and even if one feels strongly about an issue, one cannot register an opinion directly, as in the market mechanism, but only indirectly, through a candidate. It is as if we were forced to buy a whole market basket of goods in order to indicate our desire for *one* of the products. The political process does not allow us to give direct signals on resource allocation and does not provide a direct incentive for the voter to seek information. Paradoxically, it is rational for individuals to be somewhat uninformed, since it costs a person time and money to become informed. It is in this environment that the elected official operates.

Elected Officials

Elected officials make most of government's major policy decisions. Yet in their decision-making behavior, one of the highest priorities is the desire to be reelected, if already in office, or to win election, if out of office. No matter how sincere and dedicated, an official cannot be effective if he or she is not in office. Presumably politicians' chances of being elected are greatly enhanced if their voting patterns do not offend voters (staying out of jail and/or lack of scandal also helps) and if they are able to accumulate sufficient resources to wage an election campaign.

Voter Preference Suppose that the people's political opinions range from liberal at one extreme to conservative at the other and that they are distributed between these extremes in a bell-shaped curve, as shown in Exhibit 20-1. In a two-person race between Stu and Ann, Stu assumes a position left of center. Voters further left will not find Stu as liberal as they would choose, but would prefer him to Ann, whose position would be nearer the middle of the political spectrum. Ann, however, gets all the votes from conservatives on the right, plus some votes from liberals closer to her than Stu. The result, as shown in Exhibit 20-1, is that Ann receives 55 percent of the votes and Stu gets 45 percent. In such a well-defined spetrum the tendency would be for any candidate to head to the middle of the road and hope that his or her opponent would adopt a more extreme position.

But why would an opponent adopt a position such as Stu's when it would obviously mean losing the election? One answer is that election platforms cover many issues, and many personalities take part. The middle ground of the spectrum is not always clear, and candidates may misjudge what the middle-of-the-road position really is. Second, the candidate usually enters a campaign with a previous record and personal ideology. Even if he or she wishes to adopt a moderate position, previous positions, taken in a party primary, for instance, might prevent changing. Still, there is a strong tendency, in a two-party system, for candidates to head to the center on issues and attempt to make personality the deciding criterion.

The presidential elections of 1960–76 illustrate this tendency. In three of these five elections there was little to distinguish between the candidates in terms of issues. The vote was very close, with one or two states determining the outcome (Kennedy and Nixon in 1960, Hum-

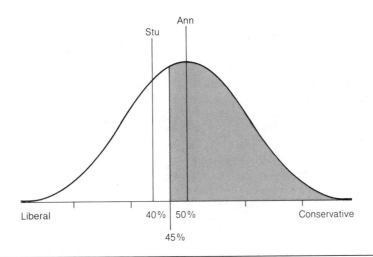

Exhibit 20-1   Hypothetical distribution of voters

In this hypothetical election, candidate Ann has adopted a middle-of-the-road position. Candidate Stu has adopted a position that is more liberal than

Ann's. The electorate votes for the candidate whose views are closest to their own. As a result, Ann receives 55% of the vote and wins.

phrey and Nixon in 1968, Carter and Ford in 1976). In 1964, Goldwater was perceived as right of center, and in 1972 McGovern took a position perceived to be left of center. Johnson (1964) and Nixon (1972), viewed as being near the center, won by landslides.

Of course, the center of the political spectrum in Nebraska is different from the center in Massachusetts. However, the "middle-of-the-road" candidates still win in those areas, and regional differences tend to cancel out. Office-holders do not wish to offend well-defined and well-organized interest groups, because those groups can influence marginal voters.

Special-Interest Groups   The average voter usually knows something about major issues like abortion, legalization of marijuana, the death penalty, and some welfare programs. There are

usually articulate spokesmen on both sides of the issue. On these issues, the center position will tend to prevail. Because so much information is available, the effects of rational ignorance do not come into play. A different picture emerges, however, when we look at the minor issues.

A simple policy of not offending constituents on major issues is not enough to keep politicians in office. They must get their messages or at least their names across to the voters—in other words, they must overcome voters' rational ignorance. This requires resources, and the usual way to obtain resources is through campaign contributions. It takes a lot of money to buy television and newspaper advertisements and to pay for travel and staff.

Many of these contributions come from special-interest groups. The contributions enable politicians to get out their messages; if a poli-

---

Special-Interest Groups

Many special-interest groups exist in the U.S. political system. The goal of each is to advance the cause of the members through the use of the political system. Among the most prominent special-interest groups are medical associations, trade unions, dairy co-ops, insurance groups, and the banking industry. Of these groups few have been as successful as the maritime unions, the relatively small unions organized from those who man U.S. registered ships. During debate on a bill affecting shipping, Senator Russell Long of Louisiana said, "There's nobody I'd rather have on my side than the Seafarers (Seafarers' International Union)."

The major thrust of the maritime unions in 1974–75 was a bill to require a fixed percentage of U.S. oil imports to be carried in tankers manned by U.S. crews. Since U.S. crews are much higher paid than any other nations this would have effectively raised the cost of transporting oil. The bill was opposed by the Department of Defense, the Federal Energy Administration, the State Department, and most outside observers. This opposition had little effect, and the maritime union influence in Congress was sufficient to get the bill through. Many observers believe the political power of the unions is due in part to

their political contributions. For example, Democrat Long received $10,000 from the Seafarers and $10,000 from the Marine Engineers. Democrat Frank Clark of Pennsylvania, the House leader for passage of the bill, received $15,000 from the Marine Engineers and $4,000 from the Seafarers. The bill was frustrated temporarily when President Ford vetoed the measure.

In 1976 the maritime unions pressured candidates for a commitment on the issue. Candidate Carter assured the unions that he would support their program. The maritime unions quickly raised $200,000 for Mr. Carter's primary election campaign.

Once elected president he got a chance to make his pledge good. The 1974 bill was reintroduced. Again leading economists and State and Defense Department officials argued that cargo preference was a very costly way to create a few jobs, would be antagonistic to free trade and disruptive to our relationships with other countries. These arguments failed to change the earlier pledge, and the president supported the bill. While the bill raised energy prices, the costs were only a part of maritime subsidy payments, which have exceeded $3.2 billion in the last 10 years.

---

tician is elected, the special-interest group receives the friendly attention of the official.

On nonmajor issues, the special-interest group will often have the politician's vote. On major issues, special-interest group influence is usually limited by voter knowledge, and by other, opposing special-interest groups. For example, labor unions tend to be very influential because they can channel both large amounts of funds and large numbers of "volunteers" to a politician. But on some issues they will be opposed by business trade associations or even other labor groups (e.g., the Teamsters versus the United

Farm Workers). In such cases the efforts of special-interest groups counteract each other.

Special-interest groups are most effective when a legislative proposal is complex and its benefits will go to a small, well-defined group but the cost will be borne by a dispersed, poorly organized group such as taxpayers or consumers. An example is a proposed bill to limit foreign steel imported to the United States. Domestic steel producers and the United Steel Workers would clearly benefit from the bill's passage, but almost all consumers would be hurt by the resulting higher prices. Yet each consumer would have difficulty estimating how much the bill will cost him or her, because of the indirect nature of the cost increase. As a result, few voters would know or care how their representative planned to vote. But the special-interest group would, and its members will write, phone, or telegraph their feelings to their representatives, and closely follow the progress of the bill in subcommittee, committee, and on the floor of Congress. Subjected to the special-interest group's knowledge, organization, and pleas, the representative will usually vote in its favor.

It is important to point out that there is no suggestion that anything illegal or immoral is going on in a case such as this. No bribes or illegal actions are taking place. We are merely discussing the incentives a political decision maker faces on a bill to reallocate resources. Although we have framed the decision in terms of a democracy, a similar set of incentives would apply in almost any political system. On minor issues special-interest groups will tend to dominate, not because of weak or immoral individuals, but because of the *incentives* facing the political decision maker.

The Bureaucracy

Although elected officials come and go, the bureaucracy goes on and on and on. There is nothing inherently good or bad about bureaucrats. Like almost everyone else, they respond to incentives and modify their behavior to maximize their personal utility. Of course there are exceptions, but in general, maximization of individual utility within the bounds of legality is a reasonable description of bureaucrats' goals.

The environment in which the bureaucrat operates has a strong effect on his or her action; it should be recognized that bureaucracies usu-

As a bureaucratic monopoly, the U.S. Postal Service tends to build up its costs to equal its revenue. *(Photo by Terry Zabala)*

ally are monopolies. Examples include the postal service, unemployment compensation, welfare, and agricultural allotment. (In a few cases alternatives are available. For example, certain crimes could be investigated by several different agencies: the Secret Service, FBI, military police, state police.)

Since government services are often a monopoly, their revenue, which is provided by Congress, could exceed cost and leave a profit. However, bureaucratic monopolies cannot legally take profits. They *can* build up costs to a point at which the costs equal revenue. Because their monetary salaries are limited, bureaucrats can maximize utility by adding to the nonpecuniary rewards of their positions—attractive furniture, thick rugs, important conferences to attend in Paris or Rome. When new agency heads move into a position, the office always needs refurbishing. A not atypical appointee to subcabinet rank spent $120,000 for carpets, tinted glass, floor-to-ceiling bookcases, and other refurbishing even though his predecessor had redecorated the office a year earlier.

Such activity is obvious to everyone and has a very minor impact on an agency's cost. Much more significant costs stem from another kind of bureaucracy—the desire to build the largest and most prestigious organization possible. The longer one serves in an organization, the greater the belief in its activities and its value. Director J. Edgar Hoover of the FBI is the classic example. Is it any wonder that a man who worked 40 years to develop an agency believed in its mission? Such bureaucrats may often provide more resources to an activity than necessary— it would be rather surprising if they didn't. Congress, of course, is supposed to determine which expenditures are and aren't necessary. But in a monopoly no test exists to determine how much or how little is rational. How does a congressman know whether the agency is equating marginal costs and marginal benefits when it is a nonprofit organization that enjoys a monopoly?

Occasionally a test of true cost emerges in rare cases where several agencies provide the same service. The Department of Defense has several such missions. The Navy and Air Force both have long-range missiles, and the Marines and Army both have a capability for amphibious landings. This potential competition may create some uncertainty about how to allocate the activity; probably some efficiency creeps in as each service seeks to show it can perform the task for lower cost. However, this incentive to improve efficiency usually is ended when an "efficiency" panel recommends consolidation to stop the competition (avoiding duplication is the term most frequently used). This solution is equivalent to saying Ford, General Motors, and Chrysler should merge to stop duplication.

Are there any incentives that work directly to assure that bureaucrats will seek optimum allocation of resources or operations at the lowest possible cost? There appear to be none.

Other Elements of the Government Decision-Making Process

Elected officials and bureaucrats make most government allocation decisions, but other officials, such as judges and heads of regulatory agencies, also play a role. It seems clear that government officials do not have direct and significant incentives to improve the allocation of resources. Furthermore, the less important the issue, the less incentive to allocate resources according to the desires of the majority of the population.

In summary, whenever there is imperfection in the market, there is a possibility for government intervention to improve the allocation of resources. Reallocation can be accomplished by prohibition, subsidies, taxes, tax breaks, and other methods. Unfortunately, the preliminary findings of research on the subject show that government intervention is not an automatic improvement over market decisions, even if the market is allocating badly. There is especially little incentive to improve the market decision on minor allocation questions or issues.

THE DILEMMA

Private markets can misallocate resources. Yet there is no direct set of incentives to assure that government intervention will improve the efficiency of the allocation. Does this mean that individuals should wring their hands and give up? Certainly not.

Both private and public economic activity have advantages and disadvantages. What is important is to use these tools skillfully, capitalizing on their strengths and deemphasizing their weaknesses. To a certain extent this is now being done. Once the decision is made to build a road— a public good—public workers seldom do the actual construction. Private contractors bid for the job, and the lowest bidder usually gets the contract. The government provides the resources for the public good; the private firm, which has a profit-motivated system, provides the service at minimum cost.

An optimum mix of public and private enterprises would recognize the strengths and weaknesses of each. These strengths and weaknesses follow from the incentives, motivations, and controls that prevail in each form of activity.

SUMMARY

1. An area of increasing importance is the nonmarket allocation of resources. The largest nonmarket allocation system is government—federal, state, and local. Other nonmarket organizations include universities, churches, and charitable organizations. In 1929 11 percent of Gross National Product was allocated by government. In 1983 government share had grown to three times that much.

2. Allocation of resources in a private market system has been criticized for a long time. The critics range from early Greek philosophers through medieval churchmen to some present-day economists. The critics argue that there is some higher goal that should be pursued and that private markets are not providing incentives that lead to that goal.

3. Private markets have been criticized for inefficiency in their allocation of scarce resources. This is true when social and private costs (and benefits) diverge, when there is monopoly or oligopoly present in the structure of industry, and/or when there are public goods involved. Traditional government intervention, such as taxes and subsidies, can correct the allocation problem.

4. A second criticism is that the market system yields results that are not equitable. However, most examples are really failures of the political system to respond directly to equity problems. Equity relationships can be separated from efficiency, and the price system still can be effective in allocating resources.

5. Even though government action *can* sometimes improve the allocation of resources, is there reason to believe it necessarily *will*? That is, what systematic influences assure that the incentives facing government will lead to improved resource allocation?

6. A review of the incentives facing different decision makers in government indicates that government intervention is not an automatic improvement over imperfect market allocation. However, this is an area in which economic research is just beginning and so there is much yet to be discovered about the government allocation system.

KEY CONCEPTS

nonmarket allocation of resources
social costs
social benefits
externalities

public goods
compensation
rational ignorance

QUESTIONS FOR DISCUSSION

1. Think of an example of a divergence between social costs and social benefits. In your example, what is the source of the divergence? What government action could be used to correct the divergence?

2. Sometimes politicians say that "human life is priceless." Is this true? In what sense? Suppose you had a choice between taking an airplane trip for $200 with present safety standards or taking the same trip on an airline that has half as many accidents per year than other airlines (it is therefore twice as safe) for a fare of $400. Which plane would you take? Is the answer to this part of the question consistent with your answer to the first part?

3. Would a judge, appointed for life, have the same incentives as a legislator elected for a two-year term?

4. Think of an example where you feel the market mechanism is allocating resources inefficiently. Does the example fall into the category of imperfect competition, externality, or public goods? Is there a way to use the price system to correct the problem?

5. Most national parks charge only a nominal fee. During the vacation season some of the parks become so overcrowded that the air pollution from automobiles begins to kill the trees. What type of problem do we have in this case and how could it be corrected?

Chapter 21

Analyzing Public Policy with Microeconomic Theory

Microeconomic analysis focuses on the efficient allocation of resources and the distribution of these resources among the population. In this chapter we use these tools to analyze public policies in four areas: environmental protection, international trade, housing, and agriculture. Our purpose in these discussions is to show how the tools of economics can be used to clarify the effects of public policies that are intended to improve the allocation of resources or designed to alter the distribution of income. The chapter also provides a useful review of some basic concepts of microeconomics.

POLICIES TO PROTECT THE ENVIRONMENT

Some people equate environmental protection with the elimination of all environmental pollution. Except for cases that constitute an absolute menace to health and welfare, the issue is seldom one of eliminating pollution but of ensuring that we have the *"optimum" level of pollution*. We say an optimum level of pollution because the existence of a negative externality like pollution does not necessarily mean that it is worthwhile for society to eliminate that externality. For example, if the production of a necessary commodity produces some smoke that does not constitute a clear danger to health, we may prefer to put up with the nuisance rather

Pollution control (through sewage treatment plants, for example) is desired if its social and private benefits exceed its costs. *(Photo by Daniel S. Brody, Stock, Boston)*

than either do without the commodity or pay large sums to eliminate the smoke. Thus the issue facing society is not clean air versus dirty air, or pure water versus polluted water, but rather between levels of air and water quality. Pollution control is desired as long as its social and private benefits exceed its costs.

It is likely that pollution control, as with goods and services, is subject to diminishing returns. In some cases its benefits are immense because of the clear threat to the environment. Such dramatic cases of environmental pollution should be controlled. Correcting less damaging forms of pollution may yield fewer benefits. One of the great challenges to policy is to gain an accurate assessment of the benefits and costs of pollution control.

Effluent Fees

Economists generally favor policies that encourage private business firms to make decisions consistent with the public interest. One great problem in controlling pollution is that polluters need not count pollution as a private cost because dumping wastes into the air and water is to them a free good. In order to eliminate this free waste disposal, some economists have proposed that private business firms and other polluters be charged an *effluent fee*.

This proposal is quite simple and is illustrated in Exhibit 21-1. On the vertical axis we have the price of pollution and on the horizontal axis the reduction of effluents. The government would set an effluent fee per unit of pollutant, which every polluter must pay. Thus, air and water resources would not be considered a free good within the decision-making processes of the private and public enterprises. Curve *S* in Exhibit 21-1 represents the cost of reducing pollutants. The rising costs reflect diminishing returns in pollution control.

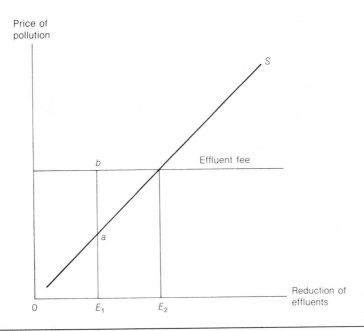

Exhibit 21-1   Effluent fees force business firms to treat pollution as a private cost

An effluent fee creates a situation in which the private firm's interests coincide with social interests until the cost of pollution control exceeds the effluent fee. If a firm reduces effluents by less than $0E_2$, it suffers unnecessary costs. This is shown by distance ab at $0E_1$. If society wants pollution reduced by more than $0E_2$, it must raise the effluent fee. (Curve S represents the cost of reducing pollutants.)

"A Clean and Gentle River Can Wash Away Your Job, Home, and Dreams."
—A Steel Worker

Steel plants have long polluted the Mahoning River in Ohio with 300 tons of metallic particles, oil, grease, cyanide, and ammonia per day. In 1976 the Environmental Protection Agency (EPA) granted these plants an exemption from pollution controls because they were so old the owners would close them rather than comply with regulation. EPA estimated that enforcing the regulation could eliminate 27 percent of the region's jobs and concluded that was too high a price to pay for a clean river.

Clearly, a business firm has an incentive to reduce the level of pollution as long as the cost of reducing effluents is below the effluent fee. If a firm decided to reduce its pollution to $0E_1$, the marginal unit of pollution control would cost the firm the vertical distance E_1a. But the government would nevertheless charge the effluent fee the distance E_1b. Therefore, the firm suffered an unnecessary cost ab that could have been avoided by more pollution control. And it could reduce the total cost of production by further reducing the level of pollution. This process would continue until the firm had eliminated $0E_2$ units of pollution. After this point the cost curve shows the firm would lose money by further reducing the level of pollution.

At any point to the left of $0E_2$, the business firm can save money by controlling pollution rather than paying the effluent fee. Assuming that the cost of environmental pollution control tends to rise for any given business firm, the imposition of a fixed effluent fee ensures that both the public and private interests coincide until $0E_2$ units of pollution are eliminated. If more than $0E_2$ units of pollution should be eliminated, the effluent fee is set too low.

The effluent fee system for environmental control is frequently cited as being simple and easy to administer. This advantage may be overstated. Setting a single effluent fee for the entire nation or even for entire regions makes little sense. The benefits of increased pollution control depend to a large extent on the capacity of the environmental receptor—the air or water into which the pollutant is discharged.

If a receptor can naturally absorb large amounts of pollution and its carrying capacity is not approached, only small social benefits are to be gained by imposing an effluent fee. On the other hand, in areas with low capacity for absorbing wastes without polluting the environment or with large populations, the benefits from pollution control are clear.

Effluent fees charged the polluter should be commensurate with the amount of damage. Consequently, different effluent fees would be needed in different regions. Similarly, effluent fees for air pollution would be different from those for water pollution. Separate fees are necessary for different kinds of effluents discharged into air and water resources. If one form of air pollution is more dangerous than another form, it would require a higher effluent fee.

Much information is required in order to set up a rational schedule of fees. One of the great advantages of the effluent fee is that it is easy to increase or lower as more information is obtained. However, there is a further problem of ensuring that polluters do not cheat on their payments. Pollution from the very large number of enterprises that degrade the environment must be monitored.

The cost of collecting fees and monitoring the effluent discharge does not make this system either simple or easy to administer. On the other hand, as we will point out, the same problems accompany any other system designed to control pollution. The advantage of a system of effluent charges is that it makes the private and public interests coincide. It requires private enterprises to account for social costs in their decision-making process.

Pollution Permits

Another strategy to force private firms to internalize the costs of environmental pollution is to create a market for pollution rights. In effect, this system would sell a specified number of *pollution permits* to the highest bidder in the private sector. To ensure that the environment is not eroded, the number of these pollution permits would be limited to the carrying capacity of the environment. The amount of pollution allowed could be held low enough that air or water would not become polluted.

This approach is shown in Exhibit 21-2. In this figure the vertical axis represents the price of pollution rights. On the horizontal axis is the quantity of pollution rights. Because we assume that the public sector will not allow pollution of the environment at any price, the supply curve of pollution rights S is perfectly inelastic at the carrying capacity of the environment. If there is a demand curve D_1 for pollution rights, we would find that the equilibrium price for them is P_1. Initially these rights would be purchased by the private sector from government. Business firms would only pollute if the cost of cleaning up their production processes exceeded the cost of pollution rights. In this sense, cre-

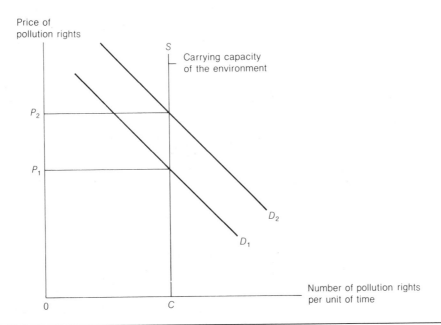

Exhibit 21-2   Creating a private market for pollution rights is another way to have business firms pay for social costs

The government can sell pollution rights to the private sector. However, as population grows, the demand for pollution rights will probably rise. This is shown by the shift from D_1 to D_2. The increase in

price will represent a windfall gain to the owners of pollution rights. To avoid this problem and to obtain funds to monitor the system, the government can sell pollution rights that expire after a period of time.

ating a private market for pollution rights resembles the system of effluent charges.

There is, however, an interesting aspect to this market for pollution rights. As population grows, the demand for pollution rights by business firms will probably increase, too. This would be reflected in demand curve D_2. As a result, the price of pollution rights would rise from P_1 to P_2 and the owners of the pollution rights would experience a capital gain the size of $P_2 - P_1 \times 0C$. This market does ration pollution rights through higher prices, but the common property right of the environment is now in private hands. Individuals or firms will realize a capital gain from the increased demand for pollution of the environment. Under this

scheme, the public sector receives only the initial payment for pollution rights. This fee, of course, is $0P_1 \times 0C$.

The disadvantage of creating a market for pollution rights is that any increased revenues as a result of an increased demand for pollution stay in the private sector and, in effect, contribute to private profits. One way to overcome this problem is to sell pollution rights for only one year. Annual auctions by the government would create a continual stream of funds to the public sector, which could be used to defray the costs of monitoring the level of pollution. A system of pollution rights must be monitored so that only those firms with pollution rights discharge effluents into the environment.

Fly Quiet Airlines

Many countries, including the United States, have either passed or are considering passing legislation designed to cut noise pollution coming from aircraft. These proposals provide for a graduated tax based on the volume of noise and the amount of disturbance it creates. A plane landing at night would be taxed more than one landing during the day. Airports in heavily populated areas would have higher taxes than remote airports. High enough taxes affect operating costs and provide an incentive for airlines to replace noisy jets or to install sound-absorbing material to quiet the engines.

Subsidies

It is sometimes suggested that the public sector should bear some of the costs of eliminating pollution by subsidizing firms to purchase pollution abatement equipment. Such a subsidy scheme suffers several disadvantages. The incentive for a private business firm to install pollution control equipment, even if it is subsidized, is zero unless the installation of this equipment will increase profits. The subsidy, therefore, offers no encouragement to the private sector to reduce its level of pollution.

A further problem with the use of subsidies to discourage pollution is the difficulty of calculating the subsidy to be paid to a new business firm. If new firms are given subsidies, it would be possible to subsidize a nonpolluting technology that costs no more than polluting technologies. The subsidy to eliminate pollution would then be a gift from the public sector to the corporation.

A third disadvantage of subsidies in the absence of any direct regulation is that it tends to violate equity principles. In general, economists

feel that people who benefit from pollution ought to pay for it. Pollution may benefit the business firm if profits rise when it uses "free" resources for the disposal of its wastes. Customers also benefit because lower costs may be reflected in lower prices. If the production of a particular good or service causes environmental pollution, each consumer should pay higher prices and the firms should realize lower profits. These effects will discourage the expansion of this industry relative to others that are less costly in social terms. A subsidy instead encourages the expansion of such industries.

Maximum Allowable Emission Approach

Although economists prefer using economic incentives to encourage firms to reduce pollution, most environmental regulations are direct regulations that limit the amount of emissions a firm may discharge into the environment. This is called the maximum allowable emission approach because firms unable to meet this standard are required to terminate production. Under this form of environmental policy, the government requires that each firm meet an emission standard. If the cost of pollution control in some firms is higher than in others, the allowable emission approach is inefficient because it does not take into account the cost of realizing the desired objective.

The advantages of an effluent fee (a tax on pollution) over the maximum allowable emission approach is easily demonstrated. Suppose there are two firms that pollute the environment, each emitting 5 units of pollution. The cost of reducing the pollution is higher for one firm than the other. Such a situation is shown in Exhibit 21-3. Society finds 10 units of pollution unacceptable and a decision is made to cut the level of pollution to 6 units: 4 units of

Exhibit 21-3   Cost of pollution control

Unit of Emission	Firm A	Firm B
1	$ 100	$ 500
2	200	1000
3	400	1500
4	800	2000
5	1200	2500

emission must be eliminated. Under the maximum allowable emission approach, each firm must eliminate 2 units of pollution. Exhibit 21-3 shows that the first unit will cost Firm A $100 and the second will cost $200, a total of $300. Firm B has a much higher cost per unit of pollution control, the 2 units totaling $1500. The social cost of eliminating 4 units of pollution using the maximum allowable emission approach is $1800. In contrast, suppose the firms were charged an effluent fee of $550 per unit of emission. Firm A would prefer to reduce pollution by 3 units rather than pay the fee because the costs of pollution control are lower than the fee. Firm B would reduce its pollution by only 1 unit because it is cheaper to pay the tax than to eliminate the second unit of pollution.

Under this $550 pollution fee the social goal has been achieved because 4 units of pollution have been eliminated. The total resource cost, however, is $700 to Firm A and $500 to Firm B, a total of $1200. The effluent fees compensate society for the damage done by the remaining pollution. Thus we see that by giving the firms that can most easily reduce pollution the incentive to do so, we are able to reduce the resources devoted to achieving a specific environmental goal by one-third. The actual savings that could be realized under a system of pollution taxes rather than the maximum allowable emission approach have been estimated to be in excess of one-third. Public policy can be greatly improved when it takes into account private incentives.

Most environmental regulations directly limit the amount of emissions a firm may discharge into the environment. *(Photo by Terry Zabala)*

SUGAR-SWEET QUOTAS

On July 9, 1982, the world price of sugar stood at 7.7¢ per pound. The price in the United States was 21.8¢ per pound. Such a price difference between the domestic and world price can exist only when there are restrictions on imports. The process of trade restriction and its economic impact provides an interesting application of political economy.

The purpose of the trade restrictions is straightforward. U.S. growers cannot produce sugar as cheaply as can foreign producers. In order to keep a domestic sugar industry, the government has protected U.S. growers for many years by restricting the admission of foreign sugar. The difference between the average world price of sugar, 7.4¢ per pound, and the U.S. average price of 19.9¢, was 12.5¢ per pound. If we assume it costs 1.5¢ per pound to transport the sugar, the cost to consumers for the 11.6 billion pounds of sugar produced domestically was approximately $1.3 billion.

There are two primary techniques used to limit imports—tariffs and quotas. A *tariff* is a charge that the importer of a good must pay when bringing the good into the country. For example, if the world price of rubber were $1 per pound and there were a 20¢ per pound tariff, the price in the United States would be $1.20 per pound. A *quota*, by contrast, is a fixed limitation on the quantity of a good that can be imported. For example, the total annual volume of foreign steel allowed to enter the United

States might be 1 million tons. No matter what happened to the price of steel, no additional amount could be imported beyond that annual quota.

The economic difference between tariffs and quotas can be shown graphically. Exhibit 21-4 shows the effect of a tariff when there is no domestic production. In the absence of a tariff, U.S. consumers would pay the world price of $1 per pound for sugar and purchase 12,000 pounds. However, when the government imposes a tariff of 50¢ per pound, the price to U.S. consumers becomes $1.50 per pound and U.S. sugar consumers purchase only 10,000 pounds. The government collects $5000 in tariffs (10,000 pounds times 50¢).

The situation changes when there are U.S. producers, because domestic producers do not have to pay the import tariff. This situation is shown in Exhibits 21-5 through 21-7.

Exhibit 21-5a shows the effect upon market supply when there is domestic production and no tariff. Those U.S. producers who are able to supply sugar at less than the world price of $1

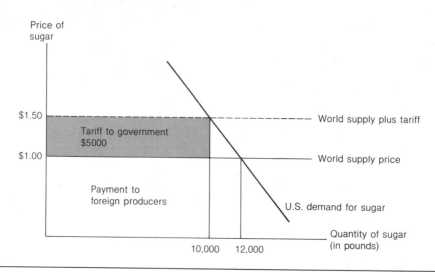

Exhibit 21-4   Effect of a tariff on a good not produced domestically

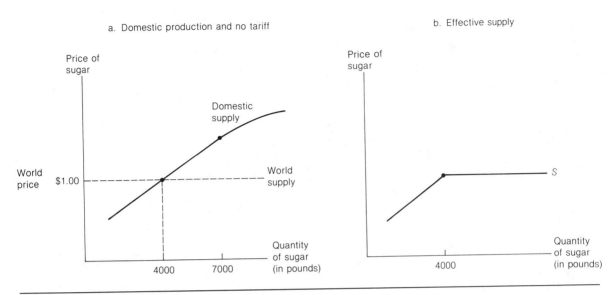

Exhibit 21-5   U.S. sugar supply curve when there are no restrictions on imports

per pound provide the first 4000 pounds. Beyond that amount, no sugar is provided by U.S. producers because there is a large volume of sugar available on the world market that can be imported for $1 per pound. Exhibit 21-4b shows

the effective supply for the U.S. market when there are no trade restrictions.

In Exhibit 21-6a the effect of restricting trade by a tariff is shown: with the tariff a firm importing sugar to the United States must pay

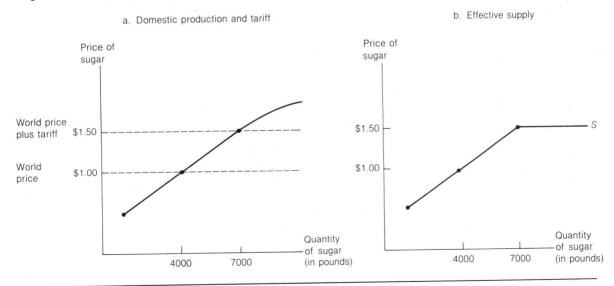

Exhibit 21-6   U.S. sugar supply curve when there is a tariff (50¢ per pound)

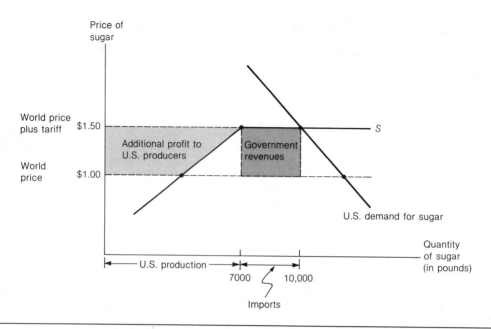

Exhibit 21-7   Effect of a tariff (50¢ per pound) when there is domestic production

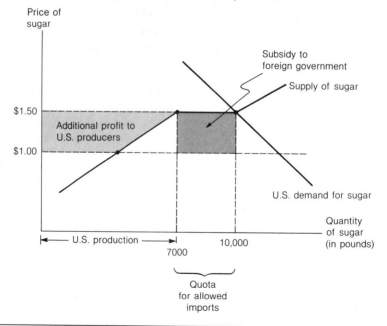

Exhibit 21-8   Effect of a quota

50¢ per pound to the government. Therefore a U.S. importer would have to sell the sugar at $1.50 per pound to cover the added cost of the tariff. This means that U.S. producers who can produce sugar for less than $1.50 are the relevant supply source. U.S. producers now provide the first 7000 pounds of sugar and the world markets provide the rest. This is shown in the effective supply curve of Exhibit 21-6b.

The effect of the tariff is shown in Exhibit 21-7. U.S. consumers purchase 10,000 pounds of sugar as they did when there was no U.S. production (as was shown in Exhibit 21-4). However, now only 3000 pounds are imported and 7000 pounds come from domestic production. The 3000 pounds of imported sugar bring in tariffs to the government. The other effect of the tariff is to raise the level of profits of the domestic producers.

The effect of the other restrictive device, the quota, is shown in Exhibit 21-8. Here an import quota of 3000 pounds of sugar has been allowed. The 3000 pounds enter the United States and a price of $1.50 is set. If only 2000 pounds were admitted, the United States price would be higher. (The student should be able to work out what would happen with the smaller quota.) As before, the domestic producers supply 7000 pounds of the good.

Since there is no tariff, the U.S. government receives no tariff revenues. What happens to the 50¢ per pound difference between the world price and the U.S. price? The $1500 difference goes to the party holding the license for importation. In practice, these licenses are often issued to the governments of the countries who are allowed to export the good to the United States. Therefore these import restrictions act as an implicit or hidden form of foreign aid. In the case of sugar, the import licenses are often given to sugar-producing Caribbean countries that are on good terms with the United States.

The sugar quota is an example of how the type of protection policy can affect the total social cost.

HOUSING POLICY

Urban Renewal

Families with low income demand inexpensive housing. This is not to say they prefer poor housing; the demand results from low family income. For two decades after passage of the Housing Act of 1949, urban renewal projects often destroyed the homes of the poor in order to use the land for some other purpose. Oppo-

Urban renewal projects do not change any of the determinants of demand (tastes and preferences, income, or prices of related products). *(Photo by Alex Webb, Magnum Photos, Inc.)*

sition to this practice led to the elimination of the urban renewal program in 1974.

We can use the tools of supply and demand to show the impact on housing of these urban renewal policies. Low-income families have a downward-sloping demand curve for housing services, which means that as the *price per unit of housing services* falls, these households will demand a larger quantity of housing services. We emphasize this point because the demand curve is not a demand for dwellings. Most families want only one dwelling unit. Larger and higher-quality dwellings offer more housing services per unit of time; since it is always possible to have a dwelling with slightly more housing services, we can draw a demand curve for housing services as shown in Exhibit 21-9. Similarly,

the supply of housing services shows a relationship between the price per unit of housing services and the quantity of housing services supplied. To understand how easy it is to increase the flow of housing services a dwelling yields when the price per unit rises, we need only consider the landlord who improves a dwelling by redecorating or fixing some broken stairs. These acts increase the number of housing services the dwelling can provide during a given period of time.

Urban renewal projects do not change any of the determinants of demand (tastes and preferences, income, or prices of related products). Thus we know that the demand curve shown in Exhibit 21-9 remains unchanged. However, the destruction of dwellings in which poor peo-

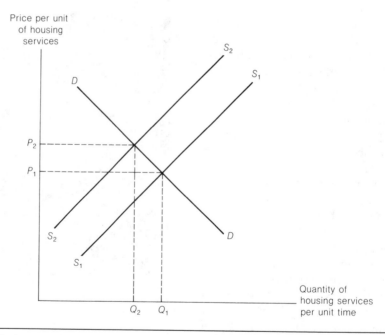

Exhibit 21-9   Effect of urban renewal on the low-income housing market

Urban renewal projects have often destroyed more low-income housing than they constructed. This

shifts the supply curve to the left, forcing the poor to pay a higher price for fewer units of housing services.

ple live shifts the supply of housing services to the left. The result is clear. The urban renewal program will cause low-income households to pay a higher price for housing services $(P_2 - P_1)$ for fewer housing services $(Q_1 - Q_2)$.

While the poor are made worse off, the improvements in the quality of housing are likely to be short-lived. Owners of deteriorating, but not slum, housing can profit by renting their property to low-income households, which now pay a higher price per unit of service. Landlord profits can be increased if they rent to low-income households and cut maintenance expenditures. Substandard housing is thus created. Many urban economists argue that if the housing market is competitive, slum clearance and urban renewal merely shift the location of substandard dwellings rather than reduce their number. If the housing market is not competitive, the poor will be forced to pay higher rents and their poverty will be accentuated. In either event, the historical experience with urban renewal has been such that federal government policy has aggravated rather than alleviated the housing problems of poor households.

Housing Subsidies

Poor housing exists because people cannot afford what we consider standard dwellings. An obvious solution is to give them more money so that they can live in better housing. Because income is a determinant of demand, the demand curve for housing among poor people would shift to the right. Given a supply curve, this means people will buy more housing.

The success of this demand-enhancing approach depends on how much of their extra income poor people will spend on housing. This amount is, of course, measured by the income elasticity of demand for housing. You will recall from Chapter 13 that the income elasticity of demand for housing is the percentage change in housing quantity divided by the percentage change in income $(\%\Delta Q_h/\%\Delta Y)$. Suppose a family of four has an income of $6400 and spends $1600 on housing. Assume we want to increase the quantity of housing consumed by such families and to do this, we give them a $1600 income supplement. Family income has risen 25 percent; the income elasticity of demand for housing will tell us how much of the $1600 will be spent on housing.

Recent research suggests that the income elasticity of demand for housing is about 0.7. This means that a 1 percent change in income will increase housing expenditures by 0.7 percent. If income rises by 25 percent, this income elasticity tells us that housing expenditures will rise by 17.5 percent $(\%\Delta Q_h/\%\Delta Y = 17.5/25 = 0.7)$. This means that only 17.5 percent of the $1600 subsidy—$280—will be spent for improved housing. The remaining $1320 will be used for other commodities that the household values more highly than additional housing.

One government housing program is designed to target assistance payments to housing. The Section 8 Existing Housing Program is a "demand-side" subsidy that requires an eligible family to spend 25 percent of its income for a "standard" housing unit. If this standard unit costs $200 per month and the household's income is $400 a month, the household participating in this program would pay $100 a month for housing and the government would pay the other $100 required for a standard dwelling. The extent to which the Section 8 program improves the housing of program participants depends on how much families spend on housing before entering the program. If before entering the program the above family spent $100 on housing, all the federal subsidy is spent on housing. However, if a household spent half of its $400 income on housing, the $100 subsidy merely replaces housing expenditures made by the family. In this case the "housing" program is simply an income transfer. Thus, the Section 8 Existing Housing Program reduces, but cannot eliminate, the problem of households spending "housing assistance" money on other commodities.

THE FARM PROBLEM

In recent years farmer groups have complained to Congress and the media, taken political actions, and driven their tractors into Washington to call attention to their plight. In this section we will discuss the economic factors behind the farm problem and evaluate public policies in this area.

Like many industries, farmers were caught during the 1970s in the squeeze of high interest rates and prices that rose slower than costs. At first glance, this situation appears similar to the problems facing the steel and auto industries. However, agriculture really was quite different with regard to efficiency and investment. The auto and steel industries were characterized by inadequate investment in modern facilities and low productivity that made them vulnerable to foreign competition. In contrast, U.S. agricultural productivity leads the world. By substituting capital for labor, the average U.S. farmer produces sufficient food to feed 75 people.

A tractor march on Washington was one way farmers found to protest U.S. policies on agricultural exports. *(Wide World Photos)*

In 1982, after years of great productivity increases, the picture was grim. Due to the forces of supply and demand, wheat that cost $6.32 a bushel to produce was selling for $3.41 a bushel in the competitive market. Every major crop was selling below farmers' real cost of production.

How did such a situation come about? The overproduction that characterized agriculture resulted largely from government policies. The 1973 OPEC decision to raise oil prices drastically created a need for increased sales of U.S. products overseas in order to pay for oil imports. Agriculture was one of these products and it received government encouragement in the form of subsidized loans. The policy was successful. The amount of land under cultivation increased from 289 million acres in 1972 to 413 million in 1982—a 43 percent increase. However, the increase in volume was not associated with increases in profit. Gross revenue rose in the nine years after 1973 but profit declined. By 1982 farmers' net income was below the interest on farm debts.

Meanwhile, the Farmers Home Administration, the government's primary source of loans to farmers, became concerned about the debts that farmers had built up. In 1982 the FHA began foreclosing on farms that had been delinquent on payments. The foreclosures brought heated protests and occasional violence from farm groups.

Usually, an overabundance of capacity will cause an exit of firms, and supply and demand will shift accordingly. Although farmers may leave the industry, their farms are sold to other farmers and the productive capacity remains in the industry.

Why had demand not increased in accordance with expectations? The answers lie in part with decisions by foreign governments and in part with decisions by U.S. politicians. Other nations responded to the political power of their farm groups by heavily subsidizing their agriculture. Thus, even though U.S. agriculture is the world's low-cost producer of many commodities, it is unable to enter many foreign markets because subsidies by foreign governments to their agricultural sectors lower the international price of their output.

Furthermore, foreign countries wanted never again to be dependent on U.S. agricultural production because they could not be confident of a continuous supply. For example, in 1973 when soybean prices began to rise sharply and threatened to raise U.S. food prices for consumers, President Nixon responded to U.S. consumer groups and severely limited the export of soybeans. The technique was effective and U.S. food prices were stabilized in the short run. However, Japan, which had been a prime export market for U.S. soybeans, was hurt by the unexpected move. The Japanese response was predictable. Japan provided millions of dollars to Brazil to establish a competing soybean capacity and the United States lost part of its best market.

A similar situation occurred when President Carter slapped an embargo on grain exports to the Soviet Union in response to the Soviet invasion of Afghanistan. Before that move, the Russians had purchased 70 percent of their grain from the United States. Now the Soviet Union buys less than 30 percent from the United States and has established trade relations with Canada, Australia, and Argentina to make itself less vulnerable to U.S. political actions.

Given the overproduction that came about in part because of government action, is there any policy to assist agriculture without drastically hurting this politically powerful industry? The answer seems to be that some land must be taken out of production. A current program provides payments to farmers who remove 15 percent of their land from production. However, all that has occurred is that the least productive land has been removed. Any serious efforts to remove land would result in higher agricultural prices and the familiar debates on income redistribution. Such issues are often the implicit factor affecting any meaningful agricultural policy. For example, a solution favored by many agricultural experts is to have the government buy land from farmers and put it in a land bank. This land would stay out of production and help bring agricultural markets into equilibrium at a higher price. If world surpluses began to go below safe levels, the land could be leased back to farmers for production. In essence, this approach would mothball capacity for that time in the future when population pressures shift demand enough that additional capacity is needed.

SUMMARY

1. This chapter uses the tools of microeconomic analysis to show the effects of various public policies.
2. Economists generally favor policies that use incentives (prices), rather than direct governmental regulation, to encourage the desired outcome. An example of this is the use of effluent fees or pollution permits instead of the maximum allowable emission approach.
3. Restriction of foreign trade raises the price of output to consumers. In the case of the sugar industry, the result is a much higher price in the United States than in the world market. The total social cost of these subsidies to the sugar industry can vary by the type of trade restriction.
4. The case of housing policy shows that the tools of supply and demand can be used even though most consumers will purchase only one house. Units of housing services, rather than number of dwellings, is the unit of analyses.
5. Housing policy designed to increase the demand for housing will be more effective when the demand for housing is highly elastic with respect to income. Recent research suggests that the income elasticity of demand for housing is about 0.7.
6. Government policies encouraged an increase in agricultural production in order to increase exports. Unfortunately, other countries have not allowed much of this increased output to be imported, resulting in a market price below the cost of production.

KEY CONCEPTS

effluent fees

pollution permits

maximum allowable emissions

tariff

quota

QUESTIONS FOR DISCUSSION

1. If the cost of reducing pollution were to fall, what would happen to the level of pollution, given a specific effluent fee? How would your answer differ if these costs fall when pollution permits are used to limit pollution? What happens if the cost of reducing pollution rises under these two policies? Which policy do you prefer?

2. Explain the effects of a quota and tariff on the U.S. sugar market when there is an increase in the demand for sugar. Assuming you must choose some trade restriction, would you prefer a tariff or a quota if you expect the demand for sugar to fall?

3. Analyze your individual demand curve for automobile transportation. Explain what a unit of automobile services means. What is the difference between a 1967 Oldsmobile and a 1983 Rolls Royce in terms of automobile services?

4. In the United States we redistribute a considerable income to poor households by means of "in-kind" transfers—notably food stamps and housing programs. Do you think food stamps will increase the quantity of food these households purchase? Why do you think we have these programs instead of straight transfers of income?

5. Many nations protect their agricultural sector from low-cost U.S. output. Show what effect tariffs and quotas might have on U.S. farmers.

Glossary

absolute advantage The advantage a nation has when it uses fewer resources to produce an item than other nations use.

AFL-CIO The union formed by a merger in 1955 of the American Federation of Labor and the Congress of Industrial Organizations.

aggregate demand The total of consumption demand, private investment demand, government demand, and net export demand.

aggregate supply schedule A table showing equilibrium levels of national income and supply, usually represented by a 45-degree line on a graph showing the income determination process.

allocation of resources The assignment of resources to various uses. Society has more demand for resources than resources. Therefore, some method has to be used to assign the resources to the best use. The market mechanism is one allocation technique.

appreciation of currency The rise in the price of a nation's currency relative to another currency.

automatic stabilizers Countercyclical fiscal policies that are built into U.S. tax and expenditure programs.

autonomous investment Investment that is independent of the level of national income.

average fixed cost The total amount spent on fixed costs divided by the number of products produced.

average product The total number of units produced divided by the number of units of the variable input.

average propensity to consume (APC) The fraction of total income being spent on consumption. In symbols, it is C/Y.

average propensity to save (APS) The fraction of total income being saved. In symbols, it is S/Y.

average total cost The total amount spent on all costs divided by the number of products produced.

average variable cost The total amount spent on variable costs divided by the number of products produced.

backward-bending labor supply curve The curve that occurs when workers prefer to increase leisure as the wage rate rises. At the higher wage rate, the worker chooses to avoid the disutility of the last unit of work.

balanced budget multiplier The increase in national income caused by a change in both taxes and expenditures.

barriers to entry Those features that would prevent firms from entering an industry.

breakeven point That level of production where total revenue and total costs are equal.

business cycles Fluctuations of economic activity.

cartel A combination of independent firms that unite to limit competition, setting prices and production levels to mutual advantage.

ceteris paribus "All other things held equal." Economists use ceteris paribus in constructing theories when they eliminate unimportant influences so that theory can focus on the most important aspects of a problem.

change in demand A shift in the demand curve caused by a change in income, tastes and preferences, or price of a related product.

change in quantity demanded A movement along a demand curve caused by a change in price.

change in quantity supplied A movement along a supply curve caused by a change in price.

change in supply A shift in the supply curve caused by a change in technology and input prices.

circular flow of income The income exchange between households and firms. It can be dia-grammed showing the flows of real resources and money payments.

classical economics The prevailing economic view during the nineteenth and early twentieth centuries. The economy was viewed as a self-adjusting, market-determined system that would return to full employment after any disruption.

collective bargaining The process by which unions and management negotiate the wages, benefits, seniority rights, and other things workers will receive.

comparative advantage A concept showing that nations can benefit from trade if they specialize in items with the lowest opportunity cost, even if they have no absolute advantage.

compensating wage differentials Variations reflecting noneconomic factors that affect the relative desirability of jobs.

complementary good A good associated with another good. The consumption of a complementary good is increased with the consumption of the complement (e.g., strawberries and shortcake).

complements When a change in consumption of one good causes a similar change in the consumption of a different good, the goods are said to be complementary.

concentration ratio A measure of the number and sizes of firms in an industry. The most common measure is based on the share of sales of the largest four firms in the industry.

conglomerate merger A merger of two firms that have unrelated products.

constant-cost industry An industry in which output can be expanded without the price of inputs changing.

constant returns to scale The costs of production do not change when a nation produces more of an item. Complete specialization of production among nations requires constant returns to scale.

Consumer Price Index (CPI) An index designed to measure the changes in prices of a representative "market basket" of goods and services purchased by a typical household in urban areas.

consumption Expenditures made by households for their personal use.

consumption function The relationship between income and consumption.

cost minimization A firm must operate where the marginal physical product/factor price ratio for all factors is equal. That is: $MPP_A/P_A = MPP_B/P_B$.

cost-push inflation A type of inflation caused by increases in costs of production, which push up selling prices.

cross elasticity of demand The responsiveness of the quantity demanded of a good when the price of another good is changed.

crowding out When the borrowing of government drives up interest rates, private borrowers cannot get credit on acceptable terms.

cyclical unemployment A type of unemployment caused by declines in economic activity over the business cycle.

decreasing-cost industry An industry in which costs decrease as the industry expands.

decreasing returns to scale The cost per unit of production rises as output increases.

demand curve A graph showing the relationship between price and quantity demanded.

demand deposits Accounts at a bank upon which a check can be written (i.e., a checking account).

demand for money People want to hold money because it facilitates transactions, provides safety for when an unexpected purchase is required, and can be used for speculation.

demand-pull inflation A type of inflation caused by excess aggregate demand.

demand schedule A table showing the quantity of a good that would be purchased at various prices.

depreciation The decrease in value of plant, equipment, and buildings caused by the production process.

depreciation of currency The decline in the price of a nation's currency relative to another currency.

derived demand The firm's demand for factors of production as derived from consumer demand for the items produced.

discount rate The interest rate for commercial banks borrowing money from the Fed.

discount rate The rate of interest used to calculate the net present value of future income.

discouraged workers Individuals who feel that they cannot get a job and who therefore quit seeking employment.

discouraged-worker effect The situation when workers drop out of the labor force because they believe they won't find jobs.

discretionary fiscal policy The manipulation of taxes and government spending to adjust the level of economic activity.

diseconomies of scale Increases in per-unit costs associated with increasing the scale of operations.

dissaving People's spending more than their income during a given time period.

dual labor-market theory The theory that there are two separate job markets: one that provides only deadend jobs and another that offers the possibility of advancement.

duopoly The situation when there are only two suppliers in a market.

ease of entry and exit An absence of obstacles to firms entering or leaving a product line. Obstacles can take the form of legal barriers, capital barriers, technological barriers, and so forth.

economic rents Payments made to workers beyond those required to bring them into production.

economies of scale Reductions in per-unit costs associated with increasing the scale of operations.

effluent fees The price set on waste discharged into the environment.

elastic demand Demand for a good in which a change in price causes a large percentage change in the quantity demanded.

employer of last resort The government can eliminate the unemployment effects of a minimum wage by employing the unemployed.

Employment Act of 1946 The act which established a national policy that the government should pursue economic policies encouraging full employment with stable prices.

entrepreneur A person who organizes the other factors of production in hopes of making a profit.

equation of exchange *(MV = PQ)* The money supply *(M)* times its annual turnover (velocity) is equal to the total amount spent (price times quantity) in that economy.

equilibrium level of income A stable income level—no forces are operating that would change it because aggregate demand equals aggregate supply.

equilibrium price The price where the quantity supplied and the quantity demanded are equal. It can be shown as the intersection of the supply and demand curves.

excess profit Profit that exceeds normal profit.

excess reserves The funds available to be used for loans, determined by actual reserves less the amount of required reserves.

exchange rate The price of one currency in terms of another.

expansions Periods of economic recovery in the business cycle.

expenditure approach to GNP The determination of GNP by measuring the expenditures that took place in an economy during the year. These expenditures are composed of (household) consumption, government expenditures, business sector expenditures, and foreign sector expenditures.

explicit or accounting costs Costs that involve a direct expenditure of funds.

exports The sale of goods or services to buyers in another country.

externalities Effects on a group of persons or on a society that result from the actions of a firm, positive or negative. The effects are such that full payment cannot be exacted from the participating parties.

factors of production (1) Land, which includes all natural resources, (2) labor, our human resources, and (3) capital, those man-made items that are used in the production process.

factor payments The compensation that the factors of production (land, labor, capital, and entrepreneurship) receive for providing their services.

fallacy of composition An error in logic when one assumes that what is true for individuals is also true for society as a whole.

Federal Open Market Committee (FOMC) The committee, made up of the Board of Governors plus presidents of five Federal Reserve District Banks, that sets policy with regard to the buying and selling of bonds in the financial markets.

Federal Reserve System Composed of the Board of Governors, Federal Reserve district banks, and the commercial banks.

fixed costs Expenses that would continue in the short run regardless of the level of production.

foreign exchange Any currency that can be used for international payments. It represents an international medium of exchange.

fractional reserves The proportion of deposits that a bank holds in the form of liquid assets.

freely floating exchange rates Exchange rates determined by market forces without government interference.

frictional unemployment A type of unemployment caused by temporary economic adjustments (e.g., a person voluntarily moves to a different state or quits a job).

gini coefficient A measure of the extent of inequality. It is the area between the Lorenz curve and the line of total equality divided by the total area under the line of total equality.

GNP deflator A price index used to calculate real GNP from money GNP. It is calculated as: (current year output valued at current year prices ÷ current year output valued at base year prices) × 100.

goals of macroeconomic policy These goals are steady economic growth, a stable price level, and minimum unemployment. Often there are trade-offs among goals, making policy formulation difficult.

government spending Expenditures by all levels of government—federal, state, and local—for finished products and direct purchase of factors.

Gross National Product (GNP) The dollar value of goods and services produced in a nation over a period of time, usually a year.

homogeneous products Goods that are viewed by potential buyers as identical or perfect substitutes.

horizontal merger The joining of firms that produce the same product to form a single firm.

human capital Workers are called human capital because investments in training and education make them more productive.

ideal long-term growth path The best possible combinations of macroeconomic goals over the long run: steady growth, full employment, and stable prices.

imperfect competition A market structure that has more suppliers than a monopoly but fewer than under competitive conditions.

imports The purchase of goods or services from suppliers in other countries.

income approach to GNP A determination of GNP by measuring the flow of payments to factors that took place in the economy during the year.

income elasticity The responsiveness of the quantity demanded to a change in income of a consumer.

incomes policy Using some form of wage and price controls to control the rate of inflation.

increasing-cost industry An industry in which costs increase as the industry expands.

indirect business taxes Taxes paid to the government by business firms; they are not levied directly on the business firm. State sales taxes are the major category of indirect business taxes.

induced investment Investment influenced by the level of national income.

inelastic demand Demand for a good in which the quantity demanded is not very sensitive to a change in price.

inflationary expectations Expectations of future price increases cause suppliers of labor and capital to raise prices, reinforcing cost-push inflation.

inflationary gap The vertical distance between the 45-degree line and aggregate demand at potential GNP when aggregate demand crosses the 45-degree line beyond the full-employment level of NNP.

interest A payment for the use of money.

investment Expenditures by business made on long-lived assets to be used in the production process.

involuntary inventory buildup Higher inventories caused by sales not being as large as expected.

kinked demand curve A discontinuous marginal revenue curve that is the result of a series of behavioral assumptions about competitors' responses.

labor-force participation rate The percentage of a population that is in the labor force.

laissez-faire A policy of little or no government interference in private economic matters. A "hands off" approach.

law of demand The law stating that the quantity demanded of a good increases as the price decreases, assuming that all other things that might affect demand—such as tastes, preferences, period of time, and the prices of other goods—remain the same.

law of diminishing marginal returns The law stating that when all inputs but one are held constant, the addition of successive units of input will yield smaller and smaller increases of output.

law of supply The law stating that the quantity of a good supplied usually varies directly with the price of the good, assuming that all other factors related to supply do not change.

legal barriers Restrictions upon new entrants to an industry based on legal limitations such as copyrights, licenses, and patents.

long-run adjustment process The process of changing the size of the plants as well as the other inputs.

long-run average-total-cost curve Sometimes called the planning curve, this curve describes the lowest average cost at which a quantity of output can be produced.

Lorenz curve A graph that shows how income is distributed among the population.

M_1 The definition of the money supply that includes coins, currency, and demand deposits.

M_2 The definition of the money supply that adds to M_1 the near money of savings accounts.

macroeconomics The study of economic growth and stability. Its purpose is to develop public policy to achieve three goals: a desired rate of growth, stable prices, and full employment.

marginal cost The cost associated with producing an additional unit.

marginal efficiency of investment (MEI) The expected rate of return on an investment.

marginal physical product The extra output produced by one additional unit of input, given that all other factors are held constant.

marginal product The change in total production associated with a one-unit change in the variable input.

marginal productivity theory The theory based on the idea that factors are paid according to their contribution to output.

marginal propensity to consume (MPC) The fraction of additional income devoted to consumption. Symbolically, $\Delta C / \Delta Y$.

marginal propensity to save (MPS) The change in saving associated with a change in income. It is $\Delta S / \Delta Y$.

marginal revenue The additional revenue that will be derived from the sale of an additional unit.

marginal revenue product The dollar value of a factor's marginal physical product.

market The interaction of supply and demand. It is not necessarily a place where buyers and sellers physically meet.

market price The price established by the interaction of supply and demand.

market system A system that uses the decentralized decision making of individuals and business firms to allocate resources. In their pursuit of self-interest, business firms produce the commodities people are willing and able to buy.

maximum allowable emissions An environmental policy whereby the government requires that each firm meet an emission standard.

medium of exchange An item that is generally accepted by people in exchange for goods and services.

microeconomics The study of how the market mechanism and government policy allocate and distribute resources.

midpoint calculation A means of determining elasticity that uses the average price and quantity as a base.

minimum-cost point The lowest point on the average total cost curve—hence, the least-cost level of production.

minimum-wage legislation Laws that are designed to guarantee workers a decent standard of living but actually cause some workers to be unemployed.

monetarists Economists who believe that controlling the money supply is the key to stabilizing macroeconomic activity.

money GNP GNP measured in terms of current prices.

money multiplier The maximum increase in the money supply caused by an increase in deposits in the system. It can be computed as the reciprocal of the reserve ratio.

money supply A dollar measure of the amount of highly liquid assets in the economy. There are several definitions of the money supply because of the variety of financial assets in the economy.

monopolistic competition A market structure characterized by many firms selling a differentiated product.

monopoly The situation when only one firm is supplying the market.

multiplier The change in income that results from a change in investment or consumption. Its numerical value is 1/MPS.

natural rate of unemployment The lowest level of unemployment that can be achieved without accelerating the rate of inflation.

near money Assets such as savings accounts and government bonds that are easily converted into coins or currency.

negative income tax A system of government payments to the poor that guarantee every family a minimum standard of living.

net exports The value of goods and services exported from an economy minus the value of those imported.

Net National Product (NNP) GNP for a year less depreciation in that year gives the net national product for that year.

net present value A determination of the value of a stream of earnings over time.

noncompeting groups Groups of workers that do not compete for the same jobs because of marked differences in education, skill, or training.

nonmarket allocation of resources Any allocation made without concern for the effects of the decision upon the profits of the organization.

normal profit The minimum profit required to keep the entrepreneur in a particular line of business.

normative economics The branch of economics that incorporates value judgments. In this area economists discuss the world as it ought to be. There is no presumption that the values of economists are better than those of other people.

oligopoly The situation when there are only a few suppliers in a market.

one-way fiscal policy A policy with a bias toward expansionary economic policies as opposed to restrictive fiscal policies.

open market operations The purchase and sale of U.S. government securities by the Fed for the purpose of controlling the money supply.

opportunity cost The best potential alternative use of resources that is given up when the resources are allocated to something else.

paradox of thrift A situation where people attempt to increase their individual savings and cause a reduction in savings for society.

perfect competition A market where there are many buyers and sellers, none of whom is able to influence the price of the product, which is homogeneous. The knowledge of price is available to all buyers and sellers, and producers can enter and leave the market with ease.

Phillips curve A graph representing the short-run tradeoff between unemployment and inflation.

pollution permits A system that allows firms to bid for the right to pollute, so that those most needing this form of waste disposal will be able to use it.

positive economics The scientific analysis of problems that describes the world as it is, keeping the analysis as free as possible of value judgments.

poverty level The definition of poverty based on the number of people in a household and on a food budget that is nutritionally inadequate for long-run use.

price elasticity The responsiveness of the quantity demanded of a good to a change in price.

price index A measure of the price level for goods and services in a nation. A base year is established and assigned a value of 100. Other years' prices are shown in relationship to the base year.

product differentiation The perception by consumers that various suppliers' products are different, whether or not they really are.

production function The relationship between the inputs into a firm and the output that can be produced by those inputs.

production-possibilities frontier A graph showing the maximum amount society can produce when fully utilizing all its resources during a given period of time.

profit The difference between total sales and the opportunity cost of all inputs.

profit maximization A firm must operate where the marginal revenue product/factor price ratio for all factors is equal. That is: $MRP_A/P_A = MRP_B/P_B$.

progressive tax A tax, paid as a percentage of income, that rises as income rises.

proportional tax A tax that is the same percentage of income for everyone.

public goods Goods that produce external benefits and do not lose value if their rates of use increase.

quota A limitation on the quantity of a good that can be imported into a country.

rational ignorance Voters' lack of familiarity with issues that do not affect them directly.

real GNP Money GNP measured in constant dollars. This measure makes possible year-to-year comparisons independent of price changes over time.

real rate of interest The nominal or money rate of interest minus the rate of inflation.

recessionary gap The vertical distance between the 45-degree line and aggregate demand at potential GNP where aggregate demand crosses the 45-degree line at less than full-employment level of NNP.

recessions Periods of economic decline in the business cycle.

regressive tax   A tax, paid as a percentage of income, that falls as income rises.

rent   A payment to the owner for the use of real property.

reserve requirement or ratio   The proportion of deposits that a bank must hold in the form of cash or as deposits with the Fed.

Say's law   The law stating that there will always be sufficient purchasing power for all of the output produced at full employment.

short run   A time period in which a firm can adjust some inputs (usually labor) but cannot change its capacity.

short-run adjustment process   The process of changing the variable inputs only, since the fixed factors cannot be changed.

short-run supply curve of a firm   The marginal cost curve above the shutdown point.

short-run supply curve of an industry   The sum of all firms' short-run supply curves.

shutdown point   That point at which out-of-pocket or variable costs exceed the revenue received for a product.

social benefits   The advantages to society of an action.

social costs   The costs (monetary or nonmonetary) of an action to society.

stabilization function   Formulation of policies that control fluctuations in economic activity.

stagflation   A term coined to describe high levels of unemployment occurring simultaneously with high levels of inflation.

store of value   An item that allows the accumulation of wealth to be used for later purchases.

structural unemployment   A type of unemployment caused by a mismatch between the skills that available workers have and the skills needed by employers.

substitute good   A good that provides a function or service similar to that provided by another good and can be used in place of that good.

supply curve   A graph showing the relationship between price and the quantity supplied.

supply schedule   A list showing the quantity of a good that would be produced at various prices.

supply shock   A disruption in specific markets that results in rising prices in the entire economy.

supply-side economics   A school of thought that focuses on the economic factors that account for economic growth. This school was formed to counter the emphasis on demand factors that was typical of the monetarists and Keynesians.

tariff   A charge that an importer of a good must pay when bringing the good into the country.

tax incidence   The tax burden—the taxes paid by various income groups.

terms of trade   The exchange ratio for commodities traded between nations.

total cost   Includes all expenses associated with a level of production. It is composed of total fixed costs plus total variable costs.

total product   The number of units produced with a set of inputs.

transfer payments   Payments to individuals for which no services are performed (e.g., unemployment compensation, Medicare payments).

unemployment rate   The proportion of the labor force that is not employed but is seeking work.

unit of value   The common commodity (money) used to express the prices of all other goods and services.

unitary elasticity   Demand for a good such that a change in price brings forth a proportional change in quantity. The total revenue for unitary elasticity remains the same even though the price changes.

value added   The difference between the value of a product when it starts a production process and its value when it finishes that process.

variable costs   Expenses that can be changed by changing the level of production.

velocity of money   The number of times the same money will be spent during some given period.

vertical merger   The creation of a single firm from two firms, one of which was a supplier of the other.

wages   A payment for providing labor resources.

Index